a
first
reader in
physiological
psychology

Harper's Experimental Psychology Series
Under the Editorship of H. Philip Zeigler

a
first
reader in
physiological
psychology
joel f. lubar

The University of Tennessee

Harper & Row, Publishers
NEW YORK   EVANSTON   SAN FRANCISCO   LONDON

A First Reader in Physiological Psychology
Copyright © 1972 by Joel F. Lubar
Printed in the United States of America. All rights reserved. No part of this book may be
used or reproduced in any manner whatsoever without written permission except in the
case of brief quotations embodied in critical articles and reviews. For information address
Harper & Row, Publishers, Inc., 49 East 33rd Street, New York, N.Y. 10016.

Standard Book Number: 06-044089-9

LIBRARY OF CONGRESS CATALOG CARD NUMBER: 79-165027

contents

preface

One of the main difficulties in teaching introductory material in any field is that most of the information to be conveyed to the student has to be gleaned from textbooks. Textbooks have many virtues, but they also have several faults. One of the main problems of the textbook approach is that one or several authors have taken upon themselves the task of interpreting a vast body of information for the student. Often too many topics are covered in too little space, and the student is left with a rather fragmentary understanding of the areas that are presented. There have been numerous attempts, particularly in teaching psychology, to overcome this problem. One of the best approaches is to have a textbook which is analytical in the presentation of its content. This means that it should not only cover the individual areas of psychology in such a manner as to present the data—which is where many textbooks stop—but should also present an interpretation of the significance of data gathered in the various psychological disciplines. That is, it should explain how theories are built, how they are tested, and what is the state of the art at present in the various areas.

In physiological psychology this is particularly important since physiological psychology is a rapidly developing and complex field which draws upon many other sciences and is now beginning to develop its own methodologies and strategies for solving problems. The accompanying textbook to this reader, A Primer of Physiological Psychology, incorporates many of these important advances in textbook writing. It deals with a variety of subjects in an analytical manner. It describes not only the subject matter germane to the various areas of physiological psychology but also tries to explain where progress has been made and where progress has not been made, looking at some of the reasons why it has not been made in some areas. It tells the student where we stand. However, even in a textbook of this kind there is still one thing that is missing—the feel of what it is actually like to be involved directly in a research problem and seeing how things really are.

The purpose of this book of readings is to bring the student into contact with the research, whether it takes place in the outside world or in an academic or medical setting. To this purpose a relatively large body of materials from many sources has been gathered together under headings paralleling the chapter headings in the Primer. Some of the material was collected from semipopularized sources written by experts in the field. Other material is taken directly from the various scholarly journals. All of the material was chosen to meet the needs of a student taking his first course in physiological psychology.

A large proportion of the material in this book is recent, but some older material was included purposely to give the student a feel for the continuity of various problems which are of persistent importance in psychology. A wide range of topics is covered starting with the basic anatomy and physiology of the nervous system and progressing to consideration of complex processes such as higher brain functions in man and animals. The readings were chosen not only for appropriate level of difficulty but all were also chosen for their readability and for their interest. It is hoped that pursuing these readings in conjunction with the various textbook chapters, the student will gain both an interpretative coverage of what is going on in the various areas of physiological psychology and firsthand information of what research is being carried out and what has been accomplished.

One other point should be mentioned. The readings in this text are of general use and not idiosyncratic to the specific textbook, A Primer of Physiological Psychology, even though it was designed with this book in mind. These readings will supplement any basic textbook in the area of physiological psychology as well as most introductory psychology texts.

Complete references for original sources of the articles are given in the text. Also included are acknowledgments for permissions from authors and publishers or any other copyright holders of the articles. The author wishes to thank all of the publishers and authors who were extremely cooperative in providing the material for this text. Particular thanks is given to Carol Umstaedter who devoted many hours of hard work to the job of gathering permission material, helping to organize the manuscript, and her general editorial assistance. I wish also to thank Dr. H. Philip Zeigler for his help and advice in the preparation of this book.

Joel F. Lubar

introduction
chapter 1

Physiological psychology is a vital and rapidly developing science. It is a fascinating field which deals with the relationship between the brain and behavior. It is a hybrid science which draws upon many sciences for its methodology and data; particularly important are the areas of anatomy, physiology, neurophysiology, neurochemistry, pharmacology, psycho-pharmacology, psychology, zoology, and endocrinology. The physiological psychologist has to be proficient in many areas of biological science and at the same time must be a psychologist. He must be able to gather information from many scientific sources in order to study the subject of his field: the biological foundations of behavior.

A large proportion of physiological psychology deals with those functions of the nervous system that are relevant to behavior. The physiological psychologist deals with topics ranging from basic questions of how individual nerve cells operate, how sensory organs transform information from the environment into coded electrical impulses to the complex problems of memory storage, and the neurological basis of intelligence. He may ask these questions: Are there biological substrates for mental illness? What is the relationship between genetics, behavior, and brain structure? Do early experiences in the development of the child affect neural capacities and even the development of neural structures?

During the past two decades tremendous strides have been made in the area of brain research. We are beginning to understand the basis for some of the motivational states, such

*as hunger and thirst. Some of the basic emotional responses
have been localized to certain groups of brain structures by
means of brain stimulation. There is even evidence that memory
might have a molecular basis and that chemicals can be used to
disrupt storage of information and perhaps even to enhance
memory functions. Analyses of complex electrical signals in the
brain, which for many years have been relatively uninterpretable, are now beginning to yield, with the aid of the
electroencephalogram, correlations with various behavioral
states. Electrical signals can be used to gauge the state of
attention or alertness of an organism. They can tell the scientist
whether dreaming is taking place. By means of complex computer analyses of electrical wave forms, it is sometimes possible
to predict the specific responses an animal will make in a
highly structured learning situation.*

*Physiological psychology holds a great promise for the future
because through this field it may be possible to improve our
basic mental qualities, such as intelligence and memory. It may
be possible to stave off degenerative processes of aging,
diseases of the nervous system, and perhaps as a by-product
extend the general vitality of the organism. In fact, there is a
strong possibility that within the next half century significant
advances will be made toward managing severe forms of
mental illness through knowledge gained in physiological
psychology. Many of the recent developments in the area of
basic brain research and physiological psychology are presented in the following readings. Certainly when one talks
about relevance, physiological psychology is in the forefront
because it offers the hope for dramatically improving the human
condition and perhaps through the individual ultimately to
help heal some of the wounds within society itself.*

the anatomy and physiology of the nervous system
chapter 2

The readings selected for this section present a picture of the organization of the nervous system. They describe in a readily understandable manner how nerves operate to transform physical stimuli into electrical impulses, which are the basis of neural coding. A great deal of progress has been made in the area of neurophysiology—the study of nerves and their function. It is an interesting fact that several Nobel prizes, including the most recent ones in medicine, were awarded on the basis of research dealing with either the chemical or electrical properties of the nerves or receptors. It is quite clear to many scientists and laymen that such research has great importance as far as the general scope of scientific knowledge is concerned and because it has implications for medicine.

By understanding the electrical properties of the nervous system, it may be possible in the near future to understand the basic coding in the nervous system. The understanding of neural coding would make it possible for us to understand and define better such vague notions as emotion, drive, and other psychological entities.

The
ionic basis
of
nervous conduction
a. l. hodgkin

Trinity College, Cambridge, which I entered in 1932, has a long-standing connection with neurophysiology. As an undergraduate I found myself interested in nerves and was soon reading books or papers by Keith Lucas (1), Adrian (2), Hill (3), and Rushton (4), all of whom are, or were, fellows of Trinity. I had a particular reason for looking at Lucas's papers because my father and Lucas had been close friends and both lost their lives during the first world war. My reading introduced me to Bernstein's membrane theory (5), in the form developed by Lillie (6), and I thought it would be interesting to test their assumptions by a simple experiment. A central point in the theory is that propagation of the impulse from one point to the next is brought about by the electric currents which flow between resting and active regions. On this view, the action potential is not just an electrical sign of the impulse, but is the causal agent in propagation. Nowadays the point is accepted by everyone, but at that time it lacked experimental proof. By a roundabout route I came across a fairly simple way of testing the idea. The method depended on firing an impulse at a localized block, and observing the effect of the impulse on the excitability of the nerve just beyond the block. It turned out that the impulse produced a transient increase in excitability over a distance of several millimeters, and that the increase was almost certainly caused by electric currents spreading in a local circuit through the blocked region (7). More

From Science, **145**, 1148–1154, 11 September 1964. Copyright 1964 by the American Association for the Advancement of Science.

striking evidence for the electrical theory was obtained later, for instance when it was shown that the velocity of the nerve impulse could be changed over a wide range by altering the electrical resistance of the external fluid (8). But this is not the place to describe these experiments, and I would like to take up the story again in 1938, when I had the good fortune to spend a year in Gasser's laboratory at the Rockefeller Institute in New York. Before leaving Cambridge I had found, by a lucky accident, that it was quite easy to isolate single nerve fibers from the shore crab, Carcinus maenas. This opened up several interesting lines of investigation, and I became increasingly impressed with the advantages of working on single nerve fibers. Carcinus fibers are very robust, but they are at most $\frac{1}{30}$ millimeter in diameter and for many purposes this is inconveniently small. There was a good deal to be said for switching to the very much larger nerve fibers which J. Z. Young (9) had discovered in the squid and which were then being studied by Curtis and Cole (10) in Woods Hole. Squids of the genus Loligo are active creatures, 1 or 2 feet long, which can swim backward at high speed by taking water into a large cavity and squirting out a jet through a funnel in the front of the animal. The giant nerve fibers, which may be as much as a millimeter in diameter, run in the body wall and supply the muscles that expel water from the mantle cavity. Although these fibers are unmyelinated, their large size makes them conduct rapidly, and this may be the teleological reason for their existence. It should be said that large nerve fibers conduct faster than small ones (11) because the conductance per unit length of the core increases as the square of the diameter, whereas the electrical capacity of the surface increases only as the first power.

You may wonder how it is that we get along without giant nerve fibers. The answer is that vertebrates have developed myelinated axons in which the fiber is covered with a relatively thick insulating layer over most of its length, and the excitable membrane is exposed only at the nodes of Ranvier. In these fibers, conduction is saltatory and the impulse skips from one node to the next. I regret that shortage of time does not allow me to discuss this important development, with which the names of Kato, Tasaki, and Takeuchi (12) are particularly associated.

Early in 1938, K. S. Cole asked me to spend a few weeks in his laboratory at Woods Hole where squid are plentiful during the summer. I arrived in June 1938 and was greeted by a sensational experiment, the results of which were plainly visible on the screen of the cathode-ray tube. Cole and Curtis (13) had developed a technique which allowed them to measure changes in the electrical conductivity of the membrane during the impulse; when analyzed, their experiment proved that the membrane undergoes a large increase in conductance which has roughly the same time course as the electrical change (Figure 1). This was strong evidence for an increase in ionic permeability, but the experiment naturally did not show what ions were involved, and this aspect was not cleared up until several years after the war. At first sight, Cole and Curtis's results seemed to fit in with the idea that the membrane broke down during activity, as Bernstein and Lillie had suggested. However, there was one further point which required checking. According to Bernstein, activity consisted of a momentary breakdown of the membrane, and on this view the action potential should not exceed the resting potential. Huxley and I started to test this

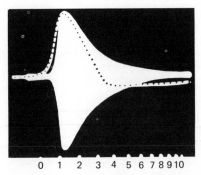

0 1 2 3 4 5 6 7 8 9 10   msec

Figure 1. Action potential (dotted curve) and increase in conductance (white band) in squid axon at about 6°C. [From Cole and Curtis (13)]

point early in 1939. We measured external electrical changes from *Carcinus* fibers immersed in oil with a cathode-ray tube, direct-current amplifier, and cathode followers as the recording instrument. The resting potential was taken from the steady potential between an intact region and one depolarized by injury or by isotonic potassium chloride. To our surprise we found that the action potential was often much larger than the resting potential—for example, 73 millivolts for the action potential as against 37 millivolts for the resting potential. [Although I was not aware of it until much later, Schaefer (14) had previously reported a similar discrepancy in the sartorius and gastrocnemius muscles of the frog.] Our results did not give the absolute value of the membrane potentials because of the short-circuiting effect of the film of sea water which clings to a fiber in oil. However, there is no reason why short-circuiting should affect one potential more than another, and the discrepancy seemed much too large to be explained by some small difference in the way the two potentials were recorded. Nevertheless, we were extremely suspicious of these results with external electrodes, and before they could be published both of us were caught up in the war.

Before going further with the discrepancy, it seemed important to establish the absolute value of the membrane potentials by recording potential differences between an electrode inside the nerve fiber and the external solution. Osterhout and his colleagues (15) had recorded internal potentials by introducing electrodes into the vacuoles of large plant cells, but for obvious reasons the comparable experiment had not been attempted with nerve. The best preparation on which to try such an experiment was the giant axon of the squid, and the first measurements of this kind were made during the summer of 1939 by Curtis and Cole (16) at Woods Hole, and by Huxley and myself (17) at Plymouth. There were minor differences in technique, but the general principle was the same. A microelectrode consisting of a long glass capillary, filled with saline or metal, was inserted at one end of the fiber and pushed in for a distance of 10 to 30 millimeters. The fiber was damaged at the point where the capillary entered it, but an insertion of 10 to 30 millimeters was sufficient to take the electrode into intact nerve. During the insertion the electrode has to be kept away from the membrane; if it scraped against the surface the axon was damaged. However, if kept clear of the membrane, the electrode did no harm, and it has since been shown that axons will conduct impulses for many hours after being impaled in this way. Figure 2A shows an electrode inside an uncleaned axon; Figure 2B is similar, but the small nerve fibers round the giant axon have been removed and dark ground illumination has been used.

In 1939 both the Woods Hole and Plymouth groups found that large action potentials could be recorded between an internal electrode and the external solution, thus providing strong evidence for the idea that the action potential arises at the surface membrane. With this technique Huxley and I again obtained the disturbing result that the action potential was much greater than the

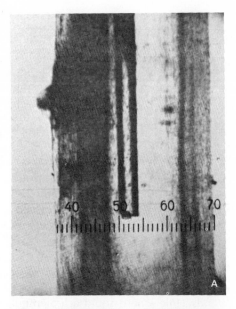

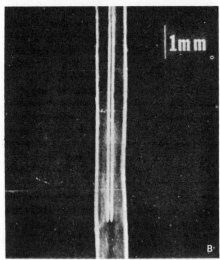

Figure 2. (A) Photograph of a recording electrode inside a giant axon of Loligo forbesi. The giant axon, which shows as a clear space, was left with small nerve fibers on either side; one division = 33 microns. [From Hodgkin and Huxley (17)] (B) Cleaned giant axon of Loligo forbesi with glass tube 0.1 millimeter in diameter inside it; dark ground illumination. [From Hodgkin and Keynes (55)]

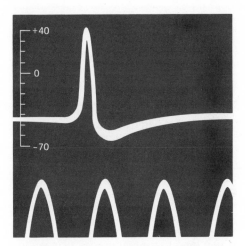

Figure 3. Action potential and resting potential recorded between inside and outside of axon with capillary filled with sea water. Time marker, 500 cy/sec. The vertical scale indicates the potential of the internal electrode in millivolts, the sea water outside being taken as at zero potential. [From Hodgkin and Huxley (17); see also 23]

resting potential (17). Figure 3, which illustrates one of these experiments, shows an action potential of 86 millivolts and a resting potential of 45 millivolts. In their 1939 experiments Curtis and Cole (16) recorded the action potential with a condenser-coupled amplifier; later measurements with a D.C. amplifier gave an average action potential of 108 millivolts and an average resting potential of 51 millivolts (18). Curtis and Cole also showed that the resting potential could be abolished, reversibly, by increasing the external potassium concentration until it was about the same as that in the axoplasm; at high concentrations the membrane behaved like a potassium electrode, as predicted by Bernstein's theory.

The small size of most nerve or muscle fibers made it difficult to extend the technique employed for the giant axon to other preparations. However, another very convenient and powerful method was developed by Graham, Gerard, and Ling, who showed that extremely small glass capillaries could be inserted transversely into muscle fibers without causing appreciable damage (19). In order to obtain consistent results it is desirable that the electrodes should have an external diameter of less than 0.5 micron. This small diameter means that the electrodes have a high resistance, and special precautions must be taken with the recording system. Initially the electrodes were used to measure the resting potential, but increasing the concentration of the potassium chloride in the electrode to 3 molar enabled the action potential to be recorded as well (20). Many types of excitable cell have now been examined, and in nearly every case it has been found that the action potential exceeds the resting potential, often by 40 to 50 millivolts.

Yet another method is required for myelinated nerve fibers, which do not take kindly to impalement. A useful way of eliminating external short circuiting was introduced by Huxley and Stämpfli in 1950 (21), and their method has been refined in a very elegant way by Frankenhaeuser (22). The values found by applying these methods to amphibian nerve fibers are: action potential, 120 millivolts; resting potential, 70 millivolts. Absolute values for mammalian nerve fibers are not known, but they are probably not very different from those reported for frog.

At the end of the war, the position was that several of Bernstein's assumptions had been vindicated in a striking way, but that in one major respect the classical theory had been shown to be wrong. By 1945 most neurophysiologists agreed that the action potential was propagated by electric currents, and that it arose at the surface membrane; it was also clear that the resting potential was at least partly due to the electromotive force of the potassium concentration cell. On the other hand, there was impressive evidence that in both crab and squid fibers the action potential exceeded the resting potential by 40 to 50 millivolts (17, 18, 23). This was obviously incompatible with the idea that electrical activity depended on a breakdown of the membrane; some process giving a reversal of electromotive force was required.

THE SODIUM HYPOTHESIS

There were several early attempts to provide a theoretical basis for the reversal, but most of these were speculative and not easily subject to experimental test. A simpler explanation, now known as the sodium hypothesis, was worked out with Katz and Huxley and tested during the summer of 1947 (24). The hypothesis, which undoubtedly owed a good deal to the classical experiments of Overton (25), was based on a comparison of the ionic composition of the axoplasm of squid nerve with that of blood or sea water. As in Bernstein's theory, it was assumed that the resting membrane is selectively permeable to potassium ions and that the potential across it arises from the tendency of these ions to move outward from the more concentrated solution inside a nerve or muscle fiber. In the limiting case, where a membrane which is permeable only to potassium separates axoplasm containing 400 mM K from plasma containing 20 mM K, the internal potential should be 75 millivolts negative to the external solution. This value is obtained from the Nernst relation

$$V_K = \frac{RT}{F} \ln \frac{[K]_o}{[K]_i} \qquad (1)$$

where V_K is the equilibrium potential of the potassium ion defined in the sense internal potential minus external potential and $[K]_o$ and $[K]_i$ are potassium concentrations (strictly, activities) inside and outside the fiber. Resting potentials of 70 millivolts have been observed in undissected squid axons (26); the smaller values found in isolated axons may be explained by a leakage of sodium into the fiber. If the permeability to sodium were 1/12 that to potassium, a potential of about 50 millivolts is predicted for an isolated axon in sea water (350 mM K, the mM Na in axoplasm 10 mM K, 450 mM Na in sea water).

From Bernstein's theory it might be assumed that when the membrane broke down, the ratio of the permeabilities to Na and K would approach that of the aqueous mobilities of these ions, about 0.7 to 1. In that case, the action potential could not exceed the resting potential and would in fact be less by at least 8 millivolts. However, it is simple to rescue the hypothesis by assuming that the active membrane undergoes a large and selective increase in permeability to sodium. In the extreme case, where the membrane is much more permeable to sodium than to any other ion, the potential should approach that given by the Nernst formula; that is,

$$V_{Na} = \frac{RT}{F} \ln \frac{[Na]_o}{[Na]_i} \qquad (2)$$

This gives a limiting value of + 58 millivolts for the tenfold concentration ratio observed by Steinbach and Spiegelman (27) and accounts satisfactorily for the reversal of 50 millivolts commonly seen in intact axons.

A simple consequence of the sodium hypothesis is that the magnitude of the action potential should be greatly influenced by the concentration of sodium ions in the external fluid. For the active membrane should no longer be capable of giving a reversed electromotive force if the concentration of sodium is equalized on the two sides of the membrane. The first quantitative tests were made with Katz, in the summer of 1947. They showed that the action potential, but not the resting potential, was reduced by replacing external sodium chloride with choline chloride or with glucose. If all the external sodium was removed the

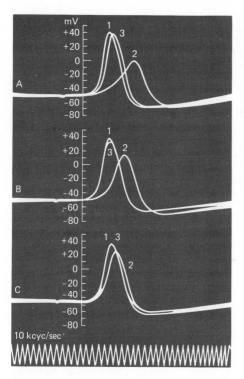

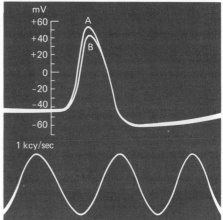

Figure 5. Effect of sodium-rich external solution on the action potential of a giant axon. Record B, in sea water; record A, 50 seconds after applying sea water containing additional NaC1 (Na concentration, 1.56 times that in sea water). [From Hodgkin and Katz (24)]

Figure 4. Effect of sodium-deficient external solutions on the action potential of a giant axon. Records labeled 1 and 3 were with the axon in sea water; A2, with 0.33 sea water, 0.67 isotonic dextrose; B2, with 0.5 sea water; 0.5 isotonic dextrose; C2, with 0.7 sea water, 0.3 isotonic dextrose. [From Hodgkin and Katz (24)]

axon became reversibly inexcitable, in agreement with Overton's experiment on frog muscle. Figure 4 illustrates one of the experiments. In the physiological region, the overshoot varied with external sodium concentrations in the same manner as a sodium electrode (24).

It was also shown that a solution containing extra sodium increased the overshoot by about the amount predicted by Equation 2. This is a particularly satisfactory result, because it seems most unlikely that an increase beyond the normal could be brought about by an abnormal solution. Figure 5 illustrates one of these experiments. Later Stämp-

fli (28) showed that at the node of Ranvier an increase of about 35 millivolts in the overshoot is brought about by a fourfold increase of external sodium.

The effect of varying external sodium concentration has now been studied on a number of excitable tissues: for example, frog muscle (20), myelinated nerve (29), Purkinje fibers of the heart (30), and crustacean nerve (31). In all these cases the results were very similar to those in the squid axon.

There are at least two cases where the mechanism is thought to be basically different. These are crab muscle, in which an entry of calcium, or other divalent cations, provides the inward current (32), and the plant cell, *Chara*, where an exit of chloride ions from the vacuolar sap may be the primary process (33).

IONIC MOVEMENT DURING ACTIVITY

During the period 1947–1951 several investigators started to measure the effect of stimulation on the movements of labeled sodium across the surface membrane of giant axons. As often happens, work proceeded independently and more or less simultaneously on the two sides of the Atlantic, the principal investigators being Keynes (34) in England and Rothenberg (35) and Grundfest and Nachmansohn (36) in America. In 1949 Keynes reported that stimulation of *Sepia* axons at 100 per second caused a 15-fold increase in the rate of uptake of ^{24}Na. There was also a substantial increase in the outflow of labeled sodium, and at first it was difficult to decide whether activity was associated with a net uptake of sodium. Keynes and Lewis (37) resolved the difficulty by measuring the sodium concentration in axoplasm by activation analysis, and there is now general agreement that at 20°C the net entry of sodium in one impulse amounts to 3 to 4×10^{-12} mole per square centimeter. Other experiments showed that a similar quantity of potassium ions leave the fiber during an impulse (38). It is perhaps easier to get an idea of what these quantities mean by saying that one impulse is associated with an inward movement of 20,000 sodium ions through 1 square micron of surface.

An entry of 4×10^{-12} mole of sodium per square centimeter is more than enough to account for the action potential. From the work of Cole and his colleagues it is known that the electrical capacity of the membrane is about 1 microfarad per square centimeter (10). The quantity of charge required to change the voltage across a 1-microfarad condenser by 120 millivolts is 1.2×10^{-7} coulomb; this is equivalent to 1.2×10^{-12} mole of monovalent cation, which is only one-third of the observed entry of sodium. A discrepancy in this direction is to be expected. In addition to charging the membrane capacity during the rising phase of the action potential, a good deal of sodium exchanges with potassium, particularly during the early part of the falling phase. From the quantitative

theory which Huxley and I developed, the size of the ionic movements can be predicted from electrical measurements. As Huxley describes (39), the theoretical quantities turn out to be in reasonable agreement with experimental values.

The quantity of sodium which enters a myelinated axon during an impulse is much less than in an unmyelinated fiber of comparable size (40). This is presumably because the ionic exchange is confined to the node of Ranvier and the capacity per unit length of the axon is reduced by the thick myelin sheath.

ANALYSIS OF MEMBRANE CURRENTS: VOLTAGE CLAMP EXPERIMENTS

In pursuing the evidence for the ionic theory I have departed from the strict order of events. During the summer of 1947 Cole and Marmont (41, 42) developed a technique for impaling squid axons with long metallic electrodes; with this technique they were able to apply current uniformly to the membrane and to avoid the complications introduced by spread of current in a cable-like structure. Cole (41) also carried out an important type of experiment in which the potential difference across the membrane is made to undergo a steplike change and the experimental variable is the current which flows through the membrane. In Cole's experiments a single internal electrode was used for recording potential and passing current; since the current may be large, electrode polarization introduces an error and makes it difficult to use steps longer than a millisecond. However, the essential features of the experiment, notably the existence of a phase of inward current over a range of depolarizations, are plainly shown in the records which Cole obtained in 1947 (41). It was obvious that the method could be improved by inserting two internal electrodes, one for current the other for voltage, and by employing electronic feedback to supply the current needed to maintain a constant voltage. Cole, Marmont, and I discussed this possibility in the spring of 1948, and it was used at Plymouth the following summer by Huxley, Katz, and myself (*43*). Further improvements were made during the winter, and in 1949 we obtained a large number of records which were analyzed in Cambridge during the next 2 years (*44*). Huxley describes these results in more detail (*39*); here all that need be said is that by varying the external ionic concentrations it was possible to separate the ionic current flowing through the membrane into components carried by sodium and potassium, and hence to determine how the ionic permeability varied with time and with membrane potential.

To begin with, we hoped that the analysis might lead to a definite molecular model of the membrane. However, it gradually became clear that different mechanisms could lead to similar equations and that no real progress at the molecular level could be made until much more was known about the chemistry and fine structure of the membrane. On the other hand, the equations that we developed proved surprisingly powerful, and it was possible to predict much of the electrical behavior of the giant axon with fair accuracy. Examples of some of the properties of the axon which are fitted by the equations are: the form, duration, and amplitude of the action potential; the conduction velocity, impedance changes, ionic movements; and sub-threshold phenomena, including the oscillatory behavior.

EXPERIMENTAL WORK ON GIANT AXONS SINCE 1952

In the last part of this lecture I should like to mention some of the more recent developments in the ionic theory of nervous conduction. One major problem, which has interested a number of physiologists and biochemists, is to find out how cells use metabolic energy to move sodium and potassium ions against concentration gradients. In excitable tissues this process is of particular interest because it builds up the ionic concentration differences on which conduction of impulses depends. When a nerve fiber carries an impulse it undergoes a rapid cycle of permeability changes which allow first sodium and then potassium ions to move down concentration gradients. In giant axons, the changes associated with an impulse are exceedingly small, as can be seen from the fact that a 500-micron axon loses only one-millionth of its internal potassium in a single impulse. Large fibers can therefore conduct many impulses without recharging their batteries by metabolism. Nevertheless, if they are to be of any use to the animal, nerve fibers must be equipped with a mechanism for reversing the ionic exchanges that occur during electrical activity. The necessity for such a system was foreseen by Overton in 1902 when he pointed out that human heart muscle carried out some 2.4×10^9 contractions in 70 years, yet, as far as he knew, contained as much potassium and as little sodium in old age as in early youth (*25*). Forty years later Dean introduced the idea of a sodium pump and showed that the distribution of potassium and chloride in muscle might be a passive consequence of an active extrusion of sodium, but that active transport of potassium or chloride ions would by themselves be adequate (*45*). The concept was developed further by Krogh (*46*) and Ussing (*47*) and is now supported by experiments on a wide range of animal tissues.

Giant nerve fibers provide excellent material for studying ion pumping. One approach is to inject radioactive sodium ions and to collect the labeled ions which emerge from the fiber. Such experiments show that if the fiber is poisoned with cyanide or dinitrophenol it stops pumping, and sodium ions gradually accumulate inside. The fiber remains excitable for many hours because sodium and po-

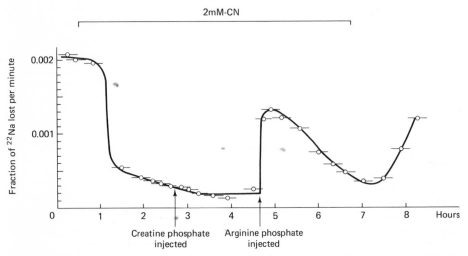

Figure 6. Effect on outflow of sodium of (i) poisoning with cyanide; (ii) injecting creatine phosphate; (iii) arginine phosphate; (iv) removal of cyanide. The mean concentrations in the axon after injection were 15.3 mM creatine phosphate and 15.8 mM arginine phosphate. [From Caldwell et al. (48)]

tassium can still move downhill during the impulse. But any sodium which gets into the fiber remains there and is not extruded as it would be in an unpoisoned axon. The ability to extrude sodium depends on the presence of adenosine triphosphate (ATP), and with an axon in which all the ATP has been broken down, sodium extrusion can be restored by injecting energy-rich phosphate in the right form (48). Figure 6 illustrates one of these experiments. It shows that the outflow of sodium is reduced to a low value by cyanide and can be restored by the molluscan phosphagen, arginine phosphate, but not by the vertebrate phosphagen, creatine phosphate. This is a satisfactory result since it is known that creatine phosphate is not handled by the enzyme which catalyzes the transfer of phosphate from arginine phosphate to adenosine diphosphate (49).

The molecular nature of the pumping mechanism is unknown, but there is much evidence to show that in most cells it is driven by compounds containing energy-rich phosphate, such as ATP or phosphagen. Recent interest in this field has been focused by Skou on an ATP-splitting enzyme which is present in the membrane and has the interesting properties of being activated by sodium and potassium and inhibited by substances which interfere with sodium transport (50).

PERFUSION OF GIANT AXONS

In conclusion I should like to mention an interesting new method which has been developed during the last few years. Since the action potential of a nerve fiber arises at the surface membrane it should be possible to replace the protoplasm inside the fiber with an aqueous solution of appropriate composition. Methods for perfusing axons were worked out by Tasaki and his colleagues at Woods Hole (51) and by Baker and Shaw at Plymouth (52). The technique used at Plymouth is based on the observation (53) that most of the axoplasm in giant nerve fibers can be squeezed out of the cut end. This has been known since

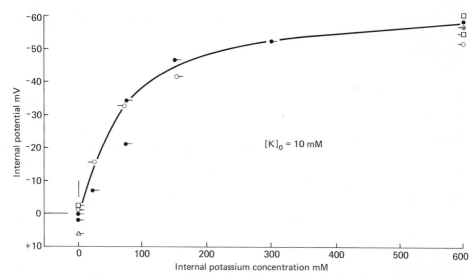

Figure 7. Effect of varying internal potassium concentration on the resting potential. External solution, sea water containing 10 mM K; internal solution, NaCl-KCl solutions isotonic with sea water. Note that the resting potential reaches a limiting value of about −55 millivolts at potassium concentration greater than 150 mM. [From Baker et al. (54)]

1937, but until fairly recently no one paid much attention to the electrical properties of the thin sheath which remained after the contents of the nerve fiber had been removed. Since extrusion involves flattening the axon with a glass rod or roler it was natural to suppose that the membrane would be badly damaged by such a drastic method. However, in the autumn of 1960 Baker and Shaw (52) recorded action potentials from extruded sheaths which had been refilled with isotonic solution of a potassium salt. On further investigation (54) it turned out that such preparations gave action potentials of the usual magnitude for several hours, and that these were abolished, reversibly, by replacing potassium with sodium in the internal solution. As can be seen from Figures 7 and 8, the resting potential and action potential vary with the internal concentrations of potassium and sodium in a manner which is consistent with the external effect of these ions.

A point of some general interest is that, although about 95 percent of the axoplasm had been removed, axon membranes perfused with isotonic potassium solutions were able to carry some 300,000 impulses. This reinforces the idea that chemical reactions in the bulk of the

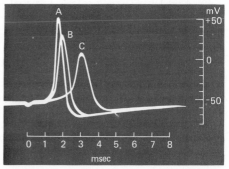

Figure 8. Effect on action potential of replacing internal potassium with sodium ions. (A) Isotonic potassium sulfate; (B) 0.25 K replaced by Na; (C) 0.5 K replaced by Na. The records were obtained in the order B, A, C. [From Baker et al. (54)]

axoplasm are not essential for conduction of impulses and that ionic concentration gradients provide the immediate source of energy for the action potential. Huxley (39) tells more about the way in which this is done.

References and notes

1. Lucas, K. *The conduction of the nervous impulse.* London: Longmans, 1917. Collected papers, mainly in *J. Physiol. London,* 1904–1914.

2. Adrian, E. D. *The basis of sensation.* London: Christophers, 1928; *The mechanism of nervous action.* Oxford: Oxford Univ. Press, 1932.

3. Hill, A. V. *Chemical wave transmission in nerve.* Cambridge: Cambridge Univ. Press, 1932.

4. Rushton, W. A. H. *J. Physiol. London,* 1927, **63**, 357; *J. Physiol. London,* 1934, **82**, 332.

5. Bernstein, J. *Elektrobiologie.* Braunschweig: Wieweg, 1912.

6. Lillie, R. S. *Protoplasmic action and nervous action.* Chicago: Chicago Univ. Press, 1923.

7. Hodgkin, A. L. *J. Physiol. London,* 1937, **90**, 183; *J. Physiol. London,* p. 211.

8. Hodgkin, A. L. *J. Physiol. London,* 1939, **94**, 560.

9. Young, J. Z. *Quart. J. Microscop. Sci.,* 1936, **78**, 367; *Cold Spring Harbor Symp. Quant. Biol.* 1936, **4** , 1.

10. Curtis, H. J., and Cole, K. S. *J. gen. Physiol.,* 1938, **21**, 757.

11. Gasser, H. S., and Erlanger, J. *Am. J. Physiol.,* 1927, **80**, 522.

12. Kato, G. *The microphysiology of nerve.* Tokyo: Maruzen, 1934; Tasaki, I. *Am. J. Physiol.,* 1937, **125**, 380; Tasaki, I. *ibid.,* 1939, **127**, 211; and Takeuchi, T. *Arch. Ges. Physiol.,* 1941, **244**, 696; Tasaki, I., and Takeuchi, T. *Arch. Ges. Physiol.,* 1942, **245**, 764.

13. Cole, K. S., and Curtis, H. J. *J. gen. Physiol.,* 1939, **22**, 649.

14. Schaefer, H. *Arch. Ges. Physiol.,* 1936, **237**, 329.

15. Osterhout, W. J. V. *Biol. Rev. Cambridge Phil. Soc.,* 1931, **6**, 639.

16. Curtis, H. J., and Cole, K. S. *J. cellular comp. Physiol.,* 1940, **15**, 147.

17. Hodgkin, A. L., and Huxley, A. F. *Nature,* 1939, **144**, 710.

18. Curtis, H. J., and Cole, K. S. *J. cellular comp. Physiol.,* 1942, **19**, 135.

19. Graham, J., and Gerard, R. W. *J. cellular comp. Physiol.,* 1946, **28**, 99; Ling, G., and Gerard, R. W. *J. cellular comp. Physiol.,* 1949, **34**, 383.

20. Nastuk, W. L., and Hodgkin, A. L. *J. cellular comp. Physiol.,* 1950, **35**, 39.

21. Huxley, A. F., and Stämpfli, R. *J. Physiol. London,* 1951, **112**, 476; *J. Physiol. London,* p. 496.

22. Frankenhaeuser, B. *J. Physiol. London,* 1957, **135**, 550.

23. Hodgkin, A. L., and Huxley, A. F. *J. Physiol. London,* 1945, **104**, 176.

24. Hodgkin, A. L., and Katz, B. *J. Physiol. London,* 1949, **108**, 37.

25. Overton, E. *Arch. Ges. Physiol.,* 1902, **92**, 346.

26. Hodgkin, A. L., and Keynes, R. D., reported in Hodgkin, A. L. *Proc. Roy. Soc. London,* 1958, **B148**, 1; Moore, J. W., and Cole, K. S. *J. gen. Physiol.,* 1960, **43**, 961.

27. Steinbach, H. B., and Spiegelman, S. *J. cellular comp. Physiol.,* 1943, **22**, 187.

28. Stämpfli, R. *J. Physiol. Paris,* 1956, **48**, 710.

29. Huxley, A. F., and Stämpfli, R. *J. Physiol. London,* 1951, **112**, 496.

30. Draper, M. H., and Weidmann, S. *J. Physiol. London,* 1951, **1 15**, 74.

31. Dalton, J. C. *J. gen. Physiol.,* 1958, **41**, 529.

32. Fatt, P., and Katz, B. *J. Physiol. London,* 1953, **120**, 171; Fatt, P., and Ginsborg, B. L. *J. Physiol. London,* 1958, **142**, 516.

33. Gaffey, C. T., and Mullins, L. J. *J. Physiol. London,* 1958, **144**, 505.

34. Keynes, R. D. *Arch. Sci. Physiol.,* 1949, **3**, 165; *J. Physiol. London,* 1949, **109**, 13P; 1951, **114**, 119.

35. Rothenberg, M. A. *Biochim. Biophys. Acta,* 1950, **4**, 96.

36. Grundfest, H., and Nachmansohn, D. *Federation Proc.,* 1950, **9**, 53.

37. Keynes, R. D., and Lewis, P. R. *J. Physiol. London,* 1951, **114**, 151.

38. Keynes, R. D. *J. Physiol. London,* 1948, **107**, 35P; *J. Physiol. London,* 1950, **113**, 99; *J. Physiol. London,* 1951, **114**, 119; Shanes, A. M. *Am. J. Physiol.,* 1954, **177**, 377.

39. Huxley, A. F. *Science,* this issue.

40. Asano, T., and Hurlbut, W. P. *J. gen. Physiol.*, 1958, **41**, 1187.

41. Cole, K. S. *Arch. Sci. Physiol.*, 1949, **3**, 253.

42. Marmont, G. *J. cellular comp. Physiol.*, 1949, **34**, 351.

43. Hodgkin, A. L., Huxley, A. F., and Katz, B. *Arch. Sci. Physiol.*, 1949, **3** , 129.

44. Hodgkin, A. L., Huxley, A. F., and Katz, B. *J. Physiol. London*, 1951, **116**, 424; Hodgkin, A. L., and Huxley, A. F. *J. Physiol. London*, p. 449; Hodgkin, A. L., and Huxley, A. F. *J. Physiol. London*, p. 473; Hodgkin, A. L., and Huxley, A. F. *J. Physiol. London*, p. 497; Hodgkin, A. L., and Huxley, A. F. *J. Physiol. London*, 1951, **117**, 500; Hodgkin, A. L., and Huxley, A. F. *J. Physiol. London*, 1953, **121**, 403.

45. Dean, R. B. *Biol. Symp.*, 1941, **3**, 331.

46. Krogh, A. *Proc. Roy. Soc. London*, 1946, **B133**, 140.

47. Ussing, H. H. *Physiol. Rev.*, 1949, **29**, 127.

48. Caldwell, P. C., Hodgkin, A. L., Keynes, R. D., and Shaw, T. I. *J. Physiol. London*, 1960, **152**, 561.

49. Ennor, A. H., and Morrison, J. F. *Physiol. Rev.*, 1958, **38**, 631.

50. Skou, J. C. *Biochim. Biophys. Acta*, 1957, **23**, 394.

51. Oikawa, T., Spyropoulos, C. S., Tasaki, I., and Teorell, T. *Acta Physiol. Scand.*, 1961, **52**, 195.

52. Baker, P. F., and Shaw, T. I. *J. Marine Biol. Assoc.*, 1961, **41**, 855.

53. Bear, R. S., Schmitt, F. O., and Young, J. Z. *Proc. Roy. Soc. London*, 1937, **B123**, 505.

54. Baker, P. F., Hodgkin, A. L., and Shaw, T. I. *Nature*, 1961, **190**, 885; *J. Physiol. London*, 1962, **164**, 330; *J. Physiol. London*, p. 355.

55. Hodgkin, A. L., and Keynes, R. D. *J. Physiol. London*, 1956, **131**, 592.

The brain
r. l. gregory

The brain is more complicated than a star and more mysterious. Looking, with imagination, back through the eyes to the brain mechanisms lying behind, we may there discover secrets as important as the secrets of the world perceived by the eye and brain.

It has not always been obvious that the brain is concerned with thinking, with memory, or with sensation. In the ancient world—including the great civilizations of Egypt and Mesopotamia—the brain was regarded as an unimportant organ. Thought and the emotions were attributed to the stomach, the liver and the gall bladder. Indeed, the echo lingers in modern speech, in such words as "phlegmatic." When the Egyptians embalmed their dead, they did not trouble to keep the brain (which was retracted through the left nostril) though the other organs were separately preserved, in special Canopic jars placed beside the sarcophagus. In death the brain is almost bloodless, so perhaps it seemed ill-suited to be the receptacle of the Vital Spirit. The active pulsing heart seemed to be the seat of life, warmth and feeling—not the cold grey silent brain, locked privily in its box of bone.

The vital role of the brain in control of the limbs, in speech and thought, sensation and experience, gradually became clear from the effects of accidents in which the brain was damaged. Later the effects of small tumors and gun shot wounds gave information which has been followed up and studied in great detail. The results of these studies are of the greatest importance to brain surgeons; for while some regions are comparatively safe, others must not be disturbed or the patient will die or suffer grievous loss.

The brain has been described as "the only lump of matter we know from the inside." From the outside, it is a pink-grey object, about the size of two clenched fists. The main parts are shown in Figure 1. It is made up of the so-called "white" and "grey" matter, the white matter being the fibers connecting the cell bodies, forming the grey matter.

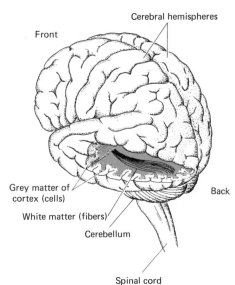

Figure 1. The brain, showing the visual part—the area striata—at the back (occipital cortex). Stimulation of small regions produces flashes of light in corresponding parts of the visual field. Stimulation of surrounding regions (visual association areas) produces more elaborate visual experiences.

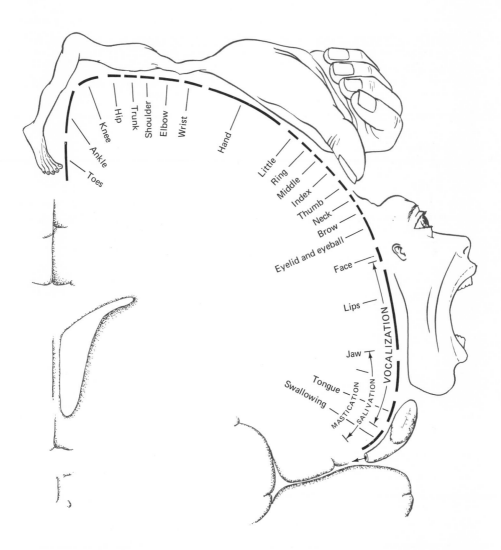

Figure 2. A "homunculus"—a graphic representation showing how much of the cortex is devoted to sensation from various regions of the body. Note the huge thumb. Different animals have very different "homunculi," corresponding to the sensory importance of the various parts of the body.

The brain has, in its evolution, grown up from the center, which in man is concerned primarily with emotion. The surface—the *cortex*—is curiously convoluted. It is largely concerned with motor-control of the limbs, and with the sense organs. It is possible to obtain maps of the association of regions of cortex with the sensation of touch on the skin—giving bizarre "homunculi" as in Figure 2. The sense of sight has its own region of cortex, as we shall see in a moment.

The nerve cells in the brain consist of *cell bodies*, each having a long thin process—or *axon*—conducting impulses from the cell. The axons may be very long, sometimes extending from the brain down the spinal cord. The cell bodies also have many finer and shorter fibers, the *dendrites*, which conduct signals to the cell (Figure 3). The cells, with their interconnecting dendrites and their axons, sometimes seem to be arranged randomly, but in some regions of the brain they form fairly well ordered rows, especially in the visual region.

The neural signals are in the form of

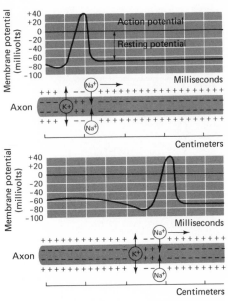

Figure 4. *Mechanism of electrical conduction in nerve. Hodgkin, Huxley, and Katz have discovered that sodium ions pass to the inside of the fiber, converting its standing negative charge to positive. Potassium ions leak out, restoring the resting potential. This can happen up to a thousand times a second, transmitting spikes of potential which run along the nerve as the signals by which we know the world, and command the muscles.*

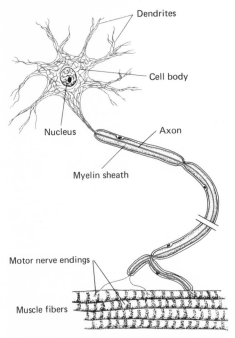

Figure 3. *A nerve cell. The cell body has a long axon, insulated by its myelin sheath, often sending control signals to muscle. The cell body accepts information from the many fine dendrites, some of which tend to make the cell fire, while others inhibit firing. The system is a simple computer element. The inter-connected elements serve to control activity and handle information for perception.*

electrical pulses, which occur when there is an alteration in the ion permeability of the cell membrane (Figure 4). At rest, the center of the fiber is negative with respect to the surface; but when a disturbance occurs, as when a retinal receptor is stimulated by light, the center of the fiber becomes positive, initiating a flow of current which continues down the nerve as a wave. It travels very much more slowly than does electricity along a wire: in large fibers it travels at about 100 meters per second, and in the smallest fibers at less than one meter per second. The thick high-speed fibers have a special fatty coating—the *myelin sheath*—which insulates the fibers from their neighbors and also serves to increase the rate of conduction of the action potential.

Nerves are joined by synapses, which are junctions where chemicals are released which serve as triggers. Most, and perhaps all, neurons have both excitatory and inhibitory synapses which act as switches.

There are many sophisticated techniques for studying the nervous system. Electrical activity of individual cells, or groups of cells, may be recorded; regions may be stimulated electrically to evoke not only responses but even—in patients undergoing brain operations—sensations. The effects of loss of regions of brain may be discovered, resulting behavior changes being related to the regions of damage. The effects of drugs or chemicals applied directly to the surface of the brain may be investigated; this is becoming an important area of research both to establish that new drugs do not have unpleasant psychological side effects, and as a direct technique for deliberately changing the state of the brain. An advantage over destruction of regions of brain is that the changes are generally reversible, and may readily be varied in degree and in kind.

These techniques, together with examination of the way regions are joined by bundles of fibers, have made it clear that different parts of the brain are engaged in very different functions. But when it comes to discovering the processes going on in each region, even the most refined techniques look rather crude.

It may seem that the most direct way to study the brain is to examine its structure, and stimulate it and record from it. But like electronic devices, it is not at all easy to see how it works from its structure; and the results of stimulation, recording, and removal of parts are difficult to interpret in the absence of a general model of how it works. In order to establish the results of stimulating or ablating the brain, it is essential to perform associated behavior experiments. The results of recording from brain cells are also most interesting when there is some related behavior, or reported experience. This means that animal and human psychology are very important, for it is essential to relate brain activity to behavior, and this involves specially designed psychological experiments.

The brain is, of course, an immensely complicated arrangement of nerve cells but it is somewhat similar to man-made electronic devices, so general engineering considerations can be helpful. Like a computer, the brain accepts information, and makes decisions according to the available information; but it is not very similar to actual computers designed by engineers, if only because there are already plenty of brains available at very reasonable cost, and they are easy to make by a well-proved method so that computors are designed to be different.

It is easier to make a machine to solve mathematical or logical problems—or to learn or to translate languages—than to see. The problem of making machines to recognize patterns has been solved in various ways for restricted ranges of patterns, but so far there is no neat solution, and no machine comes anywhere near the human perceptual system in range or speed. It is partly for this reason that detailed study of human perception is important. Finding out what we can of human perception may suggest ways in which perception can be simulated by machines. This would be useful for many purposes—from the reading of documents and books to the exploration of space by robots.

One of the difficulties in understanding the function of the brain is that it is like nothing so much as a lump of porridge. With mechanical systems, it is usually possible to make a good guess at function by considering the structure of the parts, and this is true of much of the body. The bones of the limbs are *seen* to be levers. The position of attachment of the muscles clearly determines their function.

Mechanical and optical systems have parts whose shapes are closely related to their function, which makes it possible to deduce, or at least guess, their function from their shape. It was possible for Kepler to guess that a structure in the eye (called at that time the "crystalline") is in fact a lens from its shape. It was a rather simple matter for Scheiner to discover the image, because he knew where to look. But unfortunately the brain presents a far more difficult problem, if only because the physical arrangement of its parts and their shapes is rather unimportant to their function. When function is not reflected in structure we cannot deduce function by simply looking. We must resort to sophisticated techniques.

The electrical activity recorded by physiologists is extremely important, but unfortunately it is very difficult to get detailed information of the separate activity of more than a few cells at a time. The technical problems are immense.

Design principles may be suggested by engineering considerations. If a given possible engineering design has certain limitations, and experiments on animals or human beings show they have similar limitations, then such experiments may confirm hypotheses perhaps culled originally from engineering. In particular, perceptual experiments can be important tools for discovering or testing models of brain function. Looking out through the eyes, the brain sees the world—by looking in through the eyes via suitable experiments we can see the brain as a functional system limited by physical, engineering considerations.

THE VISUAL REGIONS OF THE BRAIN

The neural system responsible for vision starts with the retinas. These, as we have seen, are essentially outgrowths of the brain, containing typical brain cells as well as specialized light-sensitive detec-

tors. The retinas are effectively divided vertically down the middle, the fibers from the outer sides going to the same side of the back of the brain, while the fibers from the inner, nasal, sides of the retinas cross just behind the eyes—at the *optic chiasma*—and go to the opposite sides of the back of the brain (Figure 5). This visual region at the back of the brain is known as the *area striata*, from its appearance, the cells being arranged in rows (*frontispiece*).

The brain as a whole is divided down the middle, forming two hemispheres, which are really more-or-less complete brains, joined by a massive bundle of fibers the *corpus callosum*, and the smaller *optic chiasma*. On their way from the chiasma, the optic tract passes through a relay station in each hemisphere, the *lateral geniculate body*.

The central region of *area striata* is known as the "visual projection area."

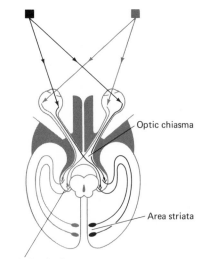

Optic chiasma

Area striata

Lateral geniculate body

Figure 5. The optic pathways of the brain. The optic nerve divides at the chiasma, the right half of each retina being represented on the right side of the occipital cortex, the left side on the left half. The lateral geniculate bodies are relay stations between the eyes and the visual cortex.

When a small part is stimulated a human patient reports a flash of light. Upon a slight change of position of the stimulating electrode, a flash is seen in another part of the visual field. It thus seems there is a spatial representation of the retinas upon the visual cortex. Stimulation of surrounding regions of the striate area also gives visual sensations, but instead of flashes of light the sensations are more elaborate. Brilliant colored balloons may be seen floating up in an infinite sky. Further away, stimulation may elicit visual memories, even complete scenes coming vividly before the eyes.

Among the most exciting of recent discoveries, is the finding of two American physiologists, Hubel and Wiesel, who recorded activity from single cells of the visual area of the cat's brain while presenting its eyes with simple visual shapes (Figure 6). These were generally bars of light, projected by a slide projector on a screen in front of the cat. Hubel and Wiesel found that some cells were only active when the bar of light was presented to the cat at a certain angle. At

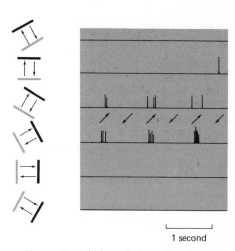

Figure 7. Hubel and Wiesel's discovery that selected single brain cells (in the cat) fire with movement of the eye in a certain direction. The arrows show the various directions of movement of a bar of light presented to the eyes. The electrical record shows that this particular cell fires only for one direction of movement.

that particular angle the brain cell would fire, with long bursts of impulses, while at other angles it was "silent." Different cells would respond to different angles. Cells deeper in the brain responded to more generalized characteristics, and would respond to these characteristics no matter which part of the retina was stimulated by the light. Other cells responded only to movement, and movement in only a single direction (Figure 7). These findings are of the greatest importance, for they show that there are analyzing mechanisms in the brains selecting certain features of objects.

We do have "mental" pictures, but this should not suggest that there are corresponding electrical pictures in the brain. It is possible to represent things in symbols but symbols will generally be very different from the things represented. The notion of brain pictures is conceptually dangerous. It is apt to suggest that these supposed pictures are themselves seen with a kind of inner eye—

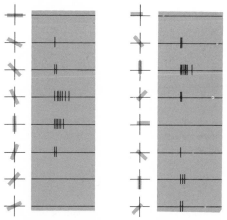

Figure 6. Hubel and Wiesel's records from single cells in the visual cortex of the cat. A line (shown on the left) was presented to the cat at various orientations. A single cell in the brain fires only at a certain orientation. This is shown by the spikes of the electrical records.

involving another picture, and another eye ... and so on.

In any case, it is not possible to suppose that sounds and smells and colors are represented by pictures in the brain—they *must* be coded in some other form. There is every reason to believe that retinal patterns are represented by coded combinations of cell activity. Hubel and Wiesel, and other electrophysiologists, are now beginning to discover the code.

We are not primarily concerned in this book with the electrical or other activity in the brain. We are concerned with the phenomena of perception, and experiments which have been devised to discover various aspects of perception. Ultimately these studies should link up with the physiological studies—when this happens we shall have deeper understanding of the eye and the brain.

evolution
of
the
nervous
system
chapter 3

Study of the evolution of the nervous system is important
because it gives us an idea of how man's behavioral capacities
are linked to his cerebral development and also how he
compares with other animals in these regards. The first paper
in this section deals with the octopus. It was included because
we now realize the octopus probably has the most complex
of invertebrate brains. In fact, not only is the brain of this
animal amazingly intricate but its behaviors are highly varied
and complex. It has been discovered that the octopus can
perform many learning tasks that challenge a rat or even a
cat. This points to something that has always been suspected
—the evolution of behavioral capacities, as is already the case
for physical traits, is not a linear function of level on the
phylogenetic scale. Clearly, many invertebrates exhibit far
more complex behaviors than many of the lower vertebrates.
One could even speculate that because man's brain is one of
the largest compared with the size of his body as well as very
complex in its structure, he may not necessarily be the most
intelligent member of the animal kingdom. There are animals
that have even larger brains proportionally to their bodies
than man; there are some animals, such as the porpoise, that
have certain cortical areas more complexly organized than in
man. It is through comparative studies of behavior that we can
set up a phylogenetic classification of behavioral capacities
which may or may not be the same as the generally acknowledged phylogenetic scale based upon physical characteristics.
When we talk about the development of man there have

even been some changes in his cerebrum over the past 500,000 years. Fascinating speculations dealing with this topic are presented in the Magoun, Darling, and Prost paper.

Finally, in lower animals as well as perhaps in higher animals, some behavior seems to be almost reflexive, automatic, and independent of learning experiences. This indicates genetic coding of specific circuitry and is discussed in detail in the Wooldridge paper.

Learning
by
touch
m. j. wells

THE SENSE ORGANS CONCERNED

The suckers of *Octopus* are exceedingly sensitive to both mechanical and chemical stimulation. They contain a great many sensory endings, some of which, deeply buried beneath the skin, are presumably mechanoreceptors stimulated by shear forces or pressure, while others with fine processes penetrating to the surface are almost certainly chemoreceptors (Figure 1). It is not known whether there is more than one functional type of chemoreceptor; certainly octopuses are sensitive to substances that we would call sweet, sour and bitter, and their sensitivity to some of these (sour and bitter) approaches that of the human tongue. But it is not known whether these tastes are distinguished from one another.

The extreme sensitivity of the suckers, and particularly of the rims of the suckers, seems to be due to the great concentration of sense organs there, several thousands per square centimeter. Elsewhere in the skin morphologically identical sensory endings occur, though in smaller numbers, and it can be shown that the whole surface of a cephalopod is to some extent sensitive to taste as well as to touch. In tactile discrimination experiments one is concerned, however, only with the receptors on the suckers, because these are invariably used to test the surface of objects with which the animal comes in contact.

In considering tactile discrimination one is concerned also with internal re-

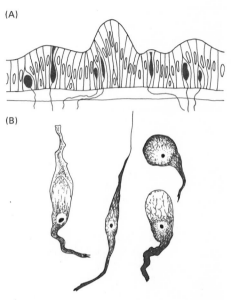

(A)

(B)

Figure 1. Sensory endings from the suckers of Octopus. *(A) is a diagram showing how some of these have processes running to the surface while others are deeply buried in the skin. (B) shows some typical sensory cells. Similar cells, with a cap of clear cytoplasm, are found in the "olfactory" organ; spindle-shaped cells are also found in the muscles surrounding the eyeball. (After Rossi and Graziadei)*

ceptors inasmuch as these can give information about external conditions. In theory internal receptors can increase the amount of information available about things touched in a number of ways. They are potentially important, for example, in registering the relative position of the surface tactile sensory endings; an octopus can hope to detect the shape or the surface pattern of an object touched only if it has accurate information about the relative position of the several very mobile individual suckers making the contact. Internal receptors are also potentially able to provide information about the weight of objects touched by registering the muscle tension needed to support them. Lastly, information from the statocysts and perhaps from muscle stretch receptors is important in that it fixes the animal's own position in space and thus, indirectly, gives information about the orientation of objects touched.

The statocysts have already been described; they are clearly capable of providing all the information needed to define the position of the animal itself in space, whether it is sitting still or moving about. Hardly anything is known about other internal receptors in cephalopods. Alexandrowicz has described a muscle receptor organ lying beneath the nerves radiating from the stellate ganglion in *Eledone* and *Octopus*; but this is the only known instance of an undoubted proprioceptor. For the rest of the body, including the arms, all that can be said at the moment is that there are many nerve endings of undetermined function in the skin and connective tissue and in the muscles. These endings must in some way provide the proprioceptive feedback that the animal needs for accurate adjustments of its own movements; the information they provide could also be available for tactile discrimination.

In practice it appears that octopuses never make use of proprioceptive information in learning to recognize things by touch. It will be shown below that they cannot be taught to make discriminations that would depend upon their taking into account either the relative position of the sense organs in contact, or the tensions developed in the muscles of the arms used to grasp objects.

THE BEHAVIOR OF BLIND OCTOPUSES

To test tactile discrimination, octopuses must be blinded, since it is otherwise impossible to be sure that they are not learning to recognize the test objects by sight. The operation, carried out under urethane anæsthesia, is easy to perform and the optic nerves do not regenerate.

Immediately after revival by passing a stream of seawater through the mantle cavity, octopuses blinded by cutting the optic nerves sit with their arms over the head, generally in a corner of the tank, pressed against the walls. They react by shrinking back if touched and if prodded will turn upside down, presenting the under surface of the arms towards the attacker. After a period of hours the animal recovers sufficiently to extend one or more arms and make cautious exploratory movements over the surfaces against which it is sitting. Small objects touched may be grasped and passed under the interbrachial web to the mouth. If the animal is touched gently on an extended arm it will, at this stage, withdraw the arm at once and may move away. Some days later the same animal will seize anything that touches it, and can then be trained. Octopuses that have been blinded for several days or weeks move freely around their tanks with the arms outspread; they can swim but seldom do so.

Unlike normal animals they do not keep to a home of rocks or bricks, but usually sit in the angle between the water surface and the side of the tank. If prodded or given electric shocks they may retreat into a corner and if repeatedly disturbed in this way will revert to the retiring sort of behavior observed immediately after operation. Blind animals are sensitive to vibration; they flush darkly if the tank is jarred, and can locate the approximate direction of disturbances in the water around them, making exploratory movements with the arms on the side of the disturbance. If touched lightly on an arm a fully-recovered blind octopus will move swiftly in the direction of the stimulus, and in this way can succeed in cornering food such as crabs wandering in its tank.

HABITUATION

A blinded octopus picks up any small unfamiliar object that it encounters, passing the object under the interbrachial web to the mouth. If the object is inedible it is rejected after a period of minutes, generally being passed down the line of suckers along one arm and thrust away by the armtip. If the same object is presented again after a short interval it will probably be retaken, but rejection is more rapid. After several successive presentations, rejection follows a cursory examination with the armtip. A second object will still be taken if it is sufficiently unlike the first. The result of a typical experiment is plotted in Figure 2.

As a means of investigating tactile discrimination the technique is not altogether satisfactory since a similar reaction to two objects does not necessarily imply that the animal is unable to distinguish between them.

REPEATED PRESENTATION, WITH SHOCKS

The process of learning to reject a particular object is greatly accelerated if the animal is given a small (6–9 volt A.C.) electric shock for passing the object under the interbrachial web. Two or three shocks are sufficient to teach an octopus to reject an object that has not previously been associated with food, while twice that number serves to reverse responses towards objects that the animal has previously been rewarded for taking.

An interesting sidelight on the organization of the brain of *Octopus* is obtained from these experiments. If trials are frequent (three to five minutes apart) and

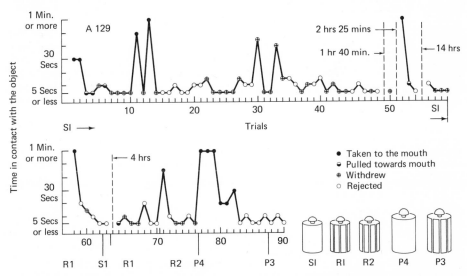

Figure 2. *Habituation as a means of testing discrimination in* Octopus. *The same object was repeatedly presented by dropping it into the water close to the octopus. The animal did not learn to recognize the object by sight, continuing to reach out an arm and grasp it whenever presented. The octopus did, however, quickly learn to recognize the object by touch, and after four attempts to eat it during the first thirteen trials, ceased to pull the object towards itself, withdrawing the arm after a cursory examination, or pushing the cylinder away. Trials were at two-minute intervals. New objects were at first taken, which shows that the animal was learning to recognize a specific stimulus pattern, and not simply becoming fatigued or learning to reject all objects. (From Wells and Wells)*

experience is limited to one arm at a time by presenting the test object always to the same arm, that arm alone learns to reject the object. In tests with the other arms the object is taken and the animal has to relearn. With trials at less frequent (twenty minute) intervals learning proceeds as before, but tests carried out on other arms show that the effect of the experience has spread; none of the arms of the octopus will accept a test object that one has learned to avoid (Figure 3). Since animals with the subesophageal lobes removed cannot be taught to reject

a test object at all, there is no question of learning within the axial cords of the eight individual arms. These results therefore imply that the tactile system of octopus is in some way functionally divided into eight sections related to the individual arms; changes taking place within any one section take time to spread through the learning system in the supraesophageal lobes.

CHEMOTACTILE AND MECHANOTACTILE DISCRIMINATION

Octopuses at least, and probably other cephalopods, can distinguish between objects, such as live and dead shellfish, by the chemical characteristics of their surfaces as well as by their surface texture. Although it is quite certain that the chemotactile sense is very important to bottom-living cephalopods we know remarkably little about it. Systematic investigation has been hampered by the technical difficulty of devising experiments in which the test objects continue to "taste" the same throughout, and of ensuring that any "smell" left after a test is eliminated from the circulating seawater before the next trial. A still more serious problem is our own inability to classify tastes in a satisfactory manner. Because of these difficulties no experiments have been done to show whether octopuses can make quantitative chemotactile discriminations or even whether the various substances to which they are sensitive taste different to them.

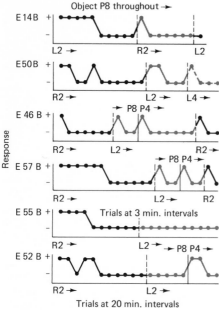

Figure 3. Results of training octopuses not to accept (+ response) an object repeatedly presented to them. Figures L2, R2, etc., show the arm of the octopus to which the test object was presented, and P8, P4, which object (see Figure 4). In the first four experiments, trials were at three-minute intervals, and a change of arm resulted in the object being taken although the animal had already learned to reject it (− response) with the original arm. In the last two experiments, with a similar number of trials more widely spaced, a change of arms had no such effect. (From Wells)

DISCRIMINATION OF TEXTURE

We know more about discrimination of the physical characteristics of objects touched. Octopuses can readily be trained to discriminate by touch between objects such as the cylinders shown in Figure 4, which must taste the same, as well as between more natural objects such as the cleaned valves of shellfish,

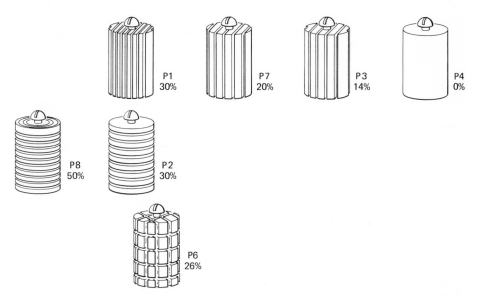

Figure 4. Perspex cylinders used as test objects in tactile training experiments. The series is arranged so that there is a decreasing proportion (given as a percentage beside each object) of grooved to flat surface from left to right. The top row is of cylinders that differ only in the frequency of standard sized vertical grooves cut into them. P1, P2 and P6 differ in the arrangement of the grooves, which represent the same, or almost the same proportion of the total surface in each case. Octopuses find these three difficult or impossible to distinguish but can readily be taught to discriminate between the members of the top row. (From Wells and Wells)

which might possibly taste different.

In training blind octopuses, advantage can be taken of the fact that such animals habitually sit with the arms outspread. An object touched against the back of one of these arms causes the arm to twist and grasp with the suckers. Once the test object has been gripped, one of three things happens. Either (i) the arm bends and the object is passed under the interbrachial web to the mouth—the normal reaction of an untrained octopus to any unfamiliar object, or (ii) the object is rejected by passing it centrifugally from sucker to sucker and finally pushing it away with the armtip, or (iii) the animal, having examined the object by grasping it with the suckers (it may change its grip several times) simply withdraws the arm, and lets the object fall away. All three sets of movements are evidently organized within the axial cords of the arms concerned, since they are also performed by brainless preparations (rejection rarely, the other two commonly). For the experiments reviewed below, no time limit was set on reaction, this being considered complete when the animal had either passed the object under the interbrachial web or let go of it. The animal was rewarded with a piece of fish for passing one of the test objects to be distinguished to the mouth, and given a small electric shock (as in the visual training experiments) if it did the same with the other. The object, attached to a line, was pulled away from the octopus immediately after giving a shock or reward. In the case of rejection of the positive object, this was presented again together with the reward, whereupon it was normally taken.

In such experiments by far the greater proportion of the errors made are by acceptance of the negative object, which the animals are punished for taking; errors by rejection of a positive object are comparatively rare. Learning is about as rapid as in visual discrimination experiments.

Experiments have been made to discover which features of things touched are distinguished by *Octopus*, using the cylinders shown in Figure 4. These were alike in weight and (presumably) in taste; they differed only in the number and arrangement of standard section grooves cut into their otherwise smooth surfaces. P1, P3 and P7 differed from P4 in being grooved ("rough") instead of smooth and from each other in the interval between grooves. The objects P2 and P8 differed from these four in groove orientation, while P6 had grooves cut into it forming a pattern of squares. Selecting pairs of objects from this series that differed in only one way (in roughness or in groove orientation, for instance), it was possible to test *Octopus's* capacity to detect particular sorts of difference between things touched. When a number of discrimination experiments was made, it was found that octopuses always failed to distinguish between P1 and P2 and that they distinguished between P1 and P6 only with the greatest difficulty. Other discriminations between the cylinders were relatively easy for them. This was a rather unexpected result, because for us P1, P2 and P6 are easy to distinguish by touch compared with P1, P3 and P7. A further analysis of the results of training experiments showed that the difficulty of any discrimination (measured as the proportion of errors made by trained animals) varied as the difference in proportion of surface cut away from the objects to form the grooves (Figure 5). Thus P8, with fifty percent of the surtace cut away, was distinguished from the smooth P4 more readily than P1, from which thirty percent was removed. P1

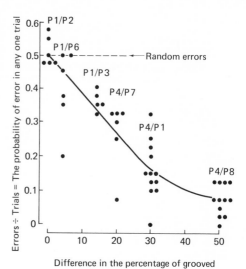

Figure 5. A summary of the results of 48 experiments in which octopuses were trained to distinguish between pairs of objects from the series shown in Figure 4. The probability of error (measured over a sample period of 40 trials, on days 8–12 of training at eight trials per day) is clearly related to the difference in proportion of grooved surface between the objects to be discriminated, and appears to be unaffected by differences in the pattern or orientation of the grooves. (From Wells and Wells)

and P2, with the same proportion of groove, were treated as identical, despite the difference in orientation of the grooves.

Evidently octopuses discriminate between these cylinders on a basis of the proportion of groove and other differences are irrelevant to them. This suggests that discrimination of the topographical features of objects touched may be based simply upon the proportion of sense organs excited in the contact areas. A measure of this can be derived directly from the cylinders, since the grooves are deep and too narrow for the rims of the suckers to penetrate. A sucker applied to one of the cylinders bridges

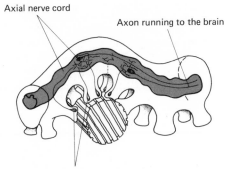

Axial nerve cord

Axon running to the brain

Sense organs in the rims of the suckers

Figure 6. Diagram of an arm of an octopus touching one of the cylinders shown in Figure 4. The proportion of sense organs excited in the suckers in contact will depend upon the proportion of the surface of the object that is cut away to form grooves into which the suckers cannot penetrate. The sense organs do not themselves send axons to the brain, but supply parts of the axial cord immediately above or close to them. It is suggested that the proportion of sense organs excited determines the rate of firing in the axons running from the nerve cord to the brain and that it is this frequency that the animal learns to recognize in identifying objects. (From Wells and Wells)

the gap made by a groove (Figure 6) and the sense organs on this bridge are likely to be differently stimulated from those on parts of the sucker in flat contact with the object. Whether it is the latter proportion (excited, presumably, by pressure) or the proportion of sense organs in the bridge (excited by stretch) that is counted is unimportant; sense organs in the suckers potentially capable of responding in either way exist. In either case, the rate of firing in the axons running from the axial nerve cord to the brain will be related to the general state of excitation within the region of the nerve cord in which they originate, and this in turn will depend upon the proportion of sense organs excited in the suckers underlying that part of the cord

If tactile discriminations are really

made simply on a basis of signals generated in this way (and there is certainly no evidence of spatial projection from the tactile sensory field, nor any indication that proprioceptive information is available for integration with the surface tactile input) then the function of the brain in touch learning is peculiarly simple. The mechanism concerned is required only to recognize the frequency of its input and to trigger off appropriate positive or negative responses. It does not have to organize details of these responses, since these are largely determined reflexedly at the arm nerve cord level. The consequences of a mechanism that is organized in this way are discussed below.

DISCRIMINATION OF SIZE AND SHAPE

It seems to be impossible to train octopuses to distinguish between cylinders of different sizes and although they can be taught to discriminate between a sphere and a cube, there is evidence that the two are distinguished only because of the irregularity represented by the corners of the cube. To the circular rims of the suckers a sphere is a flat surface, and a cube will differ from a sphere because it distorts any suckers that happen to touch corners. This seems to be the difference that *Octopus* detects. When a narrow rod was presented in place of the cube, animals already trained to distinguish between a sphere and a cube made *fewer* errors than before the change. When the rod was presented in place of the sphere, the same animals made more than random errors in discrimination—the rod, which could only be grasped by bent suckers, was a "better" cube than the original, so far as the octopuses were concerned.

In an earlier series of experiments, octopuses failed to learn to distinguish between shellfish of similar texture but different shape; all of these, however, had corners.

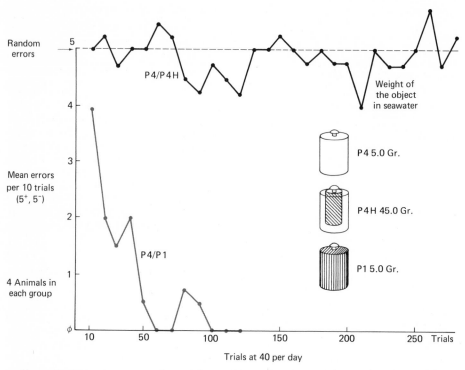

Figure 7. Octopuses cannot be taught to discriminate between objects differing only in weight. In these experiments, which are plotted as total errors, ● *shows the results of a weight discrimination experiment (P4 against P4H),* O *the result of training to make a textural discrimination (P4 against P1). Training was at a rate of 40 trials (20⁺, 20⁻) per day. (Data from Wells)*

DISCRIMINATION OF WEIGHT

Although it is easy to train octopuses to discriminate between objects differing in surface texture, it seems impossible to train them to distinguish between objects differing in weight. Unsuccessful attempts were made to teach octopuses to discriminate between pairs of perspex cylinders, weighing 5 and 15, 5 and 25, and 5 and 45 grams, while the addition of a weight difference to a pair of cylinders already discriminable on a textural basis failed to produce any noticeable difference in performance. The results of weight discrimination experiments (Figure 7) are the more

remarkable because octopuses very obviously compensate for the weight of objects that they pick up. In these experiments the objects (suspended as usual by a nylon line to ensure their recovery after acceptance or rejection) were presented in the normal manner by touching them against an arm of the animal under test. As soon as the octopus had grasped the object, this retaining line was slacked, the animal thereafter having to support the full weight of the object. The usual immediate result of this was considerable passive extension of the arm gripping the test object. The octopus, sitting on the side of its tank (as blinded octopuses do, most of the time) would then contract its arm before handling the object in the normal way. An observer is able to distinguish which of the two test objects is being handled simply by watching the animal; but the octopus itself is apparently unable to distinguish objects from the muscle tension it must exert to support them.

PROPRIOCEPTION IN LEARNING

The failure of octopuses in experiments on weight discrimination emphasizes a curious feature of the nervous organization of these animals already implied from the results of other tactile discrimination experiments and from the consequences of statocyst removal on visual discrimination. It would appear that proprioceptive information is not available for integration with other sensory inputs in learning, though it is obviously used in a number of reflex adjustments. Thus in weight discrimination experiments the animal increases muscular tone when an arm is passively extended. Animals with the supraesophageal part of the brain removed do the same, as one must suppose that this sort of response to proprioceptive input is organized in the subesophageal lobes. It will be shown later that discriminatory learning depends upon the integrity of parts of the supraesophageal brain, and the simplest explanation of the non-use of proprioceptive information in learning is that signals from proprioceptors never penetrate to so high a level. Such an explanation would be compatible with the findings derived by comparing the results of direct electrical stimulation and brain lesion experiments, which suggest that while higher motor organization within the supraesophageal lobes is not dependent upon sensory feedback, the actions normally organized at a lower level in the subesophageal part of the brain are.

A similar state of affairs, with postural information used for reflex adjustments but not available for learned responses, is revealed by the effect of statocysts removal upon the visual discrimination of orientation. The eyes are normally kept in a constant orientation with respect to gravity as a result of positional information derived from the statocysts. Removal of the statocysts abolishes this constancy, and with the retina disoriented visual recognition of horizontal and vertical becomes confused. The animal is not able to compensate for removal of its gravity receptors as a vertebrate would, by combining proprioceptive information from stretch receptors with the visual input. The whole visual system of an octopus is evidently constructed on the assumption that the retinae will remain constantly oriented with respect to the vertical and horizontal axes, and there is no provision for combining positional information about which way up the animal happens to be with the visual input.

In the case of tactile discrimination, the consequences of non-use on proprioceptive information are more far-reaching. Since the suckers are extraordinarily mobile, and the arms themselves very flexible, the relative positions of the tactile sense organs can vary within wide limits. Any projection of the tactile sensory field, as would be necessary for pattern recognition, for example, would depend upon a mechanism for assessing the relative positions of the sense organs, that is, upon the integration of proprioceptive information about the positions of the suckers with information from superficial touch receptors. It seems that this does not occur, which is scarcely surprising in view of the immense complication of mechanism that would be needed in an animal in which movement is unrestricted by joints. One effect of this is that the animal cannot learn to distinguish between objects of different shape, because it cannot take into account the bends and twists that are made by the arms. Another and possibly more important consequence is that the animal can never learn by experience to make skilled movements; manipulation is not improved by practice.

REVERSAL AND RETENTION

Octopuses trained to discriminate between two objects by touch, taking one and rejecting the other, can also be trained to reverse these responses. Typical animals at first react to the switch in rewards and punishments by continuing to discriminate in the old direction and in consequence make far more than random errors. This is commonly followed by a period during which the animals cease taking the objects altogether, and finally by relearning during which they achieve standards of accuracy of response at least approaching those attained in pre-reversal training. When animals are trained to make several reversals in succession, the number of trials required to reach a given standard of performance increases with each changeover.

Octopuses trained to discriminate and afterwards retested by means of trials without rewards or punishments show a slow steady decline in performance, though traces of training are still found after periods of from three to four weeks and perhaps endure for much longer.

The evolution of man's brain

h. w. magoun
louise darling
and
j. prost

Before the nineteenth century, the *Scala natura*, in which living forms were arranged in an order of increasing complexity, was generally conceived as the immutable product of divine creation. Early in the century, Lyell's ideas of geological evolution provided a background for Darwin's proposal of the *Origin of Species by Means of Natural Selection*, published in 1859. By this principle, Darwin wrote, "Light will be thrown on the origin of man and his history," a prophecy fulfilled in 1871 in his *Descent of Man*. Darwin's concept of man's evolution from primate ancestors anticipated the discovery of intermediate fossil forms. In the creationists' view, fossils of lower plants and animals were the consequence of periodic geological catastrophes that had wiped out all life, after which new and higher forms were created. Because, as Cuvier had pointed out earlier, man's creation had followed the last such catastrophe, "L'homme fossile n'existe pas!"

The accumulation of actual evidence for fossil man began with the discovery of Neanderthal remains in 1856. Next, Java man was found in 1891. The implications of both findings were vigorously opposed, the first on the ground that it was a pathological specimen of modern man and the second on the basis that it was a fossil ape. Throughout this period, Darwin's "bulldog," Huxley, defended the concept of man's evolution against the opposition of Richard Owen in England, while Ernst Haeckel played a similar role against Virchow in

From *The Central Nervous System Behavior*, M. A. B. Brazier, Ed © 1960 by The Josiah Macy, Jr. Foundation.

Germany. In the present century, increasing discoveries of fossil material now make possible the presentations of a well documented series of stages in hominid evolution.

Earlier concepts of the evolution of man, in which growth of the brain was considered to be the primary and determining event, have now given way to the view that man's large brain is the culmination of a series of changes which actually began caudally and only reached the cranium through successive alterations in intervening parts of the body.

It is now generally held that the initial adaptation leading to the emergence of the *Hominidae* involved the pelvis and lower extremity, permitting assumption of an upright posture. Following this, the upper extremity and hand, freed from locomotory obligations, undertook the activities of prehension and food-getting, as well as those of combat and defense, for which the jaw and teeth had previously provided the major instrumentation. The acquisition of manual skills, augmented by the use of specialized implements and weapons capable of being sequentially employed and discarded, reduced the requirements for a large jaw with its built-in incisor teeth for cutting, its large canines for attack, and its molars for grinding food. Consequent reduction of the lower face and regression of the massive jaw musculature, which had "imprisoned the cranium," was followed by an expansion of the brain-bearing portion of the head and an hypertrophy of its neural contents.

From the viewpoint of geological time, the interval over which these alterations of hominid evolution proceeded has been described as "explosively" brief. Life is presumed to have originated on this earth some 2 billion years ago, the simplest primates made their appearance 60 million years ago, and remains of fossil apes (*Proconsul*) are dated at 25 million years. By contrast, the entire scope of hominid evolution has occurred within the most recent geological period, the Pleistocene, which spans only the last one million years. Hominid evolution has occupied, therefore, about 0.05 percent of the total period of life on earth. It is customary to divide the Pleistocene into three subperiods: the Lower (500,000 years), in which the Australopithecines were the typical hominids; the Middle (350,000 years), of which the Pithecanthropoids were representative; and the Upper (150,000 years), characterized by Neanderthal types living 50,000 to 100,000 years ago, and by *Homo sapiens*, present only for the last 25,000 to 50,000 years. The span of existence of modern man is thus only about 0.00125 percent of the total period of life on earth.

The following general survey of the subject is organized both chronologically and in relation to these stages of hominid development. It is obviously introductory, and technical analysis of proposed taxonomic relations has been studiously avoided.

AUSTRALOPITHECINES

During 1924, at the Northern Lime Company, Taung, South Africa, there was blasted out of the red, sandy limestone a small fossil brain-cast and skull. The specimen was studied by Professor Raymond A. Dart, of the Department of Anatomy, Witwatersrand University in Johannesburg and, because of its seemingly obvious significance, he promptly sent off to England a preliminary account which appeared in *Nature* in 1925.

"It represents," Dart wrote, "a creature well advanced beyond modern anthropoids in just those characters, facial and

cerebral, which are to be anticipated in an extinct link between man and his simian ancestor. I proposed that a new family of man-apes be created, and that the first known species be designated *Australopithecus africanus*, vindicating Darwin's claim that this continent would prove to be the cradle of mankind." The editor of *Nature* requested the leading English anthropologists to comment, and the 5 year-old hominid—"Dart's baby" as the immature Taung skull soon came to be called—was generally condemned as a fossil ape.

In 1936, Dr. Robert Broom of the Transvaal Museum started collecting in the nearby limestone caves and, in two years' time, accumulated several skulls of adult man-apes. Most recently (1959), Dr. and Mrs. L. S. B. Leakey of the Coryndon Museum, Nairobi, discovered in Tanganyika the skull of a type with massive molar teeth, nicknamed "nutcracker man." As Dr. Broom stated: "We now know with moderate certainty that a group of higher primates lived in South Africa in Pliocene time and apparently survived into the Pleistocene. They were almost certainly bipedal and probably used their hands for the manipulation of implements. Their faces were rather larger than those of modern man, but their brains were relatively small. The group, if not quite worthy of being called men, were nearly men."

The Australopithecines now emerge as the main hominid type of the Lower Pleistocene period. Their cranial capacity averaged 550 cc. (450 to 650 cc.), which is but 100 cc. larger than that of the average anthropoid (450 cc.). These small-brained bipeds made crude and simple pebble tools, which have been found with their remains.

PITHECANTHROPOIDS

The nineteenth-century proposal, by Ernst Haeckel, that man had evolved from a gibbon-like ancestor in Indonisia led young Eugene Dubois, physician in the Royal Dutch Army, to seek assignment in Java to undertake excavations exploring Haeckel's view. In 1890, Dubois discovered a calvarium, femur, and jaw in a mid-Pleistocene stratum, on the bank of the Solo River in Trinil. These findings were described in a monograph entitled *Pithecanthropus erectus; eine menschenaehnliche Ubergangsform aus Java*, published in Batavia in 1894. Later, exhibit of his specimens in Europe was met by so much opposition that Dubois withdrew the material and locked it away from examinations for most of the rest of his long life. His confidence was not shaken, however, and he later wrote: "I believe that it now hardly admits of a doubt that this upright-walking ape-man, as I have called him, represents a so-called transition-form between men and apes. I do not hesitate now, any more than I formerly did, to regard this *Pithecanthropus erectus* as the immediate progenitor of the human race."

Confirmation of his conclusions came in 1927, when Davidson Black, Professor of Anatomy at Pecking Union Medical School, China, boldly published a paper on a fossil hominid molar tooth, excavated from the quarried of Chou-kou-tien, southwest of Peking. "The circumstances," Black wrote, "justify the proposal that the hominid be regarded as a new genus to the named *Sinanthropus*. Since the horizon from which the specimen was obtained is identical with the early Pleistocene, the hominids of Chou-kou-tien occurred contemporaneously with *Pithecanthropus*." In extensive succeeding excavations, remains of upwards of forty individuals were discovered and, following Black's death, their study was continued by Franz Weidenreich. Upon the Japanese invasion of China, U.S. Marines attempted to evacuate the collection to the Chinese coast for transport to this country but they were captured by Japanese troops. The subsequent fate of the collection has remained to this day a mystery. Meanwhile, further exploration in Java, by G. H. R. von Koenigswald,

revealed additional remains of *Pithecanthropus* which he studied with Weidenreich following World War II.

Java and Peking man are now considered members of a common Pithecanthropoid group forming the dominant hominid type of the middle Pleistocene period. The cranial capacity of Java man averaged 850 cc. (750 to 900 cc.) and that of Peking man 1,050 cc. (900 to 1,200 cc.). The latter made chopper-type tools and weapons, somewhat more elaborate than those of the Australopithecines, but crude by comparison with the later cultures. Peking man was a hunter and, above all, was distinguished by introducing the use of fire.

NEANDERTHAL MAN

Neanderthal man gained this appellation from the discovery of his remains in a cave in the Neander Gorge, near Dusseldorf, Germany, in 1856. Neanderthaloid remains, since discovered widely in other parts of Europe, and in Africa and Asia, may be considered representative of the main hominid type of the Upper Pleistocene period. His cranial capacity averaged 1,350 cc. (1,150 to 1,600 cc.), a figure within the limits of modern man. The pointed flints and hand-axes of Neanderthal man were improvements over earlier tools and weapons. Caches of bear skulls in his caves suggest the possibility of ritualistic activities. Recovery of the remains of the old man of La Chapelle aux Saints from a shallow grave provided the earliest instance of man's burial.

Limitations of his cultural advance, despite an essentially modern cranial capacity, have probably been responsible for the lowly status in which Neanderthal man was formerly held. M. Boule, who reconstructed the skeleton from La Chapelle aux Saints in a semierect, simian-like posture, wrote: "The uniformity, simplicity and rudeness of his stone implements and the probable absence of all traces of preoccupation of an aesthetic or moral kind, are quite in agreement with the brutish appearance of this energetic and clumsy body and heavy-jawed skull, which itself declares the predominance of functions of a purely vegetative or bestial kind over the functions of the mind."

Recent celebrations of the centenary of the discovery of Neanderthal man have tended to elevate his position somewhat. Straus and Cave concluded: "There is no valid reason for the assumption that the posture of Neanderthal man differed significantly from that of present-day man." Eiseley wrote: "Let us remember what was finally revealed at the little French cave near La Chapelle aux Saints. Here, across millennia of time, we can observe a very moving spectacle. Massive, flint-hardened hands had shaped a sepulchre and placed flat stones to guard the dead man's head. A haunch of meat had been left to aid the dead man's journey. Worked flints, a little treasure of the human dawn, had been poured lovingly into the grave. For these men whose brains were locked in a skull reminiscent of the ape, these men whom serious scientists had contended to possess no thoughts beyond those of the brute, had laid down their dead in grief."

FOSSIL MODERN MAN

Just as the discoveries of the Australopithecines had a particular setting in Africa, and those of the Pithecanthropoids in Asia, so the crowning stage of hominid evolution, fossil Homo sapiens, was earliest found and most thoroughly investigated in Europe. Southern France especially provided large collections of the remains of Ice Age, Stone Age, or Reindeer Age man, as he is variously called.

During the 1860s the French anthropologist, Édouard Lartet, and his patron and collaborator, the English industrialist, Henry Christy, recovered quantities of Ice Age artifacts from the Vézère Valley in Dordogne, France. This "paradise of primitive man" came to have a meaning for prehistory, like that of the Valley of the Kings in Egyptology. In 1864, Lartet's work was crowned by finding a mammoth's tusk, upon which the picture of a mammoth had been engraved, an overwhelming proof that primitive man had lived early enough to have known the mammoth. In 1868, during railway construction, the Cro-Magnon cave was discovered. In it, Lartet's son, Louis, found remains of weapons, tools, ornaments, game, and five human skeletons, including "the old man of Cro-Magnon." His striking skull, with high forehead, broad face, and prominent nose and chin, became the type-specimen of Cro-Magnon man, the earliest representative of Homo sapiens, living 50,000 to 25,000 years ago.

The skeletal remains of the Cro-Magnon cave were studied by the anthropologist, Paul Broca (1824–1880), better known today for his discovery of the cortical speech area. Broca's presentation to the French Society of Anthropology, in 1868, opened: "The innumerable objects found in the caves have not only furnished the most incontestable proof for the contemporaneity of man to mammoth, but have revealed also the most curious details of the life and manners of these ancient troglodytes. There still remained to be known, however, the anatomical characteristics of this intelligent and artistic race, whose carvings are a subject of astonishment for us. This lacuna has been filled in today by the bones presented by M. Lartet fils."

Endocranial casts of Cro-Magnon man, taken from the Predmost skulls from Moravia, had cranial capacities ranging from 1,308 to 1,568 cc. and averaging 1,435 cc. The capacities of other specimens are 1,415 cc. (Combe-Chapelle), 1,590 cc. (Cro-Magnon) and 1,530 cc. (Chancelade). An over-all average of 1,475 cc. is sometimes given, equivalent to or slightly larger than that of contemporary man (1,450 cc.).

While physical anthropological interest in fossil *Homo sapiens* has recently come to lie chiefly in technical questions of racial relationships, the cultural features of his development have been of the greatest general interest. In the long series of stone artifacts marking hominid evolution, crude and stereotyped tools and weapons of earlier manufacture can readily be distinguished from the later ones of *Homo sapiens* with their contrasting inventiveness, variety, and perfection. S. L. Washburn has stressed the important role played by tools in hominid evolution. "It is my belief," he writes, "that the decrease in the size of the anterior teeth and the tripling of the size of the brain came after man was a tool user, and were the result of new selection pressures coming in with the use of tools." Later he summarizes: "It was bipedalness which started man on his separate career. But tool use was nearly as early. Biological changes in the hand, brain, and face followed the use of tools, and were due to the new selection pressures which tools created. Tools changed the whole pattern of life—bringing in hunting, cooperation, and the necessity for communication and language. Memory, foresight, and originality were favored as never before, and the complex social system made possible by tools could only be realized by domesticated individuals. In a very real sense, tools created *Homo sapiens*."

While some of the implements of the Cro-Magnon period came to be decorated by their makers, artistic interests were by no means confined to this utilitarian association. Animal carvings on bone, prepared by Cro-Magnon man, attracted earliest attention, but his paintings, discovered later on the cave walls of Southern France and Northern Spain, formed his greatest cultural achievement. The art of Reindeer man, the hunter, was dominated by the major source of his food supply, before which he was extremely self-effacing. Vegetable forms are exceedingly rare; some fish and birds are represented, but the large mammals, which he hunted, are figured in prolific variety and abundance.

Most frequently depicted are the reindeer, cave bear, bison, rhinoceros and, most impressive of all, the now extinct mammoth. The creative artistry of these paintings suggests that they formed expressions of man's early esthetic interests. Additionally, it is likely that these animals were drawn upon the cave walls and missiles directed at them in rites promoting success in hunting, designed to insure the food supply and material welfare of the practitioners. Man did not dwell in these caves that he decorated, but seemed rather to have entered their dark interiors for magical or sacred rituals. These subterranean caverns appear to have formed early religious sanctuaries for Ice Age man. A striking instance, in the cave of Trois Frères, is "The Sorcerer" who presides over a chamber filled with paintings of animals of the hunt. He has the horns of a stag, the face of an owl, the ears of a wolf, the forelegs of a bear, and the tail of a horse. His arms are flexed and his feet appear to move as in a dance; his virile reproductive organ is paradoxically pointed backward. The archeologist, Abbé Breuil, concludes, "Such is the figure the Magdalenians considered the most important in the cave and which we judge to represent the spirit ruling over the abundance of game and the hunt's success."

The Venus of Willendorf is one of the "steatopygous aphrodites, with their voluminous breasts, prominent hips, and protruding buttocks," which seemingly characterized the feminine ideal of Ice Age man. Discovered in 1908 by a road builder in the village of Willendorf, Austria, it is attributed to the Aurignacian Period. The archeologist Hugo Obermaier remarked: "Its maker had a first-rate comprehension of the build of a human body, but was only concerned in this case with bringing out the primary and secondary sexual characteristics." A desire for increase and fertility has been proposed to account for the abundance of these forms, which emphasized prolific femininity to the point of deformation.

A number of the caves contain paintings of the hands of prehistoric man. Most of these are imprints, silhouettes, or stencils: one hand was held against the cave wall and surrounded by pigment applied with the other. The left hand is usually shown and, in one cave, thirty-five left and seven right hands were so depicted. The right hand of Ice Age man was thus more frequently employed for dextrous manipulative activity than his left. Such right-handedness is associated with left cerebral dominance and, in turn, is related to the representation of the cortical mechanism for speech in modern man. Though man's first records of written language do not appear until about 5000 B.C., frequent dots, lines, and geometric patterns in many of the caves suggest the beginning use of symbols at this much earlier period.

Most fascinating of all is the possibility that primitive man may already have developed concepts of possession of a soul and its leaving the body after death. The dramatic scene of the "Man in the Well" at Lascaux shows a rhinoceros and a disemboweled, but still standing bison, with a spear through its flank. Between them, a man lies prone and outstretched, his face masked as a bird. Obviously the man had speared the bison, possibly after it had been gored by the rhinoceros. One or the other of these beasts must then have killed the man. His conspicuous priapism may have been the consequence of injury to the spinal cord, or of autonomic discharge associated with death in struggle. Most interesting of all is a small bird perched, like a weathercock, on a rod in the foreground of the painting. Does this represent the dead man's soul?

THE BRAIN OF MODERN MAN

The extreme rapidity of human intellectual evolution, and the speed of advance of man's intelligence beyond that of his simian ancestors, in the geologically brief period of a million years, has been described by Eiseley as "an explosion of brains!" The genetic or anthropological changes that underlay the increment of a kilogram of brain, with a tripling of cerebral size, during hominid evolution through the Pleistocene Period, are still unknown. In particular, it does not yet seem possible to explain the feature that plagued Alfred Russel Wallace, i.e., why most of this increment had already been attained at the stage of Neanderthal man, about 100,000 years in advance of any significant use that was made of it. Wallace's famous remark, made in 1869, was: "Natural selection could only have endowed the savage with a brain little superior to that of an ape; whereas he actually possesses one but very little inferior to that of the average member of our learned societies."

On the other hand, once modern man had acquired a competent brain, it is feasible to propose that his rapid intellectual advance rested upon the development of processes for evolution independent of those determined by genetic means. Modern man has found it possible to substitute, for phylogenetic modification, maturational changes in his brain acquired during the course of his individual, postnatal development. In this way, he has been able to avoid dependence upon variations reproductivity transmitted through a series of generations, with preservation of favored ones by natural selection working over long intervals of time.

The deferral of maturation of the higher parts of his brain until after birth is among the most important of the factors by which modern man has, to this degree, become independent of the processes of biological evolution. In spite of a long gestation period of 38 weeks, typical of the great apes (chimpanzee, 34 weeks; orang, 39 weeks), each human infant is exceedingly immature at birth, particularly with respect to his higher neural functions and most of all those of the cerebral hemispheres, whose cortex provides the all-important organ for his maturation. Delay of cerebral growth to the postnatal period is advantageous also in the respect that man's brain is already so large at parturition as just to permit uninjured passage through the birth canal.

In the early postnatal period, growth of man's brain is more rapid than that of any other organ of the body. His brain weight doubles (from 380 to 630 gm.) in the first 6 months after birth, and more than doubles again (from 630 to 1,330 gm.) by the age of 4 years. Further increment is slight but the brain's full weight is not reached until the age of 20. While this gain is quantitative testimony for the pronounced and prolonged maturation of the brain after birth, no direct relationship can be drawn between it and the rise of functional neural capacity during individual development. For example, man's intellectual attainment is much greater between the ages of 4 and 20 years, when the weight of his brain increases only 120 gm., than during the first 4 years of life, when the brain expands by almost a kilogram. Furthermore, the ratio of brain to body weight diminishes rather than rises during postnatal growth for, while the brain increases four times by adulthood, the weight of the body has increased twenty times, or five times as much.

Maturation of the brain's functional capacity is related more to the increase of its cytological than to its gross complexity. These microscopic alterations, in which weight changes are minimal, involve the elaboration of dendritic processes of neurons; the development of new or preferential pathways and synapses associating previously unrelated parts; the rise of shifting foci of neural facilitation or inhibition, grading central activity; the formation of loop circuits and feedbacks modifying neural input and output; and the capacity, whatever its basis, by which previous activity in the nervous system can later be reinvoked, as memory, to merge with and influence current action.

In addition to these general features, more organized developments in the maturing brain lead to the formation of elaborate cortical receiving areas for each of the sensory modalities, to which all incoming information is relayed, and whose activity underlies subjective perception. Reciprocally, because the only way the brain can express itself is through motor performance, a cortical area develops which subserves "voluntary" movement of the body parts. In the monkey, no one of the parts of the body has a markedly greater representation in this motor cortex than the others, and this is in keeping with the absence of any pronounced regional specialization in the general motor performance of subhuman primates.

In man, by contrast, the hand has come to assume an almost exclusive role in all skilled, dextrous, manipulative activity. Its opposable thumb, in particular, forms man's chief prehensile organ. Correspondingly, in man a much larger area of motor cortex is devoted to representation of the hand, especially the thumb, than to that of the rest of the arm, trunk, and leg. Furthermore, in man, one of two hands, most often the right, characteristically develops a greater proficiency and comes to be used more frequently than the other. This handedness is associated with a dominance of the opposite cerebral hemisphere, because the motor paths are crossed; in a right-handed individual, the left hemisphere is the dominant one.

In man, the face, tongue, and larynx also have an extensive representation in the motor cortex, equivalent in area to that of the hand. Just as the use of the hand in complex acts, such as making or using tools, involves the cortical region ahead of the arm area proper, so the performance of the lips, tongue, and larynx in vocal speech has come to be managed by the cortical region ahead of the face area of the motor cortex. Unlike other motor representation in the brain, this special capacity for the production of sounds as symbols develops only in the dominant one of the cerebral hemispheres. In analogous relation to the cortical sensory areas for hearing and for vision, further special capacities develop for the recognition of auditory or visual signals as symbols, i.e., for the recognition of spoken or written language. Lesions in these speech areas of the dominant hemisphere result in aphasia; analogous injury to the opposite side of the brain is without this consequence.

Obviously the phylogenetic development of the sensory and motor regions of the cortex and, in the dominant hemisphere, of the areas for speech and language, have been of major significance in the evolution of modern man. Knowledge of the stages of their development would be of the greatest possible interest for anthropology. Regrettably, the brain is the softest organ in the body and its preservation after death is brief. On the other hand, its protective and supportive bony case, the cranium, has the highest preservation index of any of the body parts, except for the teeth and jaw. Fossil crania form the common currency of physical anthropology, and measurement of their capacity provides valuable information of the gross dimensions of the brain. Endocranial casts have sometimes shown frontal and temporal convolutional patterns in remarkable detail, but further efforts to establish stages of differentiation of functional cortical areas from them have invariably and, it would appear, correctly been contested. The great interest in the subject shares with the limitation of real data in accounting for the many speculative proposals which have been advanced concerning the evolution of man's brain. One of the most common of them is the proposal that man's capacity for speech evolved from abilities for emotional vocalization present in lower animals.

Animal studies suggest that vocalization in emotional expression is managed by a neural mechanism in the middle brain stem, and data from clinical neurology support the presence of such a subcortical emotional mechanism in man as well. No functional relationship is known between this deep-lying mesencephalic system for emotional vocalization, widely present through the animal kingdom, and the topographically distant cortical areas for symbolic speech, which exist only in the associational cortex of the human brain. In keeping with their phylogenetic difference, these two mechanisms for vocal communication display widely different maturation times in the ontogeny of the human infant. As might be expected, the older, more stereotyped, subcortical, emotional mechanism is fully functional at birth. By contrast, in the infant, activity of the cortical mechanism for symbolic speech is only manifest about 6 months later, as the incomprehensible babbling and jabbering, described as vocal play. Its function in understandable speech only develops between 1 and 2 years after birth. Its capacities in written language are not gained until the child is 5 or 6 years of age.

These observations oppose the view that man's capacity for speech evolved from the abilities for emotional vocalization present in lower animals. On the contrary, man's communication by symbols, both vocal and written, appears to represent an entirely novel functional increment, related to the acquisition of associational cortex, in front of the face and hand parts of the motor area, in the case of speaking and writing, and around the cortical sensory areas for audition and vision, in the case of recognition of spoken and written language. Man's capacities for communicating by symbolic language are unique also in depending upon neural mechanisms which develop only in the dominant one of the two cerebral hemispheres, rather than bilaterally.

These observations are in full agreement with Huxley's remarks, in *Evidence as to Man's Place in Nature*, in 1863: "Our reverence for the nobility of manhood will not be lessened by the knowledge that man is one with the brutes; for he alone possesses the marvelous endowment of intelligible and rational speech, whereby, in the secular period of his existence, he has slowly accumulated and organized the experience which is almost wholly lost with the cessation of every individual life in other animals."

POSTNATAL MATURATION
OF MAN'S BRAIN

The large balance of the cerebral cortex, outside of these more specifically preoccupied regions, is called associational because of its involvement with the more abstract, conceptual and ideational aspects of intellectual life. These complex functions bear a general relation to the bulk of the brain, in the sense that a large mass of neural tissue is required for their performance. Capacities in this direction increase through the phylogenetic series as the brains of animals become progressively larger. Furthermore, within man's own cerebrospinal nervous system, increasing complexity of function is encountered on moving cephalically along the neuraxis. Intrinsic function of the small spinal cord is primarily reflex in nature. That of the somewhat stouter brain stem is more elaborate, but it is still concerned largely with preserving internal homeostasis. It is primarily within the robust cerebral hemispheres, forming the main bulk of the brain, that the higher neural functions that relate man to the external world and to his fellows in it have their seat.

Without evoking the biogenetic law and recognizing that increments of weight bear only the most general and potential relationship to functional capacity, it is of interest to compare the stages of postnatal growth of the human infant's brain with the adult dimensions of earlier forms. At the age of 1 month, the weight of the human infant's brain (460 gm.) is about that of adult apes. At 3 months, his brain (550 gm.) is the size of that of the African man-apes. At 11 months, when the modern infant is first beginning to talk, his brain (850 gm.) equals that of Java man. At the age of 3 years, when he has learned to talk fairly well, his brain (1,110 gm.) is about the weight of that of Peking man; at the age of 10, the weight of the infant's brain (1,410 gm.) matches that of Neanderthal man and is essentially fully grown.

In man's capacity to substitute individual development for phylogenetic evolution, deferral of his cerebral maturation is matched in relevance by the great prolongation of each of the main periods of his postnatal life. While the duration of man's prenatal period is about the same as that of the great apes, the period of his postnatal growth has almost doubled, and his total life span is also twice that of simians. General growth is completed in 3 years in prosimians (shrews, lemurs, and tarsiers), 7 years in catarrhine monkeys, 11 years in great apes; in man, however, this period has increased to 20 years. Similarly, the total life span has grown from 25 years in monkeys to about 35 years in apes to over 70 years in modern man. While man's gestation period is not unique, except for being inadequate for his cerebral maturation, he is markedly specialized in the great prolongation of his postnatal growth and in his long postponement of the onset of senility.

As a consequence of these factors— postponement of man's cerebral maturation and the prolongation of his total life—development of the cerebral portion of his brain and its functions may be extended over a third or more of his existence. Instead of proceeding in an immutable fashion, isolated within the uterus and subject only to genetic blueprinting and the stereotyped environment of the maternal circulation, development of the cerebral part of man's brain is transported into a setting in the external world, where it becomes subject to all the parental, familial, and other interpersonal influences of modern man's social environment, as well as to features of his cultural heritage accumulated during a civilization of several thousand years.

While this individual, postnatal evolution of man's brain proceeds gradually, two clear periods can be distinguished in it. The first 2 years after birth are devoted largely to the perfection of general sensori-motor performance. From the age of 2 to 6, however, the ability to communicate by speech and writing is perfected and, thereafter, the speed of intellectual development rises precipitously. The human neonate can awaken, vocalize upon discomfort, suckle, display tonic neck reflexes related to the posture of the head, and show generalized startle reactions upon novel stimulation. This initial, stereotyped behavior is much like that of surviving anencephalic infants lacking a cerebral cortex. Increasingly, however, the human infant develops capacities related to the rise of cortical function.

His functional maturation proceeds cephalocaudally. At 3 months, he is able to focus and track visually, and a rhythm appears in his electroencephalogram, though a further period is needed before adult α-frequency and amplitude are attained. At 4 months, the infant can reach and grasp; at 11 months, he can creep and stand; and at 15 months, he can walk alone. Talking develops between the ages of 1 and 2 years, and the child begins to read and write at 6. Its further manipulation of symbols extends rapidly, and formal education in organized fields of knowledge usually continues until adolescence or longer. Indeed, most of us cherish the notion that we can continue to learn and improve intellectually until senility sets in, after which we are convinced of it.

In association with the functional im-

maturity of man's brain at birth, and along with its gradual acquisition of increasingly complex capacities, have developed the various means by which the human infant is sheltered, nourished, protected, and educated during his maturation. The period of infant dependency is 1 year in monkeys, 2 years in apes, and 6 to 8 years in modern man. Freud has remarked that the lengthy dependence of the human child upon its parents is an overwhelmingly important biological fact. Consideration of the prolonged maturational processes, leading to acquisition of intelligence, is thus of basic significance in accounting for the rapid evolution of brain function in modern man.

Of the closest relationship also is modern man's Lamarckian attainment of the ability to transmit his acquired characteristics into the future, and again by neural rather than by genetic processes. Man has found it possible, as a substitute for mutational variations transmitted by genes and chromosomes with selection pressures determining survival, to apply processes of higher nervous activity to the creation of novel ideas, concepts, and discoveries, and has developed a written language and a body of learning related to it, by which his intellectual heritage can be conveyed to future members of his race. The brain has thus come to form the chief organ responsible both for man's rapid evolutionary advance and for the perpetuation of his culture.

This neurally determined evolution of modern man has proven fantastically more rapid and, in some ways, remarkably superior to that dependent upon reproductive and genetic processes. It does not appear, however, that a continued increase in the size of the brain is to be anticipated. Von Bonin has concluded from his studies that "while the human brain is larger than that of our subhuman ancestors, no further increase has taken place since the time of Neanderthal man, and there is definite indication of a decrease, at least in Europe, within the last 10,000 or 20,000 years. All these facts suggest that size of the brain has become stable, its evolutionary path has turned a corner, and internal organization rather than bulk appears now to be of positive selective value." In considering the situation, Eiseley states: "We do not have to abandon natural selection as a principle, but it is obvious that we must seek selective factors of a sort that Darwin never envisaged, and which may be bound up with speech and social factors difficult to investigate paleontologically." Schultz has commented: "The study of mankind's past has been largely in the domain of the physical anthropologist; our future evolution represents chiefly a problem for the social anthropologist. Man's future evolution is likely to be less dependent on physical than upon psychic perfection."

References

Ariens Kappers, C. U. The fissures on the frontal lobes of *Pithecanthropus erectus Dubois* compared with those of Neanderthal men, *Homo recens* and Chimpanzee. *Proc. Sect. Sc. K. Akad. Wetensch. Amsterdam*, 1929, **32**, 182–195.

Ariens Kappers, C. U. The fissuration on the frontal lobe of *Sinanthropus pekinensis Black*, compared with the fissuration in Neanderthal men. *Proc. Sect. Sc. K. Akad. Wetensch. Amsterdam*, 1933, **36**, pt. 2, 802–812.

Ariens Kappers, C. U. Further communication on the fissures of the frontal lobes in Neanderthal men. *Proc. Sect. Sc. K. Akad. Wetensch. Amsterdam*, 1939, **32**, pt. 1, 196–205.

Bailey, P., and Von Bonin, G. *The isocortex of man.* Illinois Monogr. Med. Sc. 6, No. 1–2, 1951.

Bailey, P., von Bonin, G., and McCulloch, W. S. *The isocortex of the chimpanzee.* Urbana: Univ. of Illinois Press, 1950.

Bass, A. D. (Ed.) *Evolution of nervous control from primitive organisms to man.* Washington: American Association for the Advancement of Science, Publ. No. 52, 1959.

Bataille, G. *Prehistoric painting; Lascaux; or The birth of art.* Lausanne: Skira, 1955.

Bayley, N. On the growth of intelligence. *Am. Psychol.*, 1955, **10**, 805–818.

Black, D. On a lower molar hominid tooth from the Chou-Kou-Tien deposit. *Paleontologia sinica*, Ser. D. v. 7, 1927, fasc. **1**, 1–28.

Black, D. The Croonian lecture. On the discovery, morphology and environment of *Sinanthropus pekinensis. Phil. Trans. Roy. Soc. London*, 1934, **B 223**, 57–120.

Black, D. et al. Fossil man in China. *Mem. Geol. Surv. China*, 1933, Ser. A., No. 11.

Bonin, G. von. On the size of man's brain as indicated by skull capacity. *J. Comp. Neurol*, 1934, **59**, 1–28.

Boule, M., and Anthony, R. L'encéphale de l'homme fossile de la Chapelle-aux-Saints. *Anthropologie, Paris*, 1911, **22**, 129–196.

Boule, M., and Anthony, R. Neopallial morphology of fossil men as studied from endocranial casts. *J. Anat.*, 1917, **51**, 95–102.

Boule, M., and Vallois, H. V. *Fossil men.* New York: Holt, Rinehart and Winston, 1957.

Braidwood, R. J. *Prehistoric man.* (3rd ed.) Issued in co-operation with the Oriental Institute, University of Chicago. Chicago, 1957.

Broca, P. Sur les crânes et ossements des Eyzies. *Bull. Soc. Anthrop. Paris*, 1868, Ser. 23, 350–394.

Brook, R., and Schepers, G. W. H. The South African fossil ape-men, the *Australopithecinae.* Part I. The occurrence and general structure of the South African ape-men. *Transv. Mus. Mem.*, 1946, **2**, 1–153.

Broom, R., and Robinson, J. T. Sterkfontein ape-man Plesianthropus. Part I. Further evidence of the structure of the Sterkfontein ape-man *Plesianthropus. Transv. Mus. Mem.*, 1949, **4**, pt. 1.

Broom, R., and Robinson, J. T. Swartkrans ape-man, *Paranthropus crassidens. Transv. Mus. Mem.*, 1952, **6**, 1–123.

Brown, T. G. Note on the physiology of the basal ganglia and mid-brain of the anthropoid ape, especially in reference to the act of laughter. *J. Physiol.*, 1914–1915, **49**, 195–207.

Bucy, P. C. (Ed.) *The precentral motor cortex.* (2nd ed.) Urbana: Univ. of Illinois Press, 1949.

Clark, G. *From savagery to civilization.* New York: Schuman, 1953.

Conel, J. L. *The postnatal development of the human cerebral cortex.* Cambridge: Harvard Univ. Press, 1939–1955. 5 vols.

Dart, R. A. *Australopithecus africanus:* the man-ape of South Africa. *Nature, London,* 1925, **115,** 195–199.

Dart, R. A., and Craig, D. *Adventures with the missing link.* New York: Harper & Row, 1959.

Darwin, C. R. *The descent of man and selection in relation to sex.* London: Murray, 1871.

Donaldson, H. H. *The growth of the brain: A study of the nervous system in relation to education.* London: Scott, 1895.

Dubois, E. *Pithecanthropus erectus. Eine menschenaehnliche Ubergangsform aus Java.* Batavia: Landesdruckerei, 1894. *Jaarb. Mijnw. Nederl. Ind.,* 1895, **24,** (Part 1), 5–77.

Dubois, E. *Pithecanthropus erectus,* eine Stammform des Menschen. *Anat. Anz.,* 1896, **12,** 1–22.

Dubois, E. The shape and size of the brain in *Sinanthropus* and in *Pithecanthropus. Proc. Sect. Sc. K. Akad. Wetensch. Amsterdam,* 1933, **36,** (Part 1), 415–423.

Eiseley, L. Symposium commemorating the one hundredth anniversary of the discovery of Neanderthal man. I. Neanderthal man and the dawn of human paleontology. *Quart. Rev. Biol.,* 1957, **32,** 323–329.

Eiseley, L. *Darwin's century. Evolution and the men who discovered it.* Garden City, N. Y.: Doubleday, 1958.

Elliot Smith, G. *The evolution of man.* London: Oxford Univ. Press, 1924.

Gesell, A. *The first five years of life.* New York & London: Harper & Row, 1940.

Gesell, A. *The embryology of behavior.* New York: Harper & Row, 1945.

Greene, J. C. *The death of Adam. Evolution and its impact on western thought.* Ames: Iowa State Univ. Press, 1959.

Gregory, W. K. *Man's place among the anthropoids.* Oxford: Clarendon Press, 1934.

Haeckel, E. *The evolution of man.* New York: Appleton, 1896. 2 vols.

Haldane, J. B. S. Animal communication and the origin of human language. *Science Progress,* 1955, **43,** 385–401.

Harris, J. A., et al. *The measurement of man.* Minneapolis: Univ. of Minnesota Press, 1930.

Howell, F. C. The Villafranchian and human origins. *Science,* 1959, **130,** 831–844.

Howells, W. *Mankind in the making.* Garden City, N. Y.: Doubleday, 1959.

Hurzeler, J. *Oreopithecus bambolii* Gervais, a preliminary report. *Verhandl. naturf. Gesellsch. Basel.,* 1958, **69,** 1–48.

Huxley, T. H. *Evidence as to man's place in nature.* London and Edinburgh: Williams and Norgate, 1863.

Keith, A. *The antiquity of man.* London: Williams and Norgate, 1925. (Rev. Ed.)

Kelly, A. H., Beaton, L. E., and Magoun, H. W. A midbrain mechanism for facio-vocal activity. *J. Neurophysiol.,* 1946, **9,** 181–189.

Koenigswald, G. H. R., von (Ed.) *Hundert Jahre Neanderthaler, 1856–1956;* Gedenkbuck der Internationalen Neanderthal, Frier, Düsseldorf, August 1956. Utrech Kemink en Zoon, 1958. Pp. 26–30.

Leakey, L. S. B. A new fossil skull from Olduvai. *Nature, London,* 1959, **184,** 491–493.

LeGros Clark, W. E. *History of the primates.* (4 ed.) London, Printed by order of the Trustees of the British Museum, 1954.

LeGros Clark, W. E. *The fossil evidence for human evolution.* Chicago: Univ. of Chicago Press, 1955.

LeGros Clark, W. E., and Leakey, L. S. B. The Miocene *Hominoidea* of East Africa. Brit. Mus. (*Nat. Hist.*). *Fossil Mammals of Africa,* 1951, **1,** 1–117, Illus.

Lyell, C. *The geological evidence of the antiquity of man.* London: Murray, 1863.

Moore, R. *Man, time and fossils.* New York: Knopf, 1953.

Oakley, K. P. *Man the tool-maker.* Chicago: Univ. of Chicago Press, 1957.

Osborn, H. F. *Men of the old stone age.* (3rd ed.) New York: Scribner's, 1919.

Penfield, W., and Rasmussen, T. *The cerebral cortex of man.* New York: Macmillan, 1950.

Penfield, W., and Roberts, L. *Speech and brain mechanism.* Princeton, N. J.: Princeton Univ. Press, 1959.

Piveteau, J. *Traité de paléontologie.* Vol. VII. *Primates; paléontologie humaine.* Paris: Masson, 1957.

Pumphrey, R. J. *The origin of language.* Liverpool: University Press, 1951.

Robinson, J. T., and Mason, R. J. Occurrence of stone artifacts with *Australopithecus* at Sterkfontein. *Nature, London,* 1957, **180**, 521–524.

Schaafhausen, H. Zur Kenntniss der altesten Rassenchädel. *Arch. Anat. Physiol. Jhrg.,* 1858, 453–478.

Schepers, G. W. H. The endocranial casts of the South African ape-men. Part II. The South African fossil ape-men: the *Australopithecinae. Transv. Mus. Mem.,* 1946, **2**, 154–272.

Shirley, M. M. *The first two years. A study of twenty-five babies.* Vol. 2. *Intellectual development.* Minneapolis: Univ. of Minnesota Press, 1933.

Spuhler, J. N. Somatic paths to culture. *Human Biol.,* 1959, **31**, 1–13.

Spuhler, J. N., et al. *The evolution of man's capacity for culture.* Detroit: Wayne State Univ. Press, 1959.

Straus, W. L., Jr. The riddle of man's ancestry. *Quart. Rev. Biol.,* 1949, **24**, 200–223.

Straus, W. L., Jr., and Cave, A. J. E. Symposium commemorating the one hundreth anniversary of the discovery of Neanderthal man. III. Pathology and the posture of Neanderthal man. *Quart. Rev. Biol.,* 1957, **32**, 348–363.

Symington, J. Endocranial casts and brain form: A criticism of some recent speculations. *J. Anat. Physiol.,* 1916, **50**, 110–130.

Teilhard de Chardin, P. *The phenomenon of man.* New York: Harper & Row, 1960.

Tilney, F. The brain of prehistoric man. A study of the psychologic foundations of human progress. *Arch. Neurol. & Psychiat.,* 1927, **17**, 723–769.

Tilney, F. *The brain from ape to man.* New York: Hoeber, 1928. 2 vols.

Vierordt, H. Das Massenwachsthum der Körperorgane des Menschen. *Arch. f. Anat. u. Entwicklungsgesch.,* Suppl.-Bd., 1890, 62–94.

Wallace, A. R. *My life: A record of events and opinions.* New York: Dodd, Mead, 1905. 2 vols.

Washburn, S. L. The analysis of primate evolution with particular reference to the origin of man; *Origin and Evolution of Man. Cold Spring Harbor Symp. Quant. Biol.,* 1950, **15**, 67–78.

Washburn, S. L. The new physical anthropology. *Tr. New York Acad. Sc.* Ser. II, 1951, **13**, 298–304.

Washburn, S. L. Speculations on the interrelations of the history of tools and biological evolution. *Human Biol.,* 1959, **31**, 21–31.

Washburn, S. L., and Avis, V. Evolution of human behavior. A. Roe and G. G. Simpson (Eds.), In *Behavior and evolution.* New Haven: Yale Univ. Press, 1958. Pp. 421–436.

Weidenreich, F. Observations on the form and proportions of the endocranial casts of *Sinanthropus pekinensis,* other hominids and the great apes: a comparative study of brain size. *Paleontologia sinica,* 1936. Ser. D, v. 7, fasc. 4.

Weidenreich, F. The brain and its role in the phylogenetic transformation of the human skull. *Tr. Am. Philosoph. Soc.,* 1941, n.s. **31** (Part V), 320–422.

Weidenreich, F. The skull of *Sinanthropus pekinensis;* a comparative study on a primitive hominid skull. *Paleontologia sinica,* 1943, n.s., D. 10.

Weil, A. Measurements of cerebral and cerebellar surfaces. Comparative studies of the surfaces of endocranial casts of man, prehistoric men and anthropoid apes. *Am. J. Phys. Anthropol.,* 1929, **13**, 69–90.

Weiner, J. S. *The piltdown forgery.* London & New York: Oxford Univ. Press, 1955.

Wendt, H. *In search of Adam.* Boston: Houghton Mifflin, 1956.

Wilson, S. A. K. *The modern problems in neurology.* New York: Wood, 1929.

Permanently wired-in behavior patterns of lower animals
dean e. wooldridge

This is a book about the human brain. Nevertheless we have already devoted considerable attention to the nervous systems of other animals, and we shall continue to do so. The basis for the expectation that animal studies will prove pertinent to understanding of the human nervous system is the time-honored principle, so often verified by the biologist, that similarity in structure and similarity in function usually go hand in hand. And the fact is that the nervous tissue of the lower animals is remarkably similar to our own. We find the same neuronal building blocks with similar arrangements of dendrites and axons, and similar operating characteristics. We find the same tendency for groupings of richly interconnected neurons to occur at crossroads between the incoming streams of sensory data provided by the afferent nerves and the outgoing systems of orders sent over the efferent nerves to the muscles and other effector mechanisms. In some instances, the aggregations of neurons that appear to perform the data-processing tasks in lower animals have the semblance of a full-blown brain, although usually of modest size and complexity by comparison with the human organ. In other instances, a small animal might employ one or more groupings of neurons, or "ganglia," appearing, from their construction and from the general understanding of these matters that we have been developing, to be the sites of special-purpose neuronal reflex or control centers.

Because of these anatomical similarities the neurologist rather confidently expects to be able to transfer much of the knowledge acquired from experiments with the simpler species to man and the other higher animals. Soundness of the extrapolation is usually confirmed when an opportunity arises to observe directly the corresponding human neural phenomenon.

But if such reasoning by analogy is sound, it ought to work both ways. What is learned about the properties of neuronal aggregates through studies on the higher animals should also sometimes be capable of application to the lower ones. We have seen that the neural equipment of humans and other higher vertebrates includes a large number of reflex circuits whereby stereotyped patterns of muscular response are automatically triggered into existence by occurrence of specific sensory stimuli. This suggests an interesting possibility: could we have here the basis for an explanation of an aspect of animal life that has always been a mystery to scientist and philosopher alike—the ability of some of nature's lowliest and simplest creatures to engage in highly organized and seemingly purposeful behavior that frequently appears to involve an improbably high content of intelligence? Could their apparently reasoned acts instead be only the results of the triggering of patterns of automatic reflexes, built into the animal at birth, not involving conscious intelligence at all? To be sure, such a question does not bear directly upon the operation of the human brain, but it is believed to be a justifiable digression in view of its general interest. Therefore this chapter will be devoted to an explicit attempt to test how far we can go in explaining the puzzling behavior of the lower forms of animal life by invoking the operating properties of the same kinds of permanently wired-in reflex circuits that we have found to be so important in the central nervous system of man.

REFLEXES AND TROPISMS

Upon the approach of a possible enemy, a barnacle abruptly closes its shell, a tube worm snaps its exposed feeding tentacles back into its protective tunnel of sand, a sea squirt contracts into a gelatinous blob, burrowing bivalves withdraw their soft protruding siphons into the sand. A sea urchin turns its pointed needles in the direction of approaching danger, and the pincerlike jaws that inhabit the spiny jungle at the base of the needles stand up, ready to seize any enemy that comes too close.

These have indeed been found to be simple reflex actions. The barnacle, tube worm, sea squirt, and bivalve possess tiny photocells among their sensory neurons. The shadow cast by an approaching enemy causes these photoreceptors to generate their standardized trains of voltage impulses that stimulate the muscles employed in the resulting avoidance reaction. Even the more complex reaction of the sea urchin is of the same nature, although the receptor neurons in this case appear to be, not photoelectric, but chemical; they "taste" the surrounding salt water for signs of the characteristic flavor of an enemy. The completely automatic and local nature of the response is demonstrated by the fact that a tiny chip broken away from a living sea urchin's shell, with only a single spine or a single stalked beak attached to it, will show the same alarm and preparation.

In addition to reflexes, nature makes extensive use of tropisms in regulating the behavior of its simpler creatures. A

tropism is an automatic response differing from other reflexes only in that it affects the movement of the complete organism. When an earthworm digs down and finds the moist decaying vegetation on which it thrives and at the same time avoids the surface where it might furnish a meal for a passing sparrow, it is not the intelligent, planned procedure that it appears to be. The muscles that turn the front end of the worm and thereby determine its direction of locomotion are constructed so as to receive their electric control signals from photosensitive receptors on either side of the head. As a result, the earthworm automatically heads away from the light in such a direction as to equalize the amount of illumination received by the left- and right-hand photoreceptors. This causes the worm to travel toward the darker regions, where it finds food and safety. The completely machinelike, unreasoning nature of this performance has been nicely demonstrated by exposing a worm simultaneously to two separate sources of light of controllable intensity and observing that the path followed is always one that orients the worm, in accordance with the positions and relative intensities of the lights, to equalize the amount of illumination of its two photoreceptors; and this occurs even though it may impel the worm along a course opposite to the one in which the proper conditions for food and safety are to be found.

The machinelike nature of the reflexes and tropisms that so extensively regulate the behavior of the lower animals was not appreciated as soon as it might have been by workers in the field. This was probably because these animal responses do not have the precision and detailed reproducibility that is usually observed in the commoner reflexes of higher animals. The spines of the sea urchin are likely to display a certain restless motion, even when no stimulus is present, and the orientation toward a potential enemy may involve a certain hesitation or lack of precision, together with a persistence of some of the original restless motion, even after the enemy has been sensed. In similar fashion, an earthworm, when exposed to light, does not instantly snap into an opposite heading and pursue a precisely straight course steadily away from the source of illumination. Instead, the trajectory pursued is modulated by wormlike twistings and turnings; these deviations may become particularly severe if, for example, it is necessary for the worm to avoid an obstacle that lies in its path. The reason for such unprecise response is that most tropisms do not provide such an overriding source of control voltage to the organism's effector mechanisms as to overshadow completely the effects of other sources of command signals. While the earthworm possesses neuronal connections that provide a steady bias to its muscles so that they tend to turn it away from a source of illumination, it also possesses a behavior pattern that provides for detouring around obstacles. Its actual muscular response at any given instant is a combination of these and several other reinforcing or competing built-in reflex or tropism mechanisms.

The restlessness of the spines of the sea urchin also results from a competing control signal, but one of a different kind. The nerve cells of these lower animals, like many of those in the human body, do not always wait to receive a specific stimulus before "closing the switch" and sending a voltage pulse out over the axon. Instead, there is a certain amount of random firing of the neurons. In the large and complex nervous systems of the larger animals, so many neurons must act cooperatively to produce significant movement of principal organs that the occasional random firing of a few neurons cannot produce a conspicuous result (although an occasional flicker of an eyelid or twitch of a muscle may be due to this cause). In some of the small and primitive animals that we are now dealing with, however, there may be only a few interconnected neurons in the circuit that controls a major element of the body. Under such circumstances, the random firing of one or two neurons can easily produce observable restless movement of the affected part.

COMPLEX TROPISMS

Tropisms that are themselves turned on or off by the presence or absence of other stimulating factors, or combinations of tropisms, can increase immeasurably the apparent "purposefulness" of the behavior of a simple organism. For example, the larvae of barnacles appear to decide whether they want to swim toward the surface or away from the surface of the sea. This apparent exercise of free will has been traced to a prosaic temperature-reversible tropism that causes the barnacle larvae to seek light in the cold and avoid it in warmth; similarly, many aquatic crustaceans, such as the water flea *Daphnia*, tend to swim downward in a bright light and upward in darkness.

An interesting tropistic mechanism causes the caterpillars of the goldtail moth (*Porthesia chrysorrhoea*) to leave their hibernating nests in early spring and crawl to the only portions of the shrubs where their leafy food is to be found at that time of the year. The tropism involved is one whereby an adequate amount of warmth automatically causes the caterpillar to leave its nest and start crawling toward the light; it can be induced at any time by an experimenter simply by applying heat. This tropism results in the caterpillar climbing as high as it can go, which is to the top of the shrub where the new growth of green leaves first emerges early in spring. However, if other effects than this simple tropism were not operating, the caterpillar would be in difficulty as soon as it had eaten the green leaves at the top of the shrub, for its food from then on would have to be found at lower levels; reaching such levels would be in conflict with a tropism that continuously impels it upward. This problem has been handled by nature by causing the upward-climbing tropism to operate only when the caterpillar is hungry. Therefore, having eaten, the caterpillar is free to creep in any direction and will eventually make its way down and find the new leaves as they commence to open.

As with all tropisms, the behavior of the goldtail moth is completely unreasoning. For example, if caterpillars are taken as they are leaving the nest and put into a glass tube lying near a window, they will all collect in the end of the tube nearest the light and stay there. If a few young leaves from their food shrub are put at the other end of the tube, farthest from the light, the hungry, unfed caterpillars will remain held captive near the lighted end of the tube, and there they will stay until they starve.

Tropisms, like the reflexes of higher animals, appear to be a direct consequence of the way the nerves and muscles have been put together. Usually they contribute to the health and well-being of the organism. The latter result, of course, would be an inevitable consequence of evolutionary selection; creatures with tropisms that lessen their chances of survival would presumably not have won out in the struggle for species existence. It is only when the creature is placed in historically abnormal or unusual circumstances that tropisms can work against survival, as in the instance of the caterpillars and the lighted tube. Similarly, the prawns that accumulate around the positive pole of a pair of electrodes placed in their tank do so because of a normally unimportant feature of their construction that weakens the effectiveness of their muscles when electricity passes through them in one direction and strenghtens their effectiveness when the current is in the other direction. Moths and other phototropic insects that are irresistibly im-

pelled to seek their own destruction in a flame are accidentally constructed so that superimposed upon the random motions characteristic of their flight is a steady "downhill" pull toward the light. If electric currents in the ocean or open flames in the forests had been important features of nature in the past, it is likely that prawns and moths would not have survived the evolutionary processes.

Although combinations of tropisms and simple reflexes seem to account for a surprising portion of the behavioral responses that the lower animals need to survive, such simple "wired-in" nerve circuits do not by any means constitute the extent of nature's provision for unthinking, unlearned, but constructive and complex behavior. Let us now pass to the evidence for the existence of stored programs not dissimilar to those we found in the human brain, whereby elaborate sequences of interrelated actions may be called forth by the receipt of suitable stimuli.

"STORED PROGRAMS" OF BEHAVIOR

As these words are being dictated from a shady spot just off Waikiki Beach, several birds are moving about in the grass a few feet away, occasionally stopping to peck as whatever it is that birds peck at in such grassy areas. Two species of birds are represented; they differ greatly in size and coloring, but they also differ in another way. One species progresses across the grass by hopping on both feet; the other's gait is a walk, one step at a time. While the two species of birds are physically quite different, this difference in their method of locomotion is not a consequence of muscular requirements or any other special aspects of their construction that we ordinarily consider to be physical. The birds that hop could just as well have been designed to walk, and the birds that walk could just as practicably have been designed to hop. What is involved is a difference in behavior. Birds of the one species inevitably become hoppers, and birds of the other species inevitably become walkers. They have no capability of changing their behavior patterns; the hoppers could no more walk than they could change their size and coloring, and the walkers will go through life taking their steps one at a time.

Birds provide many instances of species-connected peculiarities of behavior. Thus, while there is a similarity among the cries of alarm of all gulls, the number, pitch, and frequency of the staccato cries that constitute such a call vary between species. Then there are the four groups of birds that constitute the conventionally recognized family of titmice (Paridae). There are no physical features to differentiate these four groups, but their nest-building habits are quite different. One group always nests in hollow trees or other cavities; a second group builds an oval nest with lateral entrance in bushes and trees; a third group builds a peculiar retort-shaped nest of plant down worked into feltlike consistency; the fourth group builds a stick nest with a lateral entrance. While these birds are apparently physically identical, their innate, unlearned, nest-building habits serve to identify them as different species as clearly as though the four groups were marked with red, yellow, blue, and green feathers. In fact, it is not unusual for behavioral characteristics to provide important clues to the proper classification of animal species. For a long time, the group of desert birds called sand grouse (Pteroclididae), which has downy young greatly resembling young grouse (Tetraonidae), was considered to be a member of a closely related family. Later, more careful analysis of physical characteristics led to the suspicion that sand grouse were more closely allied with pigeons. This suspicion was finally confirmed and the classification corrected by employment of a behavior characteristic. While nearly all birds scoop water up with their bills and then let it run down into their stomachs by lifting head and neck, pigeons have a very different drinking behavior; they stick their bills into the water and simply pump it up through the esophagus. The fact that sand grouse are the only other birds with this behavior strongly reinforced the anatomical findings which placed them next to pigeons.

Inherited behavior patterns are by no means confined to birds. Separate family classification has been assigned to different groups of grasshoppers largely because of differences in their habits of cleaning their antennae. Thus, the Acrididae place a leg on one antenna and clean the antenna by pulling it through between the leg and the ground. Physically similar, the Tetrigidae family differ in that they clean their antennae by stroking them with the legs, which in turn are cleaned by being pulled through the mouth. And in the sea there are hermit crabs with the instinct to find castoff shells as houses for their unprotected abdomens, and other crabs that protect themselves by holding stinging sea anemones in their claws. There is the elaborate flight instinct of the squid, with its ejection of ink and a right-angle turn at the crucial moment. There are the octopuses, which have the instinct to build little walls of stones behind which they can lurk unseen.

Since the ability to learn is a characteristic that is possessed, to some extent at least, by a surprisingly large proportion of animals, including some that we consider to be quite inferior, it is necessary always to be alert to the possibility that behavior patterns such as those described may be the consequence of indoctrination of the young by their parents. For many years it was in fact assumed that learning processes were responsible for most of the adaptive behavior exhibited by animals. Only with the advent of experiments in which the animals were carefully reared, from birth or from the egg, without access to others of their kind, was it determined that much of what had been assumed to have been learned existed in the organism at the time of birth as a finished and complete pattern of behavior. Certain newly hatched birds, for example, will automatically crouch down in the nest when a hawk passes overhead. This is not simply a response to a dark object in the sky. The shape must be hawklike; a robin can pass overhead without evoking the slightest reaction. Then there is the so-called thermometer bird, or bush turkey, of the Solomon Islands. It lays its eggs in a heap of mixed plant material and sand, with all the eggs arranged to lie with the blunt end upward. Each chick, on breaking out of the blunt top of its egg, wriggles and struggles in such a way that its stiff feathers, which point backward, gradually cause it to work its way up to the top of the heap. On reaching the surface, the chick dashes cross country into the shade of the nearest undergrowth. Certainly, no learning is involved in this response pattern of the newly hatched chick. Similarly, a female canary that has been isolated from birth builds a nest competently the first time suitable material is presented and the occasion arises. And a caterpillar, when it is about to pupate, spins a cocoon. It has never seen its parents or a cocoon and yet automatically sets about to construct an edifice that, when analyzed, is a masterpiece of engineering.

Although observations such as those just described show conclusively that learning from experience is not occurring, the inheritance at birth of such detailed and purposeful behavior patterns is so different from anything we humans experience that it is necessary for us to fight against the tendency to imagine that reasoning intelligence is involved. We must therefore not ignore the evidence on this point. Consider again the thermometer bird, which on emerging from the egg executes exactly the kind of wriggling motion needed to bring it to the surface of the heap and then changes to a new mode of motion

to bring it to the protection of shade. If the chick, after having emerged, is once more dug into the heap, it is quite incapable of coming out again but stays there struggling ineffectively until it dies. Its movements are now of the type adapted to running to shade, and not of the type that will bring it to the surface. And the caterpillar that builds such a wonderful cocoon displays the completely automatic nature of its performance if it is interrupted in the middle of its task and the half-finished cocoon removed; it does not start again from the beginning, but spins only what remained for it to do, in spite of the fact that the resulting half cocoon is completely useless for protection. The octopus that so "intelligently" builds a stone wall behind which it can hide unseen will with equal vigor construct the wall out of transparent pieces of glass, if this is the material that happens to be handy.

In the light of present knowledge, we can only conclude that these specific and detailed behavior patterns are built into the organisms at birth. The same kind of kinetic embryonic forces that determine the configuration of the animal, its coloring of skin or feathers, and all the millions of details that constitute the blueprint for its physical construction also act to determine the detailed pattern of interconnection of the neurons in its brain; and the patterns of behavior thus produced are as unique to the species as such obviously physical characteristics as size, shape and coloration.

"INTELLIGENCE" OF INSECTS: TRIGGERING OF SUCCESSIVE STORED SUBROUTINES

A special challenge to our hypotheses is provided by the unusually elaborate patterns of conduct exhibited by some insects, such as ants, termites, bees, and wasps. For years, man has been fascinated by the complex behavior patterns of these insects. He has read into their organized behavior strong elements of similarity to the reasoning processes of humankind. Let us see if this interpretation survives close analysis, or if our concept of permanently wired-in neuronal circuits again appears to fit the facts.

Consider, for example, the solitary wasps. When the time comes for egg laying, the wasp *Sphex* builds a burrow for the purpose and seeks out a cricket which she stings in such a way as to paralyze but not kill it. She drags the cricket into the burrow, lays her eggs alongside, closes the burrow, then flies away, never to return. In due course, the eggs hatch and the wasp grubs feed off the paralyzed cricket, which has not decayed, having been kept in the wasp equivalent of deep freeze. To the human mind, such an elaborately organized and seemingly purposeful routine conveys a convincing flavor of logic and thoughtfulness—until more details are examined. For example, the wasp's routine is to bring the paralyzed cricket to the burrow, leave it on the threshold, go inside to see that all is well, emerge, and then drag the cricket in. If, while the wasp is inside making her preliminary inspection, the cricket is moved a few inches away, the wasp, on emerging from the burrow, will bring the cricket back to the threshold, but not inside, and will then repeat the preparatory procedure of entering the burrow to see that everything is all right. If again the cricket is removed a few inches while the wasp is inside, once again the wasp will move the cricket up to the threshold and re-enter the burrow for a final check. The wasp never thinks of pulling the cricket straight in. On one occasion, this procedure was repeated forty times, always with the same result.

To the computer scientist, there must be a sense of familiarity to this type of behavior. It has the earmarks of a set of subroutines recorded in the permanent memory system of a computer and called into play by the appearance of certain conditions of the input data. In the instance of the solitary wasp, some triggering mechanism, perhaps the physiological state of the female, sets into motion the series of subroutines associated with the preparing of a nest and the laying of eggs. The first subroutine called forth is the preparation of a burrow. The completion of this subroutine is the trigger for the next, which consists in the searching down of a particular species of cricket and paralyzing it. This in turn is the trigger for the next act in the drama, bringing the cricket to the threshold of the burrow. The presence of the cricket at the threshold of the burrow is the signal for the wasp to go inside for a last check around. Emergence from the burrow and finding the paralyzed cricket at the threshold is the signal for pulling the cricket into the burrow, and so on. Just as in the design of complex programs for electronic digital computers, subroutines appear to be stored and triggered into operation by the particular combinations of stimuli called for by the stored control program of the mechanism.

This concept of stored subroutines that are triggered by specific stimuli goes a long way toward accounting for the surprising variety of detailed inherited behavior patterns exhibited by insects. A bee that has found food will, on its return to its hive, execute a characteristic wagging dance by means of which the direction, distance, amount, and quality of the food source are communicated to the other bees. But a worker that has found food will perform her dance as artistically in the absence of other bees as in the presence of an audience. All that is necessary to trigger the performance is stimulation of her antennae.

The social insects—ants, termites, and bees—all appear to be patriotic, in the sense that they will drive out and frequently sting to death individuals from other hives. But the trigger is odor. All is changed if the interloper is protected long enough to acquire the scent of the new hive. In fact, suitably odor-conditioned insects of entirely different species will frequently be allowed to live indefinitely in a colony of ants or termites.

The senses of odor and taste are used as triggers in many ways by the insects. The great devotion to their queen of termite workers, hundreds of whom are generally seen to be in attendance upon her, appears to be a simple consequence of the fact that she exudes an especially rich and fatty secretion; their apparent attentions consist in licking her to get something for themselves, sometimes so violently that they rasp holes in the royal side. Superficially similar, but for an entirely different purpose, is the phenomenon displayed by certain species of spiders, whereby the male is stimulated to suitable attentions toward the female by a doubtless agreeable substance that she exudes over her body.

Because of the specificity of the trigger mechanisms, these innate response patterns are, by human standards, ridiculously rigid and inflexible. Thus, a male nocturnal moth may fly unerringly to his mate for a distance of more than a mile; yet, if the feathery antennae that serve the male as sense organs are cut off, not only is he incapable of finding the female but, if placed alongside her, is incapable of mating. The trigger for this act apparently is the smell stimulus normally supplied by his sensory antennae. The odor that so stimulates the male moth is generated by two little scent organs located near the top of the female's abdomen. These organs can be cut out without particularly inconveniencing the female. If they and the operated female are then put in a cage with a normal male not deprived of his antennae, his built-in pattern of mating actions will be triggered, but will be entirely directed toward the source of the stimulus; he will make vain attempts to mate with the two little scent glands but will entirely ignore the female.

An invertebrate animal may starve to death in the midst of plenty if the particular plant or animal material that serves as food for its species happens to be missing. Or an insect may doom its race (or at least its local colony) to extinction because of the absence of the particular stimulus that is required to set off its pattern of nest building or egg laying. While a *Sphex* wasp provides its grubs with crickets, the *Ammophila* must find and paralyze a caterpillar before it can continue with its nest-building and egg-depositing routine; the *Sceliphron* wasp recognizes only spiders as suitable larva food, and the *Podium* uses roaches. The *Pronuba* moth can lay its eggs only in a yucca plant, and a species of Trinidad mosquito can be triggered to deposit its eggs only by the presence of the leaves of a bromeliad plant floating in a pool of stagnant water.

So there is, indeed, abundant evidence of the employment by nature in the insects and lower animals of "permanently wired-in" inherited patterns of behavior. Ranging from simple reflexes and tropisms up through complex patterns of multistage behavior triggered into performance by the occurrence of specific stimuli, these automatic, machinelike responses have many of the earmarks of the library of subroutines that can be stored in the memory of an electronic computer and triggered into operation by the occurrence of a prescribed set of relationships among the data supplied to the computer by its input devices.

When a single organism possesses a number of reflexes, tropisms, and stored subroutines, each triggered by its own prescribed input stimuli, all of which can occur concurrently and sometimes in competing fashion, the complexity of the behavior of the animal is much increased and the machinelike nature of its responses is thus obscured. The superposition on these responses of a certain degree of randomness, arising from the spontaneous firing of the neurons, also enhances the "lifelike" character of the behavior. Furthermore, it must be admitted that the kinds of automatic mechanisms discussed in this chapter do not constitute the complete story of the behavior of insects and lower animals. Like electronic computers that modify their behavior in accordance with experience, these simple natural computers have a limited ability to learn. Although this does not have nearly so large an influence upon over-all behavior as in the case of higher animals, it is nevertheless a real and complicating factor that contributes materially to the appearance of detailed unpredictability in the behavior of even some surprisingly low forms of living creatures. But this need not detract from the sense of familiarity that the computer scientist should feel for the behavior of the lower animals. The detailed performance of some of his machines can also be unpredictable.

NATURE'S COMPUTER FABRICATION TECHNIQUES

It is the existence in the nervous systems of the lower animals of permanently wired-in patterns of response to specific situations that constitutes the subject matter of this chapter; techniques employed by nature for accomplishing the construction of these computer/control circuits are essentially outside our scope. Nevertheless, in spite of the convincing nature of the evidence that we have examined, it would be disturbing if what were known about nature's methods of constructing living creatures were to be found in conflict with the requirements of a hypothesis that ascribes a major role to inherited automatic patterns of behavior. Therefore, we must conclude our present considerations by a glance at the pertinent features of the existing state of knowledge concerning the transmission of inherited characteristics in living organisms.

To be sure the immediate problem is clearly defined, let us recall that our present position, as computer scientists, is that we believe we have a sort of understanding of the automatic behavior we have been studying. By using electronic circuit elements and techniques presently available to us, we feel that we know how to build computer/control systems with permanently wired-in reflexes, tropisms, and behavior subroutines triggered by specific input stimuli; and such systems would in general exhibit the kinds of performances we have been studying. To be sure, we are a little worried about synthesis of animal responses to specific visual patterns, for our theory and laboratory experimentation has carried us only a small way toward a complete understanding of these matters, but we have made a start and have confidence that we shall one day be much less awkward in our handling of such problems than we are now. It is also true that the 250 neurons in the brain of an ant and the 900 neurons in the brain of a bee appear to us to be impressively small numbers of computer building blocks for the storage and control of the complex behavior patterns of these social insects; we are sure that we would have to use many times this number of electronic switches to accomplish the same task. A somewhat unsatisfactory rationalization for this difficulty is to say that, when we understand better than we do now the tricks that nature has worked out to control the behavior of these social insects, we shall discover the existence of a large number of short cuts like examples that have already been given—the employment of odor or taste in specific circumstances as an attraction device that directly results in the performance of acts that otherwise might require complex control machinery. A more satisfactory basis for an explanation is provided by our knowledge that a neuron is a much more complex component than a simple on/off switch—that in some circumstances, at least, a single neuron may possess a number of modes of operation which cause it all by itself to constitute a simple computer. Of course, this further emphasizes the disparity in size between the circuit elements the computer scientist has learned to build and those that nature employs. But this disparity, impressive though it is, offers no logical difficulty to the computer scientist; he too will be able to accomplish great miniaturization of his components once he has developed a technique for fabrication of devices on a molecular level.

It is, in fact, nature's techniques of miniaturized construction that we now wish to inquire about.

The molecular mechanisms of genetics

One of the most important and fascinating fields of modern science is genetics. In the last several decades, geneticists have learned a great deal about how nature prepares the blueprint and detailed plans for construction of each of its creatures. This blueprint exists in the nucleus of every cell in the body of each animal. The design information is organized into tiny specks called chromosomes, visible under a high-power optical microscope. Every human cell contains 23 pairs of chromosomes. Each cell of the fruit fly contains 4 pairs, of the mouse 20 pairs, of garden peas 7 pairs. Under the much greater magnifying power of the electron microscope, a structure is observed in each chromosome that is consistent with its division into a large number of still smaller parts. These smaller subdivisions of the chromosomes are called genes. The gene is the basic unit of heredity. It has been established that the principal working part of the gene is a gigantic molecule of *deoxyribonucleic acid*—DNA, for short. Each DNA molecule carries a coded message, written in a four-letter alphabet. Each of the four letters is represented by one of four different types of standard molecular fragments, or "nucleotides." These letters are arranged in a linear array along the "backbone" of the DNA molecule. The resulting message, conveyed by the several thousand genes that comprise the chromosomes of each cell, has a length of about ten billion letters—a few more for a man, a few less for a mosquito! This is the equivalent of one thousand large volumes of ordinary printed material. The original copy of the set of manufacturing instructions with which each animal starts its life comes to it in the fertilized egg—half from its mother, half from its father. As this original cell divides, and the resulting cells divide again and again to form the final adult organism, the one-thousand-volume library of manufacturing instructions is faithfully duplicated at each cell division until, in a human, about one hundred million million copies have been made. And it is this library of instructions, and this alone, that determines whether the resulting animal is to be a flea, an earthworm, or a man.

Of course, a set of specifications is of little value unless arrangements are provided for actual fabrication of the desired structure in accordance with these specifications. Some of nature's fabrication arrangements are now known. For example, the DNA molecules, which are exclusively confined to the nucleus of the cell, act as templates for the formation of molecules of *ribonucleic acid*, or RNA. Each RNA molecule is very similar to the DNA molecule that supervises its synthesis out of the raw materials floating around in the nucleus. In fact, the RNA molecule is believed to carry an exact duplicate of the coded message arranged along the backbone of the parent DNA. RNA differs slightly from DNA in the atomic composition of the nucleotides that make up the four-letter alphabet of its message, and in the chemical composition of its long backbone, but the accuracy of the resulting set of specifications is not diminished by these differences. The chemical differences between RNA and DNA do have an important result, however. They permit RNA to leave the nucleus and travel to the surrounding cytoplasm of the cell, where the real business of fabrication of the materials for constructing the organism is carried on.

Once in the cytoplasm, the RNA molecules guide the formation of specific kinds of protein material, the enzymes. Apparently the particular arrangement of "alphabet" nucleotides along the backbone of the RNA molecule operates in some sort of lock-and-key fashion, through the employment of chemical forces, to assemble out of the material of the surrounding cell the right kinds of ingredients and arrange them in the proper order for the fabrication of the types of enzyme molecules required by the embryonic growth processes. The enzymes accomplish their effects, in turn, by highly specific catalytic properties whereby they govern just what chemical reactions take place in the cell fluids to build the kinds of organic material that, finally, constitute the tissue, bones, and blood of the completed organism.

This brief description of how the genetic material controls the embryonic growth processes is, of course, far from complete. One obvious deficiency of the discussion, for example, is that it provides no explanation for the vital phenomenon of cell differentiation. If every nucleus of every cell contains the same, complete genetic specification for the entire organism, why do not the processes described always cause all enzymes specified in the DNA/RNA code to be indiscriminately produced, thereby resulting in a mass of homogeneous, undifferentiated cells? Obviously, mechanisms must exist that selectively activate parts of the gene-directed enzyme formation. A start has been made toward an understanding of these mechanisms by James Bonner and his associates at the California Institute of Technology.

The Caltech group has established that histone, a protein constituent of the chromosomes, inhibits the DNA-directed synthesis of RNA in the nucleus. In laboratory experiments, it was found possible to control the rate of RNA generation at will by adding or withholding this ingredient. It is also known that changes in the histone content of cells are sometimes associated with important metabolic phenomena. In some instances, at least, tumor cells have been found to possess an abnormally low concentration of the growth-inhibiting histone (Cruft et al., 1954). And there is also evidence that the transition of a plant from the vegetative to the flowering state is preceded by a massive loss of histone from the cells that participate in flower formation (Gifford, 1963). These observations, together with the determination that histone produces its effects through inhibition of the DNA-controlled synthesis of RNA in the cell nuclei, have led Bonner to put forth some very interesting speculation. He suggests that histone may possess a variety of different structures, each form of which is a specific inhibitor of the RNA-generation effectiveness of a particular DNA molecule. If so, some kind of programming mechanism, yet to be identified, could control the abundance of the different types of histone and thereby selectively turn on and off the effects of different portions of the DNA material in the genes. This, in turn, would regulate the generation of the different kinds of RNA molecules and, through them, the various types of enzyme proteins manufactured in the cytoplasm. In this way, cells could be caused to develop differently in accordance with their positions in the organism and the timing of their growth processes.

It is still too early to be sure that we have, in the results obtained in the Caltech laboratories, the basis for a complete explanation of the most important phenomenon of cell differentiation. However, new discoveries, such as those of Bonner and associates, are flowing out of research laboratories at a rapid rate. Their cumulative effect is not to upset the DNA/RNA theory of genetics, but rather to extend it and to fill in its gaps. There seems little doubt of the essential validity of these modern molecular concepts of the genetic processes.

General features of
modern genetic theory

An extensive treatment of the theory of genetics is beyond the scope of this book and certainly well beyond the competence of the author. For our present purposes, we need concern ourselves with only two or three of the features of the theory. To begin with, the blueprint, or better, the library of specifications, contained in coded form in the genes, extensive though it is, is still not complete enough to describe in detail how every cell is to be fabricated and connected with the other cells of the body. Fortunately, this degree of detail is not necessary. We have already seen an example of the kinds of short cuts nature has learned to use in its technique for ensuring proper interconnection of peripheral neurons with their corresponding components in the brain. The genetic message need not include such detail as "the neuron in the retina of the eye that is 1,048 from the left and 579 up from the bottom must make connection with the neuron in the left occipital lobe of the brain that is exactly 104,954 cells left of the center line and 3,045 cells up from the mid-line of the calcarine fissure." If this were required, the one thousand volumes of specifications to which the genetic content of the human being is equivalent would not begin to stretch far enough to permit the desired machinery to be defined. The instruction coded into the genes for this part of the job order is simply that each retinal neuron must establish contact with a cortical neuron of the same relative content of two specified chemicals and that, further, such simplified instructions are coupled with a method of design of the nerves and associated structures that permits the searching axons to wander about more or less at random during the course of the embryonic development, thus providing opportunity for close approach to any given target neuron. Hence the required end result is achieved with a great reduction in the length

of the genetic message that otherwise would be needed. It is likely that nature employs many such ingenious simplifying devices to minimize the communication problem and make it possible for the necessary specifications of the individual to be transmitted by the no more than approximately ten billion nucleotides in each cell that appear to be devoted to that purpose.

Although it is these genetic specifications coming to the new individual from its parents by means of the sperm and egg cells that determine whether it will be an amoeba or a chimpanzee, the inherited specifications are not identical for all amoebae or for all chimpanzees. The inherited characteristics that differentiate individuals, as well as those that differentiate members of different species, are a consequence of the fact that the genetic library of specifications differs in some details from one individual to another. These various libraries of specifications corresponding to individuals of different characteristics within a species seem to possess remarkable stability and permanence. Not only are the genetic specifications replicated without error thousands of billions of times as a single multicelled individual grows from the original sperm and egg cell, but also apparently they can be propagated successively through many generations without substantial modification. It is likely that those of us in the twentieth century who have light eyes or hemophilia come by this characteristic through an unbroken chain of successive reproduction and transmission of the same complex coded pattern of thousands of precisely arranged genetic molecules, through generation after generation, extending back into prehistoric times.

Although genetic libraries of specifications are remarkably stable, they are not completely changeless. A breed of cattle characterized by long legs will sometimes produce a short-legged offspring. Cats and dogs are occasionally born without tails. These spontaneous changes in content of the genetic instructions propagated from parent to offspring are known as *mutations* and appear to be a form of cosmic accident. Many, perhaps most, such mutations are produced by radiation. A high-energy charged particle arising from the cosmic radiation that continually permeates space or from natural radioactive minerals of the earth occasionally passes through the sexual equipment of a prospective parent in such a way as to disarrange the pattern of molecules in the genes of one of its cells—to produce a "typographical error" in its library of specifications. This error or change is then reproduced in the sperm cell or ovum that ultimately participates in the formation of a new individual, and a modified library of specifications is then propagated by that new individual to its offspring. Mutations, however caused, result in new genetic specifications that are as stable and reproducible as the original genetic instructions and can therefore be passed along for generation after generation. When, by X-ray-induced mutation, fruit flies are produced with white eyes, it is found that after seventy-five generations flies with the mutant gene possess eyes as white as those first produced! And the breeders of race horses, beef cattle, and new varieties of dogs all make use of the permanence and continuity of the genetic design information handed along from parent to offspring. They know that, if once developed and then kept uncontaminated, a new genetic strain producing the characteristics they desire in their animals will thenceforth breed true.

Of course, mutations provide the raw material for evolution. If the new characteristics resulting from the mutation have survival value, the individual is apt to live longer and have more offspring than its nonmutated contemporaries. Many of these offspring, in turn, will be more successful than their contemporaries in surviving until they reproduce offspring; thus the next generation will have a still higher proportion of individuals whose cells contain the new genetic specifications. Individuals with the new characteristic with higher survival value may ultimately displace completely the unfortunate inheritors of the old-fashioned set of genes.

Genetic control of behavioral characteristics; evolutionary hypothesis

Interesting and important though all this may be, what is its pertinence to our present subject of the "permanently wired-in" computer/control functions of the brain? Simply this: these behavioral characteristics are also a consequence of the physical construction of the organism—in this case, of the specific way in which the neurons are interconnected. The specifications for these interconnections, like those for the more obviously physical characteristics of the organism, are carried by the genes. The same built-in mechanism by means of which the genetic blueprints, in their interaction with the surrounding chemical materials, compel precise adherence to their design specifications in the embryonic growth of the muscles or visceral organs, automatically and accurately "wires" the neurons into the precise computing/control circuits required by heredity. And the same processes must control the evolutionary development of inherited behavior characteristics. Presumably, changes in the inherited behavior patterns of individuals are produced by mutations in the genes that specify the wiring of the neurons. If the change in behavior results in increased survivability for the individual affected, the descendants of the individual will grow more numerous from generation to generation, and the new behavioral characteristic will ultimately become typical of the species.

At least in the case of simple reflexes and tropisms, it is as easy to visualize the workings of evolutionary principles upon behavior as upon the more obviously physical characteristics of the species. A mutation in the neuronal scheme of the nocturnal moth resulting in a more effective interconnection between the sensory neurons responsive to the scent of the female and the effector neurons controlling the flight muscles could easily result in a new strain of moths of enhanced mating effectiveness. If individuals of this new strain produced on the average 20 percent more progeny than the nonmutated individuals, only four generations would be needed for a colony of moths of the new strain to attain twice the population of a colony of old-style moths of initially the same size. Of course, in an actual situation in which the new strain starts out as a tiny minority element in an unmodified population, with no artificial forces at work to speed the process by controlled interbreeding of the individuals having the desired characteristics, much longer periods of time are required by the evolutionary processes to produce noticeable changes. On the other hand, we must remember that the population in any one generation of insects and some of the other lower animals may run into many billions and also that the life span of an individual in these lower forms is so short that a complete generation may be compressed into a few weeks or months. Therefore it is easy to imagine that nature, in the millions of years it has had for working its evolutionary wonders, should have found its random statistical methods adequate for refinement to today's state of the reflexes and tropisms that form so much of the basis of behavior of some of the simpler forms of life.

But simple reflexes and tropisms are one thing—the inherited behavior pattern of a solitary wasp or of a social insect appears to be quite another. Consider the complex, precise pattern of interneuronal wiring needed in the memory and control system of a wasp to provide the set of subroutines and triggering arrangements involved in its nest-building activities. Is it really logical to assume that this pattern could have been arrived at by evolutionary selection from among the literally millions of different ways in which the dendrites and axons of only a few hundred neurons can conceivably be interconnected? This question, of course, was raised more generally a few decades back about all evolutionary processes, including those responsible for properties that appeared to be simpler than those that concern us here. The question lost much of its cogency as improved methods for determining the age of the earth revealed that nature's evolutionary processes have been going on much longer than had originally been thought. However, in the nineteenth century, prior to these geophysical developments, the Lamarckian evolutionists had a way of reconciling the apparent shortness of the time that had been available for evolution with the extensiveness of the resulting accomplishments. They believed that acquired characteristics could be inherited. If, with the passage of time, the individuals of successive generations of a species made more and more use of their legs in running down their prey, the increased musculature in the legs thus acquired by an individual would somehow be passed on to his offspring who would, as a result, start out in life with stronger legs than the parent and evolve from there. It is easy to see that such a hypothesis would be particularly effective for explaining the evolutionary development of inherited behavior. With such an approach, we could reason as follows. If, for whatever cause, a female wasp while under the influence of the biological urge to make a nest and lay eggs comes across a certain species of caterpillar, stings it, and brings it to its burrow just before the urge to lay eggs becomes controlling, the no doubt pleasurable associations in the brain of the wasp between the egg laying and the caterpillar episode could in some way produce changes in the genetic material passed on to the next generation of wasps and result in some probability that they, too, would associate the two kinds of behavior. By such a hypothesis, given many generations to work with, we could probably develop a fairly comfortable feeling about the adequacy of evolutionary processes to account for the remarkably detailed inherited behavior patterns of some of the lower animals.

Unfortunately for the Lamarckian hypothesis, all the modern science of genetics conspires against it. No one has ever succeeded in showing the slightest effects on subsequent generations of any kind of physical or behavioristic experience of previous individuals (with the exception of the special experiment of exposing the parents to radiation and thereby inducing mutations to occur at a rate higher than normal). Numerous investigators have tried every device they could think of to modify by special conditioning of the parent the genetic information transmitted to an offspring. In the course of this work, "animals and plants were drugged, poisoned, intoxicated, illuminated, kept in darkness, half smothered, painted inside and out, whirled around and around, shaken violently, vaccinated, mutilated, educated, and treated with everything except affection from generation to generation."[1]

One investigator even cut off the tails of generation after generation of mice, only to find the tails of the final progeny as long as those of the first. Not only such experimental evidence, but also the increasingly well-established basic theory of genetics, leads to the conclusion that there is nothing in the experience of the parents that can have any effect whatever on the "library of

specifications" contributed by them to their offspring. The genetic instructions that will one day be passed along to subsequent generations are precisely determined at the instant the sperm and egg cells meet and initiate the processes of embryonic cell division that finally result in the adult parent. Only unpredictable, random mutations, probably for the most part produced by radiation, but never the result of intervening activity or experience of the parent, can make changes in the "literary content" of the genetic package.

The fruitlessness of any attempt to find an accelerating factor in the evolution of inherited behavior leaves us in the position of having to rest our confidence in the validity of the existing hypothesis on the statistical effectiveness of the large numbers of individuals and generations involved. Perhaps we can be adequately comfortable in contemplation of this situation if we again recall the propensity of natural processes toward ingenious simplifying techniques. It is likely that throughout the ages the evolutionary processes of nature have automatically developed certain packaging concepts for the specification of neuronal wiring diagrams. A mutation in a gene that is involved in the specification of the nervous system probably results, not simply in the reconnection of individual neurons, but instead in a change of the method of deployment or in the weight factor associated with an aggregation of interconnected neurons, without thereby upsetting the operational integrity of this more or less self-sufficient package. If this hypothesis is correct, the number of random mutations required to carry the inherited behavior of a developing species through a wide range of variations could easily become mere hundreds instead of millions. When the science of genetics has developed to the point where the library of specifications passed on from parent to offspring can be decoded, we shall probably discover a large number

[1] A quotation from H. J. Muller, the American geneticist who received the Nobel prize in 1946 for his discovery of the production of mutations by means of X-ray irradiation.

of simplifying factors such as this. These simplifying factors, coupled with the tremendous capacity for change inherent in the basic principle of evolution when applied to billions of individuals over millions of generations, will presumably be found adequate to explain what appears today to be the remarkable specificity and sophistication of the inherited patterns of behavior of some of the insects and lower animals.

Genetic control of behavioral characteristics; direct evidence

Evolutionary hypotheses are by their very nature difficult to confirm by factual observations. However, no such uncertainty need extend to the interpretation of the experimental evidence for the genetic specification of behavioral characteristics. In experiments with rats, for example, strains have been isolated that exhibit marked differences in their behavior toward strangers. In one genetic strain, extreme aggressiveness and hostility is displayed; in another strain of rats that in other respects appear identical, the behavior is docile. These behavioral characteristics breed true, just as do the physical characteristics determined by the genes. In another animal experiment, a particular gene of a fruit fly has been identified that controls one of the details of behavior during the act of mating. Specifically, a modification in this gene decreases the strength and duration of the vibrations of the wings and antennae with which the male fly caresses the female at a certain stage in the courtship procedure!

Evidence for the hereditary control of the properties of the neurological circuits is also supplied by human victims of genetic defects. *Phenylketonuria*, a defect that often causes mental retardation, has been determined to be hereditary in nature. So is *juvenile amaurotic idiocy*. The obscure *Kuru disease*, which regularly kills nearly half of the members of a particular remote tribe in New Guinea, is another case in point. This disease, which causes progressive degeneration of the nervous system, has been traced to a single defective gene. And several other mysterious diseases of the nervous system are suspected to be genetic in nature. These include, for example, two different types of muscular tremor, each highly specific to local population groups in New Guinea, a progressive dementia found in certain islands of the Western Pacific, and so on.

With the growing understanding by physicians of the possible genetic significance of the symptoms of their patients, clues to the existence of hitherto unrecognized hereditary defects are being discovered at a rapid rate. Because so many more humans than animals come under medical scrutiny, it is from such sources, rather than from animal experiments, that most new evidence is coming for neurological genetic defects.

In summary, the inextricably intertwined modern concepts of evolution and genetics appear to provide an explanation of the development and propagation of permanently wired-in computer/control networks of the type required to account for the inherited patterns of behavior of many of the lower animals. The same evolutionary/genetic mechanisms, of course, would also appear to be responsible for the development of the many reflex mechanisms in the higher animals, which we have seen are so similar to the inherited behavior patterns of lower forms and which contribute so much to survival capability. None of this is to say that there exists today anything like a complete understanding of these complex matters. But in view of the evidence that has been secured so far, it would be difficult to question the validity of the basic concept of a library of specifications transmitted by the genes in coded form from one generation to the next. In the ensuing years, it is to be expected that great progress will be made in deciphering the genetic code. When more is known about the physical and chemical laws by means of which the structural pattern of a gene controls the molecule-building processes in the surrounding protoplasm, we may be able to work out a detailed translation of the messages conveyed by the genes of a specific individual. It is not inconceivable that eventually the designers of computer/control devices will learn to synthesize the types of genes that control the formation of the nervous system in animals. If so, they may be able to fabricate computer components from organic materials on a molecular scale, as nature does, to substitute for the current electronic devices that in future terms of reference may appear fantastically naive, large, and inefficient.

Bibliography

Asimov, I. *The intelligent man's guide to science.* New York: Basic Books, 1960. Pp. 497–551.

Bastock, M. A gene mutation which changes a behavior pattern. *Evolution*, 1956, vol. 10. Pp. 421–439.

Bonner, J., Huang, R. C., and Maheshwari, N. The control of chromosomal RNA synthesis. In press.

Cruft, H., Mauritzen, C., and Stedman, E. Abnormal properties of histones from malignant cells. *Nature*, 1954, vol. 174. Pp. 580–585.

Dobzhansky, T. Eugenics in New Guinea. *Science*, 1960, vol. 132. P. 77.

Eibel-Eibesfeldt, I. The interactions of unlearned behavior patterns and learning in mammals. In Fessard, Gerard, Konorski, and Delafresnaye (Eds.), *Brain mechanisms and learning*, Springfield, Ill.: Charles C. Thomas, 1961. Pp. 53–74.

Emerson, A. E. The evolution of behavior among social insects. In Roe and Simpson (Eds.), *Behavior and evolution*. New Haven: Yale Univ. Press, 1958. Pp. 311–335.

Gajdusek, D. C. Kuru: An appraisal of five years of investigation. *Eugenics Quarterly*, 1962, vol. 9. Pp. 69–74.

Gifford, E. M., Jr. Variations in histone, DNA and RNA content during flower induction. In press.

Horowitz, N. H. The gene. *Scientific American*, October, 1956. Pp. 79–90.

Huang, R. C., and Bonner, J. Histone, a suppressor of chromosomal RNA synthesis. *Proceedings of the National Academy of Sciences*, 1962, vol. 48. Pp. 1216–1222.

Mayr, E. Behavior and Systematics. In Roe and Simpson. *Behavior and evolution*, New Haven: Yale Univ. Press, 1958. Pp. 341–362.

Muller, H. J. The Darwinian and modern conceptions of natural selection. *Proceedings of the American Philosophical Society*, 1949, vol. XCIII. Pp. 459–470.

Pittendrigh, C. S. Adaptation, natural selection, and behavior. In Roe and Simpson (Eds.), *Behavior and evolution*. New Haven: Yale Univ. Press, 1958. Pp. 390–416.

Taylor, J. H. The duplication of chromosomes. *Scientific American*, June, 1958. Pp. 37–42.

Thompson, W. R. Social behavior. In Roe and Simpson (Eds.), *Behavior and evolution*, New Haven: Yale Univ. Press, 1958. Pp. 291–310.

Thorpe, W. H. Some characteristics of the early learning period in birds. In Fessard, Gerard, Konorski, and Delafresnaye (Eds.), *Brain mechanisms and learning*. Springfield, Ill.: Charles C. Thomas, 1961. Pp. 75–94.

Wells, H. G., Huxley, J. S., and Wells, G. P. *The science of life* Garden City, N.Y.: Doubleday, 1938. Book eight, chap. I, "Rudiments of behavior"; chap. II, "How insects and other invertebrates behave"; chap. III, "The evolution of behavior in vertebrates."

sensory
processes
chapter 4

It is currently recognized that there are seven basic sensory systems at least in higher animals. One is the somesthetic system which can be subdivided into various subsystems covering the qualities of heat sensation, cold sensation, touch sensation, pressure sensation, and pain. A second system is the kinesthetic system which deals with the perception of bodily movement and the feedback which results from movements. Another is the vestibular system dealing with equilibrium which operates jointly with the kinesthetic and somesthetic systems to control general coordination of somatic activity. Other systems include the auditory and visual, gustatory, and olfactory.

Modern research has indicated that sensory input is critical for normal functioning, and in fact restricting sensory input has deleterious effects upon the mental and physical well-being of an organism. The first papers discuss the problems which arise as a result of sensory deprivation. Following are discussions of the various sensory systems dealing with problems of how sensations are coded, how receptors operate, and how input is handled centrally at various levels within the brain. Theories are presented to account for such diverse factors as olfactory perception, color vision, discrimination of sounds of different pitch, and the general problem of what is pain.

A great deal of important information could be gained from understanding how specific sensations are coded. The reason for this actually goes back over 100 years when it was expressed by Johannes Müller in the form of "the doctrine of specific nerve energies." Müller, a physiologist, made the startling but very important observation that sensation is not an awareness directly of the environment but only of the states of neural pathways. The only thing that the nervous system "understands" is electrical energy, not what is going on directly outside. In fact, stimulation of a sensory nerve by any means, mechanical, electrical, or chemical, always elicits the same sensation. Stimulation of the optic nerve, whether by pressure, by chemicals, or by electricity, yields a visual sensation. This means that one does not have to have eyes to see or ears to hear, because the central nervous system does not respond to light or sound directly but through trans- formations of light and sound in the form of nerve impulses. Hence, if we could understand the neural code for the different colors and light intensities, it might be possible to convert physical stimuli by means of laboratory devices into electrical impulses appropriate to the code. The central nervous system would interpret these synthetic electrical messages in the same manner that it normally interprets input directly from the eye. The result would be vision but produced by an artificial device converting the sensory input into electrical information rather than using a retina. Although this is far off, it is, of course, the ultimate hope for the cure of unpreventable peripheral blindness. The same might be true of all sensory systems so that individuals deprived of their various sensory modalities might be able to regain usable sensations through electrical devices, provided the neural code is broken. This is probably one of the underlying reasons why so much research is being done in the area of sensory physiology.

Effects of
decreased variation in
the sensory environment
w. harold bexton
woodburn heron
and
thomas h. scott

This study began with a practical problem: the lapses of attention that may occur when a man must give close and prolonged attention to some aspect of an environment in which nothing is happening, or in which the changes are very regular. Watching a radar screen hour after hour is a prime example. As Mackworth (5) and others have shown, when at least something *does* happen in such circumstances the watcher may fail to respond. Such monotonous conditions exist in civilian occupations as well as in military ones (marine pilotage by radar, piloting aircraft on long flights), and here too lapses of attention may have extremely serious consequences. For example, such lapses may explain some otherwise inexplicable railroad and highway accidents.

Besides its practical significance this problem has theoretical implications of great interest. There is much evidence from recent neurophysiological studies to indicate that the normal functioning of the waking brain depends on its being constantly exposed to sensory bombardment, which produces a continuing "arousal reaction." Work now being done by S. K. Sharpless at McGill indicates, further, that when stimulation does not change it rapidly loses its power to cause the arousal reaction. Thus, although one function of a stimulus is to evoke or guide a specific bit of behavior, it also has a non-specific function, that of maintaining "arousal," probably through the brain-stem reticular formation.

In other words, the maintenance of normal, intelligent, adaptive behavior

From *Canadian Journal of Psychology*, 1954, **8**, 70–76. Reprinted by permission.

probably requires a continually varied sensory input. The brain is not like a calculating machine operated by an electric motor which is able to respond at once to specific cues after lying idle indefinitely. Instead it is like one that must be kept warmed up and working. It seemed, therefore, worthwhile to examine cognitive functioning during prolonged perceptual isolation, as far as this was practicable. Bremer (2) has achieved such isolation by cutting the brain stem; college students, however, are reluctant to undergo brain operations for experimental purposes, so we had to be satisfied with less extreme isolation from the environment.

PROCEDURE

The subjects, 22 male college students, were paid to lie on a comfortable bed in a lighted cubicle 24 hours a day, with time out for eating and going to the toilet. During the whole experimental period they wore translucent goggles which transmitted diffuse light but prevented pattern vision. Except when eating or at the toilet, the subject wore gloves and cardboard cuffs, the latter extending from below the elbow to beyond the fingertips. These permitted free joint movement but limited tactual perception. Communication between subject and experimenters was provided by a small speaker system, and was kept to a minimum. Auditory stimulation was limited by the partially sound-proof cubicle and by a U-shaped foam-rubber pillow in which the subject kept his head while in the cubicle. Moreover, the continuous hum provided by fans, air-conditioner, and the amplifier leading to earphones in the pillow produced fairly efficient masking noise.

GENERAL EFFECTS

As might be expected from the evidence reviewed by Kleitman (3) for onset of sleep following reduced stimulation in man and other animals, the subjects tended to spend the earlier part of the experimental session in sleep. Later they slept less, became bored, and appeared eager for stimulation. They would sing, whistle, talk to themselves, tap the cuffs together, or explore the cubicle with them. This boredom seemed to be partly due to deterioration in the capacity to think systematically and productively—an effect described below. The subjects also became very restless, displaying constant random movement, and they described the restlessness as unpleasant. Hence it was difficult to keep subjects for more than two or three days, despite the fact that the pay ($20 for a 24-hour day) was more than double what they could normally earn. Some subjects, in fact, left before testing could be completed.

There seemed to be unusual emotional liability during the experimental period. When doing tests, for instance, the subjects would seem very pleased when they did well, and upset if they had difficulty. They commented more freely about test items than when they were tested outside. While many reported that they felt elated during the first part of their stay in the cubicle, there was a marked increase in irritability toward the end of the experimental period.

On coming out of the cubicle after the experimental session, when goggles, cuffs, and gloves had been removed, the subjects seemed at first dazed. There also appeared to be some disturbance in visual perception, usually lasting no longer than one or two minutes. Subjects reported difficulty in focusing; objects appeared fuzzy and did not stand out from their backgrounds. There was a tendency for the environment to appear two-dimensional and colors seemed more saturated than usual. The subjects also reported feelings of confusion, headaches, a mild nausea, and fatigue; these conditions persisted in some cases for 24 hours after the session.

EFFECTS ON COGNITIVE PROCESSES

Our present concern is primarily with cognitive disturbances during the period of isolation and immediately afterwards. The subjects reported that they were unable to concentrate on any topic for long while in the cubicle. Those who tried to review their studies or solve self-initiated intellectual problems found it difficult to do so. As a result they lasped into day-dreaming, abandoned attempts at organized thinking, and let their thoughts wander. There were also reports of "blank periods," during which they seemed unable to think of anything at all.

In an attempt to measure some of the effects on cognitive processes, various tests were given to the subjects before, during, and after the period of isolation.

First, the tests given during isolation. Twelve subjects were given the following types of problem to do in their heads: multiplying two- and three-digit numbers; arithmetical problems (such as "how many times greater is twice $2\frac{1}{2}$ than one-half $2\frac{1}{2}$"); completion of number series; making a word from jumbled letters; making as many words as possible from the letters of a given word. Each subject was tested on problems of this type before going into the cubicle, after he had been in for 12, 24, and 48 hours, and three days after coming out of the cubicle. Twelve control subjects were given the same series of tasks at the same intervals. The average performance of the experimental subjects was inferior to that of the controls on all tests performed during the cubicle session. With our present small number of subjects the differences are significant only for the error scores on the second anagram task

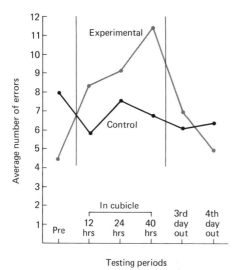

Testing periods

Errors in word-making

(wrong words, misspelling, repeats)

Figure 1. Mean error scores for experimental and control subjects, before, during, and after the isolation period.

(p = .01, see Figure 1). The groups are now being enlarged.

Secondly, tests given before entering the cubicle and immediately after leaving it. On the Kohs Block Test and the Wechsler Digit Symbol Test the experi-

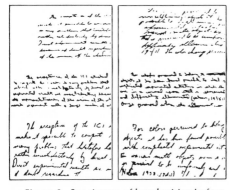

Figure 2. Specimens of handwriting before and after the isolation period.

mental subjects were inferior to the controls on leaving the cubicle (p = .01). They also tended to be slower in copying a prose paragraph (p = .10). Figure 2 gives samples of handwriting before and after the experiment. The first is from one of the subjects showing the greatest effect, the second illustrates the average effect. As the third sample shows, some subjects were not affected. This disturbance in handwriting, though perhaps due to some sensori-motor disturbance, might also reflect cognitive or motivational changes.

HALLUCINATORY ACTIVITY

Finally there were the hallucinations reported by the subjects while in the experimental apparatus. Among our early subjects there were several references, rather puzzling at first, to what one of them called "having a dream while awake." Then one of us, while serving as a subject, observed the phenomenon and realized its peculiarity and extent.

The visual phenomena were actually quite similar to what have been described for mescal intoxication, and to what Grey Walter (6) has recently produced by exposure to flickering light. There have also been rare cases of hallucinations in aged persons without psychosis (1), which, like ours, involved no special chemical or visual stimulation. As we did not ask our first subjects specifically about these phenomena we do not know the frequency among them. The last 14 subjects, however, were asked to report any "visual imagery" they observed, and our report is based on them. In general, where more "formed" (i.e., more complex) hallucinations occurred they were usually preceded by simpler forms of the phenomenon. Levels of complexity could be differentiated as follows: in the simplest form the visual field, with the eyes closed, changed from dark to light color; next in complexity were dots of light, lines, or simple geometrical patterns. All 14 subjects reported such imagery, and said it was a new experience to them. Still more complex forms consisted in "wall-paper patterns," reported by 11 subjects, and isolated figures or objects, without background (e.g., a row of little yellow men with black caps on and their mouths open; a German helmet), reported by seven subjects. Finally, there were integrated scenes (e.g., a procession of squirrels with sacks over their shoulders marching "purposefully" across a snow field and out of the field of "vision"; prehistoric animals walking about in a jungle). Three of the 14 subjects reported such scenes, frequently including dreamlike distortions, with the figures often being described as "like cartoons." One curious fact is that some of the hallucinations were reported as being inverted or tilted at an angle.

In general, the subjects were first surprised by these phenomena, and then amused or interested, waiting for what they would see next. Later, some subjects found them irritating, and complained that their vividness interfered with sleep. There was some control over content; by "trying," the subject might see certain objects suggested by the experimenter, but not always as he intended. Thus one subject, trying to "get" a pen, saw first an inkblot, then a pencil, a green horse, and finally a pen; trying to "get" a shoe, he saw first a ski boot, then a moccasin. The imagery usually disappeared when the subject was doing a complex task, such as multiplying three-place numbers in his head, but not if he did physical exercises, or talked to the experimenter.

There were also reports of hallucinations involving other senses. One subject could hear the people speaking in his visual hallucinations, and another repeatedly heard the playing of a music box. Four subjects described kinesthetic and somesthetic phenomena. One reported seeing a miniature rocket ship

Figure 3. Drawing made by a subject to show how he felt at one period in the cubicle. He reported that it was as if "there were two of me," and was momentarily unable to decide whether he was A or B.

discharging pellets that kept striking his arm, and one reported reaching out to touch a doorknob he saw before him and feeling an electric shock. The other two subjects reported a phenomenon which they found difficult to describe. They said it was as if there were two bodies side by side in the cubicle; in one case the two bodies overlapped, partly occupying the same space. Figure 3 shows this subject's subsequent drawing, made in an attempt to show what he meant.

In addition, there were reports of feelings of "otherness" and bodily "strangeness" in which it was hard to know exactly what the subject meant. One subject said "my mind seemed to be a ball of cotton-wool floating above my body"; another reported that his head felt detached from his body. These are familiar phenomena in certain cases of migraine, as described recently by Lippman (4), and earlier by Lewis Carroll in *Alice in Wonderland*. As Lippman points out, Lewis Carroll was a sufferer from migraine, and it is suggested that Alice's bodily distortions are actually descriptions of Carroll's (i.e., Charles Dodgson's) own experiences.

In summary, both the changes in intelligence-test performance and the hallucinatory activity, induced merely by limiting the variability of sensory input, provide direct evidence of a kind of dependence on the environment that has not been previously recognized. Further experimental study will be needed to elucidate the details of this relationship.

References

1. Barlet, J. E. A. A case of organized visual hallucinations in an old man with cataract and their relation to the phenomena of the phantom limb. *Brain*, 1951, **74**, 363–373.

2. Bremer, F., and Terzuolo, C. Nouvelles recherches sur le processus physiologique de reveil. *Arch. Internat. de Physiol.*, 1953, **61**, 86–90.

3. Kleitman, N. *Sleep and wakefulness.* Chicago: Univ. of Chicago Press, 1939.

4. Lippman, Caro. Certain hallucinations peculiar to migraine. *J. Nerv. Ment. Dis.*, 1952, **116**, 346–351.

5. Mackworth, N. H. *Researches on the measurement of human performance.* Med. Res Council, Spec. Rep. Ser. London. No. 268, 1950.

6. Walter, W. G. *The living brain.* New York: Norton, 1953.

Pain
as
a puzzle
for psychology
and
physiology
ernest r. hilgard

Pain is so familiar that we take if for granted, but this does not lessen its importance. Pain reduction is a primary task of the physician, second only to the preservation of life. The ubiquity of pain is clear enough from the many advertisements which pit one pain killer against another. Because pain is so important, and interest in pain is so great, it is surprising how little firm knowledge there is about pain.

WHAT IS PUZZLING ABOUT PAIN?

The very familiarity of pain may cause us to acknowledge it without questioning it. Pain appears to warn us of tissue damage, and it is easy to assign a superficial interpretation that it is merely "the cry of an injured nerve." When one does begin to question pain, however, there are many mysteries that remain to be unraveled. I wish to mention some of these before reporting some of our own experiments on pain and its reduction.

1. *Is pain a sensory modality?* The first question is this: Shall we consider pain to be a sensory modality like vision or audition? If you cut your finger or stub your toe, pain behaves very much as if it were an ordinary sensory modality. That is, there is a stimulus, there are receptors in the fingers and toes, there is an afferent transmission of impulses, a central processing of data, a perceptual response appropriate to the stimulus, and perhaps some verbal accompaniment, such as "Ouch." The perceptual response of felt pain localized in a finger

From *American Psychologist*, February 1969, **24**, 103–113. Copyright 1969 by the American Psychological Association.

or a toe is analogous to seeing a light off to the left or of hearing a sound off to your right. Perceptual responses give knowledge of environmental events, and you guide your actions accordingly. Furthermore, the stimulus to pain can be graduated, as by an electric shock of varying intensity, or by water at different degrees of hot or cold, with subsequent changes in felt pain. All that I have said thus far qualifies pain as a sensory modality.

But there are other considerations which make it less easy to assign pain the status of a sensory modality. Most defined sensory modalities have definite stimuli, definite receptors, specific sensory tracts, and localized receptive areas within the cortex. Not so for pain. Any stimulus can qualify to produce pain if it is intense enough: loud sounds and very bright lights are painful. The receptors are unspecified, despite the role traditionally assigned to free nerve endings. While there are pathways for cutaneous pain, there are at least two afferent systems, and they operate quite differently (Melzack and Wall, 1965). And there is no one pain center that has been localized in the brain.

A further problem arises in that there are so many differences in the quality of felt pain that it may be as dubious to consider pain a single sense as to consider all cutaneous experiences as belonging to a single sense of touch. Even the attempt to define pain has met numerous obstacles (e.g., Beecher, 1959; Melzack, 1968). One of the puzzles is how to deal with the distinction between mild sensory pain and the intense pains that are described as suffering or anguish; under frontal lobe operations, for example, the anguish may be reduced even though the pain remains.

We must therefore give a qualified answer to the question whether or not pain can be counted as a sensory modality.

2. *Are there any satisfactory physiological indicators of pain?* We know about pain through a subject's verbal reports, but if we expect to objectify the amount of pain he feels we would be happy to have some physiological indicators by which to compare his pain with that of others who suffer. Our second question is then: Do satisfactory indicators exist?

A satisfactory physiological indicator of pain is one which is present (or increased) when pain is felt, and absent (or reduced) when pain is not felt. The correlation between the physiological indicator and the verbal report has to be established both positively and negatively if the indicator is to be used in confidence in the absence of supplementary verbal report. Without attempting at this time a literature review, may I simply summarize the state of our knowledge of the physiological correlates of pain by saying that there is at present *no single accepted indicator of pain* that can be counted to vary in an orderly way with degrees of pain and absence of pain.[1] While in many experiments some kind of average difference in a physiological response can be detected with increase in pain, individual differences in the patterning of responses, and some individual response stereotype to different kinds of stress, complicate the problem.

3. *Where is the pain that is felt?* My third question about the puzzle of pain is this: where is the pain that the subject reports? A subject locates the pain of an

injury at the site of the injury or noxious stimulation by the same sorts of local signs and environmental references that he uses in localizing other sources of stimulation. I say, "I feel pain in my finger." My listener sees that the finger is bleeding, and replies, "No wonder you feel pain in your finger; you cut it." The pain is in my finger just as the word I read is on the printed page. The psychoneural *conditions* of feeling pain and of seeing words are within me, but it would be as uninformative to say that the pain is in my head as to say that the word I read is in my head. We have to distinguish between the *conditions* of the perception and the *informative* aspect of the perception itself. The *information* is of a pain in my finger and of a word on the printed page.

The trouble about pain as informative is that there are at least three kinds of pain which make us wonder whether or not to accept information conferred by the localized pain. The first of these is *referred* pain, in which the source of irritation is one place and the pain is felt at another place, as in heartburn as the result of indigestion. The second is *psychosomatic* pain, in which the stimulus conditions may be vague, as in a headache following a political argument. The third kind is *phantom-limb* pain, where the pain is felt in a part of the body which has been amputated from it. Of these, phantom-limb pain is particularly interesting. Our tendency to revert to a strict sensory analogy is very strong; hence we would expect phantom-limb pain to be the result of referring the stimulation of a cut nerve in the stump to the limb from which it originally received its impulses. However, phantom-limb pain probably has more to do with body image than with local signs (Melzack, 1968; Sternbach, 1968; Szasz, 1967). The reply to our question must then be that, *as information* (even if it be false), the best we can do is to accept that the pains are where they are felt, including the phantom-limb pains; as *condi-*

---

[1]There have been a great many reviews of the literature on pain, of which Melzack (1968) and Sternbach (1968) can serve as recent representatives and as sources of citations of earlier reviews.

tions for pain, there are many complex events within the nervous system.

4. *How account for the great individual differences in felt pain?* My fourth and final question about the puzzle of pain has to do with the *lack* of relationship between the conditions of noxious stimulation and the amount of pain that is felt. This is primarily a matter of individual differences, but they are very impressive. I am not talking about the extreme cases of people who are born with practically complete lack of sensitivity to cutaneous or other pains. These people correspond in their own way to the totally blind or the totally deaf. Within the normal population, however, there are widespread differences, and it is these which concern us now.

In the relief of postsurgical pain through morphine, Beecher (1959) and his associates have found results that may be summarized roughly as follows: about a third of the patients gain relief of pain through morphine that is greater than the relief following a placebo; about a third get as much relief from a placebo as they do from morphine; the final third are relieved neither by placebo nor by morphine in doses considered safe to use.

Differences in pain responses are found to be related to cognitive styles by Petrie (1967). She reports that subjects selected on the basis of a test of kinesthetic aftereffects can be classified as *augmenters* or *reducers:* the augmenters exaggerate their pain responses and the reducers tend to inhibit theirs.

Differences in pain responsiveness, particularly complaints about pain, have been found to be associated with social class, ethnic groups, and family constellation. For example, Gonda (1962a, 1962b) found that those from the working class complain more to the nurses in hospitals than do those from white-collar classes, an observation confirmed in England as well as in the United States.

Finally, pain responses in the laboratory appear to follow some of the theories of cognitive consistency, in that the pain corresponds to the amount of reward offered for participating in pain experiments—the greater the reward the greater the pain—as though some suffering is consistent with the higher pay for participation (Lewin, 1965; Zimbardo, Cohen, Weisenberg, Dworkin, and Firestone, 1966; Zimbardo, 1969).

By raising these four questions, about pain as a sensory modality, about the physiological indicators of pain, about where pain is felt, and about individual differences in pain responsiveness, I hope that you will now agree that there are sufficient unsolved problems to make a concerned attack on pain a fruitful scientific enterprise.

PAIN AS A SENSORY MODALITY: COLD PRESSOR RESPONSE AND ISCHEMIC PAIN IN THE NORMAL WAKING STATE

We have used two sources of noxious stimulation in the experiments I am about to report. In the first of these pain is produced by placing the subject's hand and forearm in circulating cold water at several temperatures. This arrangement is commonly referred to as the *cold pressor test* (Greene, Boltax, Lustig, and Rogow, 1965; Hines and Brown, 1932; Wolf and Hardy, 1941). In the second method pain is produced by first placing a tourniquet just above the elbow, and then asking the subject to squeeze a dynamometer a standard number of times. After he quits working and is quiet, the pain begins to mount. This we call *ischemic pain*, following the practice of Beecher and his associates (Beecher, 1966; Smith, Lawrence, Markowitz, Mosteller, and Beecher, 1966). Their method is a modification of the method initiated by Lewis, Pickering, and Rothschild (1931).

First, the cold pressor test. I shall not report here the details of experimental arrangements, which will appear in due course in the form of journal articles.

Suffice it to say that there are base-line conditions: first, a *vigilance* condition, in which the subject keeps alert by pressing the appropriate one of a pair of buttons, to turn off that one of two discriminable sounds which happens to be sounding; this is followed by a condition of *relaxation* for several minutes prior to the immersion of the hand and forearm in the cold water; the *immersion period*, usually of 40 seconds; then, after the hand and arm are removed from the water and dried, a repetition of the vigilance and relaxation conditions. Except as part of the situational background, the base-line conditions are not important for the present psychophysical account, but they are important for the physiological measures which were taken concomitantly with the verbal reports. While the hand and forearm are immersed in the cold water, the subject reports his felt pain on a scale of 0 to 10, 0 being no pain, and 10 being a pain so severe that he would wish to remove his

hand. We refer to this as a *critical level*, for it is the tolerance level for the pain, without special encouragement to continue to suffer. If a subject has reached the pain level of 10 before the immersion period is over, he is persuaded to keep his hand in the water a little longer and to keep on counting. This he is able to do, and the result is of course a pain report beyond 10.

That such verbal pain reports yield an orderly relationship to the conditions of stimulation, both to the temperature of the water, and to the time in the water, is shown by the mean results for 0, 5, 10, and 15 degrees Centigrade as plotted in Figure 1. The means of the pain-state reports in each of the temperatures differ significantly from each of the other temperatures by t tests, with significances of at least $p = .05$.

These data appear orderly enough to provide a test of standard psychophysical models. The model chosen is Stevens' (1966) power function because it proves to fit better than the standard Fechner logarithmic function. The test is quite simple. If both the numerical pain report and some measure of the intensity of stimulation are plotted logarithmically, the power function fits if a straight-line function results.

There is the single scale for verbal pain reports, but there are two possibilities for describing the intensity of stimulation: one, the *temperature* of the water, on the simple assumption that the colder the water the greater the pain; two, the *time* in the water, on the assumption that the pain mounts the longer the hand and forearm are exposed to the cold. The two measures have a common intermediary, which is the relationship between cold and pain, but there is not a priori reason for both of them to fit the same mathematical function.

Let us first see how pain varies as a function of water temperature. Other workers have found that the threshold for cold pressor pains is near 18 degrees Centigrade. This is well below skin tem-

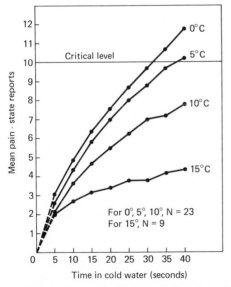

Figure 1. Reported pain as a function of time in water at temperatures of 0, 5, 10, and 15 degrees Centigrade.

perature, but water can feel cold without feeling painful. If we then plot the average pain-state reports at 15, 10, 5, and 0 degrees on a scale which assumes that as the water gets colder the pain will be a power function of the difference in water temperature from the threshold value of 18 degrees we get the plot shown in Figure 2. The four plotted points fall quite well along a straight line, and the line projects to a threshold value of pain near 18 degrees.

Now we may ask whether a similar result will be obtained if we plot pain as a power function of the time in water of a given temperature. Because we have four temperatures, we have a family of four lines, as shown in Figure 3. Again the straight lines fit well enough to indicate the appropriateness of the power function.[2]

Turning now to ischemia, as our second form of laboratory pain, and using the same scale of pain reports, we again find a power function with time, although now the time units are in minutes rather than in seconds (Figure 4).

Thus far I have shown that pain reported verbally on a simple numerical scale yields not only orderly results, but valid results, in the sense that the pain reported bears a systematic relationship to the temperature of the water and to the time of exposure to the noxious stimulus. The lawfulness is supported by the fit of the power function which holds

[2]There are limitations in the fit of the power functions for both the cold pressor response and the ischemic response, when the stimulating conditions endure too long. In the cold pressor response numbing begins to set in at about 60 seconds for 0 degrees Centigrade water; in the case of ischemia there may be a sudden upturn of pain as the critical tolerance level is passed. We have elsewhere proposed a more complex function which can be used when there are inflections in the rate of change of pain or when the pain change is not monotonic (Voevodsky, Cooper, Morgan, and Hilgard, 1967).

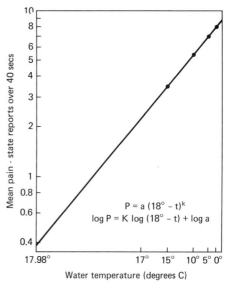

$$P = a (18° - t)^k$$
$$\log P = K \log (18° - t) + \log a$$

Figure 2. Pain as a power function of the differences in water temperature from the threshold value of 18 degrees Centigrade.

within so many other perceptual modalities.

I emphasize these findings as a reply to those who would degrade the subject's statements as being "merely"

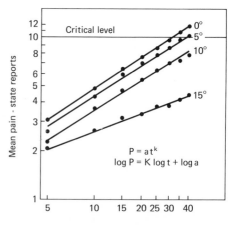

$$P = at^k$$
$$\log P = K \log t + \log a$$

Figure 3. Pain as a power function of time in cold water.

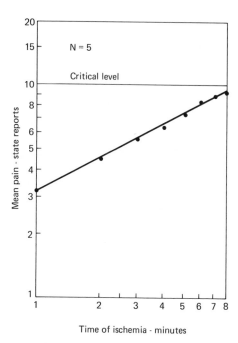

Figure 4. *Pain as a function of time of isch-emia.*

verbal reports, as though some sort of physiological response would be sounder. I wish to assert flatly that there is no physiological measure of pain which is either as discriminating of fine differences in stimulus conditions, as reliable upon repetition, or as lawfully related to changed conditions, as the subject's verbal report.

PHYSIOLOGICAL ACCOMPANIMENTS OF PAIN

If I seem to disparage physiological indicators of pain, it is not because we have not studied them, nor indeed because results are negative, for I shall have some positive results to report. We have studied a number of measures, but I shall confine my discussion to one indicator, systolic blood pressure as measured from a finger on the hand opposite to that which is suffering the pain. We place

a small inflatable cuff around one finger, with a plethysmographic transducer on the finger tip to indicate when the pulse is occluded. Another plethysmograph on an adjacent finger helps us to monitor heart responses. An automatically operated air pump inflates the finger cuff until the circulation is cut off, as indicated by the record from the plethysmograph on that finger, and then a device automatically releases the air from the cuff until the pulse again appears and is restored to normal, when the cycle automatically repeats itself. Thus a record is obtained on the polygraph of the systolic blood pressure every 10 seconds or so. By connecting these measurements as they appear on the polygraph we have an essentially continuous record of the blood pressure.

The rise in pain in the cold water is accompanied by a rise in blood pressure, and the rise in ischemic pain is also accompanied by rise in blood pressure. Thus, under appropriate conditions, blood pressure appears to be the kind of indicator of pain for which we have been searching. A record of the blood pressure rise within cold water at four temperatures is given in Figure 5, which corresponds closely to the verbal pain reports earlier shown in Figure 1. The

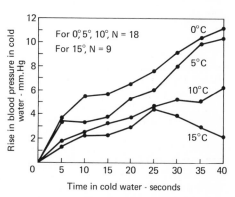

Figure 5. *Blood pressure as a function of time in water at temperatures of 0, 5, 10, and 15 degrees Centigrade.*

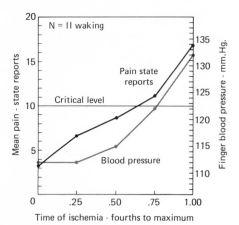

Figure 6. Pain reports and blood pressure as a function of time in ischemia. (The tourniquet was removed when pain became intolerable, which varied from 12 to 32 minutes for these 11 subjects. Hence the time to intolerable pain was divided into fourths for purposes of obtaining the means that are plotted.)

average results hold also for individual subjects. That is, those who suffer less at a given temperature also show less rise in blood pressure. Thus, for water at 0 degrees Centigrade, a correlation between mean pain reports and blood pressure rise for 22 subjects reaches $r = .53$, a satisfactorily significant correlation ($p = .02$). Othere have reported similar findings (e.g., Tétreault, Panisset, and Gouger, 1964).

Blood pressure also rises as pain rises in ischemia. Rise in pain reports and rise in blood pressure yield the curves shown in Figure 6. These are means for 11 subjects. The abscissa has been converted to ratios of time in ischemia in order to plot the several subjects in comparable units. The time to maximum tolerable pain (at which the torniquet had to be removed) fell between 12 and 32 minutes, by contrast with the water pain which was measured over a fraction of a minute only.

Thus we have established blood pressure as a candidate to serve as an in-

dicator of pain. At least, in two stressful situations, it mounts as the pain mounts. As we shall see later, this does not satisfy all the requisites for a physiological pain indicator.

PAIN REDUCTION UNDER HYPNOSIS: COLD PRESSOR RESPONSE

Now I wish to turn to the reduction of pain, under the identical physical conditions of stressful stimulation, when that reduction is by way of hypnosis.[3] First we shall consider reduction of cold pressor pain.

College students or high school students who come to the laboratory for their first experience of hypnosis differ widely in their responses to a standard induction procedure followed by a standard list of suggestions. By making use of some scales earlier standardized in our laboratory (Weitzenhoffer and Hilgard, 1959, 1962, 1967) we are able to sort our subjects according to their degree of hypnotic susceptibility before they take part in the experiments concerned with pain. Then, at some later time, they experience the cold pressor pain in the waking condition, and learn to use the verbal pain report to indicate how much pain they feel. On a subsequent occasion we may hypnotize them, without suggesting any pain reduction, and then expose them to

[3]The experimental literature on pain reduction (and pain production) in hypnosis is very confused, despite the well-established clinical successes in childbirth, dentistry, major surgery, and the successful relief of pain through hypnosis in severe burns and terminal cancer. A few of the major reports from other laboratories of experimental studies are listed here for the benefit of those who may care to explore this literature: Barber and Hahn (1962, 1964), Brown and Vogel (1938), Doupe, Miller, and Keller (1939), Dudley, Holmes, Martin, and Ripley (1964, 1966), Dynes (1932), Levine (1930), Sears (1932), Shor (1962), Sutcliffe (1961), West, Neill, and Hardy (1952), Wolff and Goodell (1943).

immersion in the cold water, or we may hypnotize them and tell them that they will feel no pain in the cold water. This is the condition which we call attempted hypnotic analgesia. The subjects who entered the ice water experiments had had very little experience of hypnosis, and they were not trained in pain reduction. Our purpose was not to see how completely we could wipe out pain, but rather to see what individual differences in pain reduction would appear under standard conditions.

Because we did not have blood pressure measures on the subjects of our first reported experiment,[4] I shall turn to our second experiment which was partially a replication of the first one, but also introduced some modifications. We used high school students as subjects in this second investigation, instead of college students, largely because they were conveniently available in large numbers during the summer when the experiment was conducted. The subjects had already served in the experiment with water at different temperatures, in the normal waking state, so that they came to the hypnotic portion of the experiment well familiar with reports of pain on the verbal pain-state scale. They served three days, one in the normal waking condition, one in hypnosis without analgesia, and one in hypnosis with suggested analgesia; the orders of the latter two days were randomized, to correct for any demand characteristics associated with having the hand in ice water in the midst of hypnosis. The advantages of comparing a day of hypnosis *without* suggested analgesia and hypno-

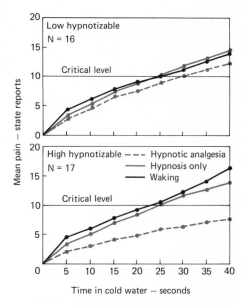

Figure 7. *Pain as a function of time in water of 0 degrees Centigrade in waking state, and following attempted hypnotic induction without analgesia instructions and with analgesia instructions. (Low subjects, scores of 0–9 on combined Forms A and C–Mean = 7.1; High subjects, scores of 18–24 on combined Forms A and C–Mean = 21.6.)*

[4]Hilgard (1967). In this first experiment of the series with the cold pressor response, reactions from 55 college students were reported. The correlation between the amount of pain reduction under hypnotic analgesia and susceptibility to hypnosis was reported as $r = .37$ ($p = .01$). If one very discordant subject is eliminated, this rises to $r = .46$. See also Hilgard, Cooper, Lenox, Morgan, and Voevodsky (1967).

sis *with* analgesia are twofold. In the first place, this arrangement separates out any physiological effects that are attributable to the hypnosis as distinct from those associated with the stressful stimulus, and, in the second place, it rules out the effect upon pain of whatever relaxation is associated with hypnotic induction. It is well known that relaxation may itself reduce pain. The results for the three days are shown in Figure 7, plotted separately for the subjects low in hypnotic susceptibility and for those high in susceptibility. What we see from the figure is that hypnosis alone did not reduce pain appreciably for either group, but the suggested analgesia did indeed produce a reduction in verbally reported pain, slightly for the low hypnotizables, more for the high hypnotizables. In

Figure 7 the high and low susceptibles are the extremes of a larger distribution, so that a correlational analysis is not appropriate. For a smaller group of 19 subjects, unselected for hypnosis, and including moderates as well as highs and lows, the correlation between hypnotic susceptibility as tested prior to the pain experiment and the pain reduction under hypnosis turned out to be $r = .60$ ($p = .01$).

The verbal pain reports thus yield an orderly picture of pain reduction under hypnotic analgesia, with the greatest reduction found for those who are the most hypnotizable. Now what of the blood pressure measures? Will they continue to correlate with pain reports under these conditions? To our surprise, the blood pressure *rises* under hypnosis and is highest under the analgesic condition, for both high and low hypnotizable subjects (Figure 8). It may be noted

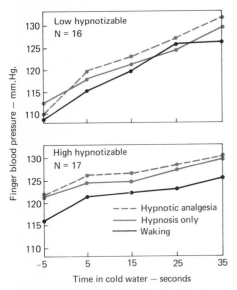

Figure 8. Blood pressure as a function of time in water of 0 degrees Centigrade in waking state, and following attempted hypnotic induction without analgesia instructions and with analgesia instructions. (Same subjects as in Figure 7)

that, particularly for the high hypnotizable subjects, the blood pressure rises before the hands are placed in the ice water, so that the initial readings are above those of the less hypnotizable.[5]

We are thus led to two propositions about the relationship between blood pressure and pain:

1. When pain is felt there is a tendency for blood pressure to rise in an amount correlated with the amount of experienced pain.
2. Blood pressure may rise in a stressful situation independent of the amount of felt pain.

The second of these statements is my reason for asserting that blood pressure is not a completely satisfactory physiological indicator of pain. It works in some situations, but not in others. There is nothing very surprising about this, because we know that there are many controls over blood pressure of which pain is but one. The two propositions, taken together, show that we have to be careful not to identify a *correlate* of pain, found in some special arrangement, with the pain itself. We may note also that we have to avoid a superficial interpretation of pain reduction under hypnosis by claiming that the effects of hypnotic analgesia rest entirely on the reduction of anxiety; it appears that excitation, possibly with some anxiety over the impending stress, may keep the blood pressure high, even while the pain is reduced.

PAIN REDUCTION UNDER HYPNOSIS: ISCHEMIC PAIN

The relationship between blood pressure and pain reduction under hypnosis

[5]The initial differences in blood pressure between waking and hypnosis days were not found in ischemia (Figure 9.), and this discrepancy sets problems for further investigation. The conclusion holds, however, that blood pressure rises in the cold pressor test even when no pain is felt.

turned out quite differently in ischemia. It is fortunate that we performed both experiments, for had we performed only one of them we might have produced misleading generalizations. There are several differences in the experiments to be noted. First, the cold water has the stress of cold, in addition to pain, while the cold is lacking in the ischemia experiment. Second, ischemic pain tends to mount very slowly at first, so that there is time for the hypnotic subject to achieve a confident analgesic state, while the shock of the ice water is immediate. Third, in the experiments to be reported the subjects were much more highly selected for their ability to reduce pain in hypnosis than they were in the cold pressor experiment, in which they were not selected at all. Still, the subjects in the ischemia experiments were selected from those in the cold pressor experiment, so we are not dealing with ideosyncrasies that can be accounted for on the basis of subject differences. These subjects behaved differently in ischemia from the way that they themselves had behaved in the ice water experiment.

It turns out that in the ischemia experiment these highly responsive subjects were able not only to rid themselves completely of pain for a matter of 18–45 minutes, but their blood pressure, which rose sharply in the waking state, *did not rise in ischemia or rose very little* even though the stressful condition was continued for many minutes beyond the time, in the waking condition, when the pain was too severe to be further endured. Results for six subjects, all of whom suffered greatly in the waking state but were able to maintain their analgesia throughout in the hypnotic state, are shown in Figure 9. The time to unbearable pain in the waking state is taken as unity; under hypnotic analgesia the tourniquet was kept on well beyond the time at which the intolerable pain would have been found in the waking state. Two subjects were unable to re-

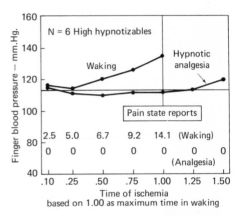

Figure 9. Blood pressure in ischemia, in waking state and in hypnotic analgesia (Mean, 6 subjects).

main analgesic throughout; their blood pressures showed changes beyond the subjects reported in Figure 9. While they were eliminated from Figure 9, statistical treatment with them left in shows a significant difference ($t = 3.12$, $df = 7$, $p = .01$) between the rise in blood pressure in the waking state over hypnotic analgesia for the whole group of subjects tested.

The three additional subjects, whose responses to ischemia in the waking state were reported earlier (in Figure 6), were subjects refractory to hypnosis, who were intended to be used as simulators in the hypnotic analgesia experiment, according to the experimental design recommended by Orne (1959, 1962). It turned out that the stress was too great, however, and none of them could tolerate the pain for the time required to parallel the behavior of the "true" hypnotic analgesia subjects. While this in some respects spoiled the experimental design, the conclusions are the same regarding the reality of the hypnotic analgesia for the "true" subjects, substantiated by the lack of any appreciable rise in blood pressure.

We are now prepared to add a third proposition regarding the relationship between blood pressure and pain:

3. When stressful conditions which normally lead both to reported pain and to an increase in blood pressure do not lead to an increase in blood pressure, it may be assumed that pain is absent.

This now brings us to a conclusion regarding the reality of hypnotic analgesia and to a summary assertion about the role of blood pressure. The absence of pain, reported by the hypnotically analgesic subject, is confirmed by the absence of a rise in blood pressure. Thus we have a physiological validation for the reality of hypnotic analgesia, but the validator works in one direction only. That is, *absence* of the blood pressure rise may be taken as an indication of absent pain under specified conditions, but pain may be absent *even if blood pressure rises.* This is a logical problem which has caused a good deal of confusion in earlier efforts to deal with the question of pain reduction under hypnotic analgesia (see especially Barber, 1963, Barber and Hahn, 1962; Sutcliffe, 1961).

CLINICAL RELEVANCE OF THE LABORATORY STUDY OF PAIN AND HYPNOTIC ANALGESIA

I wish to close my remarks with a few comments on the practical implications of the kind of experiments I have reported. There are continuing arguments over the relative amounts of money and energy to be expended on basic research and on research aimed at the applications of science. There are those who take the position that basic research is an end in itself, designed to satisfy curiosity, to seek the truth, to discover and order knowledge for its own sake. There are others who take the position that basic science will ultimately pay off in its contributions to society, although immediate payoff is not to be expected; this is the essence of the position that "there is nothing so practical as a good theory." On the more general issues, I

take a moderate position: I believe that science has multiple aims, that there is a division of labor along the spectrum from pure science to the arts of practice, that there should be mutual respect and encouragement for those who work at any point along this spectrum, so long as their work is imaginative and sound.

When, however, there is an evident application for laboratory results, I believe there is an obligation on the scientific enterprise as a whole to provide the bridging investigations that move from the laboratory to the real world. Thus the psychology of learning is incomplete if it is not reflected in educational practices, and the study of pain is incomplete if it does not contribute to the relief of pain outside the laboratory.

One may well ask how the experiments which I have reported bear upon the relief of pain through hypnosis by dentists, obstetricians, surgeons, and others who are confronted with the practical problems of suffering people. The answer is that the studies alone will not make much of a contribution unless they are extended to deal with the practical problems, either by those within laboratories such as ours, or by others who build upon our findings.

The potential contributions fall along the following lines:

1. First, our hypnotic susceptibility scales make it possible to determine what kinds of responsiveness to hypnosis are essential if a patient is to profit from the use of hypnosis in pain reduction. Not all people can be helped, and one obligation upon science is to be diagnostic regarding those who can be served by particular applications. It must be pointed out, however, that until normative data are obtained in the practical setting, the scales cannot be used effectively.

2. Second, the further study of the physiological consequences of pain, and the alterations of these consequences by hypnotic analgesia, can yield better understanding of what is happening in otherwise stressful conditions, such as

the preparation for surgery or surgery itself. If hypnosis can reduce surgical pain or postoperative shock, it is important to know what is happening inside the body. Again, unless these studies are carried out eventually in the hospital, the information gained in the laboratory will tend to be idle and useless.

We have accepted this as part of the responsibility of our own laboratory, and have undertaken studies of some patients suffering the pains of terminal cancer, others with migraine headaches. Clinicians are at present far ahead of our laboratories in the hypnotic reduction of pain, but the laboratory worker has a contribution to make. The contribution will be made, however, only if he takes his obligation seriously, and goes to the necessary trouble to tailor his findings to the needs of the world outside the laboratory.

References

Barber, T. X. The effects of "hypnosis" on pain: A critical review of experimental and clinical finding. *Psychosom. Med.*, 1963, **24**, 303–333.

Barber, T. X., and Hahn, K. W., Jr. Physiological and subjective responses to pain-producing stimulation under hypnotically suggested and waking-imagined "analgesia." *J. abnorm. soc. Psychol.*, 1962, **65**, 411–418.

Barber, T. X., and Hahn, K. W., Jr. Experimental studies in "hypnotic" behavior: Physiologic and subjective effects of imagined pain. *J. nerv. ment. Dis.*, 1964, **139**, 416–425.

Beecher, H. K. *Measurement of subjective responses.* New York: Oxford Univ. Press, 1959.

Beecher, H. K. Pain: One mystery solved. *Science*, 1966, **151**, 840–841.

Brown, R. R., and Vogel, V. H. Psychophysiological reactions following painful stimuli under hypnotic analgesia contrasted with gas anesthesia and Novocain block. *J. appl. Psychol.*, 1938, **22**, 408–420.

Doupe, J., Miller, W. R., and Keller, W. K. Vasomotor reactions in the hypnotic state. *J. Neurol. Psychiatr.*, 1939, **2**, 97–106.

Dudley, D. L., Holmes, T. H., Martin, C. J., and Ripley, H. S. Changes in respiration associated with hypnotically induced emotion, pain, and exercise. *Psychosom. Med.*, 1964, **24**, 46–57.

Dudley, D. L., Holmes, T. H., Martin, C. J., and Ripley, H. S. Hypnotically induced facsimile of pain. *Arch. gen. Psychiat.*, 1966, **15**, 198–204.

Dynes, J. B. Hypnotic analgesia. *J. abnorm. soc. Psychol.*, 1932, **27**, 79–88.

Gonda, T. A. The relation between complaints of persistent pain and family size. *J. Neurol. Neurosurg., and Psychiat.*, 1962, **25**, 277–281. (a)

Gonda, T. A. Some remarks on pain. *Bulletin, Brit. Psychol. Soc.*, 1962, **47**, 29–35. (b)

Greene, M. A., Boltax, A. J., Lustig, G. A., and Rogow, E., Circulatory dynamics during the cold pressor test. *Amer. J. Cardiol.*, 1965, **16**, 54–60.

Hilgard, E. R., A quantitative study of pain and its reduction through hypnotic suggestion. *Proceedings of the National Academy of Sciences*, 1967, **57**, 1581–1586.

Hilgard, E. R., Cooper, L. M., Lenox, J., Morgan, A. H., and Voevodsky, J. The use of pain-state reports in the study of hypnotic analgesia to the pain of ice water. *J. nerv. ment. Dis.*, 1967, **144**, 506–513.

Hines, E. A., and Brown, G. W. A standard stimulus for measuring vasomotor reactions: Its application in the study of hypertension. *Proceedings of Staff Meetings, Mayo Clinic*, 1932, **7**, 332.

Levine, M. Psychogalvanic reaction to painful stimuli in hypnotic and hysterical anesthesia. *Bulletin, Johns Hopkins Hospital*, 1930, **46**, 331–339.

Lewin, I. The effect of reward on the experience of pain. In *Dissertations in cognitive processes*. Detriot, Mich.: Center for Cognitive Processes, Wayne State University, 1965.

Lewis, T., Pickering, G. W., and Rothschild, P. Observations upon muscular pain in intermittent claudication. *Heart*, 1931, **15**, 359–383.

Melzack, R. Pain. *International Encyclopedia of the Social Sciences.* Vol. 11. New York: Macmillan and Free Press, 1968. Pp. 357–363.

Melzack, R., and Wall, P. D. Pain mechanisms: A new theory. *Science*, 1965, **150**, 971–979.

Orne, M. T. The nature of hypnosis: Artifact and essence. *J. abnorm. soc. Psychol.*, 1959, **58**, 277–299.

Orne, M. T. On the social psychology of the psychological experiment: With particular reference to demand characteristics and their implications. *Amer. Psychologist*, 1962, **17**, 776–783.

Petrie, A. *Individuality in pain and suffering.* Chicago: Univ. of Chicago Press, 1967.

Sears, R. R. Experimental study of hypnotic anesthesia. *J. exp. Psychol.*, 1932, **15**, 1–22.

Shor, R. E. Physiological effects of painful stimulation during hypnotic analgesia under conditions designed to minimize anxiety. *Int. J. clin. exp. Hypnosis*, 1962, **8**, 151–163.

Smith, G. M., Lawrence, D. E., Markowitz, R. A., Mosteller, F., and Beecher, H. K. An experimental pain method sensitive to morphine in man: The submaximum effort tourniquet technique. *J. Pharmacol. exp. Therapeutics*, 1966, **154**, 324–332.

Sternbach, R. A. *Pain: A psychophysiological analysis.* New York: Academic Press, 1968.

Stevens, S. S. Matching functions between loudness and ten other continua. *Perception and Psychophysics*, 1966, **1**, 5–8.

Sutcliffe, J. P. "Credulous" and "skeptical" views of hypnotic phenomena: Experiments on esthesia, hallucination, and delusion. *J. abnorm. soc. Psychol.*, 1961, **62**, 189–200.

Szasz, T. S. *Pain and pleasure.* New York: Basic Books, 1967.

Tétreault, L., Panisset, A., and Gouger, P. Etude des facteurs, emotion et douleur dans la reponse tensionnelle au "cold pressor test." *L'Union Medicale du Canada*, 1964, **93**, 177–180.

Voevodsky, J., Cooper, L. M., Morgan, A. H., and Hilgard, E. R. The measurement of suprathreshold pain. *Amer. J. Psychol.*, 1967, **80**, 124–128.

Weitzenhoffer, A. M., and Hilgard, E. R. *Stanford Hypnotic Susceptibility Scales, Forms A and B.* Palo Alto, Calif.: Consulting Psychologists Press, 1959.

Weitzenhoffer, A. M., and Hilgard, E. R. *Stanford Hypnotic Susceptibility Scales, Form C.* Palo Alto, Calif.: Consulting Psychologists Press, 1962.

Weitzenhoffer, A. M., and Hilgard, E. R. *Revised Stanford Profile Scales of Hypnotic Susceptibility, Forms I and II.* Palo Alto, Calif.: Consulting Psychologists Press, 1967.

West, L. J., Neill, K. C., and Hardy, J. D. Effects of hypnotic suggestions on pain perception and galvanic skin response. *Arch. Neurol. Psychiat.*, 1952, **68**, 549–560.

Wolf, S., and Hardy, J. D. Studies on pain: Observations on pain due to local cooling and on factors involved in the "cold pressor" effect. *J. clin. Investi.*, 1941, **20**, 521–533.

Wolff, H. G., and Goodell, H. The relation of attitude and suggestion to the perception of and reaction to pain. *Proc. Ass. Res. nerv. ment. Dis.*, 1943, **23**, 434–448.

Zimbardo, P. G. *Cognitive control of motivation.* Chicago: Scott, Foresman, 1969.

Zimbardo, P. G., Cohen, A. R., Weisenberg, M., Dworkin, L., and Firestone, I. Control of pain motivation by cognitive dissonance. *Science*, 1966, **151**, 217–219.

Fingertip sight: fact or fiction?
d. liddle

In November, 1962, reports first began to appear in British newspapers that Soviet scientists were investigating the case of a 22-year old Russian girl who appeared to be able to "see" with her fingers. The girl, Rosa Kuleshova, from the Urals town of Nizhni-Tagil, was apparently "discovered" by Dr. Isaac Goldberg, a medical psychologist at the Sverdlov Clinic for Nervous Disorders, where she was being successfully treated for epilepsy. A conference was called, in September 1962, of the Urals branch of the All Union Society of Psychologists and before this highly skeptical audience Rosa demonstrated her ability to distinguish colors by touch, to read print and perceive accurately the contents of a photograph or postcard or even the tiny picture of a postage stamp. In these experiments, Rosa, heavily blindfolded, ran the fingers of her right hand lightly over the object, reading or describing without hesitation or error. She claimed to have developed this astounding ability simply by practice, and felt sure that anyone else could follow suit.

The next steps were obvious enough. Rosa was taken to Moscow for more intensive investigation, while tests were begun in Nizhni-Tagil to see if others did indeed have this strange ability. About one in six of those tested was found to have some degree of color perception through the skin, some to an extent suggesting that with practice they could rival Rosa's achievements.

At first it seemed possible that Rosa was not in fact distinguishing colors by

reacting differentially to light of different wavelengths, but was detecting minute differences in surface texture; she herself referred to colors feeling smooth or rough. But in later tests she read printed material through a sheet of glass, and could perceive patterns of colored light beamed on to a perfectly smooth glass screen. Her success with such patterns of colored light, even when the infra-red, heat-carrying component was filtered out, similarly removed the possibility that her fingers were detecting minute differences in reflected heat between, say, the black print and the white paper. When patterns were made up using differences in temperature Rosa failed completely to decipher them even when the differences were many times greater than any which occur in real life. The investigators were forced to conclude that her skin was reacting to light, and that her ability showed several technical parallels to the phenomenon of sight.

At this stage, Dr. W. A. H. Rushton, F.R.S., of Cambridge, an authority on the mechanisms of vision, pointed out that if Rosa's ability was genuine, we would find mechanisms in the skin of a complexity approaching that of the eye. Neither Rosa's fingertips, nor those of anyone else, appear to contain any structures approaching this.

Another explanation had to be sought, such as telepathy or fraud—possibly fraud of which Rosa was not even aware. Then along with this statement of incredulity came the news that Rosa could also "see" with the tip of her tongue and with her toes, and many people suddenly found themselves uninterested in the phenomenon of fingertip sight.

By courtesy of *Science Journal* (incorporation *Discovery*), London. September 1964, 22–26.

Not that the idea of the skin being sensitive to light is new. The famous Moscow psychologist, Alexe Leontyev, had demonstrated the sensitivity of human skin to light some ten years previously, and he had also found that this increases with training. But, of course, it is a big stride from light sensitivity to sight.

STRUCTURES IN THE SKIN

The skin is built up of several layers of cells, in various stages of growth, with a complicated network of blood vessels, sweat ducts and nerve fibers. Many of these nerve fibers end simply, and are known as free nerve endings, while the rest end in some form of disc or knob. It had always been assumed that these nerve endings could take only a limited number of forms and that each was associated with a particular type of sensation. Thus, Ruffini Cylinders are warmth receptors, Merkel Discs touch receptors, and so on. Unfortunately this neat and tidy view does not fit a growing amount of recent evidence, and many now think that the nerve endings occur in random shapes, and that shape is no guide to function. If then we must remove the labels from these minute structures, it is surely not defensible to declare categorically that none of them could be sensitive to light. But Rushton's point still stands—there is nothing which resembles the retina of the eye, or which could serve as a lens.

HISTORY OF FINGERTIP VISION

Rosa Kuleshova's ability to "see" with her fingertips is by no means unique. As long ago as the 1820s, a doctor gave an account of a patient he treated for some form of severe mental disturbance who demonstrated that he could, through his hands, perceive and describe objects in a glass case, in a dark room. This case he compared with the "authenticated" case of a sailor who learned to read print with his fingers. Interestingly this sailor was subject to hysterical symptoms from time to time. Then again a Dr. Giuseppe Calligaris, at the University of Rome, examined a Yoga who could "see" things at a distance, again through the skin. There is also the case of a blind schoolboy in Scotland, reported by Dr. Karl Konig, who could "see" through the skin; a Canadian girl who can read print with her fingers; and a well-known medium (still living) who found that as a young man he could "see quite clearly through his elbow." In 1898 Dr. Khovrin, of the Neuropsychiatric Hospital of Tamboy, published his observations of a case very like Rosa Kuleshova, and a very thorough series of experiments was carried out in France by Dr. Jules Romains about the time of the First World War. Romains found that anyone at all could be brought into the laboratory, securely blindfolded and told to read with the hands the headlines of a newspaper, and this they would proceed to do after only moments of hesitation. Nor do the results stop here; it seems that any part of the body surface could be used, although some were more sensitive than others, and the object to be perceived did not need to be touched. Romains seems to have induced some kind of hypnotic state in his subjects, and readily acknowledged that this increased the speed with which they acquired these powers. He reported how, after 150 hours of exhausting concentration, he began to experience this sort of skin-vision himself. It is interesting that he found that blind people made more rapid progress than those with sight, although people blind from birth were not as successful as those with experience of sight. His dramatic investigation was, until recently, quite forgotten, and his plan for teaching the blind to use this new form of perception gained no support.

Soviet scientists have continued to discover more and more people with varying degrees of this ability to "see" with the skin; many of the more recent claims have been such that even sight in the skin would no longer suffice as an explanation. Meanwhile, a more humble claim was investigated in the United States a few months ago by Dr. R. P. Youtz of Barnard College, New York. A series of experiments convinced Youtz that a housewife, Mrs. Stanley, had some ability to detect color through her fingers, since she appeared to be able to select whatever color was suggested from a pile of different colored strips in a lightproof box. There was no possibility that she was using her normal vision. Naturally Youtz began to test his students with the same apparatus and found one in six of the 135 tested showed some perception of colors through the skin. In experiments at Brunel College, London, Dr. M. Jahoda has found that one in eleven of her subjects can detect colors, through glass, with an accuracy that could be expected only once in a thousand times by chance.

Recent reports have dismissed claims of seeing with the fingers simply because the subjects—at least in the Soviet experimenters—were prone to epilepsy. However, there seems to be no real justification for denying the results simply because of the mental state of the subject; after all, the subject, ill or otherwise, does not presumably record the results or design the experimental situation. However if there is a real relationship in the case of Rosa, for example, between epilepsy and "fingertip vision," then we have here a possible diagnostic tool for this illness—but that, of course, is another matter. I will return to this question later.

To date, there have been more than fifty recorded cases of people perceiving color through "touch." Unfortunately, almost without exception, these cases— scattered over 140 years and eight different countries—lack rigid scientific control. Nevertheless sufficient material is now available to warrant at least a preliminary stocktaking of the claims and their possible explanations.

EXPLAINING THE CLAIMS

The claims using the fingers to actually touch the objects vary from perceiving color to patterns and printed words, both in light and darkness. Others perceive objects or printed words apparently through the skin without touching them at all, and some of these acts of perception have been in total darkness. Naturally these claims have evoked a corresponding variety of explanations:

Tactile cues. The fingers are sensitive to minute differences in the texture of surfaces, and it has often been suggested that such differences might be sufficient to reveal the color of an object either directly, because one color feels smoother than another, or indirectly because one object, of known color, can be distinguished from others. This probably explains many of the supposed cases of "seeing" fingers but, of course, minute tactile differences cannot explain those instances such as the study of Romains and several of the Soviet experiments where the objects are not touched.

Temperature cues. I have found this explanation is most generally adopted by people who actually claim to be able to perceive objects through the skin. They say that certain colors feel warmer or cooler then others. This explanation was, however, ruled out by the Soviet experiments and seems unlikely to apply where objects are "seen" at a distance.

"Skin-vision." Incredible as this may seem from our knowledge of the skin and normal vision, this has been suggested as the only possible explanation, both of the Soviet and of the French results. Many of the other cases on record are equally difficult to explain in any other way. Yet this cannot account for performances carried out in darkness, as, for instance, in the current American investigation.

Telepathy. Many of the results on the perception of color by touch could be taken as evidence for telepathic communication between the subject and someone else in the room at the time. But telepathy cannot be invoked as an explanation when pieces of colored paper or cloth are concealed in a bag or box, from which light is completely excluded, and which no one in the room can see, as in Soviet and American experiments.

Supernatural powers. There is apparently no shortage of recorded cases of this sort of perception in the literature of psychical research. However "invoking the supernatural" is not likely to produce any reasonable explanation although such cases could still provide useful information if the situation has been sufficiently controlled for the results to be admitted as evidence.

Hoaxing. Inevitably, it has been suggested that people claiming some sort of vision through the skin are deceiving the onlookers, and perhaps themselves, by continuing to use more conventional modes of perception, by peering under the blindfold or some such trick. If tactile or temperature cues are not the basis of this perception, then telepathy, supernatural powers or "seeing skin" remain. No wonder the idea of a hoax springs to mind.

While the reports differ considerably, there seems to be general agreement that perception is adversely affected if the skin is too cold or too dry, or if one is distracted by light reaching the eyes, or by emotional disturbance. Presumably, variations in the extent of such perception can be attributed to the amount of practice. What is not clear is whether light or touching is necessary. Certainly in the American investigations light and touch were needed at first. Another feature common to many of the reports is an association with abnormal mental states in the subject. Mediumistic trances, hypnosis or a history of epilepsy seem to be linked with just about all the most remarkable performances on record. Could the abnormal mental states help in this kind of perception? Romains' finding that with hypnosis every person tested could perceive sufficiently well to read the headlines of a newspaper, through the skin almost immediately, provides some support for this. Both the Soviet and American investigations, without hypnosis, find only about one person in five or six capable of learning to distinguish colors.

CARDS, COLOR AND TOUCH

In a recent experiment I tried to eliminate any possibility of deception. I used cards, each covered with colored paper. This paper was fitted to the card very carefully to prevent tactile cues such as roughening or wrinkling. In the experiments, which I carried out at spare moments over a period of about two months, I simply shuffled the cards and then tried to decide the color of the top card, either by touching with my right hand or by moving my hand just above the card. After writing down my guess, I then added the correct color, which was given by a distinguishing mark in a corner of the card—kept well away from the area I touched. As a totally blind person, I could not "accidentally" see the colors, nor was anyone else present during the tests. In two series of trials, I touched the papers lightly. I used four colors, so that I could expect to get around 25 percent correct simply by chance. The actual percentage were 48 and 69. However, a comparison of these two series suggested that despite my precautions I was learning to distinguish the papers by small tactile differences. My ability to perceive each individual color was quite different in the two series, in which I used two different sets of cards. Also, in a third series, in which the hand did not touch the paper, the percentage correct dropped to 18, with yet another different order for the perception of colors. Subsequent series with only black and white cards (and therefore doubling the number which I could expect to get right by chance), always without touching, yielded 42, 56, 65, and 55 percent correct judgments.

Three points are perhaps worth noting from this very simple experiment. The importance of even the smallest tactile cues—at least in my own case—is firmly established. Surface differences are unwittingly used even when precautions are taken to avoid it. With touch disallowed, the percentages of correct judgments fall to less than half of the earlier totals, although the 65 percent result with the black and white cards is still statistically significant.

Secondly, the 56 and 65 percent results occurred in series during which the free hand, the left, was allowed to touch a white card. This comparison card was absent in the other series although only further research will confirm whether this increase is anything more than a coincidence.

Finally, if the series with the same experimental conditions are compared, in every case there is an increase in correct results from the first series to the second: 48–69, 42–55, 56–65 percent.

Normally, this would be explained in terms of learning or practice—but what is being learned here? After all the tactile cues could not be learned: the cards were changed between each test in the first series, and they were not even touched in the other two series.

THE FINAL WORD

Even from this brief outline, it is clear that the claims vary considerably and no single explanation covers them all. However, the problem is not to ask whether this is possible but to find out conclusively whether color perception through the skin does happen. Many people seem to have been convinced that they have powers of this sort, and have also convinced other people whose opinions are difficult to ignore. And yet, without more evidence, most people, scientists and laymen alike, remain unconvinced. After all, if you are securely blindfolded, how do you convince a skeptical audience that you can read with your fingers a printed book beneath a sheet of glass? But even if all these performances are found to be hoaxes, their explanation should make interesting reading.

Why
we
have
two ears
e. colin cherry

I want to call your attention to one re-markable fact about the body, a fact which is such common experience that we may rarely think about it—namely, that it has nearly axial symmetry. There may be several biological advantages in this symmetry, but I am concerned only in this symposium with hearing and with speech, and I would refer to one psycho-logical advantage. What can we do with two ears that we cannot do with one? Many people would say that directional hearing is the result, but I believe this to be a secondary factor, a consequence of something far more fundamental. This is that, with two ears, we are able better to separate the various sources of sound; we can attend more readily to one voice in a noisy crowd, we can distinguish traffic noises and footsteps, and other myriad of sounds which surround us. And this enhanced image separation gives us better adaptation to our world.

Anyone who has the misfortune to lose his hearing in one ear complains, not about his near loss of directional hearing, but he cannot listen so well to what you are saying whilst other people are talking. To my mind, separation of the various sound images comes first because, only if we can achieve this can we speak of "space" and "direction."

As we look around us we see a world composed of things—chairs, tables, faces; and we hear separate sounds— of voices, rain dripping, footsteps; *these concrete enduring entities are called gestalten.* The sense data which fall upon

From *Advancement of Science*, September 1962, 218–221. Reprinted by permission of British Association for the Advancement of Science, London.

our eyes and ears are, of course, a jumble, an inchoate mass, but the brain carries out upon it an analysis and the chaos congeals into concrete perceptual patterns.

FUSION AND SEPARATION OF SOUND PATTERNS

What is the nature of this analysis by which gestalten are formed? This I be-lieve to be a basic problem of percep-tion. Can we describe it mathematically, as a set of operations which might then augment the physiological evidence?

Through our two ears the brain is sup-plied with two samples of sound which are not quite the same. Thus sounds may reach one ear slightly before the other, or they may differ a little in intensity or in quality. The brain seizes upon these differences and forms one, fused, image which we hear. This "binaural fusion" can take place however only inasmuch as the sounds at each ear have something in common; if utterly different, fusion cannot occur.

I can describe one simple experiment which illustrates this. (1) If you wear a pair of headphones and arrange that the two separate earpieces are driven by two separate tape recorders (for example, two different readings from two books) you will find you can attend only to one at a time, but that this will automatically inhibit your response to the other. You can attend to your right ear message, or your left, but not to both at once.

Our two ears receive slightly different sounds because they are spaced apart by some 4 inches, whilst our heads also set up a sound shadow. This spacing pro-vides a small time difference for any sound source unless it is directly in front of us, or behind. However, if the source of sound has a high pitch (a frequency greater than about 1200–1500 c.p.s.) ambiguity in this timing would result, because the sound half-wavelength is then less than the 4 inches between the ears. The brain overcomes this difficulty by a very simple operation upon the sounds. (2) It seems that in each ear there is an averaging device, with a storage time of, very roughly, one millisecond; these devices provide "running averages" of the sounds and pass this smoothed data to central processes in the brain. Such averaging extracts the fluctuating envelopes of the sounds, and rejects the high-frequency steady tones. This operation may perhaps take place in the cochlea, thereby greatly extending the range of frequencies with which gestalten are built.

Suppose you wear the headphones again—we can illustrate this envelope fusion very simply. Into one earpiece we play a steady tone of 2000 c.p.s. and into the other a slightly different tone, say 2100 c.p.s. No fusion occurs; you hear two separate tones of different pitches, one on each side of the head. Now give them both a common envelope, say varying in amplitude at 200 c.p.s., and immediately they fuse together and you hear a hum of 200 cycles in the center of your head.

As we move and turn our heads about, the sounds reaching each ear vary in characteristic ways which we come to learn to associate with muscular movements. The world appears to stand still; the sense of hearing seems to be related to the sense of balance and posture. By turning our heads time-differences can be introduced between the sounds at our two ears, positive or negative depending upon the direction of rotation.

In this way we are better able to explore the world around us, by virtue of the fluctuating acoustic evidence reaching our two ears. In real life, voices and other sources of sound appear subjectively to lie outside our bodies, not inside our heads. "Over there," we say, or "in that direction." We can regard the brain as a superb mechanism for testing hypotheses, based upon sensory evidence received, and the directions from which sounds appear to come represent most likely hypotheses, as evidenced by the particular ways in which the stimuli at our two ears vary as we turn our heads.

When we are fitted with headphones, however, turning our heads avails us nothing. The consequence is that the brain seizes on the only tenable hypothesis—that the sound source lies in the middle of our heads. And that is, in fact, where we hear it.

Clearly, it is by turning the head from side to side that the most evidence is gathered concerning the direction of a sound, since our two ears are then given the greatest movement in relation to the source. Most sources of sound which are important to us lie on the surface of the earth and we have evolved so as to deal most readily with these; with our upright posture we can rotate our heads rapidly from side to side.

In this way ambiguities of direction are resolved and we are also better enabled to attend to one person in a chatty crowd. How do we turn, to listen to one person speaking in such noisy conditions? A simple experiment shows that we do not face him, but turn sideways, so as to maximize the time difference between our ears.

This turning of the head prepares the data reaching the two ears for the brain to get to work upon; it maximizes our chances of separating one voice from others, or from other sounds. But the separation of the conglomerated sounds into distinct voices is a feat of inductive inference, remarkable in its speed and accuracy. As with any inductive inference, success depends very much indeed upon "prior probabilities" which condition or bias the judgments made.

That is, past experience makes the guesses judicious guesses. And in the case of human voices, past experience we have in abundance, by the very fact that we speak ourselves. Our own speech habits represent a vast store of probabilities, which operate upon our perception of speech. In this sense, perception and production of speech form one closely integrated activity.

So readily are our speech habits called upon when we listen to speech that many people mutter when listening attentively. But, further than this, I will demonstrate how you can listen to and speak the same text concurrently. (1, 3) (A demonstration was given; a text was read to the lecturer who repeated what he heard almost concurrently without errors.)

So ready is this mimicry, that even stammerers can do it, without stammering. (4) This, combined with other evidence, suggests that stammering is primarily not a fault of speech but a fault of hearing—that, whatever the original cause, the sufferer has developed wrong habits of listening to and monitoring his own speech, and that error in the "feedback path," as we may regard such monitoring, has resulted in the characteristic faulty motor patterns of speech.

THE "COCKTAIL PARTY" PROBLEM

I should like for a moment to return to the experiment which I quoted at the beginning of this paper, in which a listener wears headphones which provide him with two totally different readings, from two different texts, one in his right ear and the other in his left ear. If this listener is asked to mimic one of these texts, speaking concurrently with it, in the way I have just demonstrated, he can do this without error; but, in so doing, he is rendered almost totally unaware of what is reaching his other ear. He is certainly aware of sound there, and whether it is human speech or not. But, for instance, he cannot say afterwards what was the language. (1) I believe Professor Oldfield has shown more

recently that he does make a significant response, however, if his own name be injected.

But in real life we cannot listen to voices in this simple way. When we are trying to attend to what one person is saying, whilst others are chatting nearby (as at a cocktail party), *both* our ears are assailed by all the voices, but the voices have different mutual time-relationships at the right and left ears. There are other small differences, too. It is possible to conceive a logical process by which the brain takes these two slightly different samples of sound, cross-compares them, and isolates one desired voice. This is a process of inductive inference; it, too, may be regarded as a process of testing hypotheses. It would require that the brain should introduce mutual time-delays between the two sound samples (assuming such time-delays can be effected by neural networks) and test these various delays as "hypotheses." The most likely hypothesis (giving a single isolated voice) being that when the combined, cross-compared, signals most closely conform to past experience of a single voice which, as I have stressed, we have in abundance from our speech habits.

We have wanted to study this "cocktail party" problem experimentally, especially to learn what specific physical aspects of voices are used in this inferential process. We cannot often have cocktail parties in our laboratory, so we set up very simplified situations for studying the problem, using at the most two voices. A listener wears headphones, and listens to a reading by speaker A, recorded on a special tape-recorder. This machine has two heads, the space between which can be varied accurately. In this way time-intervals can be introduced between the right and left headphones, which causes the fused sound image to move from side to side in the listener's head. Now a second voice, B, is introduced, reading another text, and similarly moved from side to side. In an experiment, voice A is set in a certain position in the listener's head whilst voice B is moved right or left of it by various amounts, at random—unknown to the listener. The listener is required to guess, at each setting, whether the moved voice B is right or left of the fixed voice A.

The statistics of his guesses show some measure of uncertainty, owing to the finite subjective "size" which each sound appears to have. Now suppose we use, not two voices, but two sounds of which the listener can have no prior knowledge whatever; such sounds are readily provided by "random noise generators" (such sources sound like a breeze rustling the leaves of a tree—sh). The uncertainty as to whether one lies right or left of the other is now exactly doubled, for there are no clues whatever to establish which is A and which is B. In fact the listener hears them as one mixed sound image. (5)

Now we can either start with two voices and systematically remove clues, or we can start with random noise sources and introduce clues. In each case, the measure of uncertainty indicates the extent to which the clues are used by the listener's brain. Thus we can use male and female, to give different average larynx pitches; or we can remove larnyx pitch altogether by using recordings of whispered speech. Alternatively, to the random generator we can introduce definite structure, as by a sharp resonance (like the resonances which exist in our mouths and throats whilst speaking). This research is still proceeding, and I shall not report results yet. But the technique seems quite powerful, to examine what there is about human voices which enable them to be separated so efficiently.

CONCLUSION

Human voices, and indeed all the sounds of the world about us, possess definite structures. They are not random, except in the one special case of a random generator such as we have in the laboratory. It is this structure which gives each source a definite cohesion, and no sound has a structure better known to any of us than our own speech; perhaps no other habits are more deeply engrained.

The brain's analysis and search for structure comes into play in several ways in aural perception. Thus in binaural fusion, similarity of structure of the sounds at each ear is examined. (6) Again, the breaking-up of the conglomerated sounds into separate voices, motor horns, footsteps, and a myriad other gestalten results from the individual sources each having coherent structures, but being statistically independent.

Such analysis is set out in the mathematics of statistical inference. The elements of structure, to which I have referred, are examined and exposed by operations termed "correlation analysis"—of which there are several kinds. The recognition of aural, visual and tactile patterns involves the brain in identifying the existence of certain invariant clues under an infinite variety of uncertain transformations. We recognize a voice, for example, against all kinds of noisy background, or a face in many positions and lights. These clues then may be regarded as statistical invariants and correlations, or hierarchies of correlations, may assess them.

In our own laboratory we have dealt with one type of correlation—the so-called first order, short-term, correlation function. (6) With this, the logic of certain perceptual functions may be described, but the test of such an approach must ultimately be physiological. It seems to me that such computations may well be "natural" to the nervous system, involving as they do operations of *short-term storage, coincidence detection, averaging* of neural data.

This is a loose suggestion, but I would ask physiologists whether, when considering the perceptual nervous system as a computer, it has been looked at from this point of view, as a computer of short-term correlation functions, and correlations of correlations, in a hierarchy. Whether, in fact, such functions may be regarded as the bricks with which the house of perception is built.

References

1. Cherry, E. C. Some experiments upon the recognition of speech, with one and with two ears. *J. accoust. Soc. Amer.*, 1953, **25**, 975.

2. Leaky, D. M., Sayers, B. McA., and Cherry, E. C. Binaural fusion of low- and high-frequency sounds. *J. acoust. Soc. Amer.*, 1958, **30**, 222.

3. Cherry, E. C. Some further experiments upon the recognition of speech with one and with two ears. *J. acoust. Soc. Amer.*, 1954, **26**, 554.

4. Cherry, E. C., Sayers, B. McA., and Marland, M. P. Experiments upon the total inhibition of stammering by external control, and some clinical results. *J. Psychosomatic Res.*, 1956, **1**, 233.

5. Cherry, E. C., and Bowles, J. A. Contribution to a study of the "Cocktail Party Problem." *J. acoust. Soc. Amer.*, 1960, **32**, 884.

6. Sayers, B. McA., and Cherry, E. C. Mechanism of binaural fusion in the hearing of speech. *J. acoust. Soc. Amer.*, 1957, **29**, 973.

Current status of theories of hearing

georg von békésy

By the middle of the nineteenth century a large number of theories of hearing had been proposed. At that time the main problem was to determine which part of the inner ear is set in vibration by sound waves. Since very little was known of the anatomy of the inner ear, the possibilities for theorizing were almost limitless, and the confusion became so great that, it is said, some lecturers in physiology simply did not treat the topic of hearing at all. After 1863, however, when Helmholtz proposed his resonance theory of hearing, the topic could no longer be ignored.

Helmholtz' theory was successful because it was based on anatomic and physical facts. When the cochlea was laid open in earlier times by cracking the temporal bone or chiseling away the bony wall, a half-dry gelatinous mass was found. It was not even clear whether the cochlea was filled with fluid or not. In my opinion, it was P. F. T. Meckel who performed the first basic experiment in the physiology of hearing when, in 1777, he opened the cochlea of a cat under water. He found no air bubbles coming out of the cochlea, thus proving that it is filled with fluid.

After histologists had found that a fixative acid would hold the gelatinous mass in its natural position, the anatomy of the inner ear could be worked out in detail by Corti, Hensen, and others. With this increased knowledge of the anatomy of the inner ear, Helmholtz and Hensen were able to conclude that the sensation of hearing is determined by the vibrations of the basilar membrane, a conclusion that is still generally accepted.

From *Science*, May 4, 1956, **123**, 779–783.

The next problem was: how does the basilar membrane vibrate? Helmholtz thought that the tension of the basilar membrane is greater transversely than longitudinally. Since it was known that the width of the membrane changes continuously from one end of the cochlea to the other, he concluded that it should behave like a set of resonators whose tuning changes continuously from one end to the other. The pitch discrimination of the ear could thus be accounted for since every frequency would bring a different resonator into vibration. Helmholtz' theory of pitch discrimination was not generally accepted, and the question of how the basilar membrane vibrates became and continues to be an issue. The various answers proposed have been presented as theories of hearing.

In my opinion, the words *theory of hearing* as commonly used are misleading. We know very little about the functioning of the auditory nerve and even less about the auditory cortex, and most of the theories of hearing do not make any statements about their functioning. Theories of hearing are usually concerned only with answering the question: how does the ear discriminate pitch? Since we must know how the vibrations produced by a sound are distributed along the length of the basilar membrane before we can understand how pitch is discriminated, theories of hearing are basically theories concerning the vibration pattern of the basilar membrane and the sensory organs attached to it.

The problem under discussion is a purely mechanical one, and it may well seem, at least to the layman, that it can easily be solved by looking at the vibration patterns in the cochlea. Unfortunately, this direct approach proves difficult for without stroboscopic illumination and other special devices, we can observe almost no vibration in the nearly transparent gelatinous mass in the cochlea of a living organism.

Furthermore, the maximal physiological vibration amplitudes of the basilar membrane can be seen and measured only when they are magnified between 100 and 300 times. Although observations have been made with this magnification (1), it is important to find other methods of observing the vibration pattern of the basilar membrane. Since hearing is the common concern of many disciplines—physics, engineering, physiology, psychology, zoology, and even mathematics—it is understandable that a great variety of solutions have been proposed. Naturally, each investigator has thought primarily in terms of his own field, and it was forgotten, for example, that vibration patterns are really a physical problem and not a musical one.

VARIOUS VIBRATION PATTERNS OF THE BASILAR MEMBRANE

Reports of the various vibration patterns of the basilar membrane that have been proposed thus far are to be found in textbooks on the psychology of hearing.(2) These reviews point up the differences between the various hypotheses, and some of them are very critical. Indeed, they are so critical that they give the impression that the psychology of hearing is nearing the end of its productive period and entering a phase of unconstructive criticism. I would like to show in this paper, therefore, how the various hearing theories are interrelated and how by manipulating two independent physical variables of the basilar membrane—absolute stiffness and coupling of adjacent parts—we can obtain a continuous series of vibration patterns, each group of which is in agreement with one of the four major theories of hearing. We may proceed continuously from curves predicted by the resonance theory to curves predicted by each of the other three theories in turn. It is thus shown that the various theories form one continuous series of vibration patterns.

A schematic cross-section of the ear is presented in Figure 1. Sound enters the external meatus and sets the tympanic membrane in motion, and the vibrations are conducted through the ossicles to the fluid in the cochlea. The basilar membrane, which acts as a parti-

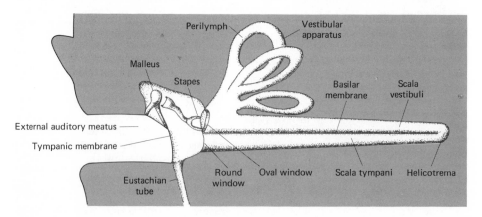

Figure 1. Schematic cross-section of the human ear.

tion between the two channels, is set in motion by any movement of the ossicles. Since the fluid is incompressible, the fluid displacement produced by the stapes is equal to the deformation of the round window. The question is, then: how is the basilar membrane displaced and how does it move during a sinusoidal vibration of the ossicles?

Although the movement of a membrane depends on other factors as well, we shall turn our attention first to the elastic properties of membranes. Three elastic properties of the membrane in a cochlear model can be varied: the absolute value of stiffness; the slope of stiffness along the length; and the coupling between adjacent parts.

1. The absolute value of the stiffness of the membrane can be changed. If the membrane is stiff, a pressure difference across the membrane causes only a small displacement or deformation.

2. The stiffness of the membrane can be constant, or it can vary along the whole length. The basilar membrane is stiffer near the stapes than it is near the helicotrema; for man and most other vertebrates, the stiffness near the stapes is about 100 times greater than it is at the other end.

3. The coupling between the adjacent parts of the membrane can be varied. In a membrane made of thin elastic fibers stretched across a frame, when there is no coupling between one strand and its adjacent strands, each strand can vibrate freely. The strands can be coupled by a thin sheet of rubber placed along the whole set. The coupling becomes larger as the thickness of the rubber sheet is increased. A membrane can also be made of a smooth sheet of rubber alone, without individual strands.

These three possibilities may be expressed mathematically by saying that we have three independent variables for the elasticity of the membrane.

There are two methods for investigating the effect of manipulating these variables on the vibration pattern of a membrane. First, we can calculate the vibrations. Unfortunately this is a time-consuming job. Or second, we can construct a model of the cochlear membrane and vary its elastic properties. I have made models the size of the human cochlea and models that were larger. The enlarged models were constructed in the same way that full-scale ships are constructed from small-scale models. As is well known, this kind of dimensional enlargement has proved quite successful.

Figures 2 and 3 show some of the effects that are obtained by varying the elastic properties of the membrane. Figure 2A shows a small section of the membrane model consisting of coupled strands acted on by a point force (needle tip). The absolute value of the elasticity of the different strands varies continuously from 100 to 1 from left to right along the membrane. Seen from the top, the deformation pattern is a group of elongated ellipses, the deformation spreading neither to the left nor to the right. The side view shows this limited lateral spread even better. This model simulates the system of almost freely vibrating elastic resonators that is postulated by the resonance theory of hearing. If we immerse this membrane in fluid, the vibra-

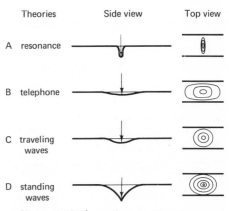

Figure 2. Deformation patterns in membranes acted upon by a point force.

Theories:

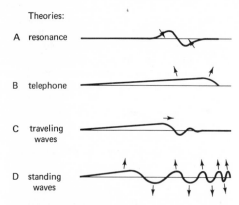

A resonance

B telephone

C traveling
    waves

D standing
    waves

Figure 3. Vibration patterns in membranes for a continuous tone (with normal damping). The arrows indicate the direction of movement at a given instant.

tion pattern seen in Figure 3A is obtained for a steady tone.

With the same slope of elasticity and the same driving frequency, but with an increase in the absolute value of the membrane stiffness, a steady tone causes the whole membrane to vibrate in phase (all parts of the membrane reaching their maximal elongation simultaneously), in the manner of a telephone diaphragm, as shown in Figure 3B. This is the pattern of vibration assumed by the telephone theory of hearing. The vibration pattern for the steady tone is independent of the coupling between adjacent parts of the membrane because the whole membrane vibrates in phase, with no force acting laterally. Because of the increase in stiffness, the same point force that was used before now produces a smaller deformation (Figure 2B); if the rubber strands are replaced by a flat plastic sheet that is stretched and clamped along the two long sides to the frame of the model, the point force produces the same lateral spread.

We obtain substantiation of two other types of hearing theories simply by decreasing the thickness of the plastic sheet. As the thickness decreases, the maximal amplitude of the displacement

becomes greater. When the thickness of the sheet is decreased slightly, the same steady tone produces a traveling wave moving away from the source (Figures 2C and 3C). When a thinner sheet is used, the same point force pushes the partition out still farther; and the same steady tone produces traveling waves that get shorter and travel farther until some are reflected from the end of the membrane and standing waves result (Figure 3D). The standing-wave theory was proposed by Ewald.

A change in the frequency of a steady tone moves the maximum of the vibrations along the basilar membrane, as the resonance theory assumes. An increase in the frequency moves the maximum of the vibrations toward the stapes. The resonance theory of hearing is a place theory in which pitch discrimination depends on locating the place along the membrane that is set in maximal vibration. According to the telephone theory, a change in frequency need not affect the displacement of the membrane, and pitch discrimination depends on some unknown function of the brain. The traveling-wave theory is also a place theory, since an increase in the frequency moves the maximum of the vibrations toward the stapes, and a decrease moves it toward the helicotrema. According to the standing-wave theory, an increase in frequency increases the number of nodes and decreases the distance between them. The brain uses this information to determine pitch.

As we can see from Figure 3, four basically different vibration patterns can be obtained for a steady sinusoidal tone simply by manipulating two variables, the absolute stiffness of the membrane and the coupling between its adjacent parts. Since it is possible to go continuously from one pattern to another, an infinite number of intermediate patterns can be obtained; but all these belong to a single family of curves. Additional vibration patterns have been proposed, some of which I have tried to verify on models, but I have come to the conclusion that they are only drawings and have no physical existence. I believe that Figure 3 shows all the principal patterns there are.

We have seen how, for a continuous tone, it is easy to substantiate each theory in turn simply by manipulating the elastic properties of the membrane. The differences among the theories depend wholly on the sizes of these variables. It is even more surprising, however, to find that for transients—for example, the onset of a steady tone—the differences between the resonance, traveling-wave, and standing-wave theories disappear completely, despite the emphasis that these differences have received. Traveling waves developed during the onset of vibrations in membranes whose vibration patterns are described by these three theories, as shown in Figure 4. (The driving frequency is the same as it is in Figure 3). Only the telephone theory assumes that all parts of the membrane vibrate in phase, in complete conformity with the movements of the driving stapes.

It is especially difficult to understand how in a system of free resonators the onset of a continuous tone produces traveling waves. A simple experiment

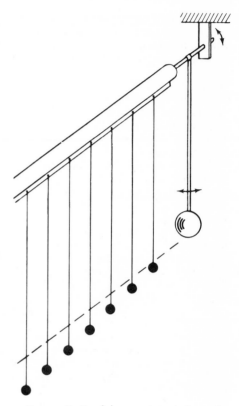

Figure 5. Pendulum system set up to demonstrate occurrence of traveling waves in a system of free resonators.

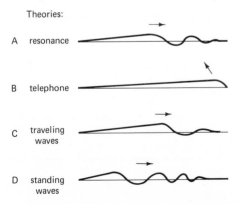

Theories:

A resonance

B telephone

C traveling waves

D standing waves

Figure 4. Vibration patterns in membranes for the transient state (with normal damping).

was set up to demonstrate the occurrence of traveling waves in a system of free resonators (Figure 5). A pendulum with a large mass was clamped to a long, horizontal driving rod from which a series of small pendulums was suspended. The lengths of the pendulums increased continuously from one end of the system to the other, from right to left in the figure. One pendulum in the middle of the series was of the same length as the heavy driving pendulum. During continuous oscillation of the driving pendulum, the resonant pendulum was set in motion by small movements that were transmitted through the oscillating supporting rod. A change in the period of the driving pendulum made a different pendulum resonate—that is, the whole series was a system of free resonators, each of which resonated at a different frequency. The onset of the oscillations of the driving pendulum set in motion a large section of the system, and a traveling wave was observed moving toward the longer pendulums.

To complete this survey of the various hearing theories, I should mention that at very low frequencies the movement of a vibrating system is independent of its mass; the displacement of the various parts of the membrane is determined solely by their elasticity. Since the slope of elasticity along the membrane is the same in all four models, the vibration patterns for low frequencies are similar, as shown schematically in Figure 6. The largest excursions appear in the standing-wave model, which has the most yielding membrane.

Another factor that affects the movement of the basilar membrane is the damping provided by the fluid in the cochlea. In our models, when the viscosity is high, the differences between the various theories tend to disappear. When the fluid friction is extremely high, the movements of the membrane are determined solely by the frictional forces in the fluid, independent of the elasticity values of the membrane. Here again the vibration patterns are identical for all the theories, and even the displacements are equal (Figure 7).

According to the foregoing discussion, the question of which hearing theory is valid reduces to the more easily answered question: what are the numerical values of the elasticity and coupling along the basilar membrane? In these experiments, when the tip of a needle was pressed perpendicularly on the surface of the basilar membrane of some lightly anesthetized vertebrates (guinea pig, mouse, cat, and pigeon), the resulting deformation was almost circular; both the top and side views

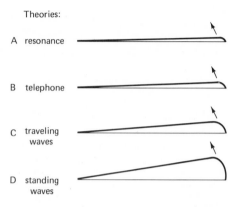

Figure 6. *Vibration patterns in membranes for continuous tones of very low frequency.*

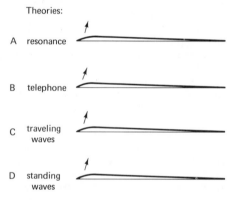

Figure 7. *Vibration patterns in membranes immersed in fluid with very high viscosity (for continuous tones).*

are identical to Figure 2C. The shape of the deformation remained the same for many hours after the death of the animal. In preparations of the human cochlea and the cochlea of very large animals such as cattle and elephants, the same circular deformation is found. The shape of the deformation proves that the coupling between the adjacent parts of the basilar membrane is so large that it invalidates the resonance theory of hearing.

The side view of the deformation makes it clear that the stiffness of the

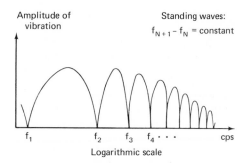

Figure 8. Hypothetical audiogram for standing-wave theory showing large fluctuations which would occur during a continuous change in frequency.

basilar membrane is too great for standing waves to occur. The formation of standing waves along the basilar membrane is improbable also because standing waves with large amplitudes occur only at certain frequencies; if standing waves were to occur, the sensitivity of the ear would undergo large fluctuations during a continuous change in frequency. Figure 8 shows the type of audiogram we would obtain under these conditions.

It is clear, therefore, that the vibration of the basilar membrane cannot be accounted for by either the resonance theory or the standing-wave theory.

Observation of the basilar membrane in mammals substantiates the traveling-wave theory. Under stroboscopic illumination, a steady tone of 1000 cycles per second produces traveling waves similar to those pictured in Figure 3. When the frequency is lowered, the maximal amplitude moves toward the helicotrema (toward the right side of Figure 3C), and the length of the membrane that is vibrating practically in phase is increased. The place of the maximum reaches that end of the membrane in the different animals at the following frequencies: mouse at 400 cycles per second, pigeon at 80, rat at 180, guinea pig at 200, man at 30, and elephant at 30. Below these frequencies

the basilar membrane vibrates in phase, as postulated by the telephone theory (Figure 3).

Below the critical frequency, pitch discrimination depends entirely on the temporal sequence of the stimulation of the nerves. Above the critical frequency, there is a second factor, the shifting of the place of maximal stimulation along the basilar membrane. We must now ask: is pitch discrimination improved by this shifting of the place of maximal stimulation as compared with the conditions under which it depends wholly on the temporal sequence of the vibrations? The problem is no longer mechanical, but one of how the nerves react to different vibration patterns on the basilar membrane.

MECHANICAL MODELS OF THE COCHLEA

In order to investigate this aspect of the problem, I built cochlear models in which the skin of the forearm was substituted for the nerve supply of the basilar membrane. Three mechanical models were made that stimulated the skin of the arm in accordance with the three vibration patterns in Figure 3A, B, and C. No model with standing waves was built because change in frequency would produce a large change in amplitude, and consequently it would be very difficult to distinguish amplitude changes from frequency changes (which is not the case in the ear).

The mechanical model for the resonance theory is shown in Figure 9, for the telephone theory in Figure 10.

The resonating model consisted of a series of tuned steel reeds attached to a metal support that oscillated slightly around its longitudinal axis. The length of the support was equal to the length of the forearm. Thirty-six reeds, tuned in equal intervals over a range of two octaves, were distributed along the whole length. A small pin on each reed, fastened close to the support, touched

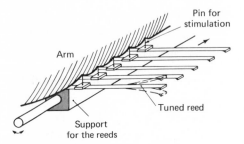

Figure 9. Mechanical model for the resonance theory, with the skin of the arm substituted for the nerve supply of the basilar membrane. The reed system transforms any change in frequency into an easily observable displacement of the stimulated area on the skin.

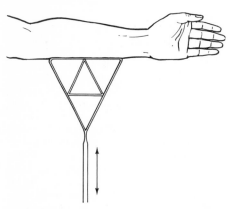

Figure 10. Mechanical model for the telephone theory, with the skin of the arm substituted for the nerve supply of the basilar membrane. All parts of the triangular frame in contact with the arm vibrate in phase.

placement of the stimulated area on the skin.

The model for the telephone theory is a triangular metal frame made of tubes (Figure 10). The frame vibrates perpendicularly to the axis of the edge in contact with the forearm. The rigidity of the frame insured that all the stimulating parts touching the skin would vibrate in phase. From time to time, phase constancy along the frame was verified by stroboscopic illumination.

The model for the traveling waves was a section of a model of the human cochlea, enlarged by dimensional analysis. The frequency range was two octaves. The model was a plastic tube case around a brass tube with a slit. The tube was filled with fluid. A vibrating piston set the fluid inside the tube in motion, and forces in the fluid produced waves that traveled from the hand to the elbow. The traveling waves thus produced were similar to those observed in preparations of human cochlea. The maximum amplitude of vibration was rather broad, and when it was observed under stroboscopic illumination, it moved along the membrane as the frequency changed. Although the maximum was quite flat as it moved along the arm, the sensation of vibration was concentrated on a relatively short length (about 2 to 4 centimeters); hence, any frequency change was easily recognized by a shift in the stimulated area. Seemingly the nerve network in the skin inhibits all the sensation to either side of the maximum of the vibration amplitude, thereby producing a sharpening of the stimulated area.

If we compare the three models, we find that the difference limen for "pitch" discrimination below 40 cycles per second is the same because the skin is able to discriminate the roughness of the vibrations as such. But for higher frequencies, displacements of the sensation along the arm, produced either by the resonating model or the traveling-wave model, permit much more accurate

the surface of the skin of the arm. The pins had rather small points, so that the skin would not pick up too much energy from the vibrating reeds; otherwise it would not have been possible to obtain a sharp resonance of the reeds. When the arm is placed carefully along the pins, so that the points just touch the skin, the reed system transforms any change in frequency into an easily observable dis-

frequency discrimination than the telephone theory model does.

The most surprising outcome of these experiments with models was that pitch discrimination did not deteriorate when the presentation time of the tone was very short. Even when the stimulus was only two cycles, the pitch discrimination for both the resonance model and the traveling-wave model was just as good as it was for a continuous tone of longer duration. Closer examination showed that in both models the place of maximal amplitude was determined during the first two cycles of the onset of a tone. Figure 4 shows that for transients there is very little difference between vibration patterns of the resonance and traveling-wave theories. In both, waves travel over quite a long section of the vibrating system. The surprising fact is the inhibitory action of the nerve supply, which suppresses all sensation except on a small spot near the maximal amplitude of vibration. In the ear the situation seems to be the same because, there too, two cycles of a tone are enough to enable us to discriminate the pitch of the tone.

SUMMARY

In summing up the current status of the hearing theories, it may be said that each of the vibration patterns of the basilar membrane postulated by the four major theories of hearing can be obtained by varying two elastic properties of the membrane—namely, the coupling between adjacent parts and the absolute value of the elasticity. If these two variables are adjusted to their numerical values in the cochlea of a living animal or a fresh preparation of the human ear, traveling waves are observed along the membrane. These traveling waves have a flat maximum that shifts its location along the membrane with a change of frequency—the place of the maximum determining the pitch. An enlarged dimensional model of the cochlea in which the nerve supply of the sensory organs on the basilar membrane was replaced by the skin of the arm indicates that the inhibitory action in the nervous system can produce quite sharp local sensations, which shift their place with changes in the frequency of the vibrations.

References and notes

1. Articles of mine that are concerned with measurement of the vibration pattern of the human cochlea have appeared in the main in *J. Acoust. Soc. Amer.* from 1947 to the present.

2. Stevens, S. S. and Davis, H. *Hearing: Its psychology and physiology.* New York: Wiley, 1938; Wever, E. G. *Theory of hearing* New York: Wiley, 1949; Ranke, O. F. *Physiologie des Gehörs* Berlin: (Springer, 1953); Wever, E. G. and Lawrence, M. *Physiological acoustics* Princeton, N.J.: Princeton Univ. Press, 1954; and Ruch T. C. Audition and the auditory pathways. In J. F. Fulton (Ed.), Howell's *Textbook of Physiology*, Philadelphia: Saunders, 17th ed. 1955. Pp. 399–423. For additional titles see Stevens, S. S. Loring, J. C. G. Cohen, D. *Biblography on hearing* Cambridge: Harvard Univ. Press, 1955.

The afferent code
for sensory quality
carl pfaffmann

One of the basic problems in the psychology and physiology of sensation is that of the mechanism by which different sensory qualities are perceived. The classical dictum on this problem was propounded by Johannes Mueller in his doctrine of the Specific Energies of Nerves. Actually Charles Bell had enunciated (Carmichael, 1926) the principle somewhat earlier, but Mueller's version is better known. This doctrine made clear that "We are aware of the state of our nerves, not of the external stimulus itself." The eye, however stimulated, gives rise to sensations of light; the ear, to sensations of sound; and the taste buds, to sensations of taste.

The further extension of the doctrine of Specific Nerve Energies to the different sensation qualities within a single modality was made by Helmholtz. According to his place theory of hearing, the perception of a particular pitch was attributed to the activity at a particular region of the basilar membrane of the inner ear, stimulation of the individual nerve fibers at these specific locations gave rise to unique tonal qualities of pitch. *Pitch* depended upon *which* nerve fiber was activated (Boring, 1950). In the less complex modalities, like the cutaneous or gustatory senses, von Frey and his school propounded the view of "modalities within modalities." The cutaneous sense was said to consist of separate modalities: touch, pressure, warm, cold, and pain, each with its specific receptors. The history of research on cutaneous sensitivity is, in large measure, a history

From *American Psychologist*, 1959, **14**, 226–232. Copyright 1959 by the American Psychological Association.

of the search for such receptors. In taste the "BIG FOUR" are familiar to all; the qualities, salty, sour, bitter, and sweet, were each mediated by a specific receptor type.

Implicit in these formulations is an isomorphism between receptor structure and phenomenology. Pure sensation as a basic psychological entity was to be reduced to a physiological entity. Psychology (at least a part thereof) was to be "explained" by the underlying physiology, hence, "Physiological Psychology." This formulation simple and direct, dominated the field of sensory psychology from the beginning with only an occasional and sporadic dissenting voice. The fact that the psychological entities were only postulated and the question of whether they were, in fact, valid were almost forgotten in the search for the "real thing."

Many of the more recent findings in sensory psychology and physiology derive from the application of electrophysiology to the study of sensory processes. The publication of E. D. Adrian's *The Basis of Sensation* in 1928 opened a new era. The invention of the electronic tube, appropriate amplifying circuits, and recording instruments made it possible to study directly the activity of the sense organs and their nerves. Since 1928, the advances in technique and instrumentation have been so dramatic that there is almost no part of the nervous system that cannot be probed by the inquisitive microelectrode. Psychologists have played a significant role in this development. One of their best known early discoveries was that of Wever and Bray (1930), on the cochlea and VIIIth nerve.

This paper will review some experiments with this procedure on another sense, that of taste, and will discuss their general implications for the theory of afferent coding. It should be emphasized that sensation itself is not being studied. Rather the investigator "taps in" on the "basis of sensation" by recording and amplifying the nerve impulse traffic in the sensory fibers "enroute" to the brain.

The sense of taste is particularly well suited to this problem because it consists of well defined differentiated structures, the taste buds, which are capable of mediating quite different sensory qualities, but the array of qualities and dimensions is not too complex for interpretation. The afferent message from receptor to brain can be studied directly in the afferent nerve fibers from the tongue, for the primary sensory nerve fibers from the receptive organs are relatively accessible with no synaptic complexities in the direct line from the receptors except for the junction between sense cell and sensory fiber.

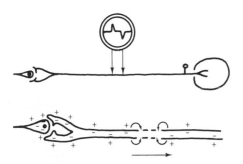

Figure 1. Diagram of electrophysiological recording from a single sensory nerve fiber. Upper diagram shows a single fiber in contact with a single sense cell to the left. A diphasic response on the cathode ray tube is shown as an impulse passes the recording electrodes en route to the central nervous system schematized to the right. The lower figure shows in more detail the positive and negative charges around the cell membranes associated with the passage of the nerve impulse.

The taste stimulus, like all stimuli, acts first upon a receptor cell. Changes in the receptor cell in turn activate or "trigger" impulses in the nerve fiber. Both the sense cell, as well as the nerve fiber, and in fact all living cells are like tiny batteries with a potential difference across the cell membrane. When stimulated, this membrane is depolarized, and it is this depolarization that can be recorded. Figure 1 schematizes such recording from a single sensory nerve fiber shown in contact with a receptor cell to the left of the figure and entering the central nervous system (CNS) to the right. The recording electrodes on the fiber connect with an appropriate recording device such as a cathode ray oscillograph shown schematically. As the impulse passes the first electrode, there is an upward deflection; as it passes the second electrode, there is a downward deflection. By an appropriate arrangement, a single or monophasic deflection only may be obtained so that at each passage of an impulse there will be a "spike" on the oscillograph tracing. The lower figure shows schematically the electrical activity associated with the passage of a nerve impulse. The message delivered along any single nerve fiber therefore consists of a train of impulses, changes in excitation of the receptor are signaled by changes in the frequency of this train. Thus, changes in strength of solution bathing the tongue change the frequency of impulse discharge per second. In any one fiber, the size of the impulse is nearly constant. The sensory nerve message, therefore, is a digital process.

Figure 2 shows a typical series of oscillograph tracings obtained from a single nerve fiber when different concentrations of sodium chloride are applied to the tongue of the rat. The "spikes" signal the passage of each impulse past the recording electrode. With stronger stimuli there is a higher frequency of discharge. Threshold for this fiber lies at approximately 0.003 M. Other fibers will show similar behavior, but

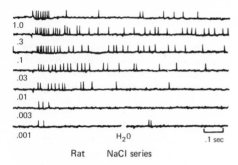

.001   H₂O
                                    .1 sec

Rat   NaCl series

Figure 2. A series of oscillograph tracings obtained from a single taste nerve fiber when different concentrations of salt solution are placed on the tongue. Note that water as well as .001 M NaCl will elicit two impulses. A concentration of .003 M NaCl will elicit three impulses and may be considered as threshold. (Reproduced from the Journal of Neurophysiology.)

may possess higher thresholds, for the tongue contains a population of taste receptors with thresholds of differing value.

This description applies to the impulse in the single sensory nerve fiber. Actually, the sensory nerve is a cable, made up of many different fibers each connected with one or more receptor cells. The single fiber recordings shown were obtained after the nerve cable had been dissected to a strand containing just one functional unit. Sometimes the same effect is achieved by using microelectrodes.

The nerve fibers subserving taste travel in three nerves from the mouth region: the lingual, glossopharyngeal, the vagus nerves which contain touch, temperature, pressure and pain fibers as well as those concerned with taste. The taste fibers from the anterior tongue branch off from the lingual nerve to form the chorda tympani nerve where it is possible to record almost exclusively from taste nerve fibers. This nerve can be exposed by appropriate surgery in the anesthetized animal and placed on the electrodes leading to the recording apparatus.

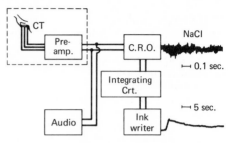

Figure 3. A block diagram of the recording apparatus showing two types of record. The upper trace shows a typical asynchronous, multifiber discharge from a large number of active fibers; the lower trace shows the integrated record of such activity. (Reproduced from the American Journal of Clinical Nutrition.)

A block diagram of the apparatus together with sample records is shown in Figure 3. The integrated record is readily adapted to quantitative treatment by measuring the magnitude of the deflection at each response and so provides a measure of the total activity of all the fibers in the nerve. An index of overall taste sensitivity can be obtained from such recordings. The curves in Figure 4 are such measures for the cat for quinine, hydrochloric acid, sodium chloride,

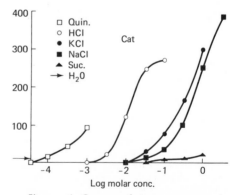

Figure 4. Curves of taste response in the cat to four different taste stimuli as indicated by the integrated response method. (Reproduced from the Journal of Neurophysiology.)

potassium chloride, and sucrose solutions (Pfaffmann, 1955).

The basic taste stimuli can be arranged in order of thresholds from low to high as follows: quinine, hydrochloric acid, sodium chloride, potassium chloride, and sucrose. In this animal, as in man, quinine is effective in relatively low concentrations. Sugar at the other end of the scale requires relatively high concentrations, and the electrolytes are intermediate. Sugar produces a nerve response of small magnitude compared with that to other stimuli. Differences in response magnitudes are found from one species to another. In the hamster or guinea pig, for example, sugar will elicit a strong discharge, and other species differences with quinine and the salts have been observed (Beidler, Fishman, and Hardiman, 1955; Pfaffmann, 1953). Recently, Carpenter (1956) has correlated certain of these species differences with behavioral data using the preference method.

The representation in Figure 4 does not show that the animal can distinguish one substance from another. Actually an animal like the rat will avoid quinine and acid, but will show a preference for NaCl and sucrose. To find how the animal can discriminate among different chemicals the single fiber analysis is required.

In the early study of the single gustatory fibers in the cat (Pfaffmann, 1941), three different kinds of fiber were found. One was responsive to sodium chloride and acid, another to quinine and acid, and a third to acid alone. Thus, acid stimulated all receptor-neural units found. This established not only that the gustatory endings were differentially sensitive to different chemicals but that the physiological receptor "types" *did not* correspond to the phenomenal categories as reported by man. In view of the more recently demonstrated species difference, this might not appear to be surprising. But, regardless of what the cat "tastes," these findings pointed to an important principle of sensory coding. This is that *the same afferent fiber may convey different information depending upon the amount of activity in another parallel fiber.* To illustrate, suppose A represents an acid-salt unit and C, an acid sensitive unit, then activity in A only would lead to salty; but activity in that same fiber A, plus discharge in C would lead to sourness. Recent studies emphasize still another important point, namely that some stimuli may decrease or inhibit the frequency of sensory discharge. Certain receptors, which can be stimulated by water (as well as other agents), may be inhibited by the application of dilute salt solutions (Liljestrand and Zotterman, 1954). Taste stimuli, therefore, may either increase or decrease, i.e., modulate, the amount of afferent nerve traffic. A diminution in activity may signal, not merely the withdrawal of a particular stimulus, but the application of a different one.

Table 1 taken from a recent paper from Zotterman's laboratory (Cohen, Hagiwara, and Zotterman, 1955) illustrates the afferent code or pattern which may be

TABLE 1. FIBER TYPE RESPONSE IN THE CAT*

Stimulus	"Water" Fiber	"Salt" Fiber	"Acid" Fiber	"Quinine" Fiber	Sensation Evoked
H₂O (0.03M Salt)	+	0	0	0	→ water
NaCl (0.05 M)	0	+	0	0	→ salt
HCL (ph 2.5)	+	+	+	0	→ sour
Quinine	+	0	0	+	→ bitter

*Cf., Cohen, Hagiwara, and Zotterman, 1955.

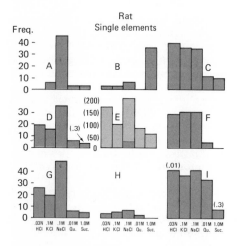

Figure 5. *The pattern of taste responses in nine different single sensory nerve fibers of the rat. The dark bar graphs give the frequency of response in impulses per second for different taste stimuli (indicated along abscissa). The light bar graph shows the relative response of the total nerve (integrated response to these same solutions). (Reproduced from the* Journal of Neurophysiology.*)*

described for the cat based on a compilation of the "types" so far discovered for that species.

But the use of the term "fiber type" harks back to some of the errors of classical thinking. Types are defined only by the range of stimuli sampled, the wider the range, the more difficult will it be to define pure "types." "Taste types" may turn out to be as varied and individual as "personality types." Figure 5 shows the variety of response patterns of nine single fiber preparations to the following standard test solutions: .03 N HCL, .1 M KCL, .1 M NaCl, .01 M quinine hydrochloride, and 1.0 M sucrose (Pfaffmann, 1955).

The bar graph shows the magnitude of response in each of the single fiber preparations in impulses per second of discharge. The central crosshatched bar graph shows the relative magnitude of response to these same solutions in the

integrated response of the whole nerve. It is apparent that the individual fibers do not all have the same pattern. The sum of the activity of all fibers is shown by the crosshatched diagram. Furthermore, fiber types are not immediately apparent in this array.

The fact that the individual receptor cells possess combined sensitivity as salt plus acid, or salt plus sugar, cannot be dismissed as the result of multiple innervation of more than one receptor cell by a single fiber. Kimura (Beidler, 1957; Kimura and Beidler, 1956) has studied the sensitivity patterns of the individual taste cells by inserting micropipette electrodes directly into the sense cells themselves. The pattern of sensitivity found in the individual sensory cells is like that already described for the single afferent fiber. Thus, within the individual sense cell there must be different sites which are selectively sensitive to different taste stimuli. These sites on the membrane may be determined by molecular configuration, the shape and size of pores in the membrane, or some such microcellular feature.

One additional principle must be introduced. This is that the relative rather than the absolute amount of activity in any one set of afferent fibers may determine the quality of sensation. Figure 6 shows frequency of discharge as a function of stimulus intensity for two units labelled A and B. Both are stimulated by both stimuli sugar and salt, but it is apparent that A is more sensitive to salt and B to sugar (Pfaffmann, 1955). Once each stimulus intensity exceeds the threshold for a particular receptor unit, the frequency of discharge increases with concentration. Thus the afferent pattern as the code for sensory quality must take account of the changing frequency of discharge with stimulus intensity. The pattern concept may be retained by recognizing that "pattern" is still apparent in the relative amount of activity of different fibers. In the two-fiber example shown in Figure 6, low

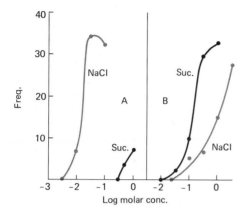

Figure 6. The relation between frequency of discharge and concentration in two fibers both of which are sensitive to sugar and salt. (Reproduced from the Journal of Neurophysiology.*)*

concentrations of salt will discharge only A, higher concentrations will discharge both A and B, but activity in A will be greater than that in B. Low concentrations of sugar will activate only B, higher concentrations will activate both B and A, but B will be greater than A. Thus the sensory code might read:

Frequency	Code
A > B	= salty
B > A	= sweet

where A or B may go to zero. It is not only the activity in parallel fibers that is important, it is the *relative amount* of such parallel activity.

Studies of the other senses indicate that these principles are not unique to taste. In the cutaneous senses there is a variety of different ending which overlap two or more of the classical skin modalities (Maruhashi, Mizuguchi, and Tasaki, 1952). For example, some pressure receptors in the cat's tongue are activated by cold (Hensel and Zotterman, 1951), and there are several different pressure, temperature, and nociceptor endings, some serving large or small areas, some adapting slowly, others

rapidly to give a variety of temporal as well as spatial "discriminanda." These findings are reminiscent of Nafe's (1934) quantitative theory of feeling, and the recent anatomical studies of Weddell (1955) and his group are of similar import.

In audition, selective sensitivity among the individual primary afferent fibers is very broad. Those fibers arising from the basal turn of the cochlea respond to tones of any audible frequency; those arising in the upper part respond only to a band of low frequency tones (Tasaki, 1954). Further, it has been suggested (Wever, 1949) that the temporal patterning of the discharge, especially in the low frequencies, provides a basis for pitch discrimination. In vision, Granit (1955) has suggested that different impulse frequencies in the *same* third order neuron from the retina may signal different spectral events at the periphery.

These electrophysiological results should not have been surprising to us. That a particular sensory dimension is not isomorphic with a particular physical dimension is well known. Auditory loudness, functionally dependent upon sound pressure level, is not synonymous with physical intensity. Pitch is not the same as frequency, although the latter is this major determinant (Stevens and Davis, 1938). Visual brightness is not the same as physical luminance. It would, indeed, have been surprising if similar nonidentities had not been found at the physiological level.

And so in attacking Mueller's classic problem with modern techniques, we have found, at least, within the modalities, a solution different from that which was first anticipated. Differential sensitivity rather than specificity, patterned discharges rather than a mosaic of sensitivities is the form of our modern view. Mueller's principle did not answer a problem so much as it posed one. In the answers that I have attempted to suggest, we see, not only the details of the mechanism for which we have searched, but we can discern broader implications for the principles governing the relation between psychology and physiology. Psychology cannot rest content with a pseudo-physiology based solely upon the phenomenology. So long as the receptor surface was conceived to be a static mosaic where phenomenal qualities were reified (in sime instances in the form of specific anatomical structures), sensory psychology and physiology were reduced to the study of how the "little pictures" were transmitted via the sensory nerves to the "sensorium" located presumably somewhere "inside the head." Such a view is not only out of date, but it diverts our attention from the proper study of the afferent influx, its dynamic properties and interactions and its relevance for all levels of neural integration and behavioral organization.

References

Adrian, E. D. *The basis of sensation.* New York: Norton, 1928.

Beidler, L. M. Facts and theory on the mechanism of taste and odor perception. In *Chemistry of natural food flavors.* Quartermaster Research and Engineering Center, 1957. Pp. 7–47.

Beidler, L. M., Fishman, I. Y., and Hardiman, C. W. Species differences in taste responses. *Amer. J. Physiol.,* 1955, **181,** 235–239.

Boring, E. G. *A history of experimental psychology.* New York: Appleton-Century-Crofts, 1950.

Carmichael, L. Sir Charles Bell: A contribution to the history of physiological psychology. *Psychol. Rev.,* 1926, **33,** 188–217.

Carpenter, J. A. Species differences in taste preferences. *J. comp. physiol. Psychol.,* 1956, **49,** 139–144.

Cohen, M. J. Hagiwara, S., and Zotterman, Y. The response spectrum of taste fibers in the cat: A single fiber analysis. *Acta. physiol., Scand.,* 1955, **33,** 316–332.

Granit, R. *Receptors and sensory perception.* New Haven: Yale Univ. Press, 1955.

Hensel, H., and Zotterman, Y. The response of mechanoreceptors to thermal stimulation. *J. Physiol.,* 1951, **115,** 16–24.

Kimura, K., and Beidler, L. M. Microelectrode study of taste bud of the rat. *Amer. J. Physiol.,* 1956, **187,** 610.

Liljestrand, G., and Zotterman, Y. The water taste in mammals. *Acta. Physiol., Scand..* 1954, **32,** 291–303.

Maruhashi, J., Mizuguchi, K., and Tasaki, I. Action currents in single afferent nerve fibers elicited by stimulation of the skin of the toad and the cat. *J. Physiol.,* 1952, **117,** 129–151.

Nafe, J. P. The pressure, pain and temperature senses. In C. Murchison (Ed.), *Handbook of general experimental psychology.* Worcester: Clark Univ. Press, 1934. Chap. 20.

Pfaffmann, C. Gustatory afferent impulses. *J. cell. comp. Physiol.,* 1941, **17,** 243–258.

Pfaffmann, C. Species differences in taste sensitivity. *Science,* 1953, **117,** 470.

Pfaffmann, C. Gustatory nerve impulses in rat, cat, and rabbit. *J. Neurophysiol.,* 1955, **18,** 429–440.

Stevens, S. S., and Davis, H. *Hearing.* New York: Wiley, 1938.

Tasaki, I. Nerve impulses in individual auditory nerve fibers of guinea pigs. *J. Neurophysiol.,* 1954, **17,** 97–122.

Weddell, G. Somesthesis and the chemical senses. *Ann. Rev. Psychol.,* 1955, **6,** 119–136.

Wever, E. G. *Theory of hearing.* New York: Wiley, 1949.

Wever, E. G., and Bray, C. W. Action currents in the auditory nerve in response to acoustical stimulation. *Proc. Nat. Acad. Sci.,* 1930, **16,** 344–350.

Number coding in association cortex of the cat

richard f. thompson
kathleen s. mayers
richard t. robertson
and
charlotte j. patterson

Bertrand Russell, in his classic analysis of the concept of number, defined number as "anything which is the number of some class; the number of a class is the class of all those classes that are similar to it" (1). Number is a property of stimuli that is independent of all the particular properties of the stimuli and is determined solely by relational class. Results of number perception and memory studies in man suggest that number of objects can be estimated and recalled relatively accurately up to about seven "plus or minus two" (2). Animal studies of counting behavior indicate that primates can learn to respond to number of objects in simultaneous presentations (3) and that cats can learn to "count" successive stimuli (4).

Higher mammals thus appear able to abstract the number of stimuli, independent of the specific aspects of the stimuli; consequently, the brain must in some manner code the number of stimuli. To demonstrate that a neural response is, in fact, coding number, it is necessary to show that the response is at least to some degree independent of particular stimulus characteristics such as quality, intensity, and frequency of presentation. A logical possibility for the locus of this coding process would be higher regions of the brain, where responses to stimuli tend to be somewhat independent of specific stimulus parameters, an example being the polysensory association-response areas of the cerebral cortex (5). Several lines of evidence have implicated these regions

in "attentive" aspects of behavior, where response is a function of the more abstract aspects of stimuli such as complexity, recency, and "significance" (6). Lindsley recently proposed that these areas may subserve the more complex aspects of behavioral alerting and attention (7). Counting number of stimuli would seem a relevant aspect of such behavior. In work on properties of polysensory cells in these regions of the cortex in the cat, we have encountered cells that do in fact appear to code number; they behave as though they are counters.

Animals were anesthetized with chloralose (70 mg/kg, intraperitoneally), and isolated single cell activity was recorded by standard techniques with glass-coated tungsten microelectrodes. Stimuli were free field click, binocular light flash, and single shock pulses (0.25 msec duration) to ipsilateral forepaw. The existence of counting cells is revealed when a sequence of stimuli is presented after a period of no stimulation. The cell typically responds to a particular stimulus in the sequence. Such cells also respond occasionally to other stimuli in the sequence, though with a much lower probability, and sometimes to more than one stimulus in the sequence. If the stimulus sequence is continued without interruption, counting cells tend to respond successively at each appropriate stimulus in the sequence, but the pattern is somewhat less clear.

An example of a "number 7" cell (a cell "coding" the concept of number 7) in the association cortex of the cat is shown in Figure 1A, both in terms of probability of first discharge in the sequence and in terms of total proportion of discharges to each stimulus in the

From *Science*, **168**, 271–273, 10 April 1970. Copyright 1970 by the American Association for the Advancement of Science.

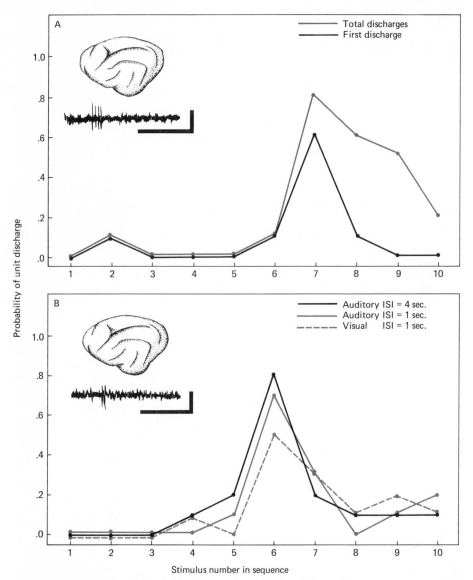

Figure 1. Counting cells obtained in the association cortex of adult cats. Inserts show the area of cortex on a standard brain drawing where the unit was found and the characteristic unit discharge. *(A) A "number 7" cell.* The probability of total discharges and of first discharge is shown as a function of stimulus number in a series of ten stimuli (here, a simultaneous click, light flash, and footshock). Time mark, 50 msec; amplitude mark, 100 μv. (B) Probability of discharge of another neuron (a "number 6" cell) in the association cortex of the cat as a function of stimulus number in a sequence for visual stimuli and for auditory stimuli at interstimulus intervals of 4 seconds and 1 second. ISI, interstimulus interval; time mark, 50 msec; amplitude mark, 50 μv.

sequence. This discharge pattern differs significantly from a random distribution ($N = 23$, $D = 0.513$, $P < .01$; Kolmogorov-Smirnov one-sample test). Ten separate sequences of ten stimuli (here a trimodal, simultaneous click, flash, and shock) were given with a 2-second interstimulus interval and a 2-minute intersequence interval. The distribution of responses shown in Figure 1A, particularly the proportion of total responses around the modal seventh stimulus, is strikingly similar to the distribution of behavioral responses in cats trained to respond to a particular stimulus (for example, sixth) in a sequence (4).

Responses of counting cells appear to be independent of stimulus modality. An example of a "number 6" cell in the association cortex of the cat is shown in Figure 1B. In ten sequences of ten stimuli at an interstimulus interval of 1 second, the cell exhibits a clear modal response to the sixth stimulus for both auditory ($N = 14$, $D = 0.429$, $P < .01$) and visual ($N = 13$, $D = 0.423$, $P < .05$) stimulation. Effect of varying the interstimulus interval is also illustrated for this cell in Figure 1B. The modal value remains the same for an interstimulus interval of 4 seconds and 1 second ($N = 16$, $D = 0.338$, $P < .05$) with an auditory stimulus. Responses of counting cells also appear to be independent of stimulus intensity, at least within certain limits. Although higher stimulus intensities occasionally result in increased overall discharge levels, the modal stimulus number does not shift.

To date we have observed five counting cells in the adult cat, which code the numbers 2, 5, 6 (two cells), and 7. With such a small sample, it is not possible to make a precise estimate of the proportion of cells in nonspecific association response areas of the cortex that "count." However, crude guesses based on the proportion of such cells that we have observed suggest that in the cat about 1 percent of the cells in association areas that respond to stimuli are counting cells (that is, five in a sample of about 500).

The data given above indicate that counting cells respond as a function of number of stimuli, independent of stimulus modality, intensity, and rate of presentation, at least over certain ranges. The independence of modality and intensity are not unexpected on the basis of previously known characteristics of cells in these association regions of the cortex (8). The independence of interstimulus interval is unexpected from past work but is, of course, crucial to the demonstration that the cells are behaving as counters. Temporal factors such as regular fluctuations in excitability are thus ruled out.

After Adrian's original definition of receptive field (9), studies have shown that the level of complexity of particular stimulus properties coded by single neurons is probably very great, particularly in sensory areas of the thalamus and cortex of higher mammals. Thus response to such relatively abstract aspects of visual stimuli as "angularity" has been found for cells in the visual cortex (10). However, as Konorski (11) notes, even this level of coding falls short of the apparent complexity of "perception," perhaps because these studies were concerned with coding that is essentially stimulus bound—that is, the cells respond only while the stimulus is being presented. Hebb observed that the coding of more abstract events may require "some sort of process that is not fully controlled by environmental stimulation yet co-operates closely with that stimulation" (12), and he proposed that complex stimulus attributes may be represented by complex phase sequences of interacting "cell assemblies." Konorski has recently developed an alternative view that the more abstract aspects of perception may be represented by single neurons, which he terms "gnostic" cells (11). We submit that the "counting" cells described here behave as though they code the abstract property of number

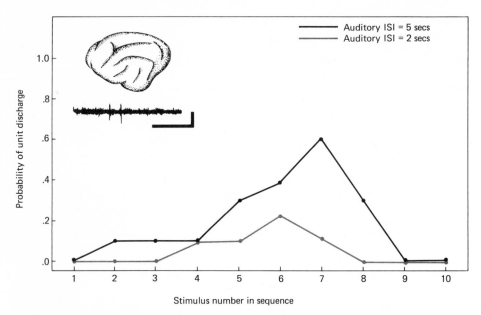

Figure 2. Probability of discharge as a function of stimulus number in a series of stimuli for a neuron ("number 6 or 7" cell) from the association cortex of an 8-day-old kitten. Auditory stimuli at interstimulus intervals of 5 and 2 seconds were used. ISI, interstimulus interval; time mark, 200 msec; amplitude mark, 40 μv.

and are by definition gnostic cells; however, it is entirely possible that the behavior of "counting" cells is the result of complex prior stimulus processing, perhaps by networks analogous to Hebb's cell assemblies.

The extent to which neural coding of stimuli develops as a result of experience is a fundamental problem, particularly for cells that code complex aspects of stimuli. Hebb (12) and Konorski (11) agree that complex coding, whether by cell assemblies or gnostic cells, is learned. At the other extreme, it has been suggested that even very complex attributes of stimuli may be coded by single neurons as a result of predetermined structural organization (13), as evidenced by Hubel and Wiesel's demonstration that complex coding of visual stimuli by cortical neurons is present in the very young kitten (14). Insofar as number coding is concerned,

Miller, Galanter, and Pribram suggested that an innate stimulus-characteristic/brainmodel comparison mechanism may form the basis of the abstract property of number (15). The data shown in Figure 2 would seem to favor this general view. The cell, a "number 6 or 7" counter, was obtained in the association cortex of an 8-day-old kitten. The counting effect is perhaps less striking here than in the cells obtained in adult animals and does not reach statistical significance ($N = 24, D = 0.233, P < .2$). Although the modal value does not appear to be completely independent of interstimulus interval, the tendency is still clear.

Studies of concept learning in humans suggest that color, shape, and number may form an ordered series of increasingly complex concepts (16). It is perhaps relevant that differential neural coding of color appears to occur at or below the level of the visual thalamus (17), that neurons coding shape are found by the level of the visual cortex (10), and that number may be coded in association areas of the cortex. However, it must be emphasized that the data presented here merely show that, under the conditions of our experiments, certain cells in the association cortex fulfill the operational requirements necessary to code the concept of number. It remains to be demonstrated that these "counting" cells function to code number of stimulus events in the organism under conditions of normal behavior.

References and notes

1. Russell, B. *Introduction to mathematical philosophy*. London: Allen and Unwin, 1919.

2. Hunter, W. S., and Sigler, M. *J. Exp. Psychol.*, 1940, **26**, 160; Miller, G. A. *Psychol. Rev.*, 1956, **63**, 81.

3. Hicks, L. H. *J. comp. physiol. Psychol.*, 1956, **49**, 212.

4. Masserman, J. H., and Rubinfine, D. L. *J. Gen. Psychol.*, 1944, **30**, 87; Wagman, A. M. *J. comp. physiol. Psychol.*, 1968, **66**, 69.

5. Albe-Fessard, D., and Rougeul, A. *Electroencephalogr. clin. Neurophysiol*, 1958, **10**, 131; Buser, P., and Borenstein, P. *Electroencephalogr. Clin. Neurophysiol.*, 1959, **11**, 285; Thompson, R. F., Johnson, R. H., and Hoopes, J. J. *J. Neurophysiol.*, 1963, **26**, 343.

6. Bettinger, L. A., Davis, J. L., Meikle, M. B., Birch, H., Kopp, R., Smith, H. C., Thompson, R. F. *Psychonom. Sci.*, 1967, **9**, 421; Thompson, R. F., and Shaw, J. A. *J. Comp. physiol. Psychol.*, 1965; **60**, 329; Thompson, R. F., Bettinger, L. A., Birch, H., Groves, P. M., and Mayers, K. S. *Neuropsychologia*, 1969, **7**, 217.

7. Lindsley, D. B., address presented before the Western Psychological Association, Vancouver, B. C., Canada (June 1969).

8. Bental, E., and Bihari, B. *J. Neurophysiol.*, 1963, **26**, 207; Shimazono, Y., Torii, H., Endo, M., Ihara, S., Narukawa, H., Matsuda, M. *Folia Psychiat. neur. jap.*, 1963, **17**, 144; Bettinger, L. A., Davis, J. L., Meikle, M. B., Birch, H., Kopp, R., Smith, H. C., Thompson, R. F. *Psychonom. Sci.*, 1967, **9**, 421.

9. Adrian, E. D. *The beasts of sensation, the action of sense organs*. London: Christophers, 1928.

10. Hubel, D. H., and Wiesel, T. N. *J. Neurophysiol.*, 1965, **28**, 229.

11. Konorski, J. *Integrative activity of the brain: An interdisciplinary approach*. Chicago: Univ. of Chicago Press, 1967.

12. Hebb, D. O. *The organization of behavior*. New York: Wiley, 1949.

13. Thompson, R. F. In J. F. Voss (ed.), *Approaches to thought*. Columbus, O.: Merrill, 1969.

14. Hubel, D. H., and Wiesel, T. N. *J. Neurophysiol.*, 1963, **26**, 994.

15. Miller, G. A., Galanter, E., and Pribram, K. H. *Plans and the structure of behavior*. New York: Holt, Rinehart & Winston, 1960.

16. Grant, D. A., Jones, O. R., Tallantis, B. *J. Exp. Psychol.*, 1949, **39**, 552; Heidbreder, E. *J. Psychol.*, 1948, **26**, 193.

17. DeValois, R. L. *J. gen. Physiol.*, 1960, **43**, 115; Svaetichin, G., Laufer, M., Mitarai, G., Fatehchand, R., Vallecalle, E., Villegas, J. In R. Jung and H. Kornhuber (Eds.), *The visual system: Neurophysiology and psychophysics*. Berlin: Springer, 1961.

motor
systems
chapter 5

Motor functions are of great importance to psychologists because behavior is measured through responses. At the present time we are not able to understand directly what is going on in the nervous system in terms of its behavioral significance although this is one of the goals of physiological psychology. We have to make inferences between observed responses and events occurring within the brain or peripheral nerves.

The motor system of higher animals is extremely complex; it involves not only direct motor pathways, which move powerful muscles, as supplied by the pyramidal tracts, but numerous feedback circuits, which control and modulate movements and make it possible for us to perform complex manipulations (playing a musical instrument or typing). This is handled by the mutual interaction of the pyramidal and extrapyramidal motor systems.

In this section we deal with the structure and function of the basic motor systems and look at the possibility of control of activity in the individual motor nerve cells by means of conscious effort.

Organization of somatic sensory and motor areas of the cerebral cortex
clinton n. woolsey

The purpose of this paper is to discuss the present status of the problem of localization in somatic sensory and motor centers of the cerebral cortex. This is relevant to the subject of this symposium because in any behavioral study involving the method of ablation it is essential that the lesions be placed according to anatomical or functional definitions of regions to be removed and spared.

We are all aware of the lack of general agreement on anatomical criteria for parcellation of cortical cytoarchitectural fields (9, 11, 13, 16, 18, 23, 24, 36) and the difficulties of determining with certainty the precise limits of homologous areas of cortex in different species. However, the electrophysiological technique for defining the afferent projection areas has provided a new method for study of localization of function in the cortex and, because it yields a very detailed story of the relations of specific parts of peripheral sensory mechanisms to specific parts of the central receiving areas, it provides not only the means of determining the extent of cortex concerned with a given sensory mechanism but, from the detailed pattern of organization of the system, it permits clear identifications of homologous parts in different species. This enables one to sidestep the immediate necessity of establishing homologies by anatomical criteria. The method provides, in fact, a new base of departure for comparative cytoarchitectural studies and for

From *Biological and Biochemical Bases of Behavior*, H. F. Harlow and C. N. Woolsey, Eds. Madison: The University of Wisconsin Press; © 1958 by the Regents of The University of Wisconsin.

more precise studies of thalamo-cortical relations, through placement of lesions in physiologically identified portions of cortical fields in various species of mammals. The opportunities for interdisciplinary research between the fields of physiology and anatomy are, in consequence, great. The method is also of value in determining the boundaries of cortical fields in behavioral studies involving local cortical destruction. Thus, by defining with the evoked potential technique the various cortical receiving areas and by the method of electrical stimulation the motor projection areas, one can determine the maximal extent of tissue potentially remaining in the category of "associational" cortex. As a matter of fact, the method has already greatly restricted the amount of cortex which can be appropriately classed as associational, because it has revealed within the classical association areas the existence of additional well-organized receiving areas with independent afferent projection pathways. These are the "second" somatic, visual and auditory receiving areas (2, 3, 44, 65).

The wealth of detail in the organization of the cortical afferent areas revealed by the evoked potential method has led to a reexamination of cortical motor systems by the electrical stimulation technique (63). By examining the "motor areas" in the detailed manner found productive in the afferent studies, new relationships have been established in the motor systems, the precentral and supplementary motor areas have been differentiated and the sensory and motor studies together have given rise to clearer conceptions of the basic plan of organization of the sensory and the motor systems and of their evolution in the mammalian series.

Moreover, it has now been firmly established that the afferent areas are not strictly afferent nor are the motor areas entirely motor. The afferent areas (SI and SII; postcentral and "second" sensory) have well-organized motor outflows which are still functional months after complete removal of the motor areas of the frontal lobe (64), while at the same time it appears that afferent connections to the frontal motor areas exist independently of the parietal afferent paths (28). Thus, the concept that the rolandic region is indeed a sensorimotor system, as held by pre-Sherringtonian workers, is reaffirmed, but with the considerable difference that the region is not an undifferentiated entity but one compounded of a number of distinguishable, individually complete, though interrelated, sensory-motor and motor-sensory representations. These facts appear to us to have important consequences for studies of the role of cortex in neurological and behavioral functions—studies which will require the close cooperation of anatomist, physiologist and behaviorist, or the mastery of multiple techniques by single individuals. Some interdisciplinary investigations based on the newer functional maps in which our laboratory has participated have already been reported (47, 48, 49); others are being discussed in this symposium (Meyer; Rose and Woolsey).

THE PATTERNS OF LOCALIZATION IN SOMATIC AFFERENT AREAS I AND II AND IN THE PRECENTRAL AND SUPPLEMENTARY MOTOR AREAS

In reviewing some of the evidence upon which the foregoing generalizations are based, we shall keep in mind the overall picture and proceed in discussion from the whole to its parts.

Figures 1 through 4 are general diagrams illustrating the evolution of the rolandic sensory and motor fields from rat and rabbit through cat, to monkey and their relations to visual, auditory and "association" cortex.

These diagrams undertake to represent the general arrangement of the somatotopical organization of the areas concerned. The orientations, propor-

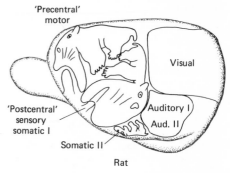

Figure 1. Diagram of rat cortex, showing general arrangement of somatic sensory areas I (SI) and II (SII), the "precentral" motor area (MI) and the gross positions of the visual and auditory areas.

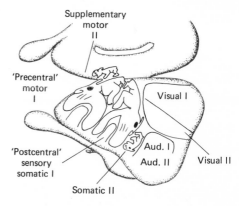

Figure 2. Diagram of rabbit cortex, showing locations and general plans of organization of "precentral" (MI) and supplementary (MII) motor areas, "postcentral" sensory (SI) and second somatic (SII) sensory areas, the visual (VI and VII) and auditory areas (AI and AII).

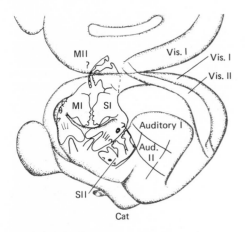

Figure 3. Diagram of cat cortex, showing locations and general arrangements of the precentral (MI) motor area, the "postcentral" (SI) and second (SII) somatic sensory areas, visual (VI and VII) and auditory (AI and AII) fields.

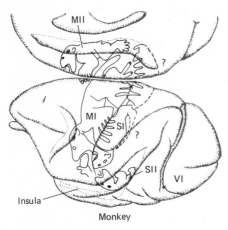

Figure 4. Diagram of monkey cortex, showing locations and general plans of organization of the supplementary motor (MII), the precentral motor (MI), the postcentral tactile (SI), and the second sensory (SII) areas. The latter lies largely on the upper bank of the sylvian fissure adjacent to the insula and the auditory area on the lower bank (not illustrated). The anterolateral boundary of the first visual area (VI) is shown by the thin line, with an asterisk placed at the center of the macular projection area.

tions and relations of parts to one another are essentially correct. The diagrams are inadequate to the actual facts in that they do not indicate the successive overlap which is characteristic of the organization of the central nervous system. This overlap is minimal between the major subdivisions of each area. The nature of the overlap is best visualized through study of detailed figurine charts, such as those of Figures 5 and 6. For rat and cat, somatic sensory areas I and II (SI and SII) and the "precentral" motor area (MI) are delineated; for rabbit and monkey these areas, plus the supplementary motor area (MII), are shown. In addition, the visual and auditory fields are outlined for rat, rabbit, and cat and the anterolateral boundary of visual area I on the lateral aspect of the hemisphere of the monkey is indicated.

The basic plan of organization of these four rolandic areas is best seen in the rabbit diagram. In essence SI and SII, and MI and MII are laid down as mirror image patterns on opposite sides of the line separating SI and MI, which corresponds to the bottom of the central sulcus of the monkey. Centers for the apices of the limbs in all four areas are nearest this line, while centers for the dorsal aspect of the animal are farther away. The symmetry is not quite complete, since SII is near the head end of SI, while MII is near the tail end of MI.

Of particular significance in the evolution of these fields is the central position of the hand areas of SI and MI. In the primates the hand achieves a high degree of corticalization in the precentral and the postcentral fields. Because of the central location of the hand areas, the simple basic pattern of organization seen in the rodent, where the parts are represented in relation to one another much as they exist in the actual animal, apparently becomes distorted in evolution as cortical representation for the hand increases, with the result that in chimpanzee (57) and in man (31) the sensory

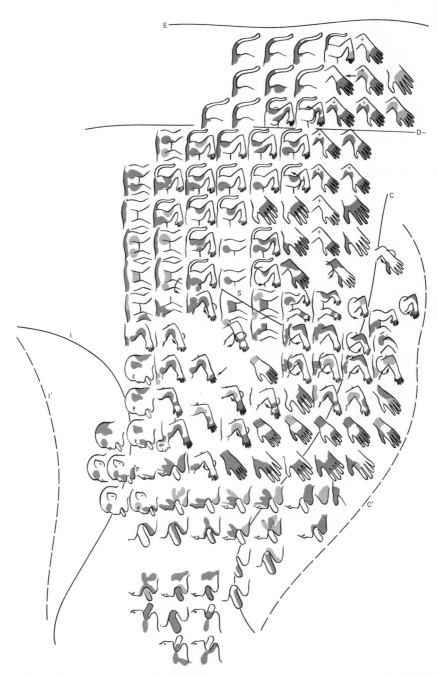

Figure 5. Figurine map of the precentral motor area of Macaca mulatta. See Figure 4 for relation of this map to the brain. Labels: C, central sulcus; C', bottom of central sulcus; D, medial edge of hemisphere; E, sulcus cinguli; I, inferior precentral sulcus; I', bottom of inferior precentral sulcus; S, superior precentral sulcus.

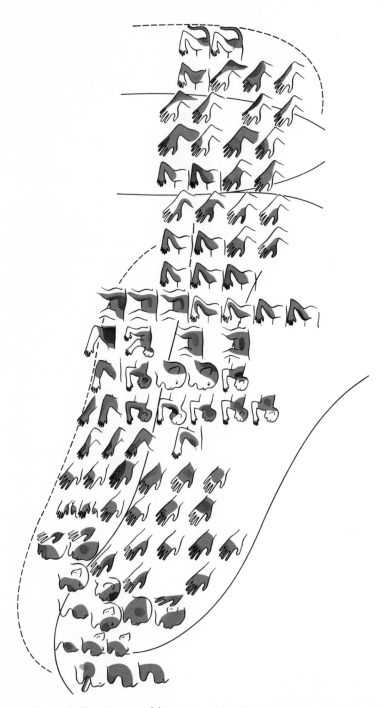

Figure 6. Figurine map of the postcentral tactile area of Macaca mulatta.

and the motor face areas lose continuity with the centers for occiput and neck, which remain associated with the trunk representations. In macaque (Figures 4, 5, 6) this separation of face from occiput has taken place in the post-central gyrus but in the precentral field the motor pattern still hangs together as it does in lower forms. Evidence for a transitional status in the postcentral area in the smooth-brained marmoset has been reported and illustrated elsewhere (56). That this separation of cortical centers for face and occiput is not the result of an *en bloc* reversal of the projections of the cervical segments upon the cortex as was once suggested (62), but rather is due to expansion of the hand area and disruption thereby of the cortical pattern (56), is supported by the finding (50) that the trigeminal nerve projects not only to the lower, classical face area but also to the "upper" head area, where not only the occiput but other parts of the head and face are represented (62). The suggestion of Petit-Butaillis et al., (33) that the upper head area of primates corresponds to the lateral face area of lower forms, while the lateral face area of primates is an elaboration of the second somatic sensory system in relation to speech function, is not in accord with our studies on the second somatic area nor with our detailed studies of somatic area I in a number of species.

Figure 1 is based on data collected by LeMessurier (25) and by Woolsey and LeMessurier (61) for the afferent systems and by Settlage, Bingham, Suckle, Borge, and Woolsey (41) for the "precentral" motor area. Detailed figurine maps of somatic sensory areas I and II and of the precentral motor area of the rat have been published elsewhere together with maps of the visual and the auditory areas (56). A supplementary motor area has not yet been sought in this species.

Figure 2 summarizes the data of several studies on the rabbit. The only one of these which has been published in full is that on the visual areas (46). The somatic afferent areas were defined by Woolsey and Wang (66); the precentral and supplementary motor areas were charted by Meyer and Woolsey, while the auditory areas were determined by focal stimulations of cochlear nerve fibers in the spiral osseous lamina by Ostenso, Lende, and Woolsey.

Figure 3 for the cat is derived from the studies of Talbot and Marshall (45) on visual area I and of Talbot (44) on visual area II, from the studies of Woolsey and Walzl (65) and of Rose (36) on the auditory system, from unpublished data on somatic afferent areas I and II by Woolsey, Hayes, Cranston, and Luethy and from motor data of a study by Borge (10). As in rat and rabbit, SI and MI in cat are arranged in a mirror image fashion but the "precentral" motor centers for the posterior half of the body are almost entirely enfolded within the cruciate sulcus. The supplementary motor area should lie near the label "MII?", although no serious attempt to define this area in the cat has yet been made.

Figure 4 shows for the monkey the general plans of organization of the precentral (MI) and supplementary (MII) motor areas as these were defined by Woolsey et al. (63), of the postcentral sensory area (SI) of Woolsey, Marshall, and Bard (62) and of the second somatic sensory area (SII) as reported by Woolsey (53, 54, 60). The latter lies for the most part on the upper bank of the sylvian fissure adjacent to the insula and auditory cortex. Only a part of the face subdivision is exposed near the lower end of the central sulcus. The question marks near SI are intended to indicate that no connection has yet been established between the "upper" head area and the laterally situated face area and that discontinuity exists between the pre- and postaxial representations for the leg and between centers for the sacral and the thoracolumbar portions of the dorsal surface, apparently as a consequence of the marked development of centers for the digits of the hindlimb

(Figure 6). Since in the precentral motor area there is continuity of centers for the dorsal axial musculature from tail to neck along the rostral border of the area (Figure 5), it is still possible that a similar continuous, but tenuous, representation for the skin of the back may exist along the caudal border of SI, but to date it has not been possible to demonstrate this. One may point out that the precentral motor and the postcentral tactile maps (Figure 5 and 6) differ in their anteroposterior extents, the former being considerably wider. The greater width of the precentral motor area, established by the identification of centers for the epaxial musculature, has only recently been demonstrated (63). Thus the "old" motor map of area 4 (20) resembles more closely the postcentral tactile map than does the "new" motor map. This again suggests that the tactile map may still be incomplete along its caudal boundary and calls for further study of this problem. In chimpanzee and man, where the distances are still greater, the discontinuities of the localization patterns are still more striking.

The figurine maps of Figures 5 and 6 provide a comparison of the patterns of organization of the precentral motor area (Figure 5) and the postcentral tactile areas (Figure 6) of *Macaca mulatta*. The motor map is reproduced from *Patterns of Organization in the Central Nervous System* (63); the tactile map is based on data used originally to construct the map for Bard's Harvey Lecture (6; see also 7) and presented with details of individual experiments by Woolsey, Marshall, and Bard (62). It has been completely redrawn in our present style of map making. The scale has also been changed, so that both the motor and the tactile maps illustrate data for points taken at two millimeter intervals on the brain. The tactile map is not complete at its lower end, where centers for the tongue are known to lie. Figure 4 may serve as a key to relate Figures 5 and 6 to the brain. Evidence for mirroring of the precentral

and postcentral patterns is seen in the face areas.

MOTOR PATHWAYS ARISING IN SI AND SII

It has long been known that electrical stimulation of the parietal lobe can produced skeletal muscle movements similar to those produced by stimulation of the frontal lobe. Schaefer's (40) map, published in 1900, of the somatic motor zone of the monkey's brain included not only the frontal areas now identified as the precentral and supplementary motor areas but it also included all of the postcentral gyrus. Similar results were reported by the Vogts (51). Stimulation of the cortex of many by Foerster (19), Penfield and Rasmussen (32) and others has demonstrated the same thing. However, since the work of Leyton and Sherrington, (27) the preeminence of the precentral gyrus in motor function has dominated teaching and thinking concerning cortical control of the somatic musculature and the motor effects of postcentral stimulation generally have been explained as the result of the spread of excessive stimulating currents to the precentral area, or on the basis of corticocortical connections with this area, or as mediated by extrapyramidal pathways (19).

In 1943, Kennard and McCulloch (22) studied the electrical excitability of the postcentral gyrus sometime after removal of Brodmann's areas 4 and 6 from infant monkeys and found that it was still possible to produce focal movements similar to those elicitable normally from the precentral gyrus. They interpreted their results as indicating a high degree of plasticity on the part of the juvenile, as contrasted with the adult, nervous system. Recently we have stimulated in detail the postcentral gyrus of several large, adult monkeys from which the precentral and supplementary motor areas were removed months earlier, and have been able to demonstrate the existence

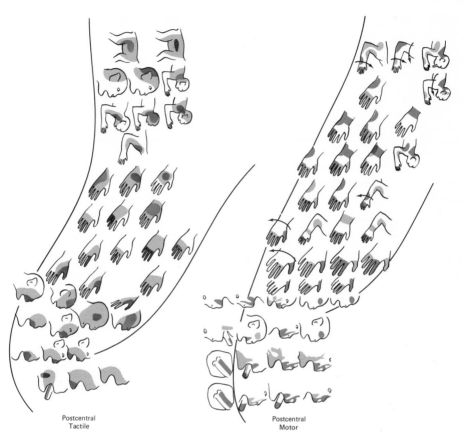

Postcentral
Tactile

Postcentral
Motor

Figure 7. Comparison of postcentral tactile localization pattern with the postcentral motor localization pattern of Macaca mulatta.

of a well-organized postcentral motor outflow after complete degeneration of of the motor pathways from both frontal lobes (*64*).

Figure 7 provides a comparison of the motor and tactile localization patterns of the postcentral gyrus for the face and arm subdivisions and for a part of the trunk area. The tactile pattern on the left is a part of the tactile map shown in Figure 6. The motor pattern on the right illustrates the results obtained in one of the experiments of Woolsey, Travis, Barnard, and Ostenso (*64*). In spite of the fact that the sensory and the

motor maps are not derived from the same animal, they show remarkable similarities in their patterns of somatotopical organization. Points receiving tactile impulses from particular parts of the face, hand, or trunk, on stimulation with 60 cycle alternating current, cause movements to occur in closely related parts of the body. Thus stimulation of cortical points (in Figure 7R) corresponding in position to those receiving afferent impulses from the occiput and neck (Figure 7L) causes movements of the dorsal neck musculature. It appears clear, then, that a basic relationship exists between the origin of the input signals to the postcentral gyrus and the destination of motor volleys leaving this area. Since the precentral motor areas (except for the left precentral face area) were absent from both frontal lobes of the animal stimulated, there must exist a well-organized postcentral motor system which can function independently of the frontal motor paths.

In addition to the motor pathway originating in the postcentral gyrus, there is another parietal motor system associated with the second somatic sensory area in the parietal operculum. This was first described by Sugar, Chusid, and French (43) and thought by them to lie rostral to the second somatic sensory area. However, studies on the squirrel monkey by Benjamin and Welker (8)

and by Welker, Benjamin, Miles, and Woolsey (52) indicate that the sensory and the motor patterns are laid down together and coincide somatotopically. A similar relationship of sensory and motor localization patterns in the second somatic area of the cat had already been found in a few experiments (55).

AFFERENT CONNECTIONS TO MI AND MII

When Poliak (35) studied the main afferent systems to the cerebral cortex of the monkey, he described strong projections to both the pre- and the postcentral regions. The total somatic afferent field defined by him coincided satisfactorily with the sensory area of the cortex delimited by Dusser de Barenne

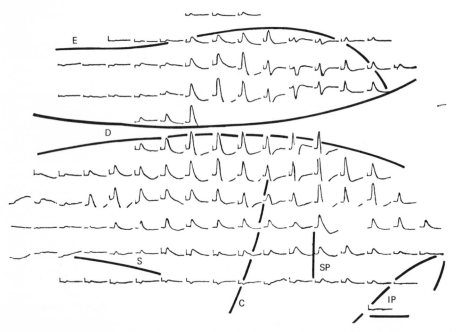

Figure 8. Potential changes (positive up) evoked pre- and postcentrally on the dorsolateral and medial surfaces of the leg region of the cerebral cortex of Macaca mulatta by single condensor discharges applied through stimulating electrodes to the right seventh lumbar dorsal root (L 7). From an unpublished experiment by Woolsey, Chang and Bard (59). Labels: SP, superior postcentral sulcus; IP, intraparietal sulcus; for others see legend of Figure 5.

with the strychnine method (17). However, the functional significance of these precentral connections has continued an open question in spite of the fact that the thalamic nucleus which projects upon the precentral cortex is known to receive connections from the cerebellum. This is so because the cerebellum is now known to receive many kinds of afferent information (4, 42) in addition to proprioceptive. Thus, it is clear that afferent information to the precentral region need not be limited to any specific sensory modality.

Under pentobarbital anesthesia, mechanical movement of hairs results in essentially monophasic surface positive evoked potentials limited to the postcentral cortex of macaque. Under the same conditions, electrical stimulation of spinal dorsal roots activates not only the postcentral but also the precentral region (57, Figure 8). Malis, Pribram, and Kruger (28) have reported that precentral responses can be evoked by electrical stimulation of cutaneous nerves alone and that the precentral responses still occur after removal of the parietal lobe and after ablation of the cerebellum. This suggests the existence of a direct spinothalamocortical path mediating some form of cutaneous sensibility to the precentral gyrus. It will be important to determine the modality concerned and the detailed pattern of somatotopic organization for this system.

Some evidence for precentral tactile responses in the porcupine (26) and the squirrel monkey (8) has been obtained, but a definitive study of the pattern of organization remains to be done. That the precentral system cannot substitute for the postcentral tactile area in the management of the tactile placing reactions has already been established by Woolsey and Bard (see Bard, 6). The functional contributions of the pre- and postcentral systems, therefore, must differ significantly. Penfield and Jasper (31) have reported for man that 25 percent of the points which on electrical stim-

ulation give rise to sensation in conscious patients are precentrally located. The character of the sensation ("numbness, tingling, feeling of electricity") is the same whether the stimulus is applied pre- or postcentrally, except that the desire to move an extremity practically always comes from precentral stimulation. Penfield also states that "sensory responses from the precentral gyrus do not depend upon activation of the postcentral gyrus, for when the postcentral gyrus has been ablated at operation, stimulation of the precentral gyrus still gives occasional sensory responses referable to the arm or leg which corresponds with the portion of postcentral gyrus just removed."

Penfield's (31, 32) observations on the supplementary motor area of man indicate that this area also may be involved in some way in sensory function. Electrical stimulation in conscious patients has been found to produce sensations referred somewhat diffusely to various parts of the body, sometimes to both sides. In addition, Penfield (31) reports some evidence for a somatic sensory representation, posterior to the postcentral foot area on the medial aspect of the parietal lobe. He refers to this as a supplementary sensory area. To date no evidence for a supplementary sensory area has been found in animals, but further study of this question is needed.

Since the evidence indicates that the rolandic region consists of at least four distinguishable, somatotopically organized areas, each of which appears to be concerned with both sensory and motor functions, it may be in order to suggest a nomenclature which is more in keeping with the facts than the terminology which we have used up to this point. We therefore propose the following designations: *somatic sensory-motor area I* (SmI) for the postcentral gyrus and its homologues in non-primate forms; *somatic sensory-motor area II* (SmII) for the "second" sensory area; *somatic motor-sensory area I* (MsI) for the pre-central motor area; and *somatic motor-sensory area II* (MsII) for the supplementary motor area. The abbreviations in parentheses indicate, by capitals and lower case letters and by order, the relative dominance of sensory and motor features of each area, as these are revealed under conditions of barbiturate anesthesia. These differences may be obscured under other circumstances, such as the absence of anesthesia, as Dr. Lilly makes clear in his presentation.

ASSOCIATION CORTEX

Comparison of Figures 1, 2, 3, and 4 reveals the striking differences in amount of cortex not devoted to sensory and motor projection systems (39). If we omit consideration of the medial aspect of the hemisphere and the limbic areas in which the mammillothalamocortical path terminates (38), it is evident that very little cortex outside the sensory and motor projection areas exists in the hemispheres of rat and rabbit. The frontal association cortex must be much less extensive in the rat than Krieg's (23) cytoarchitectural study of this animal allots to it, or has been assumed in some behavioral studies. This area is also very small in the rabbit (37). The largest area in these species not now preempted by sensory and motor projection systems lies caudal to the auditory and lateral to the visual areas in the temporal region. It seems clear that many of the identifications of homologues made on cytoarchitectural grounds, such as those of Gerebtzoff (21) for rabbit and guinea pig, are invalid. Cortex which could conceivably be classified as "associational" in these two species, therefore, must be of minimal extent.

In the cat considerably more "association" cortex exists. Some studies have been carried out to establish the nature of the connections to the association centers from the primary projection fields, such as that of Amas-sian (5) for cat parietal cortex, the studies of Clare and Bishop (15) on the visual system of the cat, and that of Ades (1) on the auditory area.

In monkey still larger portions of cortex remain after the sensory and motor projection areas have been defined. However, in this animal, it is still necessary to delimit the second visual area. This presumably includes Brodmann's area 18 and perhaps area 19. In the marmoset (58) the visual response area as defined by gross photic stimulation far exceeds the limits of the striate cortex and actually includes all the cortex designated by Peden and Bonin (30) as areas OC, OB, OA and PFG. These areas extend toward the temporal region as far as the caudal border of the auditory cortex. A part of this visual response area is probably homologous with the third visual response area of Marshall, Talbot, and Ades (29) and with the visual association area of Clare and Bishop (15). The findings, when more fully developed, should be of considerable relevance to behavioral studies involving the posterior association areas (14; see also Pribram, this symposium).

COMMENTS

The results obtained in the field of cortical localization, since the introduction of oscillographic techniques for the study of afferent systems and through the reinvestigation of motor systems, which the sensory studies have stimulated, demonstrate the inadequacies of earlier views and call for a renewed attack on the relations of anatomically and functionally differentiated regions of the cortex to both neurological and behavioral functions. Such studies should not merely refine problems already explored but may be expected to yield qualitatively different results. One need only consider the relative crudeness of even the best surgery and the lack of precise controls in the placement of lesions to appreciate how infrequently tissue removed has actually coincided with any specific anatomical or physiological system. Errors of incomplete or excessive removal have been inevitable. This comment applies both to studies on sensory and motor projection systems and to those involving so-called association areas. A region of particular difficulty in this respect is the parietal-occipital-temporal in the monkey. When in addition we find that sensory and motor projection systems are not simple, single entities but that every system appears to have multiple connections with the cortex, it is not surprising that experiments based on hypotheses visualizing simpler relationships have been disappointing. The papers on the auditory system of Neff et al. and of Rose and Woolsey in this symposium indicate that studies may become more productive when the anatomical and physiological complexities of the systems concerned are more adequately taken into consideration. They imply more complex behavioral mechanisms than present methods of testing are designed to reveal. There is opportunity for much greater control of the placement of lesions and for determination of completeness of lesions involving the sensory systems by application of oscillographic methods at time of surgery and at

sacrifice of animal than has yet been achieved. While some (9, 16, 24) have become pessimistic over the possibility of relating cytoarchitectural and functional differentiations it may well be that this pessimism is premature, since only relatively recently have the electrical methods of recording made possible the type of study through which such correlations may become possible. As yet practically no such studies have been made.

A real need, of basic importance to all studies on the effects of localized cortical lesions, is the determination of the functional capacities of the nervous system after total removal of all cortex. No really adequate study of the learned behavioral capacities of totally decorticated mammals has been carried out to date and yet studies of this kind would seem to be essential before one is justified in drawing conclusions from more limited ablations, especially when partial lesions result in transient and impermanent deficiencies. The experiences of Bromiley (12) on the decorticate dog, of Macht and Bard on decerebrate cats (see Bard, 7) and of Travis and Woolsey (49) on decorticate monkeys suggest that much could be done in the behavioral study of adequately maintained totally decorticated animals, including primates.

References

1. Ades, H. W. A secondary acoustic area in the cerebral cortex of the cat. *J. Neurophysiol.*, 1943, **6**, 59–63.

2. Adrian, E. D. Double representation of the feet in the sensory cortex of the cat. *J. Physiol.*, 1940, **98**, 16 P (Abstract).

3. Adrian, E. D. Afferent discharges to the cerebral cortex from peripheral sense organs. *J. Physiol.*, 1941, **100**, 159–191.

4. Adrian, E. D. Afferent areas in the cerebellum connected with the limbs. *Brain*, 1943, **66**, 289–315.

5. Amassian, V. E. Studies on organization of a somesthetic association area, including a single unit analysis. *J. Neurophysiol.*, 1954, **17**, 39–58.

6. Bard, P. Studies on the cortical representation of somatic sensibility. Harvey Lecture, Feb., 1938. *Bull. N. Y. Acad. Med.*, 1938, **14**, 585–607.

7. Bard, P. *Medical physiology.* (10th ed.) St. Louis: C. V. Mosby, 1956.

8. Benjamin, R. M., and Welker, W. I. Somatic receiving areas of cerebral cortex of squirrel monkey (*Saimiri sciureus*). *J. Neurophysiol.*, 1957, **20**, 286–299.

9. Bonin, G. von, and Bailey, P. *The neocortex of Macaca mulatta.* Urbana, Ill.: Univ. of Illinois Press, 1947.

10. Borge, A. F. *The motor cortex of the cat.* Unpublished master's thesis, Univ. of Wisconsin, 1950.

11. Brodmann, K. *Vergleichende Lokalisationslehre der Grosshirnrinde in ihren Prinzipien dargestellt auf Grund des Zellenbaues.* Leipsig, Germany: J. A. Barth, 1909.

12. Bromiley, R. B. Conditioned responses in a dog after removal of neocortex. *J. comp. physiol. Psychol.,* 1948, **41**, 102–110.

13. Campbell, A. W. *Histological studies on the localization of cerebral function.* Cambridge: Cambridge Univ. Press, 1905.

14. Chow, K. L., and Hutt, P. J. The "association cortex" of *Macaca mulatta.* A review of recent contributions to its anatomy and functions. *Brain,* 1953, **76**, 625–677.

15. Clare, M. H., and Bishop, G. H. Responses from an association area secondarily activated from optic cortex. *J. Neurophysical.,* 1954, **17**, 271–277.

16. Clark, W. E. LeG. A note on cortical cyto-architectonics. *Brain,* 1952, **75**, 96–104.

17. Dusser de Barenne, J. G. Experimental researches on sensory localization in the cerebral cortex of the monkey (*Macacus*). *Proc. roy. Soc., London,* 1924, **96B**, 272–291.

18. Economo, C. von, and Koskinas, G. N. *Die Cytoarchitectonik der Hirnrinde des erwachsenen Menschen.* Berlin: Springer, 1925.

19. Foerster, O. Motorische Felder und Bahnen. Bumke and Foerster, *Handbuch der Neurologie.* Berlin: Springer, 1936. Vol. 6, pp. 1–357.

20. Fulton, J. F. *Physiology of the nervous system.* New York: Oxford Univ. Press, 1949.

21. Gerebtzoff, M. A. Recherches sur l'écorce cérébrale et le thalamus du cobaye. I. Étude architectonique. *La Cellule,* 1940, **48**, 337–352.

22. Kennard, M. A., and McCulloch, W. S. Motor responses to stimulation of cerebral cortex in absence of areas 4 and 6 (*Macaca mulatta*). *J. Neurophysiol.,* 1943, **6**, 181–189.

23. Krieg, W. J. S. Connections of the cerebral cortex. I. The albino rat. A Topography of the cortical areas. *J. comp. Neurol.,* 1946, **84**, 221–275.

24. Lashley, K. S., and Clark, G. The cytoarchitecture of the cerebral cortex of Ateles: A critical examination of architectonic studies. *J. comp. Neurol.,* 1946, **85**, 223–306.

25. LeMessurier, D. H. Auditory and visual areas of the cerebral cortex of the rat. *Fed. Proc.,* 1948, **7**, 70–71 (Abstract).

26. Lende, R. A., and Woolsey, C. N. Sensory and motor localization in cerebral cortex of porcupine (*Erethizon dorsatum*). *J. Neurophysical.,* 1956, **19**, 544–563.

27. Leyton, A. S. F., and Sherrington, C. S. Observations of the excitable cortex of the chimpanzee, orang-utan and gorilla. *Quart. J. exper. Physiol.,* 1917, **11**, 135–222.

28. Malis, L. I., Pribram, K. H., and Kruger, L. Action potentials in motor cortex evoked by peripheral nerve stimulation. *J. Neurophysiol.,* 1953, **16**, 161–167.

29. Marshall, W. H., Talbot, S. A., and Ades, H. W. Cortical response of the anesthetized cat to gross photic and electrical afferent stimulation. *J. Neurophysiol.,* 1943, **6**, 1–15.

30. Peden, J. K., and Bonin, G. von. Neocortex of *Hapale. J. comp. Neurol.,* 1947, **86**, 37–63.

31. Penfield, W., and Jasper, H. *Epilepsy and the functional anatomy of the human brain.* Boston: Little, Brown, 1954.

32. Penfield, W., and Rasmussen, T. *The cerebral cortex of man.* New York: Macmillan, 1952.

33. Petit-Dutaillis, D., Chavany, J. A., Pertuiset, B., and Lobel, G., Remarques sur les représentations sensitives corticales, primaire et secondaire à propos d'une aura sensitive. *La Presse med.,* 1953, **61**, 429–431.

34. Pinto Hamuy, T. Retention and performance of "skilled movements" after cortical ablations in monkeys. *Johns Hopk. Hosp. Bull.,* 1956, **93**, 417–444.

35. Poliak, S. *The main afferent fiber systems of the cerebral cortex in primates.* Berkeley: Univ. Calif. Press, 1932. (*Univ. Calif. Publ. Anat.,* 1932, **2**).

36. Rose, J. E. The cellular structure of the auditory region of the cat. *J. comp. Neurol.,* 1949, **91**, 409–439.

37. Rose, J. E., and Woolsey, C. N. The orbitofrontal cortex and its connections with the mediodorsal nucleus in rabbit, sheep and cat. *Res. Publ. Ass. nerv. ment. Dis.,* 1948, **27**, 210–232.

38. Rose, J. E., and Woolsey, C. N. Structure and relations of limbic cortex and anterior thalamic nuclei in rabbit and cat. *J. comp. Neurol.*, 1948, **89**, 279–347.

39. Rose, J. E., and Woolsey, C. N. Organization of the mammalian thalamus and its relationships to the cerebral cortex. *EEG clin. Neurophysiol.*, 1949, **1**, 391–404.

40. Schaefer, E. A. *Textbook of physiology.* New York: Macmillan, 1898–1900. 2 vols.

41. Settlage, P. H., Bingham, W. G., Suckle, H. M., Borge, A. F., and Woolsey, C. N. The pattern of localization in the motor cortex of the rat. *Fed. Proc.*, 1949, **8**, 144 (Abstract).

42. Snider, R. S., and Stowell, A. Receiving areas of the tactile, auditory and visual systems in the cerebellum. *J. Neurophysiol.*, 1944, **7**, 331–358.

43. Sugar, O., Chusid, J. G., and French, J. D. A second motor cortex in the monkey (*Macaca mulatta*). *J. Neuropath. exper. Neurol.*, 1948, **7**, 182–189.

44. Talbot, S. A. A lateral localization in the cat's visual cortex. *Fed. Proc.*, 1942, **1**, 84 (Abstract).

45. Talbot, S. A., and Marshall, W. H. Physiological studies on neural mechanisms of visual localization and discrimination. *Amer. J. Ophthal.*, 1941, **24**, 1255–1264.

46. Thompson, J. M., Woolsey, C. N. and Talbot, S. A. Visual areas I and II of cerebral cortex of rabbit. *J. Neurophysiol.*, 1950, **13**, 227–288.

47. Travis, A. M. Neurological deficiencies after ablation of the precentral motor area in *Macaca mulatta. Brain*, 1955, **78**, 155–173.

48. Travis, A. M. Neurological deficiencies following supplementary motor area lesions in *Macaca mulatta. Brain*, 1955, **78**, 174–198.

49. Travis. A. M., and Woolsey, C. N. Motor performance of monkeys after bilateral partial and total cerebral decortications. *Amer. J. phys. Med.*, 1956, **35**, 273–310.

50. Ullrich, D. P., and Woolsey, C. N. Trigeminal nerve representation in the "upper head area" of the postcentral gyrus of *Macaca mulatta. Trans. Amer. neurol. Ass.*, 1954, 23–28 (Abstract).

51. Vogt, C., and Vogt, O. Allegemeinere Ergebnisse unserer Hirnforschung. *J. Psychol. Neurol., Lpz.*, 1919, **25**, 277–462.

52. Welker, W. I., Benjamin, R. M., Miles, R. C., and Woolsey, C. N. Motor effects of cortical stimulation in squirrel monkey (*Saimiri sciureus*). *J. Neurophysiol.*, 1957, **20**, 347–364.

53. Woolsey, C. N. "Second" somatic receiving areas in the cerebral cortex of cat, dog and monkey. *Fed. Proc.*, 1943, **2**, 55 (Abstract).

54. Woolsey, C. N. Additional observations on a "second" somatic receiving area in the cerebral cortex of the monkey. *Fed. Proc.*, 1944, **3**, 43 (Abstract).

55. Woolsey, C. N. Patterns of sensory representation in the cerebral cortex. *Fed. Proc.*, 1947, **6**, 437–441.

56. Woolsey, C. N. Patterns of localization in sensory and motor areas of the cerebral cortex. Chap. 14 in Milbank Symposium. *The biology of mental health and disease.* New York: Hoeber, 1952.

57. Woolsey, C. N. Somatic sensory areas I and II of the cerebral cortex of the chimpanzee. *19th Internat. Physiol. Congr., Abst. Communications*, 1953, 902–903 (Abstract).

58. Woolsey, C. N., Akert, K., Benjamin, R. M., Leibowitz, H., and Welker, W. I. Visual cortex, of the marmoset. *Fed. Proc.*, 1955, **14**, 166 (Abstract).

59. Woolsey, C. N., Chang, H. T., and Bard, P. Distribution of cortical potentials evoked by electrical stimulation of dorsal roots in *Macaca mulatta. Fed. Proc.*, 1947, **6**, 230 (Abstract).

60. Woolsey, C. N., and Fairman, D. Contralateral, ipsilateral and bilateral representation of cutaneous receptors in somatic areas I and II of the cerebral cortex of pig, sheep and other mammals. *Surgery*, 1946, **19**, 634–702.

61. Woolsey, C. N., and Le Messurier, D. H. The pattern of cutaneous representation in the rat's cerebral cortex. *Fed. Proc.*, 1948, **7**, 137 (Abstract).

62. Woolsey, C. N., Marshall, W. H., and Bard, P. Representation of cutaneous tactile sensibility in the cerebral cortex of the monkey as indicated by evoked potentials. *Johns Hopk. Hosp. Bull.*, 1942, **70**, 399–441.

63. Woolsey, C. N., Settlage, P. H., Meyer, D. R., Sencer, W., Pinto Hamuy, T., and Travis, A. M. Patterns of localization in precentral and "supplementary" motor areas and their relation to

the concept of a premotor area. Chap. XII in *Patterns of organization in the central nervous system. Res. Publ. Ass. nerv. ment. Dis.*, 1951, **30**, 238–264.

64. Woolsey, C. N., Travis, A. M., Barnard, J. W., and Ostenso, R. S. Motor representation in the postcentral gyrus after chronic ablation of precentral and supplementary motor areas, *Fed. Proc.*, 1953, **12**, 160.

65. Woolsey, C. N., and Walzl, E. M. Topical projection of nerve fibers from local regions of the cochlea to the cerebral cortex of the cat. *Johns Hopk. Hosp. Bull.*, 1942, **71**, 315–344.

66. Woolsey, C. N., and Wang, G. H. Somatic areas I and II of the cerebral cortex of the rabbit. *Fed. Proc.*, 1945, **4**, 79.

Conscious control of single nerve cells
john v. basmajian

For half a century, neurophysiologists have convinced themselves that the human brain can "think" or "picture" movements of joints only in a general way and that it cannot consciously call upon specific muscles to produce a desired movement. The layman who gives the matter any thought will agree with this belief, perhaps advancing as evidence his ignorance even of the names of the several hundred muscles he possesses. After all, if you do not know what muscles you have and what their functions are, how can you possibly direct your thoughts to controlling them individually?

I have carried out experiments recently which clearly show that what is obvious is wrong; a man *can* control individual muscles. In fact he can narrow his control down to a single unit of muscular contraction, one of the many tens of thousands of "motor units" in his body.

Each motor unit includes a motor nerve cell, with its microscopic body located in the spinal cord and its elongated fine nerve fiber (axone) running, as one fibre among hundreds of others, in the large nerve that enters each skeletal muscle; it also includes the small number of microscopic muscle fibers that the axone supplies with impulses (Figure 1). Whenever an impulse originates in the motor nerve cell, or motoneurone, it makes all the muscle fibers that it supplies give a brief twitch, measured in

From *New Scientist*, 12 December 1963. This article was first published in *New Scientist*, the weekly magazine of science and technology, London.

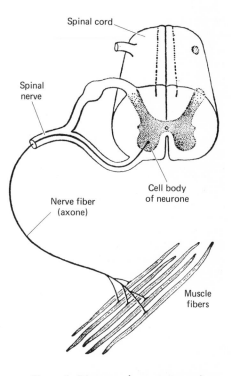

Figure 1. Diagram of one motor unit.

thousandths of a second. The increasing shower of such impulses that results from recruiting greater and greater numbers of motoneurones brings about a stronger and stronger contraction.

The impulses originating in neighboring motoneurones all have differing frequencies; one may be firing at a rate of 50 per second while a neighbor's rate may be much less—say, 10 per second. As the contractions of motor units are not synchronized, they provide a smooth contraction of the whole muscle. If all the motor units fired simultaneously at the same rate, the result would be a tremor.

Normally, the brain has a number of important areas from which impulses originate and run down to influence the motoneurones of the spinal cord. Although the most important part of the brain for initiating voluntary actions is a narrow strip of grey matter in the cortex, other important parts of the brain are involved, for example, the "red nucleus" and the "reticular formation." One generally accepted estimate is that more than 600 nerve fibers influence the activity of each spinal motoneurone. In Figure 2, only one of the many fibers from the cortex of the brain to a spinal motoneurone is shown diagrammatically. The main descending pathway from only the cortex of one side of the brain contains a quarter of a million impulse-conducting fibers. The possibility of learning to use one's motor pathways may appear even more unlikely when one realizes that each half of the brain contains more than 6000 million nerve cells and that these cells have multitudes of interconnections as well as their connections (both direct and indirect) with the spinal motoneurones.

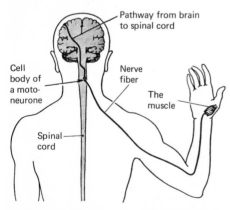

Figure 2. Diagram of a single pathway from the brain to a muscle of the thumb. In reality, hundreds of nerve fibers from the brain may influence a single motor unit, and hundreds of motor units make up a single muscle.

Employing an electronic technique developed largely during the second World War, electromyography (myos being Greek for muscle), various groups of research workers have established many of the characteristics of the motor unit, while others have been studying the connections of the motoneurones in the central nervous system.

Using electrodes made of needles and wires that are inserted right into the muscles, we can pick up the electrical discharges resulting from the contraction of individual motor units. When we amplify them and record them, we see that these discharges ("motor unit potentials"); appear as a succession of "spikes" of very brief electrical activity. But when we look more closely we see that the spikes from different motor units are not the same; each has its own peculiarities of shape, when displayed on a cathode ray oscilloscope. By its electrical "signature," the activity of an individual motor unit may be identified and followed—provided that the muscle contraction is not very strong, for in that case there is such a large shower of spikes from different units that they cannot be distinguished.

In the past decade, electromyographers have clearly demonstrated that a voluntary (skeletal) muscle can be completely relaxed by a small effort of the will. In fact, many muscles are completely or almost completely relaxed automatically as a labor-saving device. My colleagues and I have shown that ligaments, which are inert and therefore economical, then assume many functions otherwise assigned to contracted muscles. However, that is another story that does not concern us here.

What must be emphasized is that relaxation of motor units is a passive thing. An absence of impulses from the motoneurone simply results in complete rest of the muscle fibers it supplies.

As a consequence of some provocative work on motor unit contractions by Virginia Harrison and Otto Mortensen, I began to ask myself: How fine a control does the "conscious" part of the human brain have over the individual moto-neurones in the spinal cord? Harrison and Mortensen had shown that, with an electrode placed on the skin over a muscle of the leg (tibialis anterior), they could register up to six motor units in-dividually. Though their work concerned only the contraction of motor units, it immediately suggested to me a new ap-proach to finding out more about the functioning of the elusive motoneurones in the spinal cord itself. The motor unit potentials from the muscles could be regarded as the echoes of the response in the spinal motoneurones, which, for obvious reasons, have not been studied by any direct approach in man.

I therefore began a series of experi-ments on human volunteers recruited from among my colleagues and students. I shall only describe the fully analyzed findings in a group of 16 subjects. Be-cause I was concerned with functions that I assumed would require consider-able skill for the most intensive study, I chose a small muscle in the base of the thumb, the abductor pollicis brevis. Later I found that other muscles, including one in the leg, would serve as well.

The basic technique was as follows. Into the middle of the fleshy (contrac-tile) part of the muscle I injected a pair of sterilized, insulated, hair-thin wires, so fine that they are not felt by the subject. The tips were bare of insulation and acted as a pair of electrodes. The

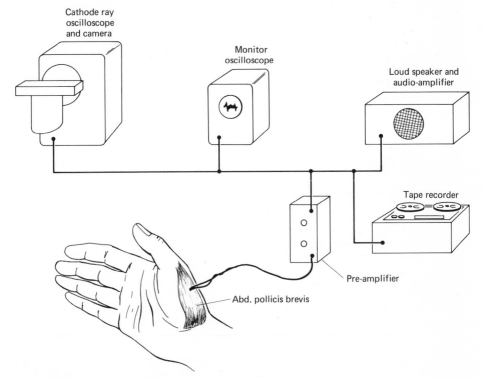

Figure 3. Apparatus for training subjects to control individual spinal motoneurones and for recordings.

wires were then connected to high-gain electronic amplifiers; thence the signals went to cathode-ray oscilloscopes for both visual monitoring and recording on photographic film, to a loudspeaker (so that the motor unit spikes could be heard by the subject as "popping" sounds) and a magnetic tape recorder for recording these sounds (Figure 3).

The experiments under discussion followed a general pattern. After the subjects had been "wired," they were given five to ten minutes to become familiar with the response of the electromyograph to a range of voluntary movements and postures. They were invariably amazed at the acute responsiveness to even the slightest effort. Then they began a short course of learning how to maintain very slight, invisible contractions which were apparent to themselves only through the response of the apparatus. This led to increasingly more demanding effort involving many procedures intended to reveal both their natural talent in controlling individual motoneurones and their skill in learning and retaining tricks with them. Individual motor units may, as I have mentioned, be identified by the characteristics of their spikes—revealed by the oscilloscope and, to a lesser extent, by the loudspeaker. Confirmatory oscillographic recordings of the potentials were made on photographic film (Figure 4). Generally, experiments on one muscle were limited to less than one day. (Recent efforts to continue for longer periods have led to technical difficulties which, fortunately, do not seem to be insurmountable.)

Within 15 to 30 minutes all the subjects had achieved notably better control at will over gentle contractions than they had at first. In this time almost all of them learned, first, to relax the whole muscle completely and instantaneously on command, and, secondly, to recruit the activity of a single motor unit on command, keeping it active for as many minutes as desired. A few persons had

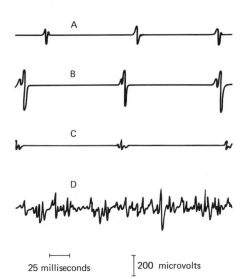

25 milliseconds   200 microvolts

Figure 4. Tracings of nerve impulses ("spikes") recorded from the cathode-ray oscilloscope. A, B, and C were recorded through the same electrodes from different motor units under conscious control. Tracing D is the result of a weak-to-moderate sustained contraction with many motor units "firing."

difficulty in maintaining the activity of such a unit, or in recruiting more units.

Of fundamental importance is the question of whether there are identifiable individual differences in subjects to which we might ascribe their differences in performance. So far, I have found no clear-cut relationship to age, manual dexterity, or anything that might be invoked as an underlying explanation. The youngest persons have been among both the worst and the best performers— but none, so far, has been under 20 years of age, and it is possible that children and young people may show different abilities. General personality traits do not seem to matter, but this impression may be based on too short an experience. Harrison recently found in a study of eight athletes of the United States Olympic team that, compared with ordinary subjects, they showed no obvious differences in their ability to recruit individual motor units in a muscle of the leg. Here again, final judgment must be reserved until many more results have been obtained.

Let us return to the details of the experiments. After about half an hour, each subject was required to learn how to repress the first motoneurone he had learned to control and to recruit another one. Most subjects were able to do this and gain mastery of the new one in a matter of minutes; only one required more than 15 minutes. More than half of the subjects could repeat the performance with a third unit a few minutes later and a few could recruit and isolate a fourth or even a fifth motoneurone.

The next problem facing a subject was to recruit, unerringly and separately, the several units over which he had gained control. Here there emerged a considerable variation in skill. About one subject in four could respond easily to the command for isolated contractions using any of three or more units. About one half of the subjects displayed much less skill than this even after several hours and even though they might later learn other bizarre tricks with single motor units. Several subjects had particular difficulty in finding the asked-for units. They groped around in their conscious efforts to locate them and sometimes, it seemed, only succeeded by accident. Tests showed that hearing the sounds of the potentials on the loudspeakers—the "aural feedback"—was more useful than watching the visual display on the cathode ray tube monitor.

The subjects who had displayed the best control were then trained to perform various tricks with their motor units. We tested several for their powers of recalling specific units into activity without any help from the aural and visual feedback that was so important to most of the subjects. Three subjects, including myself, could do so, but we were unable to explain how we managed it. To this day I cannot put into words how I was able

to call three different motoneurones unerringly into activity in the total absence of the artificial aids. This ability to recall established pathways to individual motoneurones is now one of my main concerns.

An amusing part of the experiments is introduced after about an hour when the subjects are experienced enough to be trained to produce specific rhythms on single motoneurones. Almost everyone can learn to reduce or increase the frequency of firing of a well-controlled unit. Early in the studies, it became apparent that the individual motoneurone did not have a single characteristic frequency as was previously believed. Rather, it has a maximum rate below which its firing can be varied over a wide range of frequencies. Indeed, subjects can produce single spikes, and hence isolated contractions of their motor units, on command. If, on the other hand, the rate of firing of a motor unit has been raised to its characteristic maximum, "overflow" takes place and other motoneurones are recruited.

This inherent ability to speed up and slow down the firing of motoneurones suggested the possibility of playing special rhythms on them. The success of the subjects at doing this far exceeded my expectations. Most persons became so skilled that they could produce a variety of rhythms, such as doublets, triplets, gallop rhythms, and complicated drum-rolls and drum-beats with internal rhythms. These were recorded on tape and have provided considerable amusement as well as convincing evidence for the scientific audiences to which I have played them in the U.S.A., Canada, and the Soviet Union.

Although the skills, learned in these experiments depend on aural and visual feedbacks that the nervous system normally lacks, the controls are learned so quickly, are so exquisite, and are (at least in some subjects) so well retained after the artificial feedbacks are eliminated, that one must not dismiss them as tricks. One should bear in mind that the body has its own natural sensory feedback systems indicating the state of the muscles and joints by means of the "proprioceptive" sensations.

A number of obvious problems emerged from the differences in the rates of learning of these finest motor skills by different subjects. Both my work and the newest work of Harrison (mentioned above) are still too limited to allow sweeping generalizations. Some individuals whom we would have expected to be better than average failed to show better control than the ordinary run of subjects. Much broader studies, to ascertain the relationship between rates of learning motor controls on the one hand and dexterity and special abilities on the other, are in their preliminary stages and I shall not hazard any conclusions about them here. Such information can plainly be expected to find application to the problems of teaching motor skills of all kinds at all ages. Moreover, the ability to adjust the rate of firing of individual motoneurones, as a novel physiological concept, affords the hope that detailed studies of the characteristics of individual responses should expose some of the underlying control mechanisms in the spinal cord.

memory
and
learning
chapter 6

Memory and learning are two areas of intensive study in psychology. Until recently memory was regarded, at least mechanistically, as a relatively incomprehensible phenomenon. Much work had been done during the beginning of this century, and the latter portion of the previous one, regarding some basic aspects of memory. Problems considered included the rate at which words could be memorized and the amount of recall after memorization. However, nothing was known of how memory is actually related to brain mechanisms. Recent work tends to indicate that memory might be a biochemical phenomenon—that it might actually be embodied as a coding of macromolecules in the brain. This could be in the form of RNA or proteins that are laid down in the membranes of individual neurons. It could imply that all information coming into the nervous system is stored by means of this macromolecular code to be recalled at the appropriate time.

This is a beginning, but already there are many fascinating experiments underway dealing with this phenomenon. It has been shown, for example, that there are chemicals which can interrupt protein and RNA synthesis and that these chemicals seem to produce a disruption of learning. There are other chemicals which may enhance the lying down of these protein networks, and there is some evidence that performance might be improved with certain chemicals. Specific brain regions (the hippocampus) seem to be very important in either the storage or recall of recent memory events. Also, there are electrical changes that occur during learning which can be monitored.

These fascinating possibilities are discussed in the papers in this section. There is comparative information indicating that in the cat complex learning is mediated in part by what is traditionally thought to be sensory visual cortex. It seems that the visual cortex of the cat, like that of the human, participates in more complex tasks than just vision.

The last paper in this section deals with the learning to control responses produced by the autonomic nervous system; that is, how to condition such responses as heart rate, blood pressure, and gastrointestinal activity. This is a very important emerging field that has tremendous implications for the medicine of the future. If it is possible to control the autonomic functions, it might be possible to prevent many disease processes; it opens the possibility for the treatment of already present medical abnormalities, such as cardiac arrhythmias, hypertension, and other conditions.

Loss of recent memory after bilateral hippocampal lesions
william b. scoville
and
brenda milner

In 1954 Scoville described a grave loss of recent memory which he had observed as a sequel to bilateral medial temporal-lobe resection in one psychotic patient and one patient with intractable seizures. In both cases the operations had been radical ones, undertaken only when more conservative forms of treatment had failed. The removals extended posteriorly along the mesial surface of the temporal lobes for a distance of approximately 8 cm from the temporal tips and probably destroyed the anterior two-thirds of the hippocampus and hippocampal gyrus bilaterally, as well as the uncus and amygdala. The unexpected and persistent memory deficit which resulted seemed to us to merit further investigation. We have therefore carried out formal memory and intelligence testing of these two patients and also of eight other patients who had undergone similar, but less radical, bilateral medial temporal-lobe resections. The present paper gives the results of these studies which point to the importance of the hippocampal complex for normal memory function. Whenever the hippocampus and hippogampal gyrus were damaged bilaterally in these operations some memory deficit was found, but not otherwise. We have chosen to report these findings in full, partly for their theoretical significance, and partly as a warning to others of the risk to memory involved in bilateral surgical lesions of the hippocampal region.

From *Journal of Neurology, Neurosurgery, and Psychiatry*, 1957, **20**, 11. Reprinted by permission.

OPERATIONS

During the past seven years in an effort to preserve the overall personality in psychosurgery some 300 fractional lobotomies have been performed, largely on seriously ill schizophrenic patients who had failed to respond to other forms of treatment. The aim in these fractional procedures was to secure as far as possible any beneficial effects a complete frontal lobotomy might have, while at the same time avoiding its undesirable side-effects. And it was in fact found that undercutting limited to the orbital surfaces of both frontal lobes has an appreciable therapeutic effect in psychosis and yet does not cause any new personality deficit to appear (Scoville, Wilk, and Pepe, 1951). In view of the known close relationship between the posterior orbital and mesial temporal cortices (MacLean, 1952; Pribram and Kruger, 1954), it was hoped that still greater psychiatric benefit might be obtained by extending the orbital undercutting so as to destroy parts of the mesial temporal cortex bilaterally. Accordingly, in 30 severely deteriorated cases, such partial temporal-lobe resections were carried out, either with or without orbital undercutting. All the removals have been bilateral, extending for varying distances along the mesial surface of the temporal lobes. Five were limited to the uncus and underlying amygdaloid nucleus; all others encroached also upon the anterior hippocampus, the excisions being carried back 5 cm or more after bisecting the tips of the temporal lobes, with the temporal horn constituting the lateral edge of resection. In one case only in this psychotic group all tissue mesial to the temporal horns for a distance of at least 8 cm posterior to the temporal tips was destroyed, a removal which presumably included the anterior two-thirds of the hippocampal complex bilaterally.

An equally radical bilateral medial temporal-lobe resection was carried out in one young man (H. M.) with a long history of major and minor seizures uncontrollable by maximum medication of various forms, and showing diffuse electroencephalographic abnormality. This frankly experimental operation was considered justifiable because the patient was totally incapacitated by his seizures and these had proven refractory to a medical approach. It was suggested because of the known epileptogenic qualities of the uncus and hippocampal complex and because of the relative absence of post-operative seizures in our temporal-lobe resections as compared with fractional lobotomies in other areas. The operation was carried out with the understanding and approval of the patient and his family, in the hope of lessening his seizures to some extent. At operation the medial surfaces of both temporal lobes were exposed and recordings were taken from both surface and depth electrodes before any tissue was removed; but again no discrete epileptogenic focus was found. Bilateral resection was then carried out, extending posteriorly for a distance of 8 cm from the temporal tips.

RESULTS

The psychiatric findings bearing upon the treatment of schizophrenia have already been reported (Scoville et al., 1953). Briefly, it was found that bilateral resections limited to the medial portions of the temporal lobes were without significant therapeutic effect in psychosis, although individual patients (including the one with the most radical removal) did in fact show some improvement. There have been no gross changes in personality. This is particularly clear in

the case of the epileptic, nonpsychotic patient whose present cheerful placidity does not differ appreciably from his preoperative status and who, in the opinion of his family, has shown no personality change. Neurological changes in the group have also been minimal. The incidence and severity of seizures in the epileptic patient were sharply reduced for the first year after operation, and although he is once again having both major and minor attacks, these attacks no longer leave him stuporous, as they formerly did. It has therefore been possible to reduce his medication considerably. As far as general intelligence is concerned, the epileptic patient has actually improved slightly since operation, possibly because he is less drowsy than before. The psychotic patients were for the most part too disturbed before operation for finer testing of higher mental functions to be carried out, but certainly there is no indication of any general intellectual impairment resulting from the operation in those patients for whom the appropriate test data are available.

There has been one striking and totally unexpected behavioral result: a grave loss of recent memory in those cases in which the medial temporal-lobe resection was so extensive as to involve the major portion of the hippocampal complex bilaterally. The psychotic patient having the most radical excision (extending 8 cm from the tips of the temporal lobes bilaterally) has shown a profound post-operative memory disturbance, but unfortunately this was not recognized at the time because of her disturbed emotional state. In the non-psychotic patient the loss was immediately apparent. After operation this young man could no longer recognize the hospital staff nor find his way to the bathroom, and he seemed to recall nothing of the day-to-day events of his hospital life. There was also a partial retrograde amnesia, inasmuch as he did not remember the death of a favorite uncle three years previously, nor anything of the period in hospital, yet could recall some trivial events that had occurred just before his admission to the hospital. His early memories were apparently vivid and intact.

This patient's memory defect has persisted without improvement to the present time, and numerous illustrations of its severity could be given. Ten months ago the family moved from their old house to a new one a few blocks away on the same street; he still has not learned the new address, though remembering the old one perfectly, nor can he be trusted to find his way home alone. Moreover, he does not know where objects in continual use are kept; for example, his mother still has to tell him where to find the lawn mower, even though he may have been using it only the day before. She also states that he will do the same jigsaw puzzles day after day without showing any practice effect and that he will read the same magazines over and over again without finding their contents familiar. This patient has even eaten luncheon in front of one of us (B. M.) without being able to name, a mere half-hour later, a single item of food he had eaten; in fact, he could not remember having eaten luncheon at all. Yet to a casual observer this man seems like a relatively normal individual, since his understanding and reasoning are undiminished.

The discovery of severe memory defect in these two patients led us to study further all patients in the temporal-lobe series who were sufficiently cooperative to permit formal psychological testing. The operation sample included, in addition to the two radical resections, one bilateral removal of the uncus, extending 4 cm posterior to the temporal tips, and six bilateral medial temporal-lobe resections in which the removal was carried back 5 or 6 cm to include also a portion of the anterior hippocampus; in three of these six cases the temporal-lobe resection was combined with orbital undercutting. One unilateral case was also studied in which right inferior temporal lobectomy and hippocampectomy had been carried out for the relief of incisural herniation due to malignant oedema. We found some memory impairment in all the bilateral cases in which the removal was carried far enough posteriorly to damage the hippocampus and hippocampal gyrus, but in only one of these six additional cases (D. C.) did the memory loss equal in severity that seen in the two most radical excisions. The case with bilateral excision of the uncus (in which the removal can have involved only the amygdaloid and peri-amygdaloid areas) showed excellent memory function. The unilateral operation, extensive as it was, has caused no lasting memory impairment, though some disturbance of recent memory was noted in the early postoperative period (Scoville, 1954); we now attribute this deficit to temporary interference with the functioning of the hippocampal zone of the opposite hemisphere by contralateral pressure.

The histories and individual test results for these 10 cases are reported below, and the Table summarizes the principal findings. For purposes of comparison the cases have been divided into three representing different degrees of memory impairment.

GROUP I: SEVERE MEMORY DEFECT

In this category are those patients who since operation appear to forget the incidents of their daily life as fast as they occur. It is interesting that all these patients were able to retain a three-figure number or a pair of unrelated words for several minutes, if care was taken not to distract them in the interval. However, they forgot the instant attention was diverted to a new topic. Since in normal life the focus of attention is constantly changing, such individuals show an apparently complete anterograde amnesia. This severe defect was observed in the two patients having the most radical bilateral medical temporal-lobe excisions

TABLE 1. CLASSIFICATION OF CASES

Cases	Age at Time of Follow-up (yr.)	Sex	Diagnosis	Operation
Group 1: Severe Memory Defect				
Case 1, H. M.	29	M	Epilepsy	Medial temporal
Case 2, D. C.	47	M	Paranoid schizophrenia	Medial temporal and orbital undercutting
Case 3, M. B.	55	F	Manic-depressive psychosis	Medial temporal
Group II: Moderate Memory Defect				
Case 4, A. Z.	35	F	Paranoid schizophrenia	Medial temporal
Case 5, M. R.	40	F	Paranoid schizophrenia	Medial temporal and orbital undercutting
Case 6, A. R.	38	F	Hebephrenic schizophrenia	Medial temporal and orbital undercutting
Case 7, C. G.	44	F	Schizophrenia	Medial temporal
Case 8, A. L.	31	M	Schizophrenia	Medial temporal
Group III: No Memory Defect				
Case 9, I. S.	54	F	Paranoid schizophrenia	Uncectomy
Case 10, E. G.	55	F	Incisural herniation	Inferior temporal lobectomy

(with the posterior limit of removal approximately 8 cm from the temporal tips) and in one other case, a bilateral 5.5 cm medial temporal excision. These three cases will now be described.

Case 1, H. M. This 29-year-old motor winder, a high school graduate, had had minor seizures since the age of 10 and major seizures since the age of 16. The small attacks lasted about 40 seconds, during which he would be unresponsive, opening his mouth, closing his eyes, and crossing both arms and legs; but he believed that he could "half hear what was going on."

The major seizures occurred without warning and with no lateralizing sign. They were generalized convulsions, with tongue-biting, urinary incontinence, and loss of consciousness followed by prolonged somnolence. Despite heavy and varied anticonvulsant medication the major attacks had increased in frequency and severity through the years until the patient was quite unable to work.

The aetiology of this patient's attacks is not clear. He was knocked down by a bicycle at the age of 9 and was unconscious for five minutes afterwards, sustaining a laceration of the

Bi- or Uni- lateral	Approximate Extent of Removal Along Medial Temporal Lobes (cm.)	Time Between Operation and Testing (mth.)	Wechsler Scale	
			Intelli- gence Quotient	Memory Quotient
B	8.	20	112	67
B	5.5	21	122	70
B	8	28	78	60
B	5	40	96	84
B	5	39	123	81
B	4.5	47	Incomplete	
B	5.5	41	Incomplete	
B	6	38	Incomplete	
B	4	53	122	125
U-Rt.	9	16	93	90

left supraorbital region. Later radiological studies, however, including two pneumoencephalograms, have been completely normal, and the physical examination has always been negative.

Electroencephalographic studies have consistently failed to show any localized epileptogenic area. In the examination of August 17, 1953, Dr. T. W. Liberson described diffuse slow activity with a dominant frequency of 6 to 8 per second. A short clinical attack was said to be accompanied by generalized 2 to 3 per second spike-and-wave discharge with a slight asymmetry in the central leads (flattening on the left).

Despite the absence of any localizing sign, operation was considered justifiable for the reasons given above. On September 1, 1953, bilateral medial temporal-lobe resection was carried out, extending posteriorly for a distance of 8 cm from the midpoints of the tips of the temporal lobes, with the temporal horns constituting the lateral edges of resection.

After operation the patient was drowsy for a few days, but his subsequent recovery was uneventful apart from the grave memory loss already

described. There has been no neurological deficit. An electroencephalogram taken one year after operation
showed increased spike-and-wave
activity which was maximal over the
frontal areas and bilaterally synchronous. He continues to have seizures,
but these are less incapacitating than
before.

Psychological examination. This was
performed on April 26, 1955. The
memory defect was immediately apparent. The patient gave the date as
March, 1953, and his age as 27. Just
before coming into the examining
room he had been talking to Dr. Karl
Pribram, yet he had no recollection of
this at all and denied that anyone had
spoken to him. In conversation, he
reverted constantly to boyhood events
and seemed scarcely to realize that he
had had an operation.

On formal testing the contrast between his good general intelligence
and his defective memory was most
striking. On the Wechsler-Bellevue
Intelligence Scale he achieved a full-
scale I.Q. rating of 112, which compares favorably with the pre-operative
rating of 104 reported by Dr. Liselotte
Fischer in August, 1953, the improvement in arithmetic being particularly
striking. An extensive test battery
failed to reveal any deficits in perception, abstract thinking, or reasoning
ability, and his motivation remained
excellent throughout.

On the Wechsler Memory Scale
(Wechsler, 1945) his immediate recall
of stories and drawings fell far below
the average level and on the "associate
learning" subtest of this scale he
obtained zero scores for the hard word
associations, low scores for the easy
associations, and failed to improve
with repeated practice. These findings
are reflected in the low memory quotient of 67. Moreover, on all tests we
found that once he had turned to a
new task the nature of the preceding

one could no longer be recalled, nor
the test recognized if repeated.

In summary, this patient appears to
have a complete loss of memory for
events subsequent to bilateral medial
temporal-lobe resection 19 months
before, together with a partial retrograde amnesia for the three years leading up to his operation; but early
memories are seemingly normal and
there is no impairment of personality
or general intelligence.

Case 2, D. C. This 47-year-old doctor
was a paranoid schizophrenic with a
four-year history of violent, combative
behavior. Before his illness he had
been practicing medicine in Chicago,
but he had always shown paranoid
trends and for this reason had had
difficulty completing his medical
training. His breakdown followed the
loss of a lawsuit in 1950, at which time
he made a homicidal attack on his wife
which led to his admission to hospital.
Since then both insulin and electro-
shock therapy had been tried without
benefit and the prognosis was considered extremely poor. On May 13,
1954, at the request of Dr. Frederick
Gibbs and Dr. John Kendrick, a bilateral medial temporal-lobe resection
combined with orbital undercutting
was carried out at Manteno State
Hospital (W. B. S., with the assistance
of Dr. John Kendrick). The posterior
limit of the removal was 5 cm from the
sphenoid ridge, or roughly 5.5 cm
from the tips of the temporal lobes,
with the inferior horns of the ventricles
forming the lateral edges of resection.
Recording from depth electrodes at
the time of operation showed spiking
from the medial temporal regions
bilaterally with some spread to the
orbital surfaces of both frontal lobes,
but after the removal had been completed a normal electroencephalographic record was obtained from the
borders of the excision.

Post-operative recovery was uneventful and there has been no neurological deficit. Since operation the patient has been outwardly friendly and tractable with no return of his former aggressive behavior, although the paranoid thought content persists; he is considered markedly improved. But he too shows a profound memory disturbance. At Manteno State Hospital he was described as "confused," because since the operation he had been unable to find his way to bed and seemed no longer to recognize the hospital staff. However, no psychological examination was made there, and on November 29, 1955, he was transferred to Galesburg State Research Institute where he was interviewed by one of us (B. M.) on January 12, 1956.

Psychological findings. This patient presented exactly the same pattern of memory loss as H. M. He was courteous and cooperative throughout the examination, and the full-scale Wechsler I.Q. rating of 122 showed him to be still of superior intellect. Yet he had no idea where he was, explaining that naturally the surroundings were quite unfamiliar because he had only arrived there for the first time the night before. (In fact, he had been there six weeks.) He was unable to learn either the name of the hospital or the name of the examiner, despite being told them repeatedly. Each time he received the information as something new, and a moment later would deny having heard it. At the examiner's request he drew a dog and an elephant, yet half an hour later did not even recognize them as his own drawings. On the formal tests of the Wechsler Memory Scale his immediate recall of stories and drawings was poor, and the memory quotient of 70 is in sharp contrast to the high I.Q. level. As with H. M., once a new task was introduced there was total amnesia for the preceding one; in his own words, the change of topic confused him. This man did not

know that he had had a brain operation and did not recall being at Manteno State Hospital, although he had spent six months there before the operation as well as six months post-operatively. Yet he could give minute details of his early life and medical training (accurately, as far as we could tell).

Case 3, M. B. This 55-year-old manic-depressive woman, a former clerical worker, was admitted to Connecticut State Hospital on December 27, 1951, at which time she was described as anxious, irritable, argumentative, and restless, but well-orientated in all spheres. Her recent memory was normal, in that she knew how long she had been living in Connecticut and could give the date of her hospital admission and the exact times of various clinic appointments. On December 18, 1952, a radical bilateral medial temporal-lobe resection was carried out, with the posterior limit of removal 8 cm from the temporal tips. Post-operatively she was stuporous and confused for one week, but then recovered rapidly and without neurological deficit. She has become neater and more even-tempered and is held to be greatly improved. However, psychological testing by Mr. I. Borganz in November, 1953, revealed a grave impairment of recent memory; she gave the year as 1950 and appeared to recall nothing of the events of the last three years. Yet her verbal intelligence proved to be normal.

She was examined briefly by B. M. in April, 1955, at which time she showed a global loss of recent memory similar to that of H. M. and D. C. She had been brought to the examining room from another building, but had already forgotten this; nor could she describe any other part of the hospital although she had been living there continuously for nearly three and a half years. On the Wechsler Memory Scale her immediate recall of stories and drawings was inaccurate and fragmentary, and delayed recall was impossible for her even with prompting; when the material was presented again she failed to recognize it. Her conversation centered around her early life and she was unable to give any information about the years of her hospital stay. Vocabulary, attention span, and comprehension were normal, thus confirming Mr. Borganz' findings.

GROUP II: MODERATELY SEVERE MEMORY DEFECT

In this second category are those patients who can be shown to retain some impression of new places and events, although they are unable to learn such arbitrary new associations as people's names and cannot be depended upon to carry out commissions. Subjectively, these patients complain of memory difficulty, and objectively, on formal tests, they do very poorly irrespective of the type of material to be memorized. The five remaining patients with bilateral medial temporal-lobe removals extending 5 or 6 cm posteriorly from the temporal tips make up this group. Only two of these patients were well enough to permit thorough testing, but in all five cases enough data were obtained to establish that the patient did have a memory defect and that it was not of the gross type seen in Group 1. The individual cases are reported below.

Case 4, A. Z. This 35-year-old woman, a paranoid schizophrenic, had been in Connecticut State Hospital for three years and extensive electroshock therapy had been tried without lasting benefit. She was described as tense, assaultative, and sexually preoccupied. On November 29, 1951, bilateral medial temporal-lobe resection was carried out under local anesthesia, the posterior limit of the removal being approximately 5 cm

from the tips of the temporal lobes. During subpial resection of the right hippocampal cortex the surgeon inadvertently went through the arachnoid and injured by suction a portion of the right peduncle, geniculate, or hypothalamic region with immediate development of deep coma. The injury was visualized by extraarachnoid inspection. Post-operatively the patient remained in stupor for 72 hours and exhibited a left spastic hemiplegia, contracted fixed pupils, strabismus, and lateral nystagmus of the right eye; vital signs remained constant and within normal limits. She slowly recovered the use of the left arm and leg and her lethargy gradually disappeared. By the seventh postoperative day she could walk without support and pupillary responses had returned to normal. The only residual neurological deficit has been a left homonymous hemianopia. Of particular interest was the dramatic post-operative improvement in her psychotic state with an early complete remission of her delusions, anxiety, and paranoid behavior. At the same time she showed a retrograde amnesia for the entire period of her illness.

This patient was discharged from the hospital nine months after operation and is now able to earn her living as a domestic worker. However, she complains that her memory is poor, and psychological examination (April 27, 1955) three and a half years postoperatively confirms this. But the deficit is less striking than in the three cases reported above. This patient, for example, was able to give the address of the house where she worked although she had been there only two days, and she could even describe the furnishings in some detail although she had not yet learned the name of her employer. She was also able to give an accurate, though sketchy, description of a doctor who had spoken to her briefly that morning and whom she had never seen before. However, she could recall very little of the conversation.

Formal testing at this time showed her intelligence to lie within the average range with no impairment of attention or concentration. The Wechsler-Bellevue I.Q. rating was 96. On the Wechsler Memory Scale her immediate recall of stories was normal, but passing from one story to the next was enough to make her unable to recall the first one, though a few fragments could be recovered with judicious prompting. She showed the same rapid forgetting on the "visual retention" subtest, indicating that the memory impairment was not specific to verbal material. Finally, she was conspicuously unsuccessful on the "associate learning" subtest, failing to master a single unfamiliar word association. This examination as a whole provides clear evidence of an impairment of recent memory.

Case 5, M. R. This 40-year-old woman, a paranoid schizophrenic with superimposed alcoholism, had been a patient at Norwich State Hospital for 11 years, receiving extensive electro-shock therapy. Bilateral medial temporal-lobe resection combined with orbital undercutting was carried out on January 17, 1952, the posterior extent of removal being roughly 5 cm from the temporal tips. The patient has shown complete remission of psychotic symptoms and was discharged from the hospital on September 16, 1954, to the care of her family.

Psychological examination. This was performed on April 29, 1955. Tests showed this woman to be of superior intelligence, with a full-scale I.Q. rating of 123 on the Wechsler Scale. However, she complained of poor memory, adding that she could remember faces and "the things that are important," by that, to her great em-

barrassment, she forgot many ordinary daily happenings. Upon questioning she gave the year correctly but did not know the month or the day. She knew that she had had an operation in 1952 but did not recognize the surgeon (W. B. S.) nor recall his name. Formal testing revealed the same pattern of memory disturbance as A. Z. had shown, and the memory quotient of 81 compares most unfavorably with the high I.Q. rating. In conversation, she reverted constantly to discussion of her work during the years of depression and showed little knowledge of recent events.

Case 6, A. R. This 38-year-old woman had been in hospital for five years with a diagnosis of hebephrenic schizophrenia. Before operation she was said to be noisy, combative, and suspicious, and electro-shock therapy had caused only transient improvement in this condition. On May 31, 1951, bilateral medial temporal-lobe resection combined with orbital undercutting was carried out, the posterior limit of removal being slightly less than 5 cm from the bisected tips of the temporal lobes. After operation the patient gradually became quieter and more cooperative and on September 29, 1952, she was discharged to her home. There have been no neurological sequelae.

Psychological examination. This was performed in April, 1955. Examination revealed a hyperactive woman, too excited and talkative for prolonged testing. She showed a restricted span of attention but scores on verbal intelligence tests were within the dull normal range. Moreover, she appeared to recall some recent happenings quite well. Thus, she knew that her daughter had caught a 7 o'clock train to New York City that morning to buy a dress for a wedding the following Saturday. She could also describe the clothes worn by a secretary who had shown her into the office. However, on formal testing some impairment of recent memory was seen, although unlike the other patients in this group she did succeed on some of the difficult items of the "associate learning" test. As with A. Z. and M. R., the deficit appeared most clearly on tests of delayed recall after a brief interval filled with some other activity. Thus, on the "logical memory" test she gave an adequate version of each story immediately after hearing it, but passing from one story to the next caused her to forget the first almost completely; similar results were obtained for the recall of drawings. We conclude that this patient has a memory impairment identical in type to that of the other patients in this group, but somewhat milder. It is interesting that she had a relatively small excision.

Case 7, C. G. This 44-year-old schizophrenic woman had been in the hospital for 20 years without showing any improvement in her psychosis. On November 19, 1951, bilateral medial temporal-lobe resection was carried out under local anesthesia, the posterior limit of removal being 5.5 cm. from the tips of the temporal lobes. There was temporary loss of consciousness during the resection but the patient was fully conscious at the end of the procedure and postoperative recovery was uneventful. There has been no neurological deficit. She is considered to be in better contact than before but more forgetful.

This patient was examined at Norwich State Hospital in April, 1955, and although she was too distractible for prolonged testing, it was possible to show that she remembered some recent events. For example, she knew that she had been working in the hospital beauty parlor for the

past week and that she had been washing towels that morning. Yet formal memory testing revealed the same deficit as that shown by A. Z. and M. R., though less extensive data were obtained in this case.

Case 8, A. L. This 31-year-old schizophrenic man had been a patient at Norwich State Hospital since October, 1950. He had first become ill in August, 1950, demonstrating a catatonic type of schizophrenia with auditory and visual hallucinations. On January 31, 1952, bilateral medial temporal-lobe resection combined with orbital undercutting was carried out, the removal extending posteriorly for a distance of 6 cm along the mesial surface of the temporal lobes. Recovery was uneventful and no neurological deficit ensued. The patient has been more tractable since the operation but he is still subject to delusions and hallucinations. He is said to have a memory defect. When interviewed by B. M. in April, 1955, he was found to be too out of contact for extensive formal testing. However, he was able to recall the examiner's name and place of origin 10 minutes after hearing them for the first time, and this despite the fact that the interval had been occupied with other tasks. He could also recognize objects which had been shown to him earlier in the interview, selecting them correctly from others which he had not seen before. But his immediate recall of drawings and stories was faulty and these were forgotten completely once his attention was directed to a new topic.

In this patient we stress the negative findings: despite his evident psychosis he did not show the severe memory loss typical of the patients in Group I. Yet the brief psychological examination and the hospital record both indicate some impairment of recent memory, though no reliable quantitative studies could be made.

GROUP III:
NO PERSISTENT MEMORY DEFECT

Case 9, I. S. This 54-year-old woman had a 20-year history of paranoid schizophrenia, with auditory hallucinations and marked emotional lability. She had attempted suicide on several occasions. On November 16, 1950, six months after admission to a state hospital, a bilateral medial temporal lobectomy was carried out under local anesthesia with sectioning of the tips of the temporal lobes and subpial suction removal of the medial portion, extending back 4 cm to include the uncus and amygdala. Thus this was a conservative bilateral removal, sparing the hippocampal region. The operation was complicated by accidental damage to the midbrain from the electrocautery, causing the patient to give a convulsive twitch which was followed by coma and extensive rigidity. After operation she was somnolent for a time with continuing rigidity, more marked on the left side than on the right. Vital signs were normal. She required traction to prevent flexure spasm contractures. There was slow improvement over the ensuing two months, with some residual clumsiness and spasticity of gait. For a time the patient's mental state was worse than before operation, but within three months she had improved markedly, with increased gentleness, diminished auditory hallucinations, and no depression. She ultimately showed the best result of all the cases in this series and was discharged from the hospital five months after operation.

This patient was reexamined on May 11, 1956. She shows a complete remission of her former psychotic behavior and is living at home with her husband and leading a normal social life. Her hallucinations have ceased. Upon neurological examination she shows

some 25 percent residual deficit, manifested chiefly by spastic incoordination of gait and similar but less marked incoordination of the arms. The deep leg reflexes are increased to near clonus, but there is no Babinski sign. Arm reflexes are moderately increased and abdominal reflexes absent. Smell is completely lost but all other sense modalities are intact and other cranial nerves normal.

Psychological findings. The patient was examined psychologically in April, 1955. From the standpoint of memory, this patient presents a complete contrast to the cases reported above, obtaining excellent scores for both immediate and delayed recall of stories, drawings, and word associations, and describing accurately episodes from the relatively early post-operative period. The memory quotient of 125 is consistent with the I.Q. level of 122, and both would be classed as superior. This is so despite prolonged psychosis, intensive electro-shock therapy, and brainstem damage of undetermined extent.

Case 10, E. G. This 55-year-old woman developed malignant oedema after removal of a huge, saddle-type meningioma from the right sphenoid ridge; the pupils were dilated, she lost consciousness, and vital signs began to fail. A diagnosis of incisural hippocampal herniation was made, and, as a life-saving measure, unilateral nondominant inferior temporal lobectomy was carried out, with deliberate resection of the hippocampus and hippocampal gyrus to a distance of 9 cm from the tip of the temporal lobe. Vital signs improved immediately and consciousness gradually returned, but for a few weeks the patient showed a disturbance of recent memory resembling that seen in our bilateral cases. However, follow-up studies in April, 1955, 16 months after operation, showed no residual memory loss. Both immediate and delayed recall were normal and the memory quotient of 90 was completely consistent with the I.Q. level of 93. Neurological examination at this time showed a left homonymous visual field defect with macular sparing but no other deficit.

DISCUSSION

The findings in these 10 cases point to the importance of the hippocampal region for normal memory function. All patients in this series having bilateral medial temporal-lobe resections extensive enough to damage portions of the hippocampus and hippocampal gyrus bilaterally have shown a clear and persistent disturbance of recent memory, and in the two most radical excisions (in which the posterior limit of removal was at least 8 cm from the temporal tips) the deficit has been particularly severe, with no improvement in the two or more years which have elapsed since operation. These observations suggest a positive relationship between the extent of destruction to the hippocampal complex specifically and the degree of memory impairment. The correlation is not perfect, since D. C., who had only a 5.5 cm removal, showed as much deficit as did the two cases of most radical excision. Moreover, in the absence of necropsy material we cannot be sure of the exact area removed.

In all these hippocampal resections the uncus and amygdala have also of course been destroyed. Nevertheless the importance of the amygdaloid and periamygdaloid region for memory mechanisms is open to question, considering the total lack of memory impairment in the bilateral uncectomy case (I. S.), in which a 4 cm medial-temporal lobe removal was made. But not enough is known of the effects of lesions restricted to the hippocampal area itself to permit assessment of the relative contributions of these two regions. This is a question on which selective ablation studies in animals could well shed important light, but unfortunately the crucial experiments have yet to be done (Jasper, Gloor, and Milner, 1956).

The role of the hippocampus specifically has been discussed in some clinical studies. Glees and Griffith (1952) put forward the view that bilateral destruction of the hippocampus in man causes recent-memory loss and mental confusion, citing in support of this a somewhat unconvincing case of Grünthal (1947) and also a case of their own in which the hippocampus, the hippocampal and fusiform gyri, and 75 percent of the fornix fibers had been destroyed bilaterally by vascular lesion, but in which the rest of the brain appeared normal at necropsy. Interestingly enough, the amygdaloid nuclei were found to be intact as were the mamillary bodies. This patient showed marked anterograde and retrograde amnesia.

More recently Milner and Penfield (1955) have described a memory loss similar in all respects to that shown by our patients, in two cases of unilateral partial temporal lobectomy in the dominant hemisphere. In one case the removal was carried out in two stages separated by a five-year interval, and the memory loss followed the second operation only, at which time the uncus, hippocampus, and hippocampal gyrus alone were excised. Although these authors had carried out careful psychological testing in over 90 other cases of similar unilateral operation, only in these two cases was a general memory loss found. To account for the unusual deficit, they have assumed that there was in each case a pre-operatively unsuspected, but more or less completely destructive lesion of the hippocampal area of the opposite hemisphere. The unilateral operation would then deprive the patient of hippocampal function bilaterally, thus causing memory loss. The present study provides strong support for this interpretation.

Memory loss after partial bilateral

temporal lobectomy has been reported by Petit-Dutaillis, Christophe, Pertuiset, Dreyfus-Brisac, and Blanc (1954) but in their patient the deficit was a transient one, a finding which led these authors to question the primary importance of the temporal lobes for memory function. However, their temporal lobe removals were complementary to ours in that they destroyed the lateral neocortex bilaterally but spared the hippocampal gyrus on the right and the uncus and hippocampus on the left. It therefore seems likely that the memory loss was due to temporary interference with the functioning of the hippocampal system, which later recovered.

We have stated that the loss seen in patients with bilateral hippocampal lesions is curiously specific to the domain of recent memory; neither in our cases nor in those of Milner and Penfield was there any deterioration in intellect or personality as a result of hippocampal resection. It appears important to emphasize this, since Terzian and Dalle Ore (1955) have described gross behavioral changes (affecting memory, perception, and sexual behavior) after bilateral temporal lobectomy in man; they consider these changes comparable to Klüver and Bucy's (1939) findings after radical bilateral temporal lobectomy in the monkey. But Terzian and Ore included not only the uncal and hippocampal areas, but also the lateral temporal cortex in their bilateral removal. In contrast to the grossly deteriorated picture they describe, we find that bilateral resections limited to the mesial temporal region cause no perceptual disturbance, even on visual tests known to be sensitive to unilateral lesions of the temporal neocortex (Milner, 1954).

The findings reported herein have led us to attribute a special importance to the anterior hippocampus and hippocampal gyrus in the retention of new experience. But the hippocampus has a strong and orderly projection to the mamillary bodies (Simpson, 1952), and as early as 1928 Gamper claimed that lesions of the mamillary bodies were commonly found in amnesic states of the Korsakoff type. Moreover, Williams and Pennybacker (1954) have carried out careful psychological studies of 180 patients with verified intracranial lesions and find that a specific deficit in recent memory is most likely to occur when the lesion involves the mamillary region. It is possible, then, that when we have two interrelated structures (hippocampus and mamillary bodies) damage to either can cause memory loss, a point which has been emphasized by Jasper and others (1956). In view of these findings it is interesting that sectioning the fornix bilaterally, and thereby interrupting the descending fibers from the hippocampus, appears to have little effect on behavior (Dott, 1938; Garcia Bengochea, De la Torre, Esquivel, Vieta, and Fernandez, 1954), though a transient memory deficit is sometimes seen (Garcia Bengochea, 1955).

To conclude, the observations reported herein demonstrate the deleterious effect of bilateral surgical lesions of the hippocampus and hippocampal gyrus on recent memory. The relationship between this region and the overlying neocortex in the temporal lobe needs further elucidation, as does its relationship to deeper-lying structures.

SUMMARY

Bilateral medial temporal-lobe resection in man results in a persistent impairment of recent memory whenever the removal is carried far enough posteriorly to damage portions of the anterior hippocampus and hippocampal gyrus. This conclusion is based on formal psychological testing of nine cases (eight psychotic and one epileptic) carried out from one and one-half to four years after operation.

The degree of memory loss appears to depend on the extent of hippocampal removal. In two cases in which bilateral resection was carried to a distance of 8 cm posterior to the temporal tips the loss was particularly severe.

Removal of only the uncus and amygdala bilaterally does not appear to cause memory impairment.

A case of unilateral inferior temporal lobectomy with radical posterior extension to include the major portion of the hippocampus and hippocampal gyrus showed no lasting memory loss. This is consistent with Milner and Penfield's negative findings in a long series of unilateral removals for temporal-lobe epilepsy.

The memory loss in these cases of medial temporal-lobe excision involved both anterograde and some retrograde amnesia, but left early memories and technical skills intact. There was no deterioration in personality or general intelligence, and no complex perceptual disturbance such as is seen after a more complete bilateral temporal lobectomy.

It is concluded that the anterior hippocampus and hippocampal gyrus, either separately or together, are critically concerned in the retention of current experience. It is not known whether the amygdala plays any part in this mechanism, since the hippocampal complex has not been removed alone, but always together with uncus and amygdala.

References

Dott, N. M. In W. E. Clark, Beattie J. Le Gros, G. Riddoch, and N. M. Dott. *The hypothalamus: Morphological, functional, clinical and surgical aspects.* Edinburgh: Oliver and Boyd, 1938.

Gamper, E. *Dtsch. Z. Nervenheilk.*, 1928, **102**, 122.

Garcia Bengochea, F. Personal Communication, 1955.

Garcia Bengochea, F., De la Torre, O., Esquivel, O., Vieta, R., and Fernandez, C. *Trans. Amer. neurol. Ass.*, 1954, **79**, 176.

Glees, P., and Griffith, H. B. *Mschr. Psychiat. Neurol.*, 1952, **123**, 193.

Grünthal, E. *Mschr. Psychiat. Neurol.*, 1947, **113**, 1.

Jasper, H., Gloor, P., and Milner, B. *Ann. Rev. Physiol.*, 1956, **18**, 359.

Klüver, H., and Bucy, P. C. *Arch. Neurol. Psychiat. (Chicago)*, 1939, **42**, 979.

MacLean, P. D. *Electroenceph. clin. Neurophysiol.*, 1952 **4**, 407.

Milner, B. *Psychol. Bull.*, 1954, **51**, 42.

Milner, B., and Penfield, W. *Trans. Amer. neurol. Ass.*, 1955, **80**, 42.

Petit-Dutaillis, D., Christophe, J., Pertuiset, B., Dreyfus-Brisac, C., and Blanc, C. *Rev. neurol. (Paris)*, 1954, **91**, 129.

Pribram, K. H., and Kruger, L. *Ann. N.Y. Acad. Sci.*, 1954, **58**, 109.

Scoville, W. B. *J. Neurosurg.*, 1954, **11**, 64.

Scoville, W. B., Dunsmore, R. H., Liberson, W. T., Henry, C. E., and Pepe, A. *Res. Publ. Ass. nerv. ment. Dis.*, 1953, **31**, 347.

Scoville, W. B., Wilk, E. K., and Pepe, A. *J. Amer. J. Psychiat.*, 1951, **107**, 730.

Simpson, D. A. *Journal of Neurology, Neurosurgery and Psychiatry*, 1952, **15**, 79.

Terzian, H., and Dalle Ore, G. *Neurology*, 1955, **5**, 373.

Wechsler, D. *J. Psychol.*, 1945, **19**, 87.

Williams, M., and Pennybacker, J. *Journal of Neurology, Neurosurgery and Psychiatry*, 1954, **17**, 155.

Molecular theories of memory

wesley dingman and michael b. sporn

Recently there has been a surge of interest, both theoretical and experimental, in what might be called "the molecular basis of memory." The spectacular success of recent investigations of the molecular basis of transmission of genetic information has suggested that there may be an analogous molecular mechanism for storing and utilizing experiential information during the life of the individual—that is, that the memory of an experiential event is stored in the nervous system by the formation or alteration of a particular molecule or set of molecules, which may be regarded as a molecular engram or memory trace. Various types of molecules, including DNA, RNA, proteins, and lipids, have been suggested as the actual engram. This article is an attempt to provide a critique, rather than a comprehensive review, of certain theoretical and experimental approaches to this general hypothesis. Since the particular hypothesis that specific changes in neuronal RNA represent the molecular engram of memory has received special attention of late, we consider it in some detail here. Our aim is to use this particular molecular theory to illustrate the problems that are fundamental to all purely molecular theories which fail to consider the cellular environment within which molecules exist.

RNA AND MEMORY

A large number of experiments have now been performed which support the

From *Science*, **144**, 26–29, 3 April 1964. Copyright © 1964 by the American Association for the Advancement of Science.

view that RNA metabolism may be intimately connected with memory storage and learning. Although there is still a definite controversy about some of the methods and techniques that have been used in these investigations, we limit this discussion to interpretations of experimental data and do not discuss experimental methods. The most direct suggestion that RNA metabolism is involved in memory storage is the report (Hyden and Egyhazi, 1962) that a significant change in the base composition of nuclear RNA of Deiters' nerve cells occurs when a rat learns a balancing task (the adenine-to-uracil ratio of the nuclear RNA of these cells was reported to be increased significantly) and that this change persists for at least 48 hours after the end of the learning experiment. Changes in the base composition of RNA in associated glial cells were also reported in these studies (Hyden and Egyhazi, 1963).

The formation of an epileptogenic mirror focus, a neurophysiological model of memory, has been shown to be correlated with an increase in the total amount of neuronal RNA in the cells involved (Morrell, 1961). Furthermore, studies on planarians have indicated that ribonuclease blocks the retention of a conditioned response in regenerating planarian tails (Corning and John, 1961), and it has been claimed that learning is transferable from one planarian to another by way of cannibalistic ingestion (McConnell, 1962). However, the interpretation of the cannibalism data is by no means straightforward, since it appears that in these experiments it was transfer of the general capacity to learn, rather than transfer of the specific learning of a particular task, that was being measured. 8-Azaguanine, a purine analog which can cause formation of nonfunctional RNA (Creaser, 1956), has been found to depress a rat's ability to learn a new maze without impairing its ability to traverse and recall a previously well-learned maze (Dingman and Sporn, 1961). This same antimetabolite was also shown to prolong the interval required for "fixation of experience" in an assay in which the spinal cord of rats was used (Chamberlain, Rothschild, and Gerard, 1963); moreover, in the latter report it was noted that 1,1,3-tricyano-2-amino-1-propene, a drug believed to increase the RNA concentration of neurons (Egyhazi and Hyden, 1961), shortens the interval required for "fixation of experience." Finally, long-term administration of yeast RNA has been reported to improve memory function in human subjects with cerebral arterisclerotic and presenile dementia (Cameron and Solyom, 1961); and, in animal experiments, long-term treatment with yeast RNA increased the rate at which the animal required a behavioral response motivated by shock (Cook et al., 1963).

CRITERIA FOR A
PERMANENT MEMORY TRACE

None of the experiments just described directly tests the proposition that an RNA molecule, or set of molecules, represents the molecular engram which is the permanent memory trace; they merely stress the fact that RNA metabolism is an important parameter of neuronal function. In order to prove that a given molecule or set of molecules may be regarded as a permanent memory trace, a more rigorous set of criteria should be met.

We suggest that the following criteria must be satisfied in order to demonstrate that a given molecule, set of molecules, structure, or set of structures is indeed a permanent memory trace. (1) It must

undergo a change of state in response to the experience to be remembered. (2) The altered state must persist as long as the memory can be demonstrated. (3) Specific destruction of the altered state must result in permanent loss of the memory.

If these criteria are applied to the experimental data relating RNA and memory, it is apparent that the evidence that RNA molecules are specific memory traces is highly circumstantial at present. In particular, a change in the base composition of nuclear RNA in cells involved in a learning task does not necessarily signify that these RNA molecules are permanent memory traces; it might signify that they are transient intermediates in the formation of permanent memory traces, or merely that changes in RNA occur concomitantly with learning. The effects of ribonuclease on learning in planarians may also be regarded in this fashion, since this enzyme was applied during the time the "trained" tail was regenerating a head, and presumably, then, during the process of formation of permanent memory traces in the regenerating head. Likewise, in the experiments in which drugs were used to affect RNA metabolism during the fixation of experience, the drugs were active at the time the proper functioning of transient intermediates in the formation of memory traces would be expected to be important.

In summary, not all the experiments cited have yet satisfied criteria 2 and 3 for establishing a set of molecules as a permanent memory trace. Indeed, any attempt to show the specific destruction of a particular set of molecules results in the permanent loss of an already established memory trace would appear to be beset with great experimental difficulties. Thus, in experimental work on the RNA hypothesis, it has not yet been possible to distinguish between the following alternatives:

(1) RNA molecules, like many other types of molecules, are important con-

stituents of the nervous system, whose structural and functional state may change dramatically during a learning experience, but they do not function as permanent memory traces; or

(2) RNA molecules do have a unique role in the nervous system, that of serving as the final engram of experiential memory, the permanent memory trace.

A RESTATEMENT OF THE PROBLEM

It should be apparent that there is now an abundance of data which suggests some relationship between RNA metabolism in brain and the process of memory storage. What, however, is known about the specificity of this relationship? The major function of all known types of RNA is participation in protein synthesis (Watson, 1963); no other function has thus far been demonstrated for RNA in the brain. Since protein synthesis is one of the most fundamental of all cellular processes, and since the proteins of a cell are largely responsible for its behavior, one would expect that the process of memory storage in a neuron might well involve some participation of the protein-synthesizing mechanism (Waelsch and Lajtha, 1961). It is not surprising to find that this mechanism may undergo some change of state during cellular activity, or that interference with this mechanism may cause changes in the overall behavior of a cell. Indeed, it would be more surprising if it could be unequivocally demonstrated that RNA function is in no way involved in memory storage. The important point is that proponents of the RNA hypothesis have yet to demonstrate that a unique set of RNA molecules functions as specific permanent memory traces. Criticisms of the RNA hypothesis similar to this one have also been made by Briggs and Kitto (1962).

At this point one might raise the question: is there perhaps an inherent difficulty in any hypothesis which attempts to explain the encoding of memory solely in terms of one set of molecules? Cellular metabolism is not merely a rigid hierarchy whereby DNA controls the synthesis of RNA, RNA controls the synthesis of proteins, and proteins control the synthesis of other metabolites in the cell. Rather, the cell has many regulatory mechanisms, whereby proteins, hormones, and metabolites of low molecular weight may regulate the synthesis of RNA by DNA, as well as many feedback mechanisms for the regulation of functional activity of enzymes (Karlson, 1963). Thus, one cannot logically specify one set of molecules as totally controlling the activities of another set. Furthermore, in the neuron, in which certain functional activities (for example, RNA synthesis) are localized in the cell body and other functional activities (for example, synaptic transmission) are localized in peripheral processes of the cell, the cell body and peripheral synaptic structures exert mutual regulatory effects. Consequently, proper functioning of the nucleic-acid- and protein-synthesizing mechanisms of the cell body is necessary for the proper maintenance of synaptic structure (Waelsch and Lajtha, 1961), and the phenomenon of axoplasmic flow would appear to provide the necessary communication channel whereby centrally synthesized metabolites reach the peripheral synaptic regions (Weiss and Hiscoe, 1948). Moreover, proper synaptic function is necessary for the proper performance of the nucleic-acid- and protein-synthesizing structures of the cell body. A great deal of experimental work indicates that pronounced changes in the state of RNA and proteins occur in the cell body of a neuron that is actively stimulated (Hyden, 1960), and, conversely, that removal of afferent stimulation of a neuron can also cause marked changes in its cell body (Mendelson and Ervin, 1962). The latter phenomenon is dramatically illustrated by the extreme degeneration of cell bodies of retinal ganglion cells of rabbits that were born and raised in darkness and never received visual stimulation (Brattgard, 1952). Moreover, there is much evidence, from the neuro-embryological literature, which indicates that the nature of efferent connections of neurons may influence the structure and function of the cell body (Weiss, 1955). Whereas we now understand the details of some aspects of the synthetic mechanisms (for example, RNA and protein synthesis) whereby the metabolism of the cell body may control synaptic function, we have almost no understanding of the mechanisms whereby synaptic function may control the metabolism of the cell body.

Thus we may perhaps more adequately investigate the structural basis of the permanent memory trace if we seek to answer the following questions: what permanent changes in neuronal structure and function result from stimulation of the neuron; and what is the mechanism of production of these changes? In such an approach an attempt is made to bridge the gap between current investigations, which emphasize the importance of particular molecules in memory storage, and the more cytologically and physiologically oriented theories of Raman y Cajal (1910), Hebb (1949), and Sholl (1956), in which emphasis is on the importance of synaptic interrelationships between neurons. These older theories stressed the role of growth of new axonal and dendritic connections as a fundamental process in memory storage and learning. At the time they were formulated, little was known of the molecular biochemistry of nucleic acid and protein synthesis, and thus there is an incompleteness in these formulations. It is now apparent that the molecular and the cytological approaches to the problem of memory are by no means mutually exclusive, especially if one postulates that a major function of the synthetic mechanisms of the cell body is to provide molecules necessary

for the growth and maintenance of axonal and dendritic connections. Weiss (1961) has stressed that the adult neuron, as well as the immature neuron, appears to be in a perpetual state of growth or regeneration, or both, and he has emphasized the importance of axoplasmic flow for this process. The axonal termination of a synapse is essentially devoid of ribosomes (Palay, 1956), which are necessary for protein synthesis; hence, any new proteins required for new axonal growth would, presumably, have to be synthesized in the cell body and reach new synapses by the process of axoplasmic flow. The major advantage of including synaptic structure and function in any hypothesis of memory storage is that one thereby takes into consideration a unique cytological feature of the neuron—namely, the fact that such a vast amount of its surface area (Sholl, 1956) and functional mass (Lowry et al., 1954; Friede, 1961) is located a great distance from the central cell body. As Sholl (1956) has noted, "The activity of a single cortical neuron may well affect that of 4000 other neurons, [while] a single neuron may have more than 50 dendritic branches." No other type of cell in the body has thus become specialized for direct intercellular communication. Moreover, consideration of possible changes in synaptic structure during memory storage may provide an experimental approach to test for satisfaction of criteria 2 and 3; hypotheses which consider memory storage solely at the molecular level have been weakest at this point. Therefore, we may be able to achieve a more comprehensive understanding of the phenomenon of memory if we regard this process as a property of a neuron or set of neurons rather than solely as a property of individual molecules. The molecular approach to the problem has already elucidated certain crucial biochemical processes which might underlie this phenomenon, but the picture is by no means complete at present.

SOME FUTURE PROBLEMS

In biochemical studies of memory, little attention has been paid, so far, to the lipids of the nervous system, in spite of the fact that lipids are such an important constituent of synaptic membranes. Little is known about the turnover of phospholipids and sphingolipids in such cell membranes. Are such lipids synthesized peripherally, or must they, too, reach the synapse by axoplasmic flow after being synthesized in the cell body? Are new membranes formed as part of the establishment of the memory trace? The recent description of specific inhibitors of fatty-acid synthesis (Brady, 1963; Robinson, Brady, and Bradley, 1963) should make possible an experimental approach to some of these problems.

The kinetics of the behavioral effects of drugs which have been used to produce a specific inhibition or acceleration of synthesis of essential metabolites is another problem which has so far received scant attention. If synthesis of certain necessary metabolites for synaptic growth occurs in the cell body, inhibition or acceleration of such synthetic activities may not be immediately reflected at the synapse. The rate of axoplasmic flow has been estimated to be of the order of 1 to several millimeters per day (Droz and Leblond, 1962; Ochs, Dalrymple, and Richards, 1962; Weiss and Hiscoe, 1948); thus, in neurons with long processes, there may be a considerable delay between the time a molecule is synthesized and the time it reaches peripheral regions of the neuron. It is thus suggested that, in studies of the kinetics of memory-trace formation, both the initial learning and the later retention trials should be carried out at varying intervals after administration of drugs whose principal mechanism of action is upon synthetic activities in the cell body, since such drugs may fail to produce an immediate behavioral effect but may have a pronounced delayed effect. Some of these problems have been approached in the recent and intriguing investigations of Flexner et al. (1962, 1963) on the effects of puromycin (an inhibitor of protein synthesis) on learning and memory in mice. These workers investigated the effect of injecting the drug at various sites and the effect of varying the interval between the initial learning experience and the subsequent administration of puromycin, and they found that under certain conditions puromycin caused loss of memory. Further experiments, on the effect of varying the interval between an initial injection of puromycin and a subsequent learning experience, would be of interest in evaluating the hypothesis that axoplasmic transport of newly synthesized proteins to synaptic terminals is necessary for the fixation of new experiences by means of synaptic growth.

The mechanism of synaptic influence on the metabolism of the cell body is yet another major problem to be solved. It has been suggested (Briggs and Kitto, 1962; Krech, Rosenzweig, and Bennett, 1960; Rosenzweig et al., 1962; Smith, 1962) that the phenomenon of enzyme induction brought about by synaptic stimulation may be important in establishing memory traces, but experimental evidence is scanty. The finding of changes in base ratios of RNA in response to learning situations does not prove that there has been induction of a new type of RNA; since there are many types of RNA in the cell, a change in the relative proportions of the different types being synthesized could produce the same result as induction of a new type. Further studies on the specificity of any such evoked changes in the metabolism of the cell body are critically needed.

SUMMARY

If one establishes a rigorous set of criteria for defining a given type of molecule as a memory trace in the nervous system, then no one type of molecule may at present be regarded as the sole engram of a permanent memory trace. Much evidence already exists that RNA and protein metabolism are intimately involved in the process of memory storage, but the role of other molecules, such as lipids, must also be considered. Sophisticated techniques of molecular biology and enzymology will undoubtedly provide valuable data on biochemical processes involved in memory storage. However, a comprehensive theory of the structural basis of memory must also consider the function of the entire neuron, with consequent emphasis on the reciprocal relationships between the cell body and the synapse, as well as the complex functional interrelationships between neurons.

References

Brady, R. O. Studies of inhibitors of fatty acid biosynthesis: III. Mechanism of action of tetrolyl-coenzyme A. *Biochem. Biophys. Acta*, 1963, **70**, 467–468.

Brattgard, S. O. The importance of adequate stimulation for the chemical composition of retinal ganglion cells during early post-natal development. *Acta Radiol. Suppl.*, 1952, **96**, 1–80.

Briggs, M. H., and Kitto, G. B. The molecular basis of memory and learning. *Psychol. Rev.*, 1962, **69**, 537–541.

Cameron, D. E., and Solyom, L. Effects of ribonucleic acid on memory. *Geriatrics*, 1961, **16**, 74–81.

Chamberlain, T. J., Rothschild, G. H., and Gerard, R. W. Drugs affecting RNA and learning. *Proc. Natl. Acad. Sci.*, 1963, **49**, 918–924.

Cook, L., Davidson, A. B., Davis, D. J., Green, H., and Fellows, E. J. Ribonucleic acid: Effect on conditioned behavior in rats. *Science*, 1963, **141**, 268–269.

Corning, W. C., and John, E. R. Effect of ribonuclease on retention of conditioned response in regenerated planarians. *Science*, 1961, **134**, 1363–1365.

Creaser, E. H. The assimilation of amino acids by bacteria: The effect of 8-azaguanine upon enzyme formation in staphylococcus aureus. *Biochem. J.*, 1956, **64**, 539–545.

Dingman, W., and Sporn, M. B. The incorporation of 8-azaguanine into rat brain RNA and its effect on maze learning by the rat: An inquiry into the biochemical basis of memory. *J. Psychiat. Res.*, 1961, **1**, 1–11.

Droz, B., and Leblond, C. P. Migration of proteins along the axons of the sciatic nerve. *Science*, 1962, **137**, 1047–1048.

Egyhazi, E., and Hyden, H. Experimentally induced changes in the base composition of the ribonucleic acids of isolated nerve cells and their oligodendroglial cells. *J. biophys. biochem. Cytol.*, 1961, **10**, 403–410.

Flexner, J. B., Flexner, L. B., and Stellar, E. Memory in mice as affected by intracerebral puromycin. *Science*, 1963, **141**, 57–59.

Flexner, J. B., Flexner, L. B., Stellar, E., de la Haba, G., and Roberts, R. B. Inhibition of protein synthesis in brain and learning and memory following puromycin. *J. Neurochem.*, 1962, **9**, 595–605.

Friede, R. L. Thalamocortical relations reflected by local gradations of oxidative enzymes. In S. S. Kety and J. Elkes (Eds.), *Regional neurochemistry*. New York: Pergamon, 1961. Pp. 151–159.

Hebb, D. O. *The organization of behavior*. New York: Wiley, 1949.

Hyden, H. The neuron. In J. Brachet and A. E. Morsky (Eds.), *The cell*. Vol. 4. New York: Academic Press, 1960. Pp. 215–323.

Hyden, H., and Egyhazi, E. Nuclear RNA changes of nerve cells during a learning experiment in rats. *Proc. Natl. Acad. Sci.*, 1962, **48**, 1366–1373.

Hyden, H., and Egyhazi, E. Glial RNA changes during a learning experiment in rats. *Proc. Natl. Acad. Sci.*, 1963, **49**, 618–623.

Karlson, P. New concepts on the mode of action of hormones. *Perspect. Biol. Med.*, 1963, **6**, 203–214.

Krech, D., Rosenzweig, M. R., and Bennett, E. L. Effects on environmental complexity and training on brain chemistry. *J. comp. physiol. Psychol.*, 1960, **53**, 509–519.

Lowry, O. H., Roberts, N. R., Leiner, K. Y., Wu, M., Farr, A. L., and Albers, R. W. The quantitative histochemistry of brain: III. Ammon's horn. *J. biol. chem.*, 1954, **207**, 39–49.

McConnell, J. V. Memory transfer through cannibalism in planarians. *J. Neuropsychiat.*, 1962, **3** (suppl. 1), 542–548.

Mendelson, J. H., and Ervin, F. R. Influences of afferent neurons on efferent neurons: I. Effects of deafferentation on brain function and behavior. In R. G. Grenell (Ed.), *Progress in neurobiology*. Vol. 5. New York: Hoeber, 1962. Pp. 178–210.

Morrell, F. Electrophysiological contributions to the neural basis of learning. *Physiol. Rev.*, 1961, **41**, 443–494.

Ochs, S., Dalrymple, D., and Richards, G. Axoplasmic flow in ventral root nerve fibers of the cat. *Exp. Neurol.*, 1962, **5**, 349–363.

Palay, S. L. Synapses in the central nervous system. *J. biophys. biochem. Cytol.*, 1956, **2**, (suppl.), 193–202.

Ramon y Cajal, S. *Histologie du systeme nerveu de l'homme et des vertebres*. Paris: A. Maloine, 1910.

Robinson, J. D., Brady, R. O., and Bradley, R. M. Biosynthesis of fatty acids: IV. Studies with inhibitors. *J. Lipid Res.*, 1963, **4**, 144–150.

Rosenzweig, M. R., Krech, D., Bennett, E. L., and Diamond, M. C. Effects of environmental complexity and training on brain chemistry and anatomy: A replication and extension. *J. comp. physiol. Psychol.*, 1962, **55**, 429–437.

Sholl, D. A. *The organization of the cerebral cortex*. London: Methuen, 1956.

Smith, C. E. Is memory a matter of enzyme induction? *Science*, 1962, **138**, 889–890.

Waelsch, H., and Lajtha, A. Protein metabolism in the nervous system. *Physiol. Rev.*, 1961, **41**, 709–736.

Watson, J. D. Involvement of RNA in the synthesis of proteins. *Science*, 1963, **140**, 17–26.

Weiss, P., Nervous system (neurogenesis). In B. H. Willier, P. Weiss, and V. Hamburger (Eds.), *Analysis of development*. Philadelphia: Saunders, 1955. Pp. 346–401.

Weiss, P. The concept of perpetual neuronal growth and proximo-distal substance convection. In S. S. Kety and J. Elkes (Eds.), *Regional neurochemistry*. New York: Pergamon, 1961. Pp. 220–242.

Weiss, P., and Hiscoe, J. B. Experiments on mechanism of nerve growth. *J. exp. Zool.*, 1948, **107**, 315–395.

Conditioned reflexes established by coupling electrical excitation of two cortical areas
r. w. doty
and
c. giurgea

Is the mere coincidence of action of two stimuli sufficient to form a learned association between them, or is some motivational factor also required? This has been a persistent question in psychology (and psychiatry) and is of major importance in any attempt to solve the riddle of the neural mechanisms subserving learning. Human experience is too complex to provide an answer despite the long history of "associationism" as a science. In animal experimentation, on the other hand, it has been difficult to demonstrate learning or establish conditioned reflexes when motivation or "drive reduction" have been unequivocally absent.

The pertinent evidence has been reviewed elsewhere (Giurgea, 1953a). The experiments of Loucks (1935), however, are of special interest since they are the direct antecedents of our own. In several dogs Loucks stimulated the "motor" cortex through permanently implanted electrodes effecting a movement of one of the animal's limbs. With each animal on as many as 600 occasions over several days he preceded the motor stimulation with an auditory conditional stimulus (CS). The CS never came to evoke the movement with which it was so thoroughly paired, nor any other movements. A food reward was then introduced to follow the CS and the induced movement. Within a few trials the animal began moving to the CS. Loucks drew the justifiable conclusion from these experiments that the motivational

From *Brain Mechanisms and Learning,* A. Fessard, R. W. Gerard, J. Konorsky, and J. F. Delafresnaye, Eds., 1961. With permission of Blackwell Scientific Publications.

element was essential to the formation of conditioned reflexes and these results have had a wide and well-deserved influence on psychological theory since that time.

Loucks's position was apparently confirmed by Masserman (1943) who failed to obtain any signs of conditioning when stimulation of the hypothalamus was used as US. However, Brogden and Gantt (1942) were able to produce movements by presenting a CS alone after repeated pairing of CS and stimulation of the cerebellum. In some animals the "conditioned response" (CR) so elicited was very similar to the movement induced by cerebellar stimulation. Motivation seemed to be absent here. In 1951, while working in the laboratories of P. S. Kupalov seeking further confirmation of the hypothesis of "shortened conditioned reflexes," it was discovered that conditioned reflexes could readily be formed by pairing stimuli at two cortical points (Giurgea, 1953a, 1953b). Stimulation of occipital cortex which is initially without apparent effect ultimately produces movement highly similar to that elicited by the stimulation of the sigmoid gyrus with which it is paired. This direct contradiction of the results of Loucks seems best explained by differences in the timing of presentation of stimuli. In all his experiments Loucks (1935) used intertrial intervals of 2 minutes or less, usually 30–60 seconds, whereas an intertrial interval of 3–5 minutes was used in our experiments. If the intertrial interval is reduced to 2 minutes even after such CRs have been established, the CRs disappear in the majority of dogs tested so far (Giurgea, 1953a, 1953b), although the unconditioned response (UR) is unaffected.

Continuing these studies, it has been shown that formation of CRs by cortical stimulation is not dependent upon sensory endings in the meninges since the CR may be readily established after destruction of the Gasserian ganglion (Raiciulescu, Giurgea and Savescu, 1956). A CR established to stimulation of parietal-occipital cortex as CS was also elicited by a tonal or photic CS (Giurgea and Raiciulescu, 1957). In two animals with total, histologically confirmed section of the corpus callosum CRs were established even though CS and US were applied to different hemispheres (Raiciulescu and Giurgea, 1957; Giurgea, Raiciulescu, and Marcovici, 1957). The electrical activity recorded from the US area does not appear to be changed by this conditioning procedure and is within normal limits of low voltage, fast activity very shortly after the US is applied (Giurgea and Raiciulescu, 1959). In none of these experiments does the behaviors of the dogs indicate even the slightest element of motivation. This impression has now been confirmed objectively in the experiments reported below.

TECHNIQUE

The experiments at Michigan have so far been performed on four dogs, two cats and two cynomolgous monkeys. The dogs are restrained easily by placing their legs through plastic loops. Cats are held by placing their heads through a heavy plastic stock leaving their limbs free. Monkeys are kept permanently seated in a Lilly-type chair (Mason, 1958). All animals are adapted to restraint prior to electrode implantation. During the experiment the animals are isolated and observed through a "one-way" glass.

The cortex is stimulated through platinum electrodes, usually resting on the pial surface or just beneath it although in some dogs the thickness of the skull made such adjustment difficult.

Two of four electrodes are carried in 7 mm diameter plastic buttons which are held in trephine holes by means of screws (Doty, Rutledge, and Larsen, 1956). Flexible 0.5 mm diameter polyethylene insulated wires connect and electrodes to an 18 or 34 contact receptacle permanently secured to the skull by stainless steel posts (Doty, 1959).

Stimulation consists of 1 msec rectangular current pulses at a frequency of 50/sec and is monitored on a cathode-ray oscilloscope with a long-persistence screen. Great care is taken to keep the stimulating circuits and the animals isolated from ground and to avoid any other possibility of stimulation outside that intended.

Prior to pairing CS and US the effects of stimulation are observed for each electrode pair. It is advantagous to have several pairs of electrodes in "motor" cortical areas so that the chances are increased for procuring a relatively simple movement to serve as an UR. By means of automatic and silent control the CS is presented for 3–4 seconds and is slightly over-lapped by the US of 1–1.5 seconds duration. Six to ten combinations of CS and US are made daily.

After study of CS-US coupling is complete, the animals are trained in the same experimental chamber to press a lever to obtain food. The lever is then connected to administer cortical stimulation with each press.

RESULTS

Dog Alpha

All stimulation in the "motor" cortical regions produced stiff, complex and unnatural movements. That finally chosen as an UR was a lifting and extension of the right hind leg, a slight lifting and curling of the tail, and a rotation of the head to the midline and down. The US was 1.8 mA applied just posterior to the left post-crucial sulcus. The CS of 1.1 mA was applied to the left posterior supra-sylvian gyrus. It elicited no response for the first 42 CS-US pairings. The CS current was then increased to 2.2 mA and elicited an opening of the eyes and turning of the head to the right, a response judged to be inherent to stimulation of this area. It was still obtained, when, later in the experiment, the CS was again reduced to 1.0 mA. The first distinct CR was seen on the thirtieth post-operative day after 108 CS-US pairings. It was a turning of the head to the midline and down, a movement similar to the head movement seen to the US and in opposition to that inherently evoked by the CS. Movement of the leg or tail was never elicited by the CS. This CR subsequently occurred up to 100 percent of the time in some sessions and had a threshold of about 0.3 mA. It could also be elicited by 0.4 mA applied to a second pair of electrodes about 2 mm distant from the original CS pair.

The same CR was evoked by a CS of 3/ second clicks after one session (eight trials) combining this CS with the UR. A second UR was coupled with 9/second clicks as CS. This at first produced the previous CR which gradually became modified to a sidewise oscillation of the head with nose pointing down. This new "CR," however, had nothing in common with the second UR.

It was very difficult to teach this dog to eat in the experimental situation. Once trained, however, the animal pressed the lever repeatedly despite accompanying CS or US stimulation which in the case of the US produced violent movements. In contrast, if the side of the cage was tapped gently each time the lever was pressed, two or three taps abolished all pressing for the rest of the session.

Dog Beta

A US of 2.0 mA at the right postcruciate gyrus produced a brisk, well-integrated flexion of the left hind leg as its only apparent effect. The CS at the right marginal gyrus gave no overt sign at intensities up to 2.2 mA. The first sign of movement to the CS occurred during the sixth session, forty-fifth pairing. The slight tossing of the head and indefinite movements such as stepping or shifting posture seen then subsequently became very common. On the sixty-sixth pairing two 10-cm flexions of the left hind leg, held for about 1 second each, were seen as the only movement to the CS. This was the first CR. This type of CR occurred 74 times in 171 subsequent CS presentations (including extinction) and had a threshold of 0.95 mA. It was not extinguished by 84 presentations of the CS alone at 2–3 minute intervals for 11 sessions. These CRs were also obtained to stimulation of the right posterior ectosylvian gyrus indicating some generalization had occurred.

Technical difficulties prevented testing this dog in the lever-pressing situation. However, the animal was extraordinarily sensitive and yelped violently even when grasped gently by the scruff of the neck. Yet there was no evidence of pain or emotion during the training sessions, and the animal ran each day to the experimental room and jumped into the enclosure to be harnessed.

Dog Gamma

Stimulation at 0.4 mA 1.5 mm above the right pyramid in the field H_1 of Forel was used as US. It produced a forceful extension of the neck and rotation of the head over the right shoulder, wider opening of the eyes, flaring of the nostrils and occasionally a lifting of the right lip. This response was elicited 68 times in 10 sessions with no particular alteration in the animal's behavior. Pairing of the US with a CS of 3/second clicks was then begun. A CR of turning the head up and 130° right was elicited by the CS on the sixteenth trial and similar CRs occurred on 48 of 96 subsequent presentations. The CS also evoked great agitation, whining and yelping. Both the CRs and this agitation to the CS were extinguished in three sessions totalling 22 presentations of the CS alone.

Lever-pressing behavior was little altered by coupling with stimulation of the postcruciate gyrus producing a hind-leg left. It was slowed greatly by the click CS or other sounds, and abolished immediately by the US.

Dog Epsilon

Stimulation at right or left postcruciate gyri produced well coordinated, maximal flexions of left or right forelegs respectively. Stimulation of left posterior ecto-sylvian gyrus with 1.8 mA or right mid-marginal gyrus with 1.6 mA produced no responses when tested initially. Stimulation at the latter points was then used as CS and at the former as US. For convenience the prefix "R" or "L" will be used to designate to which hemisphere the stimulus was applied, e.g., L-CS with R-US means CS applied to left posterior ectosylvian gyrus, US to right post cruciate.

For the first 40 pairings of R-CS with R-US there was no response to the R-CS. During the next few sessions the R-CS frequently elicited a lowering of the head and flexion of the right foreleg, the limb opposite that in which the UR was induced. The first left foreleg CR occurred on the eighty-first presentation of R-CS and in the next 113 trials occurred 58 times. These CRs were discrete, 4–20 cm elevations of the left foreleg held for several seconds and frequently returned to the floor prior to the UR. The threshold for CR elicitation was 0.5–0.7 mA. Other movements, not so specific, occurred regularly, so that movement now occurred 95 percent of the time to this CS.

L-CS was now paired four times with R-US, and except for the first presentation produced flexions of the right foreleg (again opposite to the UR) each time. Two sessions later differentiation was begun and continued for 12 sessions with results as shown in Table 1. Obviously no differentiation occurred under these conditions; CRs were maintained to stimulation of either area though the

TABLE 1. INITIAL FAILURE OF DIFFERENTIATION IN DOG EPSILON

Stimulus Location	Total Differen-tiation Trials	LFL CRS	REL "CRS"
R-CS, R-US	50	11	7
L-CS, no US	44	14	5

percentage of occurrence to R-CS may have declined.

It is characteristic of these animals (Giurgea, 1953a, 1953b) that just prior to the appearance of the first CRs and frequently thereafter, movements of the affected limb occur sporadically during the intertrial period. This phenomenon was observed in *Dogs Beta* and *Epsilon*. These movements might possibly arise from some "irritative" process consequent to the repeated presentation of the US, but the following experiments show this is not the case. Using the usual timing and parameters, the L-US alone was presented 100 times in 12 sessions producing a forceful right foreleg flexion each time. No spontaneous lifts of this limb occurred in this period. Another 150 presentations were then given in which L-US preceded L-CS by irregular intervals. Initially L-CS still gave some left foreleg CRs or other movements, but these reactions were extinguished by this procedure since for the last 70 presentations there was no response whatever to L-CS. Orthodox temporal relations for L-CS and L-US were then used. At first this restored the nonspecific movements, then left foreleg CRs and ultimately right foreleg CRs occurred about 50 percent of the time to L-CS at a threshold of 0.7 mA.

The R-CS was then presented for the first time in 79 days. The left foreleg was lifted 15 cm flexing at the wrist, and was held so for about 5 seconds. Ultimately it was possible to obtain right leg flexions to L-CS and left leg flexions to R-CS.

Coupling L-CS, L-US or R-US with the animal's lever-pressing had no effect, whereas auditory stimuli or R-CS completely abolished pressing. The effect of R-CS had been predictable on the basis of behavior changes seen as soon as the use of R-CS was resumed (after the hiatus described above). Since more than 5 months had then elapsed from time of electrode implantation, it seems likely trigeminal fibers had grown into the medial electrode location.

Monkey 1

The CS of 1.0 mA applied to the left occipital pole consistently produced movement of the eyes, and sometimes the head, down and to the right. At any time during this stimulation, however, the eyes might be moved elsewhere if attention was so directed. The 0.2 mA US (300/second) in the left precentral cortex produced a smooth, vigorous flexion of the right forearm and contraction of the muscles on the right side of the neck and face causing the mouth to open. Coupling of the CS and US was begun 2 weeks after surgery and continued for 4 weeks, 200 trials in 24 sessions. In these 200 trials the right arm made random movements during the CS eleven times. Obviously there was no conditioning. During the next 25 weeks the animal was used sporadically for testing various lever-pressing procedures with fruit juice rewards.

Coupling of CS and US was then resumed. The effects of these stimuli were still exactly as they had been 7 months earlier. Using a two-minute intertrial interval for the first 51 trials in five sessions there was no sign of conditioning. A four-minute interval was then used for trials 52 to 84. The first CR was seen on the sixty-seventh pairing. The right arm was flexed to the level of the restraining collar, then extended along its lower surface with fingers fluttering as though seeking an object. In the next 47 trials a movement similar to this occurred to the CS 31 times. At the threshold current

of 0.55 mA or during the later phases of subsequent extinction sessions the movement was more likely to be a simple flexion very similar to that evoked by the US. Even when the movement was vigorous, it often terminated prior to the US. In 91 presentations of the CS given in five sessions without the US this CR was elicited 56 times. One-minute intervals were frequently employed. In two sessions after repeated presentations of the CS without the US, the CR was absent for five or more consecutive trials. The head and eye movements evoked by the CS were still present during this period of extinction. On several occasions it was noted, however, that the eyes closed at the onset of the CS and the animal appeared to drowse even though eyes could be seen moving beneath the lids.

Stimulation with an electrode pair within 2–3 mm of those used as CS gave no eye movements if the polarity of the stimulus was negative for the electrode separated from the others by a small sulcus. None the less the CR was evoked from this pair with this polarity three times in six stimulations, never using the US. Stimulation in the right posterior parietal lobe elicited eye and head movements which were almost the exact counterpart of those elicited by the CS save they were to the left. No CRs were elicited by this stimulation in nine attempts during two sessions.

With four-minute intervals and the same US there was no CR to an auditory CS despite 110 pairings in nine sessions. After this, giving the auditory CS simultaneously with the CS to the occipital pole often produced "external inhibition" of the CR to the latter stimulus. Seventeen tests with the auditory CS alone (plus the US) elicited no CRs even though the tests were given randomly throughout 24 presentations in which simultaneous auditory and cortical CS (plus US) was used.

The effect of coupling various stimuli with lever-pressing was then studied.

On July 11th the animal pressed the lever 41 times in a five-minute period and with each press received a US of 0.4 mA (double the intensity used routinely) which produced violent movements, and often convulsive after-discharges, with each press. There was no hesitation whatever in lever-pressing behavior beyond that attributable to the physical handicap consequent to the induced movement. Coupling with cortical CS was similarly without effect. On the following day, a novel clicking stimulus completely disrupted the behavior when coupled with each lever-press.

The animal was then taught in sessions of 20 trials per day to press a lever to avoid a shock to its tail. The first response to a tonal CS occurred on the thirty-third trial and a criterion of 12 avoidances in 20 CS presentations was reached in 128 trials. Generalization to 20/sec and 5/sec clicks as CS was immediate. The cortical CS, however, produced the former CR, a flexion of the right hand towards the chin rather than the extension to press the lever at the level of the abdomen. After 25 combinations of this cortical CS with the tail-shock, the animal began making lever presses to avoid this US. It took more than 100 trials, however, before the former CR was fully extinguished under these conditions. The threshold for the shock-avoidance response to cortical CS was 0.2 mA which is significantly less than the 0.55 mA threshold at the same electrodes for the flexion CR established without motivational context.

Monkey 2

The CS and US elicited responses very similar to those seen in *Monkey 1* save that the seizure threshold was much lower in this animal and the UR was frequently followed by a few clonic movements. The animal struggled almost continuously in the experimental situation (even when being given fruit juice) and no CRs were ever observed. Using three-minute intervals 91 couplings were

administered in 12 sessions. Then after a hiatus of 25 weeks another 116 combinations were given with two-minute intervals in three sessions and 85 combinations at four-minute intervals in four sessions. Finally, 265 couplings were given automatically at four-minute intervals in two overnight sessions, but still without indication of conditioning.

The animal was then conditioned to avoid a shock to the tail by pressing a lever. The first CR to a tonal CS required 105 trials and 238 trials to attain 12 avoidances in 20 CS presentations. Generalization to other auditory conditional stimuli was immediate and complete. The cortical CS was then employed. For 300 combinations of this CS with the tail-shock US there was, judging by the animal's general behavior and visually observed respiration, no anticipation whatever of the impending shock during a four-second CS. Yet on every presentation the CS was patently effective since the eyes moved persistently down and to the right during each stimulation. The first CRs occurred after the CS was increased to 1.2 mA. The threshold was ultimately determined to be 0.6 mA for the elicitation of this CR.

Cat 425

Conditioning with cortical stimulation was likewise a failure in this animal; but so too was conditioning using an auditory CS and foot-shock as US. The animal was also seizure-prone. A total of 345 pairings of a right middle ectosylvian gyrus CS with right ansate gyrus US produced no CRs, and 420 pairings of a tonal CS with foot-shock US was almost equally ineffective although a few CRs were seen.

Cat 489

This animal has been thoroughly studied by Allan Minster. The CS applied to right middle ectosylvian gyrus usually elicited no overt response initially at the currents used. At higher currents the animal looked up and to the left. The US in the right ansate area produced an abrupt turn of the head to the left and flexion of the left foreleg. The first CR occurred on the thirty-ninth pairing, fifth session. These CRs, however, never became consistent from one session to the next. In 100 trials after the first CR there was a total of only 32 and 15 of these were made in three of the 15 sessions. At first, the CR was a vigorous lifting and extension of the left foreleg, but after the seventy-second pairing the right foreleg executed this same movement to the CS more often than did the left. The threshold for CR elicitation by stimulation of middle ectosylvian gyrus was probably about 0.8 mA. Stimulation of the right posterior ectosylvian gyrus at 0.35 mA yielded seven right and one left foreleg CRs in 11 presentations. To date, 97 pairings of the right ansate US with a CS applied to left middle suprasylvian gyrus produced only four leg lifts that could equivocally be called CRs, yet the current for this suprasylvian CS has been kept high enough that head movements initially seen to this stimulation still occurred frequently.

Ten-channel EEG records taken for each trial in this cat have not yielded much new information. Confirming Giurgea and Raiciulescu (1959) there is rarely any electrical abnormality even in the immediate vicinity of the electrodes following either CS or US. No changes characteristic of the conditioned state could be detected and it could not be predicted from the electrical record whether a CR would or would not occur. The CS in middle or posterior ectosylvian gyrus usually produced immediate electrocortical arousal whereas slower patterns frequently persisted through most of the middle suprasylvian CS. The arousal produced by CS and US, however, was minimal since 8–12 sec rhythms returned often within 1–2 seconds after stimulus cessation.

INTERPRETATION OF RESULTS

There can be no question that conditioned reflexes can be established with cortical stimulation as US. To the thirty dogs successfully conditioned in this manner in the laboratory in Bucharest and the cats observed by Nikolayeva (1957) can be added the animals of this study extending the phenomenon to the monkey and to a wide variety of cortical electrode placements. The vagaries in the appearance of this phenomenon undoubtedly arise not only from its complexity but from ignorance of its nature and the procedures most favorable for its induction. Such problems are not unknown in the study of more usual types of conditioning.

With equal assurance one can state that, in the usual sense of the word, there is no motivation involved in the formation of CRs by coupling cortical stimulations. The animals tested so far have remained entirely insouciant to self-administered cortical stimulation of near convulsive strength inducing violent movement, yet were profoundly inhibited by moderate and innocuous auditory stimuli. There is little reason to expect the cortical stimulation might be rewarding, and there was nothing in our observations to suggest this. On the other hand where motivational factors were expected as with the possible meningeal involvement (Dog Epsilon) or in the field of Forel (Dog Gamma), the method readily confirmed this impression. It is of some interest that in Dog Gamma the presence of this aversive factor did not preclude some form of motor conditioning.

Besides the direct evidence gained from coupling the cortical CS and US with lever-pressing there is equally convincing circumstantial evidence for the absence of motivation in these conditioning procedures. The extreme brevity of electrocortical arousal following the CS-US combination in Cat 489, or Monkey 1 closing its eyes to doze with onset of the CS, is scarcely expected from motivational stimuli. Nor are these CR movements purposeful; rather they are physiological absurdities. They seldom prepare the animal posturally for the ensuing UR and more often than not the CR is terminated before the UR begins. Watching Monkey 1 day after day raise its arm to stimulation of its "visual" cortex one could not escape the feeling that his nonsensical yet persitent movement was somehow analogous to the compulsive movements of neurotic humans.

The work of Segundo and his colleagues, reported at this meeting and elsewhere (Segundo, Roig, and Sommer-Smith, 1959), in which a tonal CS evokes movements similar to those elicited by electrical stimulation of center median or the mesencephalic reticular formation as US, provide excellent confirmation of our observations—movements produced by central stimulation can be conditioned. Masserman's failure to obtain such results from hypothalamic stimulation (Masserman, 1943) stands in sharp contrast to the results with Dog Gamma and the work of Segundo et al. Obviously the hypothalamus must be carefully reexamined in this regard. The US in the experiments of Segundo et al. probably produced motivational effects in some of their animals, but in others it appears less clear. In any event it would be difficult to ascribe some "biological significance" or appropriateness to the movements induced by the CS. It is equally difficult to find a motivational basis for the "backwards" type of conditioning linking the US with the CS as analyzed by Asratyan in this volume.

Since CRs can be established without a motivational factor, there is more hope that the basic phenomena of learning can be sought in neural systems sufficiently simple for meaningful analysis, perhaps with purely electrophysiological techniques. The temporal factor appears to be critical and the experiments with Dog Gamma and especially Dog Epsilon show the conditioned state is not established by the repeated, randomized excitation of US and CS systems.

Several observations support Sperry's hypothesis (1955) that the significant alteration is to be sought in the effector system. In motivated conditioning an alteration in excitability specific to the limb being conditioned can be observed some time before any CRs appear (Doty and Rutledge, 1959). In the present and earlier experiments (Giurgea, 1953a, 1953b) movements similar to the CR, never seen previously in the animal's behavior, often appeared spontaneously at about the same time the CRs were first noted. The threshold of the neural hierarchy controlling the complex CR thus seems to have been lowered. The frequent generalization of these CRs to other stimuli supports this view and in Dog Epsilon and Cat 489 it was observed that convulsions induced accidentally by high-current CS began with remarkably prolonged CRs.

Some animals seem to have inherently low thresholds for particular movement complexes so that stimulation at widely separated points within the nervous system will evoke the same response. For instance in Cat 523 stimulation in sensorimotor cortex, posterior ectosylvian and middle suprasylvian gyri, and the caudate nucleus produced an abrupt turning of the head which was highly similar for the different stimulus points. Stimulation in middle ectosylvian gyrus, ventral anterior and ventral posterolateral nuclei did not produce this effect but a convulsion elicited from middle ectosylvian gyrus began with prolonged turning of the head 180° to the rear. In Cat 365 flexion and, at higher currents, attack movements of the foreleg could be elicited by stimulation in the anterior portion of the caudate nucleus, septal region, ventral hippocampus, and periaqueductal grey. This motor response was not correlated with the motivational effects of this stimulation since caudate and septal stimulation increased lever-pressing, periaqueductal stimulation was avoided and hippocampal stimulation was "neutral." Stimulation of the median forebrain bundle, pyriform area and habenula which produced aversive effects in this animal did not elicit the foreleg attack movement.

The data are too limited to know whether electrodes in these areas in any cat would give these responses. The impression is gained, however, that they would not and that somehow a particular type of movement has in a given individual come to be "prepotent" over others. The stimulating electrodes may thus be revealing the existence of "individually acquired reflexes" (Berittoff, 1924) established through the animal's own activities. At least they are not different from the individually acquired reflexes deliberately given the animal by the stimulating electrodes during the course of our experiments. However, the relation, if any, between these phenomena must, as so many questions raised by these experiments, await further experimental analysis.

GROUP DISCUSSION

Segundo. I shall first comment on the finding that motor cortical stimulation is relatively "indifferent." It agrees with other observations, for excitation of this region in the sleeping monkey produced no arousal unless a generalized seizure occurred and, under the latter conditions, one should doubt whether wakefulness derived from stimulation itself or from proprioceptive "feed back" resulting from clonic movements. The same "indifference" was shown by the visual area: when the animal was awake, excitation with few volts produced investigation movements directed towards the contralateral field; when the animal was asleep, stimulation of up to 80 volts produced no effect. A different result occurred when excitation was applied to

temporal pole, cingular cortex or hippocampus: with low voltages, animals were immediately aroused, both behaviorally and electroencephalographically (Segundo, Arana, and French, 1955). Therefore, and as far as we can infer from the influence of animal brain stimulation upon sleeping state or tendency to excite itself, certain areas are "indifferent" and others are not.

Dr. Doty mentioned that stimulation of subcortical structures may be conditioned. In our laboratory, brief tones have been reinforced by direct excitation of mesencephalic reticular formation, center median, basolateral amygdala or head of caudate nucleus and learned responses to tones have eventually appeared. In some cases (center median, mesencephalic reticular formation, certain amygdaloid or caudate placements) conditioned effects were practically identical to the absolute responses. In other cases, responses from different points in caudate or amygdala, could not be conditioned *in toto*; some of their components, however, could and consequently conditioned responses were similar to a part of the absolute response. In a third group of animals (also caudate or amygdala) the conditioned reaction, though consistent, was completely different to the absolute effect. This variable relationship has been found in other types of conditioning and, therefore, though difficult to interpret here, is not altogether surprising (Hilgard and Marquis, 1940).

To summarize we can say that stimulation effects of certain areas of the brain can be conditioned. The latter term seems justified in the sense that the process has many features (technique, effects, inhibitions) of classical conditioning. These studies may help to understand the physiology of learning and that of tested nuclei (Roig, Segundo, Sommer-Smith, and Galeano, 1959; Segundo, Roig, and Sommer-Smith, 1959).

Chow. In your monkey work, do you worry about whether your stimulus would activate the pain sensation in your animal?

Doty. We are very much aware that the factor of meningeal stimulation must be considered. Dr. Rutledge and I have shown that stimulation of the dura mater of the saggital sinus in the cat can serve as a conditional stimulus and is undoubtedly also a noxious stimulation. However, I feel satisfied that, as outlined in the text, this factor can be detected by the self-stimulation procedure employed and was present only as stated. In addition, Dr. Giurgea has established these responses in dogs after destruction of the Gasserian ganglion.

Hernandez-Peon. The conditioned response obtained by Dr. Doty using cortical stimuli as conditioned and unconditioned stimuli provides a method for testing definitely whether there might be some cortico-cortical connections in some cases of conditioning. And I wonder whether he has done transcortical cutting isolating the respective cortical areas and testing whether these conditioned responses persist after the transection or not.

Doty. I think the experiments of Giurgea and his colleagues showing these conditional reflexes to be established after callosal section when the conditional stimulus and unconditioned stimulus are in different hemispheres, indicate that a subcortical pathway is likely to be involved in the production of this phenomenon. Perhaps pertinent also are experiments which Dr. Rutledge and I have been doing using electrical stimulation of marginal gyrus in the cat as conditional stimulus and shock to the foreleg as unconditioned stimulus. If the stimulated cortical zone is circumsected so that most of the pathways available for intracortical elaboration of the excitation are severed, conditioned reflexes still occur to the cortical conditional stimulus. If, on the other hand, the stimulated cortical zone is undercut for a total length of more than about 8 mm the conditioned reflexes are lost. They often return, however, after about a month of training. The critical factors are not fully determined in the reappearance of conditional reflexes after this undercutting of the stimulated cortex, but it may be that "U" fibers are necessary. It is also not certain whether that mere passage of time is sufficient or whether it is the retraining which is critical.

Konorski. Did you try to extinguish these reflexes that you have established and how did you obtain the extinction?

Doty. Dr. Giurgea taught me a lot about extinction. Apparently it is extremely difficult to bring about a total extinction of a salivary conditioned reflex. Those "temporary connections" are surprisingly permanent. Hence a technique of "acute" extinction is used wherein the conditional stimulus is presented as one might expect without the unconditioned stimulus, but also at much shorter time intervals than employed during the establishment of the conditioned state. I objected that this alteration of procedure would not yield a proper comparison so we tried extinguishing by rather long intervals between conditioned stimulus presentations. In *Dog Beta* we got no extinction in 85 presentations. Hence in *Monkey 1* shown in the film, we used shorter intervals of 1–2 minutes and on the two occasions produced "acute" extinction in which the conditioned reflexes were totally absent to the conditional stimulus and in five or more consecutive presentations of the conditioned stimulus, although the animal remained alert. Giurgea has also published extinction data on some of his dogs. Our *Dog Gamma* in which an aversive factor, was present in the unconditioned stimulus showed rapid extinction.

Anokhin. Much of the recently gathered data points to the possibility of obtaining "conditioned responses" by an association between the most distinct points of the brain. In fact, this trend of thought covers also some of the better-known conditioned reflexes, as the one induced by training with sound and light.

Yet a question comes reasonably to our mind: what aspect of the activity of the brain taken as a whole, do such facts reveal? Dr. Doty's interesting experiments may be taken as instances of the brain tissue's ability to act as a specialized substratum, and to establish instant links between any two stimuli which affect it simultaneously.

Our team considers that such aptitude proves the capacity of the nervous tissue to unite any separate elements during stimulation. This capacity is the basic physiological ground of any spontaneous conditioned response. But if we assume at the start that conditioned responses are a physiological function of the animal, we must consider them as the outcome of a complex physiological system, leading necessarily to an adaptation process which involves the organism as a whole.

Dr. Doty tells us that he finds it difficult to draw objectively a difference between the leg-lifting response which he has induced, and the one obtained in the classical Pavlovian test by direct application of an electric shock to the animal's paw. Yet to us, the difference seems considerable. In Pavlov's test, the subject draws away the paws from the source of stimulation, thus displaying an adaptative behavior, which terminates in a reverse afferent drive, in our sense of the word, indicating that the animal has avoided the impact of the electric current. Besides, Dr. Doty in his experiment shows the movement of limbs as the mechanical effect of a stimulation which, after having been subject to association, is now conveyed outwards onto the motor system. This proves admirably the capacity of the brain tissue to register any sequence of induced stimuli.

I wish, in concluding, to draw your attention to one important factor, which is of particular relevance, to Dr. Hernandez-Peon's remark on the possibility of showing pure cortico-cortical connections. Our laboratory has shown that the most insignificant stimuli, as well as lesions of the cortical tissue will instantly involve subcortical formations, and possibly, reticular ones. This is why, by the very nature of the process, no subsequent effects of stimulation can be *only cortical*.

Doty. In reply to Dr. Anokhin—I think we must simply adopt the mechanistic, objective approach which Pavlov used so successfully. If I form a conditioned reflex by using an avoidable, painful, "biologically significant" stimulus to a forepaw so that the animal lifts it when a tonal conditional stimulus is sounded, and for the other paw proceed as Giurgea and I have done so that the other paw is lifted when the "auditory analyzer" is stimulated directly at the cortex, you would be unable to tell me simply by looking at the animal's behavior, which conditioned reflex was which. True, by careful analysis I suspect you would find great differences in the autonomic nervous system responses to the stimuli employed, at least during some stages of the training. But their absence in the latter case only proves them to be an unnecessary complication in the process of establishing the neural alteration responsible for the change in effect of the conditional stimulus. Both tone and direct electrical stimulation of the "auditory analyzer" are initially without effect on somatic musculatures save possibly for an "orientation reflex" which is soon lost. Both become effective on the same motor apparatus in approximately the same number of trials. Both states are subject to the laws of conditioning, i.e., there is no apparent backward conditioning, there can be external inhibition, they can be extinguished. Why then call them different states or infer for them different mechanisms?

We have shown that if the ventral roots are crushed and an animal immobilized with bulbocapnine, it can still be conditioned to make conditioned reflexes with its hind leg even though the leg has never moved during conditioning. Thus we can show proprioceptive feedback from the unconditioned reflex to be unnecessary for the formation of conditioned reflexes. This does not say that such factors are not normally present; only that they need not be. Such experimental simplification of the situation certainly does not alter significantly the process we desire to elucidate, nor change its name. In similar vein the elimination of motivational factors must not be construed to infer qualitatively different processes to be operative in "cortical-cortical" conditoning as compared to the more usual procedures which involve such unknowns as "biological purpose" or unanalyzable emotional and subjective factors.

References

Beck, E. C., and Doty, R. W. Conditioned flexion reflexes acquired during combined catelepsy and de-efferentation. *J. comp. physiol. Psychol.*, 1957, **50**, 211–216.

Doty, R. W., and Rutledge, L. T. Conditioned reflexes elicited by stimulation of partially isolated cerebral cortex. *Fed. Proc.*, 1959, **18**, 37.

Doty, R. W., Rutledge, L. T., and Larsen, R. M. Conditioned responses established to electrical stimulation of cat cerebral cortex. *J. Neurophysiol.*, 1956, **19**, 401–415.

Giurgea, G., Raiciulescu, N., and Marcovici, G. Reflex condition–at interhemisferic prin excitarea directa corticala dupa sectionarea corpului calos. Studiu anatomo-histologic. *Revista Fiziol. Norm. Patol.*, 1957, **4**, 408–414.

Electrophysiological correlates of a conditioned response in cats

robert galambos
guy sheatz
and
vernon g. vernier

The search for neurophysiological correlates for psychological phenomena such as learning and emotion has a long history that cannot profitably be treated here. This report presents a brief account of some electric changes that are observable in the brain when animals are conditioned and extinguished to an auditory stimulus.

The animals under study lived in a box measuring 0.5 by 1.0 by 0.5 m that contained a loudspeaker through which clicks (at constant intensity) were delivered at a rate of 1 click/3 sec along with noise generated by a thermionic noise generator. The noise intensity was adjusted at the outset so that it was sufficient to mask most ambient sounds. Recording from brain structures was achieved through electrodes of the Delgado type that were implanted stereotaxically at sterile operation some weeks or months prior to the testing; as many as 14 separate brain locations were thus made available for study in each animal. To date, ten cats with implantations in or on auditory and visual cortex, cochlear nucleus, hippocampus, caudate nucleus, septal area, and amygdala have been examined in the conditioning process. The electrodes were directly connected through a plug to the amplifiers of a Grass EEG machine and thereafter, alternately or simultaneously, to ink-writers and a cathode-ray oscilloscope. The cats also wore a harness bearing two metal brushes, each making contact with one side of the thorax; the output of a Grass stimulator could be delivered to these brushes, and thus shocks could be applied, at will, across the chest of the animal.

The plan and results of the experiments are as follows. The animals were placed in the box for periods of many days or weeks, clicks being delivered continuously day and night throughout. From time to time their electrodes were connected to the recording devices, and the activity evoked by the clicks was visualized. The report (1) that under such conditions the response at the cochlear nucleus becomes, with time, much reduced in size ("habituation," "adaptation") was readily confirmed; in addition, we found that responses evoked in various other brain loci diminished in a similar manner. Responses so attenuated in the cochlear nucleus can be seen in the left column of Figure 1.

After an animal had been in the box for hours or days, the tracings from its brain showed small, absent, or irregular evoked potentials caused by the clicks, and consistent behavior toward the stimuli was absent. At this point single strong shocks were given across the chest contiguously with randomly selected clicks. After these shocks had been discontinued—perhaps some 10 or 20 having been given—the behavior in response to the click stimuli was noticeably different. The animals crouched, appeared alert, and most of them twitched, snarled, or otherwise responded to many individual clicks. When exhibiting this behavior, the animals were considered to have been "conditioned" to the auditory stimulus; records from the cochlear nucleus of such an animal are shown in the right column of Figure 1. As the click continued without shock reinforcement, both motor and electric responses

From *Science*, **123**, 376–377, 2 March, 1955.

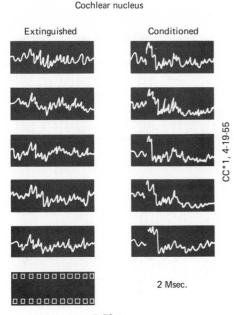

Cochlear nucleus

Extinguished   Conditioned

CC*1, 4-19-55

2 Msec.

I 50 μv

Figure 1. Cochlear nucleus responses to successive identical click stimuli before ("extinguished") and after ("conditioned") application of three shocks to a cat. The increase in response magnitude after shocks as noted here has been observed eight times in this animal, two of them previous to the instance given here.

tended to disappear (motor long before electric), and the "extinguished" condition invariably returned after hours or days. In most of our animals, the cycle of conditioning and extinction thus defined has been repeated many times.

In view of the motor behavior accompanying the conditioned state, the possibility that the responses recorded are somehow generated by muscle activity or its consequences must obviously be ruled out. Although such considerations can hardly be held to apply to the phenomenon shown in Figure 1, where the entire event is substantially completed within some 15 msec after the application

of the stimulus, it must seriously be considered as a possibility for responses that have longer latency and duration.

Of all our attempts to settle this point, the experiments of the sort illustrated in Figure 2 are perhaps the most conclusive. The upper record shows the extinguished record from an animal that had previously been conditioned and extinguished five times. The lower record, made about 1 hour after the upper one, shows evoked responses regularly in the stations along the classical auditory pathway (cochlear nucleus and auditory cortex) as well as in at least two of the electrodes in the hippocampus. Between the times at which the upper and lower records were made, the animal had received conditioning shocks and, additionally, gallamine triethiodide (Flaxedil, Lederle) 4 mg/kg intravenously in two divided doses within 1 minute. This dosage was sufficient to cause apparent complete muscular paralysis, and artificial respiration via an endotracheal tube was required. The only muscle activity noted was constriction of the iris as an object was brought close to the eye of the animal. Pupillary dilation was also observed coincident with the conditioning shocks or with clicks alone immediately after shock. Certainly there was no movement of the animal that could account for the responses shown in the lower half of Figure 2, during the recording of which, of course, only clicks were being applied at the times indicated in the top trace. It may parenthetically be stated here that, in extinguished animals that have been immobilized by Flaxedil, applied shocks promptly change the records of responses to those typical of the conditioned state.

From the data, only some of which have been presented here, the following general statements appear to be justified. When cats with indwelling electrodes are subjected to a relatively simple auditory conditioning technique, changes in electric activity of the brain apparently related to conditioning and extinction

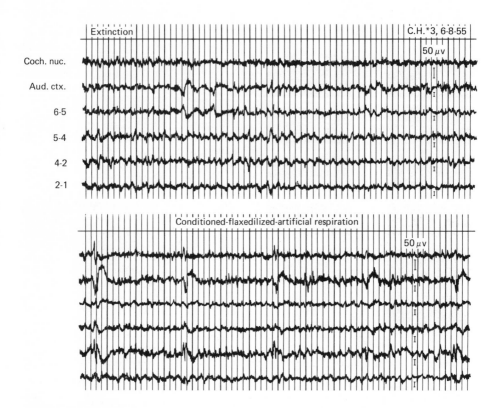

Figure 2. EEG responses to identical clicks (indicated by artifact in upper trace) before (top records) and after a shock had been delivered for a time with each click. Bipolar recording from cochlear nucleus (second trace), monopolar from auditory cortex. The bottom four traces are derived from a hippocampal array (as yet not histologically verified) inserted in a dorsoventral line, the active tips being 2 mm apart with No. 1 the deepest. The animal had received Flaxedil prior to the bottom recording and thus exhibited no motor activity whatever.

can be realiably recorded. Evoked auditory responses are larger and are seen more frequently and in more numerous locations when a given animal is in the conditioned as opposed to the extinguished state. Such changes occur near the origin of the classical auditory pathway (cochlear nucleus) as well as at its termination (auditory cortex), in portions of such limbic system structures as the hippocampus and septal area and in the head of the caudate nucleus.

Reference

1. Hernandez-Peon, R. and Scherrer, H. *Federation Proc.*, 1955, **14**, 71.

Nonvisual functions
of visual cortex
in the cat
joel f. lubar
clifford j. schostal
and
adrian a. perachio

During the last decade many studies utilizing shuttle-box avoidance tasks have indicated that, in both the cat and rat, cingulectomy produces deficits in active-avoidance response (AAR) behavior (6, 8, 10, 11, 12). Recently, however, Lubar and Perachio (6) and Lubar et al (7) showed that, in the cat, AAR deficits previously attributed to cingulate ablations probably resulted from secondary damage to those fibers of passage which underline the cingulate cortex. These fibers in part constitute optic radiations that originate in the lateral geniculate body and terminate in the mesial portion of the lateral and posterolateral gyrus (area striata), which, in turn, lie dorsal to the cingulate gyrus. Furthermore, ablation of these mesial portions of the striate cortex in themselves results in a severe deficit in the acquisition of a two-way AAR response task in which an auditory conditioning stimulus (CS), a buzzer, is employed (7).

Several hypotheses had been presented in our previous study to account for this AAR deficit (7). These included an impairment of general learning ability, facilitation of responses other than avoidance, and finally the suggestion that the ablation produced a visual or perceptual loss. Although the latter hypothesis appears most plausible in view of the fact that the lesions were placed in primary visual cortex, the importance of this factor was questionable since no gross changes in visually guided behavior were apparent. Furthermore the lesions were quite restricted in size.

The present study was designed to

From *Physiology and Behavior*, 1967, 2, 179–184. By permission of Pergamon Press Ltd.

examine in some detail the effects of lateral and posterolateral lesions on visually mediated discrimination behavior. Another purpose was to test the effect of these lesions on AAR behavior after a considerably longer post-operative delay than that employed previously to determine whether the degree of deficit is as severe as that reported in the prior study, or whether recovery of function occurs.

METHODS

Animals

The animals used in this study were 34 adult cats. Each cat was housed in a separate cage. In Experiment I, four groups of animals were used. Seven animals served as normal controls, five animals received lesions of the mesial aspect of the lateral gyrus (laterals), five animals received lesions of the mesial aspect of the posterolateral gyrus (posterolaterals), and six subjects with scattered lesions in the same cortical areas were assigned to a small striate lesion group. In Experiment II three groups of animals were used, laterals (N = 4), posterolaterals (N = 3) and normal controls (N = 3).

Surgery and histology

The cortical ablations were performed by subpial aspiration under aseptic procedures. Subjects were anesthetized with sodium pentobarbital (60mg/kg) given IP. Ablations of both the lateral and posterolateral gyri were intended to replicate in overall size and depth the lesions made in our previous study (7). The small striate lesion group (Experiment I) consisted of animals that sustained much smaller and nonsymmetrical lesions than were originally intended.

After completion of all behavioral testing, each operated animal was perfused with physiological saline and 10 percent formalin in saline. Brains were removed, split mid-sagittally, and the lesions reconstructed. The brains were then embedded in 12 percent celloidin and coronally sectioned in the stereotaxic plane at 30μ. Sections were stained with cresyl-violet and were examined to ascertain depth of the lesions and degree of retrograde degeneration in the lateral geniculate.

Apparatus

In this study, both a Yerkes-Alley discrimination apparatus and a two-way active-avoidance apparatus were used to assess visual pattern discrimination and active-avoidance behavior respectively. The Yerkes-Alley consisted of a plywood start box $6\frac{1}{2}$ in wide × $22\frac{1}{2}$ in long × 18 in high, a runway area 36 in long, and two goal boxes, separated by a partition that extended 10 in into the runway area. The entire apparatus was painted a flat grey. Stimulus cards were 4 in square and constructed of heavy white cardboard. Stimuli consisted of a black circle and square equated for area (4 in²) and luminous flux, and were placed on the stimulus cards. The stimulus cards were hung on the goal box doors, which in turn were attached to the apparatus with hinges and small springs. Small concealed magnets served to maintain the doors in a closed position. At the slightest touch, the doors would quietly spring open revealing metal food dishes within the

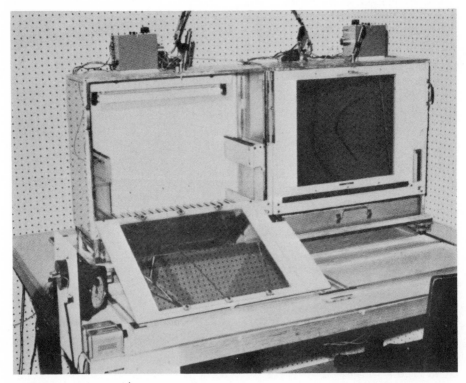

Figure 1. Active-avoidance apparatus.

goal box. Canned mackerel was used for food reinforcement. The stimulus cards and entire apparatus were evenly illuminated from above.

The two-way active-avoidance apparatus consisted of two identical boxes (24 in long × 12 in wide × 18 in high) placed end to end. The apparatus is shown in Figure 1. Each box contained sliding doors and a hurdle at each end, $8\frac{1}{4}$ in wide × 8 in high × $2\frac{1}{2}$ in long, with electrifiable bars mounted on top. During the operation of the apparatus, response latencies, the number of shocks manually delivered to the animal on each trial and the trial number were automatically recorded and transferred to punch cards by an IBM 024 key punch. A programming device automatically presented the conditioning stimulus (CS), a 75 dB buzzer mounted above the apparatus. The programmer also controlled the time interval between the CS and occurrence of shock (unconditioned stimulus) and the length of the intertrial interval. Both the programmer and keypunch were isolated from the active-avoidance apparatus so that noise generated by its operation would not interfere with the subject's performance.

Power for the shock was supplied by a 1600 V A.C. transformer. The unconditioned stimulus (US) was a constant current shock of 2 mA, delivered at 1530 V A.C. with a 0.76 M Ω resistor in series with the animal.

EXPERIMENT I

Effect of striate cortex lesions on the acquisition of a visual pattern discrimination and two-way active avoidance response

Procedure. Yerkes-Alley pattern discrimination training was begun 2–4 weeks postoperatively. A "blind" procedure was used in training the operated subjects; that is, during all behavioral work the experimenter did not know whether the subject was a lateral operate, or a posterolateral operate. First, each

cat received from 4 to 6 days of adaptation to the discrimination apparatus. Throughout both the adaptation and training procedure all animals were maintained on 23-hr food deprivation. During the adaptation period the blank side of the stimulus cards were exposed. First, the animals were trained to eat from either food dish, next they were trained to push either door open for food reward, and finally they were trained to approach the choice doors when released from the start box. Adaptation was terminated if the subject did not perseverate to the same choice door for more than three successive trials.

Experimental acquisition training began on the day following adaptation. Each animal received 24 trials per day with an intertrial interval of 1 min. The sequence of stimuli presentation was based on a modified Gellerman series. A noncorrection procedure for errors was employed. Criterion for acquisition was arbitrarily set at 20 or more correct responses for two successive days.

Following completion of the visual pattern discrimination, task acquisition training was begun in the active-avoidance task. Active-avoidance training was initiated between post-operative weeks 4–8. The daily procedure consisted of placing the animal into the apparatus and turning on the programmer. After an initial silent interval of 60 sec, the buzzer (CS) was automatically activated. Five sec after the buzzer was activated, shock was administered until either the subject escaped over the hurdle into the other box or a 60-sec interval had elapsed. Either event automatically terminated the CS and US and initiated the 60-sec intertrial interval. Response latencies were recorded photoelectrically. During the intertrial interval, the doors between the boxes were closed and would remain so until the onset of the next trial. Indicator lights warned the experimenter of each trial onset. All animals were given five shock-trials daily. Thus, for each avoidance response made, a trial was added until either the subject made five escape responses or achieved criterion. The shock-trial schedule has been shown to be the optimal procedure for achieving rapid and stable learning in cat avoidance conditioning (14). Acquisition criterion was nine AARs out of 10 consecutive trials during a single daily session.

On the day an animal had attained criterion, an extinction procedure was started. All subjects were given 20 extinction trials daily. To meet extinction criterion, the animal was required to remain in the box where the trial was initiated for 30 sec of CS presentation on nine out of 10 successive trials. The programming apparatus was set so that during extinction, after 30 sec of CS presentation without a response, the buzzer could be terminated by the experimenter and the intertrial interval begun.

Statistical analysis of the data. All data in both Experiments I and II were analyzed by means of t-tests for independent means. The level of significance was set at $p < 0.05$ for a two-tailed analysis.

RESULTS

The results for Experiment I are shown in Figure 2. There were no significant differences between any of the groups of animals for the number of trials to acquisition on the visual pattern discrimination. This result clearly indicates that there can be no gross disruption of the primary visual process, as measured by the circle-square discrimination, as a result of these restricted striate lesions.

In the acquisition of the active-avoidance response, both the lateral and posterolateral operated animals were severely deficient as compared with the normal controls ($p < 0.01$ for both comparisons). On the other hand, the normal and the small striate lesion groups did not differ significantly. These results replicate our previous findings (7), and indicate, as would be expected, that the lesion must exceed a certain size limit in order to disrupt AAR performance.

Figure 3 illustrates the speed of acquisition (reciprocal latency) for all groups for the first 50 trials. On this measure, the lateral operated animals were significantly slower than either the normal controls ($p < 0.05$) or the small lesion

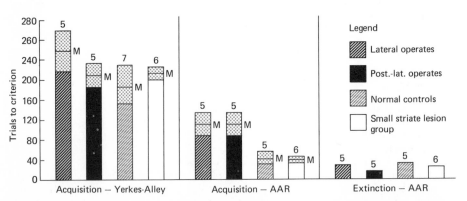

Figure 2. Trials to acquisition in Yerkes-Alley; trials to acquisition and extinction in active avoidance for lateral operates, posterolateral operates, small striate lesion group, and normal control animals (Experiment I). The number of subjects for each group is indicated above each bar. The mean for each group is designated by the letter M. Stippling above and below the mean represents the standard deviation for each group on acquisition tasks.

group ($p < 0.01$). Although there were no other significant differences, posterolateral operated animals showed a trend in the direction of that found for the lateral group. These results indicate that the nature of the AAR deficit appears to differ for the two striate operated groups although the mean number of trials to criterion was essentially the same for both. This was also clear in the course of acquisition training in that many of the lateral animals took longer than the posterolateral animals to begin making any avoidance responses. Posterolaterals, in contrast, often made avoidance responses early in the training sequence but were unable to pool enough of these responses to achieve a criterion run until many days had elapsed.

Data on extinction confirm our previous findings (7). There were no significant differences for any of the groups on this measure.

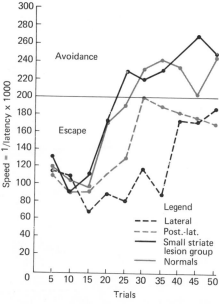

Figure 3. Running speeds for lateral operates, posterolateral operates, small striate lesion operates and normal controls for the first fifty trials of active avoidance (Experiment I).

In all other behavioral respects the animals with striate lesions appeared normal. There was no indication of impairment of tactual or visual placing responses or any loss of visually guided locomotion. In the active-avoidance apparatus the animals were able to make escape or avoidance responses without colliding with the hurdle. Thus, it appears that any effect that these restricted cortical lesions may have had on vision or perception must be very subtle.

EXPERIMENT II

Effect of striate cortex lesion on the retention and relearning of a visual pattern discrimination

Since it had been shown that there were no differences in the acquisition of the pattern discrimination task among the various experimental groups of animals in Experiment I, the possibility still remained that animals with damage to visual cortex might be deficient in the retention and relearning of a previously acquired discrimination. Retention measures also provide control for individual differences in the base performance for the discrimination task. In order to examine these possibilities, new groups of animals (lateral operated, posterolateral operated and normal) were assembled.

Procedure. Eleven adult cats were given acquisition training in the Yerkes-Alley, using the same stimuli and procedure as were employed in the previous experiment. Two to three days after criterion performance, aspiration of the requisite regions of the striate cortex was performed on eight of the animals. Four cats received lesions of the lateral gyrus, three received lesions of the posterolateral gyrus, and the rest remained as normal controls. Operative procedures and lesion placements were intended to duplicate those in Experiment I. An eighth operated animal which was to receive a posterolateral lesion died during surgery. Two weeks later all animals were given 24 retention test trials. The identical, modified Gellerman series was used for every animal. On the following day all subjects were begun on reacquisition (relearning) training, again following previous procedures. Criterion performance again was the same as that required for acquisition. However, if an animal made four or less errors on the day of the retention test, these retention trials then constituted the first day of the two-day relearning criterion.

RESULTS

The results of this experiment are presented in Table 1. Since both the posterolateral and lateral operated animals performed similarly in both the AAR and discrimination tasks in the previous experiment, their data is pooled into a single striate operated group. The acquisition performance of the normal subjects in Experiment II replicates that found for normals in Experiment I. Furthermore there were no significant retention or relearning differences between the operated and normal animals. Hence, it is clear that restricted lesions of the mesial aspect of the lateral and posterolateral gyrus do not produce deficits in the acquisition, retention, or relearning of the type of pattern discrimination used in this study.

"General anatomical considerations."

Reconstructions of representative lesions for the different operated groups are

TABLE 1. TRIALS TO ACQUISITION; TRIALS TO RELEARNING; PERCENTAGE OF RETENTION[1] FOR STRIATE OPERATED ANIMALS AND NORMAL CONTROLS IN YERKES-ALLEY FOR EXPERIMENT II

Subjects		Trials to Acquisition	Trials to Relearning	Percentage of Retention
Striates				
Laterals				
396		168	24	86
408		312	48	95
411		240	48	65
473		84	0	100
	Mean	201	30	86
Posterolaterals				
434		120	48	86
449		168	0	90
447		96	24	82
	Mean	128	24	83
Pooled mean of striates		170	27	85
Normals				
457		408	0	100
461		72	0	95
471		144	48	62
	Mean	208	16	86

[1]Percentage of retention =

$$\frac{\text{number of correct responses on first day of retention}}{\text{number of correct responses on second day of acquisition criterion}}$$

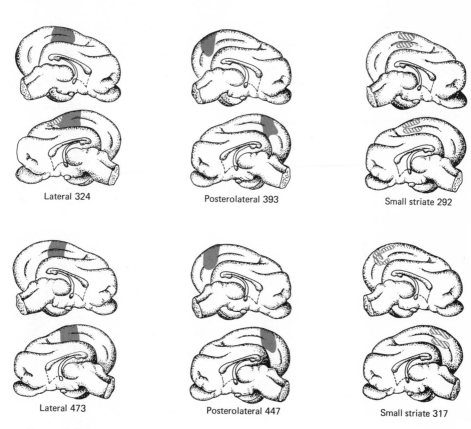

Figure 4. Reconstructions of lesions for lateral operate 324, posterolateral operate 393 and small striate operates 292 and 317 (Experiment I), and for lateral operate 473 and posterolateral operate 447 (Experiment II). The black area designates regions where the lesion invaded white matter; crosshatched area represents regions where lesions did not extend beneath the cortex to underlying fibers.

Lateral 324

Posterolateral 393

Small striate 292

Lateral 473

Posterolateral 447

Small striate 317

shown in Figure 4. In the animals with lateral gyrus ablations, the lesions were located within the region bounded by stereotaxic planes A 0.5–A 12.2 with the mean placement between A 4.3–A 8.2. The mean lesion length was 4.5 mm. The mesial surface of the lateral gyrus was ablated to the underlying white matter but did not undercut fibers to the dorsal-lying cortex. Furthermore, the lesions extended from the dorsal crown of the mesial surface of the lateral gyrus to the upper bank of the cingulate sulcus.

For the posterolateral animals, the lesions were bounded by planes −7.0 and + 2.2, with a mean placement between − 4.4 and + 0.4, and a mean length of 4.8 mm. These lesions also extended down to underlying fiber tissue and generally covered the dorsoventral extent of the mesial aspect of the posterolateral gyrus.

In the case of the small striate lesion group subjects, placements were bounded by planes − 5.5 and + 10.8, with an average lesion length of 3.7 mm. However, these lesions were much smaller in dorsoventral extent than were those in the main experimental groups and were restricted to the upper layers of the cortex. Reference to Figure 5 clearly illustrates the differences between experimental lesions and group with small striate lesions.

All of the lesions in this study were confined to area striata, and in no case was there any damage to the underlying cingulate cortex.

The pattern of retrograde degeneration for such lesions has been described in detail in our previous study (7). Such degeneration was again found for the present lesions. It is important to emphasize that, in all cases, degeneration was very restricted due to limited extent of the lesions, and in the group of animals with very small lesions degeneration was sometimes not seen at all. In the case of the lateral operated animals, the most extensive area of degeneration was in the rostral portion of the geniculate. More posteriorly, degeneration was found in the ventral part of the nucleus. For the posterolateral operates, degeneration

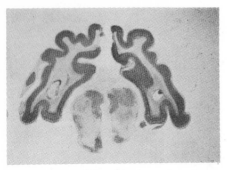

Posterolateral
operate 310

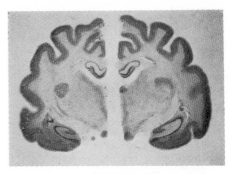

Lateral
operate 285

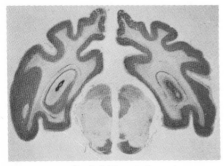

Small striate operate
posterolateral 317

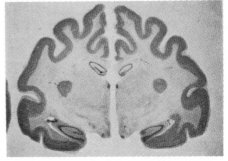

Small striate operate
lateral 282

Figure 5. Photomicrographs of coronal sections of the brain of posterolateral operate 310, lateral operate 285, and small striate lesion operates 317 (posterolateral) and 282 (lateral). Magnification × 1.75. Scale is in centimeters.

was confined to the posterior portion of the nucleus. It was primarily limited to the central portion of cell layer A as defined by Thuma (*13*) in anterior planes and extended into layer A1 in more posterior planes.

DISCUSSION AND CONCLUSIONS

The results of the present study lend support to the proposal that the deficit in AAR performance following partial ablation of striate cortex in the cat is not a reflection of a defect in visual discrimination. After sustaining bilateral ablation of mesial portions of striate cortex, cats performed a circle versus square discrimination normally but were significantly impaired in acquiring an AAR.

The failure of our small lesions to produce a deficit in the pattern discrimination task is not surprising. Lashley (*4*) showed that in the rat even complex pattern discriminations may be performed as long as a small amount of striate cortex is left intact after an extensive ablation.

These results do not rule out the possibility that the cortical ablation caused some change in visual perception. Such a decrement might be revealed by the use of the more difficult successive discrimination problem. Kimble (*3*) found that rats sustaining bilateral hippocampectomies were deficient on successive discrimination tasks but normal on simultaneous discrimination tasks.

The present experiment does demonstrate that the AAR decrement in striate ablated cats is a stable one and persists despite a long postoperative interval. Experience in the Yerkes-Alley did not benefit the normal or operated cats since their performance was the same as that of

the experimentally naive cats of the previous experiment (*7*). This suggests a further possibility concerning visual performance deficits following destriation. Normal visual discrimination in an approach task might not accurately predict visual performance in an avoidance problem. The present experiment, thus, does not allow an unequivocal rejection of the hypothesis that a visual discrimination defect underlies the AAR deficit and, for the present, the specific nature of the AAR deficit still remains obscure.

If, however, visual performance defects are not a factor in the slow AAR acquisition in the operated animals, other nonvisual factors must account for the results in the AAR task.

The view that striate cortex mediates nonvisual functions is not new. Lashley (*5*) suggested this might be the case in the rat since maze learning was more severely disrupted in those subjects that had sustained both striate cortical ablation and peripheral blindness than it was in peripherally blinded animals. Furthermore, since units in area 17 are known to respond to somesthetic, auditory, and noxious stimuli (*1, 2, 9*), perhaps this cortical region is part of a chain of structures essential to the normal rate of acquisition of the AAR by performing some integration of the multiple cues available (e.g., buzzer CS, location of the hurdle, and electric shock to the foot pads). Such recent electrophysiological findings may make it necessary for investigators to view striate function as encompassing more than just the mediation of visual processes. Our results support this view and generalize the findings of Lashley (*5*) by suggesting that perhaps visual cortex in the cat may be involved in nonvisual functions.

References

1. Horn, G. The effect of somesthetic and photic stimuli on the activity of units in the striate cortex of unanesthetized, unrestrained cats. *J. Physiol.*, 1965, *179*, 263–277.

2. Jung, R., Kornbuher, H. H., and da Fonesca, J. S. Multisensory convergence on

cortical neurones. Neuronal effects of visual, acoustic, and vestibular stimuli in the superior convolutions of the cat's cortex. In G. Morrizzi, A. Fessard, and H. H. Jasper (Eds.), *Progress in brain research—I. Brain Mechanisms.* Amsterdam: Elsevier, 1963. Pp. 207–234.

3. Kimble, D. P. The effects of bilateral hippocampal lesions in rats. *J. comp. physiol. Psychol.*, 1963, **56**, 273–282.

4. Lashley, K. S. The mechanism of vision. XVI. The functioning of small remnants of the visual cortex. *J. comp. Neurol.*, 1939, **70**, 45–67.

5. Lashley, K. S. Studies of cerebral functions in learning. XII: Loss of the maze habit after occipital lesions in blind rats. *J. comp. Neurol.*, 1943, **79**, 431–462.

6. Lubar, J. F., and Perachio, A. A. One-way to two-way learning and transfer of an active avoidance response in normal and cingulectomized cats. *J. comp. physiol. Psychol.*, 1965, **60**, 46–52.

7. Lubar, J. F., Perachio, A. A., and Kavanagh, A. J. Deficits in active-avoidance behavior following lesions of the lateral and posterolateral gyrus of the cat. *J. comp. physiol. Psychol.*, 1966, **62**, 163–269.

8. McCleary, R. A. Response specificity in the behavioral effects of limbic system lesions in the cat. *J. comp. physiol. Psychol.*, 1961, **54**, 605–613.

9. Murata, K., Cramer, H., and Bach-y-Rita, P. Neuronal convergence of noxious, acoustic, and visual stimuli in the visual cortex of the cat. *J. Neurophysiol.*, 1965, **28**, 1223–1239.

10. Thomas, G. J., and Ortis, L. S. Effects of rhinencephalic lesions on conditioning of avoidance responses in the rat. *J. comp. physiol. Psychol.*, 1958, **51**, 130–134.

11. Thomas, G. J., and Slotnick, B. M. Effects of lesions in the cingulum on maze learning and avoidance conditioning in the rat, *J. comp. physiol. Psychol.*, 1962, **55**, 1085–1091.

12. Thomas, G. J., and Slotnick, B. M. Impairment of avoidance responding by lesions in cingulate cortex in rats depends on food drive. *J. comp. physiol. Psychol.*, 1963, **56**, 959–964.

13. Thuma, B. D. Studies on the diencephalon of the cat. I. The cytoarchitecture of the corpus geniculatum laterale. *J. comp. Neurol.*, 1928, **46**, 173–199.

14. Wolfe, J. W., Kavanagh, A. J., and Lubar, J. F. Avoidance behavior of the cat as a function of shock intensity and training schedule. *Psychol. Rep.*, 1966, **18**, 287–294.

Learning
of
visceral
and
glandular
responses
neal e. miller

There is a strong traditional belief in the inferiority of the autonomic nervous system and the visceral responses that it controls. The recent experiments disproving this belief have deep implications for theories of learning, for individual differences in autonomic responses, for the cause and the cure of abnormal psychosomatic symptoms, and possibly also for the understanding of normal homeostasis. Their success encourages investigators to try other unconventional types of training. Before describing these experiments, let me briefly sketch some elements in the history of the deeply entrenched, false belief in the gross inferiority of one major part of the nervous system.

HISTORICAL ROOTS
AND MODERN RAMIFICATIONS

Since ancient times, reason and the voluntary responses of the skeletal muscles have been considered to be superior, while emotions and the presumably involuntary glandular and visceral responses have been considered to be inferior. This invidious dichotomy appears in the philosophy of Plato (1), with his superior rational soul in the head above and inferior souls in the body below. Much later, the great French neuroanatomist Bichat (2) distinguished between the cerebrospinal nervous system of the great brain and spinal cord, controlling skeletal responses, and the dual chain of ganglia (which he called "little brains") running

From *Science*, **163**, 434–445, 31 January 1969. Copyright 1969 by the American Association for the Advancement of Science.

down on either side of the spinal cord in the body below and controlling emotional and visceral responses. He indicated his low opinion of the ganglionic system by calling it "vegetative"; he also believed it to be largely independent of the cerebrospinal system, an opinion which is still reflected in our modern name for it, the autonomic system. Considerably later, Cannon (3) studied the sympathetic part of the autonomic nervous system and concluded that the different nerves in it all fire simultaneously and are incapable of the finely differentiated individual responses possible for the cerebrospinal system, a conclusion which is enshrined in modern textbooks.

Many, though not all, psychiatrists have made an invidious distinction between the hysterical and other symptoms that are mediated by the autonomic nervous system. Whereas the former are supposed to be subject to a higher type of control that is symbolic, the latter are presumed to be only the direct physiological consequences of the type of intensity of the patient's emotions (see, for example, 4).

Similarly, students of learning have made a distinction between a lower form, called classical conditioning and thought to be involuntary, and a superior form variously called trial-and-error learning, operant conditioning, type II conditioning, or instrumental learning and believed to be responsible for voluntary behavior. In classical conditioning, the reinforcement must be by an unconditioned stimulus that already elicits the specific response to be learned, therefore, the possibilities are quite limited. In instrumental learning, the reinforcement, called a reward, has the property of strengthening any immediately preceding response. Therefore, the possibilities of reinforcement are much greater; a given reward may reinforce any one of a number of different responses, and a given response may be reinforced by any one of a number of different rewards.

Finally, the foregoing invidious distinctions have coalesced into the strong traditional belief that the superior type of instrumental learning involved in the superior voluntary behavior is possible only for skeletal responses mediated by the superior cerebrospinal nervous system, while, conversely, the inferior classical conditioning is the only kind possible for the inferior, presumably involuntary, visceral and emotional responses mediated by the inferior autonomic nervous system. Thus, in a recent summary generally considered authoritative, Kimble (5) states the almost universal belief that "for autonomically mediated behavior, the evidence points unequivocally to the conclusion that such responses can be modified by classical, but not instrumental, training methods." Upon examining the evidence, however, one finds that it consists only of failure to secure instrumental learning in two incompletely reported exploratory experiments and a vague allusion to the Russian literature (6). It is only against a cultural background of great prejudice that such weak evidence could lead to such a strong conviction.

The belief that instrumental learning is possible only for the cerebrospinal system and, conversely, that the autonomic nervous system can be modified only by classical conditioning has been used as one of the strongest arguments for the notion that instrumental learning and classical conditioning are two basically different phenomena rather than different manifestations of the same phenomenon under different conditions. But for many years I have been impressed with the similarity between the laws of classical conditioning and those of instrumental learning, and with the fact that, in each of these two situations, some of the specific details of learning vary with the specific conditions of learning. Failing to see any clear-cut dichotomy, I have assumed that there is only one kind of learning (7). This assumption has logically demanded that instrumental training procedures be able to produce the learning of any visceral responses that could be acquired through classical conditioning procedures. Yet it was only a little over a dozen years ago that I began some experimental work on this problem and a somewhat shorter time ago that I first, in published articles (8), made specific sharp challenges to the traditional view that the instrumental learning of visceral responses is impossible.

SOME DIFFICULTIES

One of the difficulties of investigating the instrumental learning of visceral responses stems from the fact that the responses that are the easiest to measure —namely, heart rate, vasomotor responses, and the galvanic skin response —are known to be affected by skeletal responses, such as exercise, breathing, and even tensing of certain muscles, such as those in the diaphragm. Thus, it is hard to rule out the possibility that, instead of directly learning a visceral response, the subject has learned a skeletal response the performance of which causes the visceral change being recorded.

One of the controls I planned to use was the paralysis of all skeletal responses through administration of curare, a drug which selectively blocks the motor end plates of skeletal muscles without eliminating consciousness in human subjects or the neural control of visceral responses, such as the beating of the heart. The muscles involved in breathing are paralyzed, so the subject's breathing must be maintained through artificial respiration. Since it seemed unlikely that curarization and other rigorous control techniques would be easy to use with human subjects, I decided to concentrate first on experiments with animals.

Originally I thought that learning would be more difficult when the animal was paralyzed, under the influence of curare, and therefore I decided to postpone such experiments until ones on nonparalyzed animals had yielded some definitely promising results. This turned out to be a mistake because, as I found out much later, paralyzing the animal with curare not only greatly simplifies the problem of recording visceral responses without artifacts introduced by movement but also apparently makes it easier for the animal to learn, perhaps because paralysis of the skeletal muscles removes sources of variability and distraction. Also, in certain experiments I made the mistake of using rewards that induced strong unconditioned responses that interfered with instrumental learning.

One of the greatest difficulties, however, was the strength of the belief that instrumental learning of glandular and visceral responses is impossible. It was extremely difficult to get students to work on this problem, and when paid assistants were assigned to it, their attempts were so half-hearted that it soon became more economical to let them work on some other problem which they could attack with greater faith and enthusiasm. These difficulties and a few preliminary encouraging but inconclusive early results have been described elsewhere (9).

SUCCESS WITH SALIVATION

The first clear-cut results were secured by Alfredo Carmona and me in an experiment on the salivation of dogs. Initial attempts to use food as a reward for hungry dogs were unsuccessful, partly because of strong and persistent un-conditioned salivation elicited by the food. Therefore, we decided to use water as a reward for thirsty dogs. Preliminary observations showed that the water had no appreciable effects one way or the other on the bursts of spontaneous salivation. As an additional precaution, however, we used the experimental design of rewarding dogs in one group whenever they showed a burst of spontaneous salivation, so that they would be trained to increase salivation, and rewarding dogs in another group whenever there was a long interval between spontaneous bursts, so that they would be trained to decrease salivation. If the reward had any unconditioned effect, this effect might be classically conditioned to the experimental situation and therefore produce a change in salivation that was not a true instance of instrumental learning. But in classical conditioning the reinforcement must elicit the response that is to be acquired. Therefore, conditioning of a response elicited by the reward could produce either an increase or a decrease in salivation, depending upon the direction of the unconditioned response elicited by the reward, but it could not produce a change in one direction for one group and in the opposite direction for the other group. The same type of logic applies for any unlearned cumulative aftereffects of the reward; they could not be in opposite directions for the two groups. With instrumental learning, however, the reward can reinforce any response that immediately precedes it; therefore, the same reward can be used to produce either increases or decreases.

The results are presented in Figure 1, which summarizes the effects of 40 days of training with one 45-minute training session per day. It may be seen that in this experiment the learning proceeded slowly. However, statistical analysis showed that each of the trends in the predicted rewarded direction was highly reliable (10).

Since the changes in salivation for the

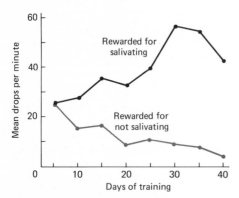

Figure 1. *Learning curves for groups of thirsty dogs rewarded with water for either increases or decreases in spontaneous salivation.* [*From Miller and Carmona (10)*]

two groups were in opposite directions, they cannot be attributed to classical conditioning. It was noted, however, that the group rewarded for increases seemed to be more aroused and active than the one rewarded for decreases. Conceivably, all we were doing was to change the level of activation of the dogs, and this change was, in turn, affecting the salivation. Although we did not observe any specific skeletal responses, such as chewing movements or panting, which might be expected to elicit salivation, it was difficult to be absolutely certain that such movements did not occur. Therefore, we decided to rule out such movements by paralyzing the dogs with curare, but we immediately found that curare had two effects which were disastrous for this experiment: it elicited such copious and continuous salivation that there were no changes in salivation to reward, and the salivation was so viscous that it almost immediately gummed up the recording apparatus.

HEART RATE

In the meantime, Jay Trowill, working with me on this problem was displaying great ingenuity, courage, and persistence in trying to produce instrumental learning of heart rate in rats that had been paralyzed by curare to prevent them from "cheating" by muscular exertion to speed up the heart or by relaxation to slow it down. As a result of preliminary testing, he selected a dose of curare (3.6 milligrams of d-tubocurarine chloride per kilogram, injected intraperitoneally) which produced deep paralysis for at least 3 hours, and a rate of artificial respiration (inspiration-expiration ratio 1:1; 70 breaths per minute; peak pressure reading, 20 cm-H_2O) which maintained the heart at a constant and normal rate throughout this time.

In subsequent experiments, DiCara and I have obtained similar effects by starting with a smaller dose (1.2 milligrams per kilogram) and constantly infusing additional amounts of the drug, through intraperitoneal injection, at the rate of 1.2 milligrams per kilogram per hour, for the duration of the experiment. We have recorded, electromyographically, the response of the muscles, to determine that this dose does indeed produce a complete block of the action potentials, lasting for at least an hour after the end of infusion. We have found that if parameters of respiration and the face mask are adjusted carefully, the procedure not only maintains the heart rate of a 500-gram control animal constant but also maintains the vital signs of temperature, peripheral vasomotor responses, and the pCO_2 of the blood constant.

Since there are not very many ways to reward an animal completely paralyzed by curare, Trowill and I decided to use direct electrical stimulation of rewarding areas of the brain. There were other technical difficulties to overcome, such as devising the automatic system for rewarding small changes in heart rate as recorded by the electrocardiogram. Nevertheless, Trowill at last succeeded in training his rats (*11*). Those rewarded for an increase in heart rate showed a statistically reliable increase, and those rewarded for a decrease in heart rate showed a statistically reliable decrease. The changes, however, were disappointingly small, averaging only 5 percent in each direction.

The next question was whether larger changes could be achieved by improving the technique of training. DiCara and I used the technique of shaping—in other words, of immediately rewarding first very small, and hence frequently occurring, changes in the correct direction and, as soon as these had been learned, requiring progressively larger changes as the criterion for reward. In this way, we were able to produce in 90 minutes of training changes averaging 20 percent in either direction (12).

KEY PROPERTIES OF LEARNING: DISCRIMINATION AND RETENTION

Does the learning of visceral responses have the same properties as the learning of skeletal responses? One of the important characteristics of the instrumental learning of skeletal responses is that a discrimination can be learned, so that the responses are more likely to be made in the stimulus situations in which they are rewarded than in those in which they are not. After the training of the first few rats had convinced us that we could produce large changes in heart rate, DiCara and I gave all the rest of the rats in the experiment described above 45 minutes of additional training with the most difficult criterion. We did this in order to see whether they could learn to give a greater response during a "time-in" stimulus (the presence of a flashing light and a tone) which indicated that a response in the proper direction would be rewarded than during a "time-out" stimulus (absence of light and tone) which indicated that a correct response would not be rewarded.

Figure 2 shows the record of one of the rats given such training. Before the beginning of the special discrimination

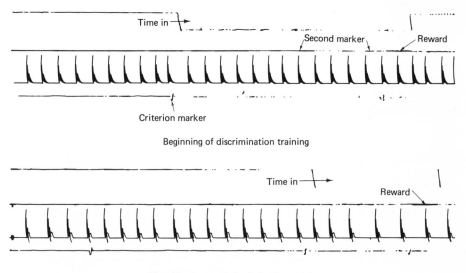

Beginning of discrimination training

After 45 minutes of discrimination training

Figure 2. Electrocardiograms at the beginning and at the end of discrimination training of curarized rat rewarded for slow heart rate. Slowing of heart rate is rewarded only during a "time-in" stimulus (tone and light). [From Miller and DiCara (12)]

training it had slowed its heart from an initial rate of 350 beats per minute to a rate of 230 beats per minute. From the top record of Figure 2 one can see that, at the beginning of the special discrimination training, there was no appreciable reduction in heart rate that was specifically associated with the time-in stimulus. Thus it took the rat considerable time after the onset of this stimulus to meet the criterion and get the reward. At the end of the discrimination training the heart rate during time-out remained approximately the same, but when the time-in light and tone came on, the heart slowed down and the criterion was promptly met. Although the other rats showed less change than this, by the end of the relatively short period of discrimination training their heart rate did change reliably (P < .001) in the predicted direction when the time-in stimulus came on. Thus, it is clear the instrumental visceral learning has at least one of the important properties of instrumental skeletal learning—namely, the ability to be brought under the control of a discriminative stimulus.

Another of the important properties of the instrumental learning of skeletal responses is that it is remembered. DiCara and I performed a special experiment to test the retention of learned changes in heart rate (13). Rats that had been given a single training session were returned to their home cages for 3 months without further training. When curarized again and returned to the experimental situation for nonreinforced test trials, rats in both the "increase" and the "decrease" groups showed good retention by exhibiting reliable changes in the direction rewarded in the earlier training.

ESCAPE AND AVOIDANCE LEARNING

Is visceral learning by any chance peculiarly limited to reinforcement by the unusual reward of direct electrical stimulation of the brain, or can it be reinforced by other rewards in the same way that skeletal learning can be? In order to answer this question, DiCara and I (14) performed an experiment using the other of the two forms of thoroughly studied reward that can be conveniently used with rats which are paralyzed by curare—namely, the chance to avoid, or escape from, mild electric shock. A shock signal was turned on; after it had been on for 10 seconds it was accompanied by brief pulses of mild electric shock delivered to the rat's tail. During the first 10 seconds the rat could turn off the shock signal and avoid the shock by making the correct response of changing its heart rate in the required direction by the required amount. If it did not make the correct response in time, the shocks continued to be delivered until the rat escaped them by making the correct response, which immediately turned off both the shock and the shock signal.

For one group of curarized rats, the correct response was an increase in heart rate; for the other group it was a decrease. After the rats had learned to make small responses in the proper direction, they were required to make larger ones. During this training the shock signals were randomly interspersed with an equal number of "safe" signals that were not followed by shock; the heart rate was also recorded during so-called blank trials—trials without any signals or shocks. For half of the rats the shock signal was a tone and the "safe" signal was a flashing light; for the other half the roles of these cues were reversed.

The results are shown in Figure 3. Each of the 12 rats in this experiment changed its heart rate in the rewarded direction. As training progressed, the shock signal began to elicit a progressively greater change in the rewarded direction than the change recorded during the blank trials; this was a statistically reliable trend. Conversely, as

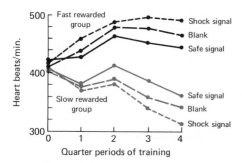

Figure 3. Changes in heart rate during avoidance training. [From DiCara and Miller (14)]

training progressed, the "safe" signal came to elicit a statistically reliable change in the opposite direction, toward the initial base line. These results show learning when escape and avoidance are the rewards; this means that visceral responses in curarized rats can be reinforced by rewards other than direct electrical stimulation of the brain. These rats also discriminate between the shock and the "safe" signals. You will remember that, with noncurarized thirsty dogs, we were able to use yet another kind of reward, water, to produce learned changes in salivation.

TRANSFER TO NONCURARIZED STATE: MORE EVIDENCE AGAINST MEDIATION

In the experiments discussed above, paralysis of the skeletal muscles by curare ruled out the possibility that the subjects were learning the overt performance of skeletal responses which were indirectly eliciting the changes in the heart rate. It is barely conceivable, however, that the rats were learning to send out from the motor cortex central impulses which would have activated the muscles had they not been paralyzed. And it is barely conceivable that these central impulses affected heart rate by means either of inborn connections or of classically conditioned ones that had been accompanied by an increase in

heart rate and relaxation had been accompanied by a decrease. But, if the changes in heart rate were produced in this indirect way, we would expect that, during a subsequent test without curare, any rat that showed learned changes in heart rate would show the movements in the muscles that were no longer paralyzed. Furthermore, the problem of whether or not visceral responses learned under curarization carry over to the noncurarized state is of interest in its own right.

In order to answer this question, DiCara and I (15) trained two groups of curarized rats to increase or decrease, respectively, their heart rate in order to avoid, or escape from, brief pulses of mild electric shock. When these rats were tested 2 weeks later in the noncurarized state, the habit was remembered. Statistically reliable increases in heart rate averaging 5 percent and decreases averaging 16 percent occurred. Immediately subsequent retraining without curare produced additional significant changes of heart rate in the rewarded direction, bringing the total overall increase to 11 percent and the decrease to 22 percent. While, at the beginning of the test in the noncurarized state, the two groups showed some differences in respiration and activity, these differences decreased until, by the end of the retraining, they were small and far from statistically reliable ($t = 0.3$ and 1.3, respectively). At the same time, the difference between the two groups with respect to heart rate was increasing, until it became large and thus extremely reliable ($t = 8.6$, d.f. $= 12$, $P < .001$).

In short, while greater changes in heart rate were being learned, the response was becoming more specific, involving smaller changes in respiration and muscular activity. This increase in specificity with additional training is another point of similarity with the instrumental learning of skeletal responses. Early in skeletal learning, the rewarded correct response is likely to be accompanied by many unnecessary movements. With additional training during which extraneous movements are not rewarded, they tend to drop out.

It is difficult to reconcile the foregoing results with the hypothesis that the differences in heart rate were mediated primarily by a difference in either respiration or amount of general activity. This is especially true in view of the research, summarized by Ehrlich and Malmo (16), which shows that muscular activity, to affect heart rate in the rat, must be rather vigorous.

While it is difficult to rule out completely the possibility that changes in heart rate are mediated by central impulses to skeletal muscles, the possibility of such mediation is much less attractive for other responses, such as intestinal contractions and the formation of urine by the kidney. Furthermore, if the learning of these different responses can be shown to be specific in enough visceral responses, one runs out of different skeletal movements each eliciting a specific different visceral response (17). Therefore, experiments were performed on the learning of a variety of different visceral responses and on the specificity of that learning. Each of these experiments was, of course, interesting in its own right, quite apart from any bearing on the problem of mediation.

SPECIFICITY:
INTESTINAL VERSUS CARDIAC

The purpose of our next experiments was to determine the specificity of visceral learning. If such learning has the same properties as the instrumental learning of skeletal responses, it should be possible to learn a specific visceral response independently of other ones. Furthermore, as we have just seen, we might expect to find that, the better the rewarded response is learned, the more specific is the learning. Banuazizi and I

worked on this problem (18). First we had to discover another visceral response that could be conveniently recorded and rewarded. We decided on intestinal contractions, and recorded them in the curarized rat with a little balloon filled with water thrust approximately 4 centimeters beyond the anal sphincter. Changes of pressure in the balloon were transduced into electric voltages which produced a record on a polygraph and also activated an automatic mechanism for delivering the reward, which was electrical stimulation of the brain.

The results for the first rat trained, which was a typical one, are shown in Figure 4. From the top record it may be seen that, during habituation, there were some spontaneous contractions. When the rat was rewarded by brain stimulation for keeping contractions below a certain amplitude for a certain time, the number of contractions was reduced and the base line was lowered. After the record showed a highly reliable change indicating that relaxation had been learned (Figure 4, second record from the top), the conditions of training were reversed and the reward was delivered whenever the amplitude of contractions rose above a certain level. From the next record (Figure 4, middle) it may be seen that this type of training increased the number of contractions and raised the base line. Finally (Figure 4, two bottom records) the reward was discontinued and, as would be expected, the response continued for a while but gradually became extinguished, so that the activity eventually returned to approximately its original base-line level.

After studying a number of other rats in this way and convincing ourselves that the instrumental learning of intestinal responses was a possibility, we designed an experiment to test specificity. For all the rats of the experiment, both intestinal contractions and heart rate were recorded, but half the rats were rewarded for one of these responses and half were rewarded for the other response.

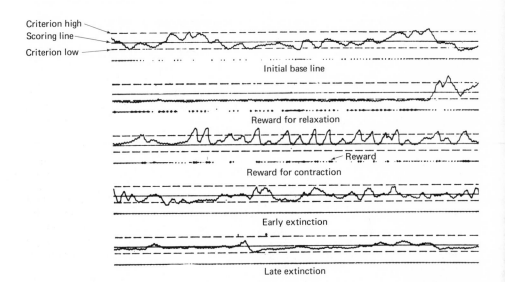

Criterion high
Scoring line
Criterion low

Initial base line

Reward for relaxation

Reward

Reward for contraction

Early extinction

Late extinction

Figure 4. Typical samples of a record of instrumental learning of an intestinal response by a curarized rat. (From top to bottom) Record of spontaneous contraction before training; record after training with reward for relaxation; record after training with reward for contractions; records during nonrewarded extinction trials. [From Miller and Banuazizi (18)]

Each of these two groups of rats was divided into two subgroups, rewarded, respectively, for increased and decreased response. The rats were completely paralyzed by curare, maintained on artificial respiration, and rewarded by electrical stimulation of the brain.

The results are shown in Figures 5 and 6. In Figure 5 it may be seen that the group rewarded for increases in intestinal contractions learned an increase, the group rewarded for decreases learned a decrease, but neither of these groups showed an appreciable change in heart rate. Conversely (Figure 6), the group rewarded for increases in heart rate showed an increase, the group rewarded for decreases showed a decrease, but neither of these groups showed a change in intestinal contractions.

The fact that each type of response changed when it was rewarded rules out the interpretation that the failure to secure a change when that change was not rewarded could have been due to either a strong and stable homeostatic

regulation of that response or an inability of our techniques to measure changes reliably under the particular conditions of our experiment.

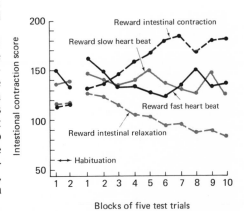

Figure 5. Graph showing that the intestinal contraction score is changed by rewarding either increases or decreases in intestinal contraction but is unaffected by rewarding changes in heart rate. [From Miller and Banuazizi (18)]

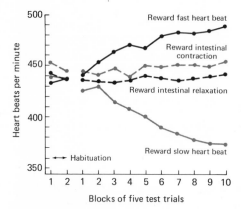

Figure 6. Graph showing that the heart rate is changed by rewarding either increases or decreases in heart rate but is unaffected by rewarding changes in intestinal contractions. Comparison with Figure 5 demonstrates the specificity of visceral learning. [From Miller and DiCara (20)]

Each of the 12 rats in the experiment showed statistically reliable changes in the rewarded direction; for 11 the changes were reliable beyond the $P < .001$ level, while for the 12th the changes were reliable only beyond the .05 level. A statistically reliable negative correlation showed that the better the rewarded visceral response was learned, the less change occurred in the other, nonrewarded response. This greater specificity with better learning is what we had expected. The results showed that visceral learning can be specific to an organ system, and they clearly ruled out the possibility of mediation by any single general factor, such as level of activation or central commands for either general activity or relaxation.

In an additional experiment, Banuazizi (19) showed that either increases or decreases in intestinal contractions can be rewarded by avoidance of, or escape from, mild electric shocks, and that the intestinal responses can be discriminatively elicited by a specific stimulus associated with reinforcement.

KIDNEY FUNCTION

Encouraged by these successes, DiCara and I decided to see whether or not the rate of urine formation by the kidney could be changed in the curarized rat rewarded by electrical stimulation of the brain (20). A catheter, permanently inserted, was used to prevent accumulation of urine by the bladder, and the rate of urine formation was measured by an electronic device for counting minute drops. In order to secure a rate of urine formation fast enough so that small changes could be promptly detected and rewarded, the rats were kept constantly loaded with water through infusion by way of a catheter permanently inserted in the jugular vein.

All of the seven rats rewarded when the intervals between times of urine-drop formation lengthened showed decreases in the rate of urine formation, and all of the seven rats rewarded when these intervals shortened showed increases in the rate of urine formation. For both groups the changes were highly reliable ($P < .001$).

In order to determine how the change in rate of urine formation was achieved, certain additional measures were taken. As the set of bars at left in Figure 7 shows, the rate of filtration, measured by means of ^{14}C-labeled inulin, increased when increases in the rate of urine formation were rewarded and decreased when decreases in the rate were rewarded. Plots of the correlations showed that the changes in the rates of filtration and urine formation were not related to changes in either blood pressure or heart rate.

The middle set of bars in Figure 7 shows that the rats rewarded for increases in the rate of urine formation had an increased rate of renal blood flow, as measured by ^{3}H-p-aminohippuric acid, and that those rewarded for decreases had a decreased rate of renal blood flow. Since these changes in blood flow were not accompanied by

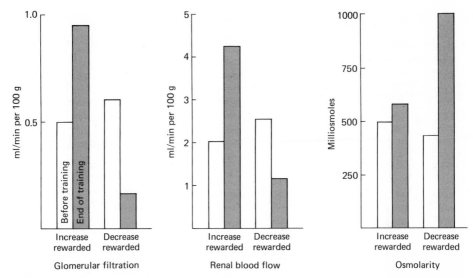

Figure 7. Effects of rewarding increased rate of urine formation in one group and decreased rate in another on measures of glomerular filtration, renal blood flow, and osmolarity. [From data in Miller and DiCara (20)].

changes in general blood pressure or in heart rate, they must have been achieved by vasomotor changes of the renal arteries. That these vasomotor changes were at least somewhat specific is shown by the fact that vasomotor responses of the tail, as measured by a photoelectric plethysmograph, did not differ for the two groups of rats.

The set of bars in Figure 7 shows that when decreases in rate of urine formation were rewarded, a more concentrated urine, having higher osmolarity, was formed. Since the slower passage of urine through the tubules would afford more opportunity for reabsorption of water, this higher concentration does not necessarily mean an increase in the secretion of antidiuretic hormone. When an increased rate of urine formation was rewarded, the urine did not become more diluted—that is, it showed no decrease in osmolarity; therefore, the increase in rate of urine formation observed in this experiment cannot be accounted for in terms of an

inhibition of the secretion of antidiuretic hormone.

From the foregoing results it appears that the learned changes in urine formation in this experiment were produced primarily by changes in the rate of filtration, which, in turn, were produced primarily by changes in the rate of blood flow through the kidneys.

GASTRIC CHANGES

In the next experiment, Carmona, Demierre, and I used a photoelectric plethysmograph to measure changes, presumably in the amount of blood, in the stomach wall (21). In an operation performed under anesthesia, a small glass tube, painted black except for a small spot, was inserted into the rat's stomach. The same tube was used to hold the stomach wall against a small glass window inserted through the body wall. The tube was left in that position. After the animal had recovered, a bundle of optical fibers could be slipped snugly into the glass tube so that the light beamed through it would shine out through the unpainted spot in the tube inside the stomach, pass through the stomach wall, and be recorded by a photocell on the other side of the glass window. Preliminary tests indicated that, as would be expected, when the amount of blood in the stomach wall increased, less light would pass through. Other tests showed that stomach contractions elicited by injections of insulin did not affect the amount of light transmitted.

In the main experiment we rewarded curarized rats by enabling them to avoid or escape from mild electric shocks. Some were rewarded when the amount of light that passed through the stomach wall increased, while others were rewarded when the amount decreased. Fourteen of the 15 rats showed changes in the rewarded direction. Thus, we demonstrated that the stomach wall, under the control of the autonomic nervous system, can be modified by instrumental learning. There is strong reason to believe that the learned changes were achieved by vasomotor responses affecting the amount of blood in the stomach wall or mucosa, or in both.

In another experiment, Carmona (22) showed that stomach contractions can be either increased or decreased by instrumental learning.

It is obvious that learned changes in the blood supply of internal organs can affect their functioning—as, for example, the rate at which urine was formed by the kidneys was affected by changes in the amount of blood that flowed through them. Thus, such changes can produce psychosomatic symptoms. And if the learned changes in blood supply can be specific to a given organ, the symptom will occur in that organ rather than in another one.

PERIPHERAL VASOMOTOR RESPONSES

Having investigated the instrumental learning of internal vasomotor responses, we next studied the learning of peripheral ones. In the first experiment, the amount of blood in the tail of a curarized rat was measured by a photoelectric plethysmograph, and changes were rewarded by electrical stimulation of the brain (23). All of the four rats rewarded for vasoconstriction showed that response, and, at the same time, their average core temperature, measured rectally, decreased from 98.9° to 97.9°F. All of the four rats rewarded for vasodilatation showed that response and, at the same time, their average core temperature increased from 99.9° to 101°F. The vasomotor change for each individual rat was reliable beyond the $P < .01$ level, and the difference in change in temperature between the groups was reliable beyond the .01 level. The direction of the change in temperature was opposite to that which would be expected from the heat conservation caused by peripheral vasoconstriction or the heat loss caused by peripheral vasodilatation. The changes are in the direction which would be expected if the training had altered the rate of heat production, causing a change in temperature which, in turn, elicited the vasomotor response.

The next experiment was designed to try to determine the limits of the specificity of vasomotor learning. The pinnae of the rat's ears were chosen because the blood vessels in them are believed to be innervated primarily, and perhaps exclusively, by the sympathetic branch of the autonomic nervous system, the branch that Cannon believed always fired nonspecifically as a unit (3). But Cannon's experiments involved exposing cats to extremely strong emotion-evoking stimuli, such as barking dogs, and such stimuli will also evoke generalized activity throughout the skeletal musculature. Perhaps his results reflected the way in which sympathetic activity was elicited, rather than demonstrating any inherent inferiority of the sympathetic nervous system.

In order to test this interpretation, DiCara and I (24) put photocells on both ears of the curarized rat and connected them to a bridge circuit so that only differences in the vasomotor responses of the two ears were rewarded by brain stimulation. We were somewhat surprised and greatly delighted to find that this experiment actually worked. The results are summarized in Figure 8. Each of the six rats rewarded for relative vasodilatation of the left ear showed that response, while each of the six rats rewarded for relative vasodilatation of the right ear showed that response. Recordings from the right and left forepaws showed little if any change in vasomotor response.

It is clear that these results cannot be by-products of changes in either heart rate or blood pressure, as these would be expected to affect both ears equally. They show either that vasomotor responses mediated by the sympathetic nervous system are capable of much greater specificity than has previously been believed, or that the innervation of the blood vessels in the pinnae of the

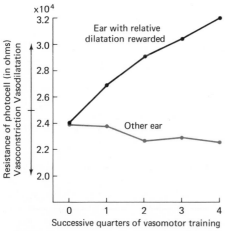

Figure 8. Learning a difference in the vasomotor responses of the two ears in the curarized rat. [From data in DiCara and Miller (24)]

ears is not restricted almost exclusively to sympathetic-nervous-system components, as has been believed, and involves functionally significant parasympathetic components. In any event, the changes in the blood flow certainly were surprisingly specific. Such changes in blood flow could account for specific psychosomatic symptoms.

BLOOD PRESSURE INDEPENDENT OF HEART RATE

Although changes in blood pressure were not induced as by-products of rewarded changes in the rate of urine formation, another experiment on curarized rats showed that, when changes in systolic blood pressure are specifically reinforced, they can be learned (25). Blood pressure was recorded by means of a catheter permanently inserted into the aorta, and the reward was avoidance of, or escape from, mild electric shock. All seven rats rewarded for increases in blood pressure showed further increases, while all seven rewarded for decreases showed decreases, each of the changes, which were in opposite directions, being reliable beyond the $P < .01$ level. The increase was from 139 mm-Hg, which happens to be roughly comparable to the normal systolic blood pressure of an adult man, to 170 mm-Hg, which is on the borderline of abnormally high blood pressure in man.

Each experimental animal was "yoked" with a curarized partner, maintained on artificial respiration and having shock electrodes on its tail wired in series with electrodes on the tail of the experimental animal, so that it received exactly the same electric shocks and could do nothing to escape or avoid them. The yoked controls for both the increase-rewarded and the decrease-rewarded groups showed some elevation in blood pressure as an unconditioned effect of the shocks. By the end of training, in contrast to the large difference in the blood pressures of the two groups specifically rewarded for changes in opposite directions, there was no difference in blood pressure between the yoked control partners for these two groups. Furthermore, the increase in blood pressure in these control groups was reliably less ($P < .01$) than that in the group specifically rewarded for increases. Thus, it is clear that the reward for an increase in blood pressure produced an additional increase over and above the effects of the shocks per se, while the reward for a decrease was able to overcome the unconditioned increase elicited by the shocks.

For none of the four groups was there a significant change in heart rate or in temperature during training; there were no significant differences in these measures among the groups. Thus, the learned change we relatively specific to blood pressure.

TRANSFER FROM HEART RATE TO SKELETAL AVOIDANCE

Although visceral learning can be quite specific, especially if only a specific response is rewarded, as was the case in the experiment on the two ears, under some circumstances it can involve a more generalized effect.

In handling the rats that had just recovered from curarization, DiCara noticed that those that had been trained, through the avoidance or escape reward, to increase their heart rate were more likely to squirm, squeal, defecate, and show other responses indicating emotionality than were those that had been trained to reduce their heart-rate. Could instrumental learning of heart-rate changes have some generalized effects, perhaps on the level of emotionality, which might affect the behavior in a different avoidance-learning situation? In order to look for such an effect, DiCara and Weiss (26) used a modified shuttle avoidance apparatus. In this apparatus, when a danger signal is given, the rat must run from compartment A to

compartment B. If he runs fast enough, he avoids the shock; if not, he must run to escape it. The next time the danger signal is given, the rat must run in the opposite direction, from B to A.

Other work had shown that learning in this apparatus is an inverted U-shaped function of the strength of the shocks, with shocks that are too strong eliciting emotional behavior instead of running. DiCara and Weiss trained their rats in this apparatus with a level of shock that is approximately optimum for naive rats of this strain. They found that the rats that had been rewarded for decreasing their heart rate learned well, but that those that had been rewarded for increasing their heart rate learned less well, as if their emotionality had been increased. The difference was statistically reliable ($P < .001$). This experiment clearly demonstrates that training a visceral response can affect the subsequent learning of a skeletal one, but additional work will be required to prove the hypothesis that training to increase heart rate increases emotionality.

VISCERAL LEARNING WITHOUT CURARE

Thus far, in all of the experiments except the one on teaching thirsty dogs to salivate, the initial training was given when the animal was under the influence of curare. All of the experiments, except the one on salivation, have produced surprisingly rapid learning—definitive results within 1 or 2 hours. Will learning in the normal, noncurarized state be easier, as we originally thought it should be, or will it be harder, as the experiment on the noncurarized dogs suggests? DiCara and I have started to get additional evidence on this problem. We have obtained clear-cut evidence that rewarding (with the avoidance or escape reward) one group of freely moving rats for reducing heart rate and rewarding another group for increasing heart rate produces a difference between the two groups (27). That this difference was not due to the indirect effects of the overt performance of skeletal responses is shown by the fact that it persisted in subsequent tests during which the rats were paralyzed by curare. And, on subsequent retraining without curare, such differences in activity and respiration as were present earlier in training continued to decrease, while the differences in heart rate continued to increase. It seems extremely unlikely that, at the end of training, the highly reliable differences in heart rate ($t = 7.2$; $P < .0001$) can be explained by the highly unreliable differences in activity and respiration ($t = .07$ and 0.2, respectively).

Although the rats in this experiment showed some learning when they were trained initially in the noncurarized state, this learning was much poorer than that which we have seen in our other experiments on curarized rats. This is exactly the opposite of my original expectation, but seems plausible in the light of hindsight. My hunch is that paralysis by curare improved learning by eliminating sources of distraction and variability. The stimulus situation was kept more constant, and confusing visceral fluctuations induced indirectly by skeletal movements were eliminated.

LEARNED CHANGES IN BRAIN WAVES

Encouraged by success in the experiments on the instrumental learning of visceral responses, my colleagues and I have attempted to produce other unconventional types of learning. Electrodes placed on the skull or, better yet, touching the surface of the brain record summative effects of electrical activity over a considerable area of the brain. Such electrical effects are called brain waves, and the record of them is called an electroencephalogram. When the animal is aroused, the electroencephalogram consists of fast, low-voltage activity; when the animal is drowsy or sleeping normally, the electroencephalogram consists of considerably slower, higher-voltage activity. Carmona attempted to see whether this type of brain activity, and the state of arousal accompanying it, can be modified by direct reward of changes in the brain activity (28, 29).

The subjects of the first experiment were freely moving cats. In order to have a reward that was under complete control and that did not require the cat to move, Carmona used direct electrical stimulation of the medial forebrain bundle, which is a rewarding area of the brain. Such stimulation produced a slight lowering in the average voltage of the electroencephalogram and an increase in behavioral arousal. In order to provide a control for these and any other unlearned effects, he rewarded one group for changes in the direction of high-voltage activity and another group for changes in the direction of low-voltage activity.

Both groups learned. The cats rewarded for high-voltage activity showed more high-voltage slow waves and tended to sit like sphinxes, staring out into space. The cats rewarded for low-voltage activity showed much more low-voltage fast activity, and appeared to be aroused, pacing restlessly about, sniffing, and looking here and there. It was clear that this type of training had modified both the character of the electrical brain waves and the general level of the behavioral activity. It was not clear, however, whether the level of arousal of the brain was directly modified and hence modified the behavior; whether the animals learned specific items of behavior which, in turn, modified the arousal of the brain as reflected in the electroencephalogram; or whether both types of learning were occurring simultaneously.

In order to rule out the direct sensory consequences of changes in muscular tension, movement, and posture, Carmona performed the next experiment on rats that had been paralyzed by means

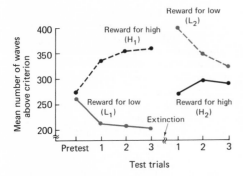

Figure 9. *Instrumental learning by curarized rats rewarded for high-voltage or for low-voltage electroencephalograms recorded from the cerebral cortex. After a period of nonrewarded extinction, which produced some drowsiness, as indicated by an increase in voltage, the rats in the two groups were then rewarded for voltage changes opposite in direction to the changes for which they were rewarded earlier. [From Carmona (29)].*

of curare. The results, given in Figure 9, show that both rewarded groups showed changes in the rewarded direction; that a subsequent nonrewarded rest increased the number of high-voltage responses in both groups; and that, when the conditions of reward were reversed, the direction of change in voltage was reversed.

At present we are trying to use similar techniques to modify the functions of a specific part of the vagal nucleus, by recording and specifically rewarding changes in the electrical activity there. Preliminary results suggest that this is possible. The next step is to investigate the visceral consequences of such modification. This kind of work may open up possibilities for modifying the activity of specific parts of the brain and the functions that they control. In some cases, directly rewarding brain activity may be a more convenient or more powerful technique than rewarding skeletal or visceral behavior. It also may be a new way to throw light on the functions of specific parts of the brain (30).

HUMAN VISCERAL LEARNING

Another question is that of whether people are capable of instrumental learning of visceral responses. I believe that in this respect they are as smart as rats. But, as a recent critical review by Katkin and Murray (31) points out, this has not yet been completely proved. These authors have comprehensively summarized the recent studies reporting successful use of instrumental training to modify human heart rate, vasomotor responses, and the galvanic skin response. Because of the difficulties in subjecting human subjects to the same rigorous controls, including deep paralysis by means of curare, that can be used with animal subjects, one of the most serious questions about the results of the human studies is whether the changes recorded represent the true instrumental learning of visceral responses or the unconscious learning of those skeletal responses that can produce visceral reactions. However, the able investigators who have courageously challenged the strong traditional belief in the inferiority of the autonomic nervous system with experiments at the more difficult but especially significant human level are developing ingenious controls, including demonstrations of the specificity of the visceral change, so that their cumulative results are becoming increasingly impressive.

POSSIBLE ROLE IN HOMEOSTASIS

The functional utility of instrumental learning by the cerebrospinal nervous system under the conditions that existed during mammalian evolution is obvious. The skeletal responses mediated by the cerebrospinal nervous system operate on the external environment, so that there is survival value in the ability to learn responses that bring reward such as food, water, or escape from pain. The fact that the responses mediated by the autonomic nervous system do not have such direct action on the external environment was one of the reasons for believing that they are not subject to instrumental learning. Is the learning ability of the autonomic nervous system something that has no normal function other than that of providing my students with subject matter for publications? Is it a mere accidental by-product of the survival value of cerebrospinal learning, or does the instrumental learning of autonomically mediated responses have some adaptive function, such as helping to maintain that constancy of the internal environment called homeostasis?

In order for instrumental learning to function homeostatically, a deviation away from the optimum level will have to function as a drive to motivate learning, and a change toward the optimum level will have to function as a reward to reinforce the learning of the particular visceral response that produced the corrective change.

When a mammal has less than the optimum amount of water in his body, this deficiency serves as a drive of thirst to motivate learning; the overt consummatory response of drinking functions as a reward to reinforce the learning of the particular skeletal responses that were successful in securing the water that restored the optimum level. But is the consummatory response essential? Can restoration of an optimum level by a glandular response function as a reward?

In order to test for the possible rewarding effects of a glandular response, DiCara, Wolf, and I (32) injected albino rats with antidiuretic hormone (ADH) if they chose one arm of a T-maze and with the isotonic saline vehicle if they chose the other, distinctively different, arm. The ADH permitted water to be reabsorbed in the kidney, so that a smaller volume of more concentrated urine was formed. Thus, for normal rats loaded in advance with H_2O, the ADH interfered with the excess-water ex-

cretion required for the restoration of homeostasis, while the control injection of isotonic saline allowed the excess water to be excreted. And, indeed, such rats learned to select the side of the maze that assured them an injection of saline so that their glandular response could restore homeostasis.

Conversely, for rats with diabetes insipidus, loaded in advance with hypertonic NaCl, the homeostatic effects of the same two injections were reversed; the ADH, causing the urine to be more concentrated, helped the rats to get rid of the excess NaCl, while the isotonic saline vehicle did not. And, indeed, a group of rats of this kind learned the opposite choice of selecting the ADH side of the maze. As a further control on the effects of the ADH per se, normal rats which had not been given H_2O or NaCl exhibited no learning. This experiment showed that an excess of either H_2O or NaCl functions as a drive and that the return to the normal concentration produced by the appropriate response of a gland, the kidney, functions as a reward.

When we consider the results of this experiment together with those of our experiments showing that glandular and visceral responses can be instrumentally learned, we will expect the animal to learn those glandular and visceral responses mediated by the central nervous system that promptly restore homeostasis after any considerable deviation. Whether or not this theoretically possible learning has any practical significance will depend on whether or not the innate homeostatic mechanisms control the levels closely enough to prevent any deviations large enough to function as a drive from occurring. Even if the innate control should be accurate enough to preclude learning in most cases, there remains the intriguing possibility that, when pathology interferes with innate control, visceral learning is available as a supplementary mechanism.

IMPLICATIONS AND SPECULATIONS

We have seen how the instrumental learning of visceral responses suggests a new possible homeostatic mechanism worthy of further investigation. Such learning also shows that the autonomic nervous system is not as inferior as has been so widely and firmly believed. It removes one of the strongest arguments for the hypothesis that there are two fundamentally different mechanisms of learning, involving different parts of the nervous system.

Cause of psychosomatic symptoms. Similarly, evidence of the instrumental learning of visceral responses removes the main basis for assuming that the psychosomatic symptoms that involve the autonomic nervous system are fundamentally different from those functional symptoms, such as hysterical ones, that involve the cerebrospinal nervous system. Such evidence allows us to extend to psychosomatic symptoms the type of learning-theory analysis that Dollard and I (7, 33) have applied to other symptoms.

For example, suppose a child is terror-stricken at the thought of going to school in the morning because he is completely unprepared for an important examination. The strong fear elicits a variety of fluctuating autonomic symptoms, such as a queasy stomach at one time and pallor and faintness at another; at this point his mother, who is particularly concerned about cardiovascular symptoms, says, "You are sick and must stay home." The child feels a great relief from fear, and this reward should reinforce the cardiovascular responses producing pallor and faintness. If such experiences are repeated frequently enough, the child, theoretically, should learn to respond with that kind of symptom. Similarly, another child whose mother ignored the vasomotor responses but was particularly concerned by signs of gastric distress

would learn the latter type of symptom. I want to emphasize, however, that we need careful clinical research to determine how frequently, if at all, the social conditions sufficient for such theoretically possible learning of visceral symptoms actually occur. Since a given instrumental response can be reinforced by a considerable variety of rewards, and by one reward on one occasion and a different reward on another, the fact that glandular and visceral responses can be instrumentally learned opens up many new theoretical possibilities for the reinforcement of psychosomatic symptoms.

Furthermore, we do not yet know how severe a psychosomatic effect can be produced by learning. While none of the 40 rats rewarded for speeding up their heart rates have died in the course of training under curarization, seven of the 40 rats rewarded for slowing down their heart rates have died. This statistically reliable difference (chi square = 5.6, $P < .02$) is highly suggestive, but it could mean that training to speed up the heart helped the rats resist the stress of curare rather than that the reward for slowing down the heart was strong enough to overcome innate regulatory mechanisms and induce sudden death. In either event the visceral learning had a vital effect. At present, DiCara and I are trying to see whether or not the learning of visceral responses can be carried far enough in the noncurarized animal to produce physical damage. We are also investigating the possibility that there may be a critical period in early infancy during which visceral learning has particularly intense and long-lasting effects.

Individual and cultural differences. It is possible that, in addition to producing psychosomatic symptoms in extreme cases, visceral learning can account for certain more benign individual and cultural differences. Lacey and Lacey (34) have shown that a given individual may have a tendency, which is stable over a number of years, to respond to a variety of different stresses with the same profile of autonomic responses, while other individuals may have statistically reliable tendencies to respond with different profiles. It now seems possible that differential conditions of learning may account for at least some of these individual differences in patterns of autonomic response.

Conversely, such learning may account also for certain instances in which the same individual responds to the same stress in different ways. For example, a small boy who receives a severe bump in rough-and-tumble play may learn to inhibit the secretion of tears in this situation since his peer group will punish crying by calling it "sissy." But the same small boy may burst into tears when he gets home to his mother, who will not punish weeping and may even reward tears with sympathy.

Similarly, it seems conceivable that different conditions of reward by a culture different from our own may be responsible for the fact that Homer's adult heroes so often "let the big tears fall." Indeed, a former colleague of mine, Herbert Barry III, has analyzed cross-cultural data and found that the amount of crying reported for children seems to be related to the way in which the society reacts to their tears (35).

I have emphasized the possible role of learning in producing the observed individual differences in visceral responses to stress, which in extreme cases may result in one type of psychosomatic symptom in one person and a different type in another. Such learning does not, of course, exclude innate individual differences in the susceptibility of different organs. In fact, given social conditions under which any form of illness will be rewarded, the symptoms of the most susceptible organ will be the most likely ones to be learned. Furthermore, some types of stress may be so strong that the innate reactions to them produce damage without any learning. My colleagues and I are currently investigating the psychological variables involved in such types of stress (36).

Therapeutic training. The experimental work on animals has developed a powerful technique for using instrumental learning to modify glandular and visceral responses. The improved training technique consists of moment-to-moment recording of the visceral function and immediate reward, at first, of very small changes in the desired direction and then of progressively larger ones. The success of this technique suggests that it should be able to produce therapeutic changes. If the patient who is highly motivated to get rid of a symptom understands that a signal, such as a tone, indicates a change in the desired direction, that tone could serve as a powerful reward. Instruction to try to turn the tone on as often as possible and praise for success should increase the reward. As patients find that they can secure some control of the symptom, their motivation should be strengthened. Such a procedure should be well worth trying on any symptom, functional or organic, that is under neural control, that can be continuously monitored by modern instrumentation, and for which a given direction of change is clearly indicated medically—for example, cardiac arrhythmias, spastic colitis, asthma, and those cases of high blood pressure that are not essential compensation for kidney damage (37). The obvious cases to begin with are those in which drugs are ineffective or contraindicated. In the light of the fact that our animals learned so much better when under the influence of curare and transferred their training so well to the normal, nondrugged state, it should be worthwhile to try to use hypnotic suggestion to achieve similar results by enhancing the reward effect of the signal indicating a change in the desired direction, by producing relaxation and regular breathing, and by removing interference from skeletal responses and distraction by irrelevant cues.

Engel and Melmon (38) have reported encouraging results in the use of instrumental training to treat cardiac arrhythmias of organic origin. Randt, Korein, Carmona, and I have had some success in using the method described above to train epileptic patients in the laboratory to suppress, in one way or another, the abnormal paroxysmal spikes in their electroencephalogram. My colleagues and I are hoping to try learning therapy for other symptoms—for example, the rewarding of high-voltage electroencephalograms as a treatment for insomnia. While it is far too early to promise any cures, it certainly will be worth while to investigate thoroughly the therapeutic possibilities of improved instrumental training techniques.

References and notes

1. *The Dialogues of Plato*, B. Jowett, Transl., (2nd ed.). London: Univ. of Oxford Press, 1875. Vol. 3, *Timaeus*.
2. Bichat, X. *Recherches physiologiques sur la vie et le mort*. Paris: Brosson, Gabon, 1800.
3. Cannon, W. B. *The wisdom of the body*. New York: Norton, 1932.
4. Alexander, F. *Psychosomatic medicine; Its principles and applications*. New York: Norton, 1950. Pp. 40–41.
5. Kimble, G. A. *Hilgard and Marquis' conditioning and learning* (2nd ed.). New York: Appleton-Century-Crofts, 1961. P. 100.
6. Skinner, B. F. *The behavior of organisms*. New York: Appleton-Century-Crofts, 1938; Mowrer, O. H. *Harvard Educ. Rev.*, 1947, **17**, 102.
7. Miller, N. E., and Dollard, J. *Social learning and imitation*. New Haven: Yale Univ. Press, 1941; Dollard, J., and Miller, N. E. *Personality and psychotherapy*. New York: McGraw-Hill, 1950; Miller, N. E. *Psychol. Rev.*, 1951, **58**, 375.
8. Miller, N. E. *Ann. N. Y. Acad. Sci.*, 1961, **92**, 830; Miller, N. E. in M. R. Jones (Ed.), *Nebraska Symposium on Motivation*, Lincoln: Univ. of Nebraska Press, 1963; Miller, N. E. in *Proc. 3rd World Congr. Psychiat., Montreal, 1961*, 1963, vol. 3. P. 213.
9. Miller, N. E. in *Proceedings, 18th International Congress of Psychology, Moscow, 1966*. In press.
10. Miller, N. E., and Carmona, A. *J. comp. physiol. Psychol.*, 1967, **63**, 1.
11. Trowill, J. A. *J. comp. physiol. Psychol.*, p. 7.
12. Miller, N. E., and DiCara, L. V. *J. comp. physiol. Psychol.*, p. 12.
13. DiCara, L. V., and Miller, N. E. *Commun. Behav. Biol.* 1968, **2**, 19.
14. DiCara, L. V., and Miller, N. E. *J. comp. physiol. Psychol.*, 1968, **65**, 8.
15. DiCara, L. V., and Miller, N. E. *J. comp. physiol. Psychol.* In press.
16. Ehrlich, D. J., and Malmo, R. B. *Neuropsychologia*, 1967, **5**, 219.
17. "It even becomes difficult to postulate enough different thoughts each arousing a different emotion, each of which in turn innately elicits a specific visceral response. And if one assumes a more direct specific connection between different thoughts and different visceral responses, the notion becomes indistinguishable from the ideo-motor hypothesis of the voluntary movement of skeletal muscles." W. James, *Principles of Psychology*. New York: Dover, new ed., 1950. Vol. 2, Chap. 26.
18. Miller, N. E., and Banuazizi, A. *J. comp. physiol. Psychol.*, 1968, **65**, 1.
19. Banuazizi, A. Thesis, Yale University, 1968.
20. Miller, N. E., and DiCara, L. V. *Amer. J. Physiol.*, 1968, **215**, 677.
21. Carmona, A., Miller, N. E., and Demierre, T. In preparation.
22. Carmona, A. In preparation.
23. DiCara, L. V., and Miller, N. E. *Commun. Behav. Biol.*, 1968, **1**, 209.
24. DiCara, L. V., and Miller, N. E. *Science*, 1968, **159**, 1485.
25. DiCara, L. V., and Miller, N. E. *Psychosom. Med.*, 1968, **30**, 489.
26. DiCara, L. V., and Weiss, J. M. *J. comp. physiol. Psychol.* In press.
27. DiCara, L. V., and Miller, N. E. *Physiol. Behav.* In press.

28. Miller, N. E. *Science*, 1966, **152**, 676.

29. Carmona, A. Thesis, Yale University, 1967.

30. For somewhat similar work on the single-cell level, see Olds, J., and Olds, M. E. In J. Delafresnaye, A. Fessard, J. Konorski, (Eds.) *Brain mechanisms and learning*. London: Blackwell, 1961.

31. Katkin, E. S., and Murray, N. E. *Psychol. Bull.*, 1968, **70**, 52; for a reply to their criticisms, see Crider, A., Schwartz, G., and Shnidman, S. In press.

32. Miller, N. E., DiCara, L. V., and Wolf, G. *Amer. J. Physiol*, 1968, **215**, 684.

33. Miller, N. E. In D. Byrne and P. Worchel (Eds.), *Personality Change*. New York: Wiley, 1964. P. 149.

34. Lacey, J. I., and Lacey, B. C. *Amer. J. Psychol.*, 1958, **71**, 50; *Ann. N.Y. Acad. Sci.*, 1962, **98**, 1257.

35. Barry, H., III, personal communication.

36. Miller, N. E. *Proc. N.Y. Acad. Sci.* In press.

37. Objective recording of such symptoms might be useful also in monitoring the effects of quite different types of psychotherapy.

38. Engel, B. T., and Melmon, K. T., personal communication.

emotion
and
motivation
chapter 7

Emotion and motivation are topics which lie at the very heart of psychology. Both are typical chapter headings and both are difficult to define. Generally, emotional states are defined by means of specific configurations of behavior. We have operational definitions of fear in terms of defensive behaviors or the conditioned emotional response. Anger is similarly defined in terms of attack behavior. The various primary motivational states (hunger, thirst, sexual drive, and the more subtle motivations—such as the need for stimulation, manipulation, and varied environment) are areas of tremendous importance to behaviorists.

An extensive collection of papers is presented in this section: it deals with theories of emotion and motivation. Stressed are the neural basis and cerebral localization of specific motivational and emotional states. In addition there is a fascinating paper by Schachter dealing with obesity and eating which presents a unique theory of obesity based upon early feeding experiences in the child. There are papers, such as one by Neal Miller, dealing with chemical aspects of behavior. There is a paper dealing with the neural basis of violence, a topic of great interest and importance today.

One thing to be gained from these readings is the notion that for many years emotion was very poorly understood. In the early part of this century several theories of emotion—the James-Lange Theory, the Cannon-Thalamic Theory, and others—were proposed; but there was little data to support these points of view. Recent research dealing with the limbic system has opened the way for understanding the basic mechanisms which underly different varieties of behavior considered to fall in the category of emotion.

Epinephrine
chlorpromazine
and
amusement
stanley schachter
and
ladd wheeler

In their study of cognitive and physiological determinants of emotional states, Schachter and Singer (1962) have demonstrated that cognitive processes play a major role in the development of emotional states. Given a common state of physiological arousal, subjects can be readily induced into states of euphoria or of anger by means of cognitive manipulations. To what extent the state of physiological arousal is a necessary component of an emotional experience is not, however, completely clear in that study.

The technique employed by Schachter and Singer (1962) to produce a state of physiological arousal was simply the injection of the sympathomimetic amine, epinephrine. With slight exceptions, this agent provokes a pattern of physiological activation which is a virtual replica of the state produced by active discharge of the sympathetic nervous system. In experimental situations designed to make subjects euphoric, those subjects who received injections of epinephrine were, on a variety of indices, somewhat more euphoric than subjects who received a placebo injection. Similarly, in situations designed to make subjects angry and irritated, those who received epinephrine were somewhat angrier than subjects who received placebo. In both sets of conditions, however, these differences between epinephrine and placebo subjects were significant, at best, at borderline levels of statistical significance.

Assuming, for the moment, that phys-

From *Journal of Abnormal and Social Psychology*, 1962, **45**, 121–128. Copyright by the American Psychological Association.

iological arousal is a necessary component of emotional states, one of the factors that might account for this failure to find larger differences between epinephrine and placebo subjects seems reasonably apparent. The experimental situations employed were fairly effective. The injection of placebo does not, of course, prevent the subject from self-arousal of the sympathetic system, and indeed there is considerable evidence (Woodworth and Schlosberg, 1958) that the arousal of an emotional state is accompanied by general excitation of the sympathetic nervous system.

A test of the proposition at stake, then, would require comparison of subjects who have received injections of epinephrine with subjects who, to some extent, are rendered incapable of self-activation of the sympathetic nervous system. Thanks to a class of drugs known generally as autonomic blocking agents, such blockage is, to some degree, possible. If the proposition that a state of sympathetic discharge is a necessary component of an emotional experience is correct, it should be anticipated that whatever emotional state is experimentally manipulated, it should be most intensely experienced by subjects who have received epinephrine, next by placebo subjects, and least of all by subjects who have received injections of an autonomic blocking agent.

PROCEDURE

In order to conceal the purposes of the study and the nature of the injection, the experiment was cast in the framework of a study of the effects of vitamins on vision. As soon as a subject arrived, he was taken to a private room and told by the experimenter:

> I've asked you to come today to take part in an experiment concerning the effects of vitamins on the visual processes. We know a great deal about vision, but only night vision has been studied in relation to nutrition. Our experiment is concerned with the effects of suproxin on vision. Suproxin is a high concentrate vitamin C derivative. If you agree to take part in the experiment, we will give you an injection of suproxin and then subject your retina to about 15 minutes of continuous black and white stimulation. This is simpler than it sounds; we'll just have you watch a black and white movie. After the movie, we'll give you a series of visual tests.
>
> The injection itself is harmless and will be administered by our staff doctor. It may sting a little at first, as most injections do, but after this you will feel nothing and will have no side effects. We know that some people dislike getting injections, and if you take part in the experiment, we want it to be your own decision. Would you like to? [All subjects agreed to take part.]

This much said, the experimenter gave the subject a test of visual acuity and of color vision, took the subject's pulse and left the room. Shortly thereafter, the doctor arrived, gave the subject a quick ophthalmoscopic examination, then gave him an injection and informed him that the experimenter would be back for him shortly "in order to take you and some other subjects who have also received shots of suproxin into the projection room."

Injections

There were three forms of suproxin administered — epinephrine, placebo, and chlorpromazine.

1. Epinephrine. Subjects in this condition received a subcutaneous injection of $\frac{1}{2}$ cubic centimeter of a 1.1000 solution of Winthrop Laboratory's Suprarenin.

2. Placebo. Subjects in this condition received a subcutaneous injection of $\frac{1}{2}$ cubic centimeter of saline solution.

3. Chlorpromazine. Subjects in this condition received an intramuscular injection of a solution consisting of 1 cubic centimeter (25 milligrams) of Smith, Kline, and French Thorazine and 1 cubic centimeter of saline solution.

The choice of chlorpromazine as a blocking agent was dictated by considerations of safety, ease of administration, and known duration of effect. Ideally, one would have wished for a blocking agent whose mechanism and effect was precisely and solely the reverse of that of epinephrine—a peripherally acting agent which would prevent the excitation of sympathetically innervated structures. Though it is certainly possible to approach this ideal more closely with agents other than chlorpromazine, such drugs tend to be dangerous, or difficult to administer, or of short duration.

Chlorpromazine is known to act as a sympathetic depressant. It has a moderate hypotensive effect, with a slight compensatory increase in heart rate. It has mild adrenergic blocking activity for it reverses the pressor effects of small doses of epinephrine and depresses responses of the nictitating membrane to preganglionic stimulation. Killam (1959) summarizes what is known and supposed about the mechanism of action of chlorpromazine as follows:

> Autonomic effects in general may be attributed to a mild peripheral adrenergic blocking activity and probably to central depression of sympathetic centers, possibly in the hypothalamus (p. 27).

Popularly, of course, the compound is known as a "tranquilizer."

It is known that chlorpromazine has effects other than the sympatholytic effect of interest to us. For purposes of experimental purity this is unfortunate but inevitable in this sort of research. It is clear, however, that the three conditions do differ in the degree of manipulated sympathetic activation.

Subjects

Subjects were male college students taking classes in introductory psychology at the University of Minnesota. Some 90 percent of the students in these classes volunteer for a subject pool, for they receive two extra points on their final exam for every hour that they serve as experimental subjects. The records of all potential subjects were cleared with the Student Health Service in order to insure that no harmful effects would result from injections of either epinephrine or chlorpromazine.

Each experimental group was made up of three subjects—one from each of the injection conditions. Their appointments were staggered slightly so as to insure sufficient time for the particular drug to be absorbed. Thus, the chlorpromazine subject received his injection about 15 minutes before the movie began. Pretests had revealed that, with this dosage and mode of administration, about this time interval was required for the onset of sympathetic effects. Placebo subjects were injected 5–10 minutes before onset of the movie. Epinephrine subjects were injected immediately before the movie so that at most 3–4 minutes went by between the time they were injected and the beginning of the film. Pretests had shown that the effects of epinephrine began within 3–5 minutes of injection. It was, of course, basic to the experimental design that these effects begin only after the movie had started.

Film

Rather than the more complicated devices employed in the Schachter and Singer (1962) experiment, an emotion inducing film was used as a means of manipulating the cognitive component of emotional states. In deciding on the type of film, two extremes seemed possible—a horror, fright, or anxiety provoking film or a comic, amusement provoking film. Since it is a common stereotype that adrenalin makes one nervous and that the tranquilizer, chlorpromazine, makes one tranquil and mildly euphoric, the predicted pattern of results with a horror film would be subject to alternative interpretation. It was deliberately decided, then, to use a comedy. If our hypothesis is correct, it should be anticipated that epinephrine subjects would find the film somewhat funnier than placebo subjects who, in turn, would be more amused than chlorpromazine subjects.

The film chosen was a 14-minute 40-second excerpt from a Jack Carson movie called *The Good Humor Man*. This excerpt is a self-contained, comprehensible episode involving a slapstick chase scene.

The projection room was deliberately arranged so that the subjects could neither see nor hear one another. Facing the screen were three theatre-type seats separated from one another by large, heavy partitions. In a further attempt to maintain the independence of the subjects, the sound volume of the projector was turned up so as to mask any sounds made by the subjects.

Measurement

Observation. During the showing of the movie an observer, who had been introduced as an assistant who would help administer the visual tests, systematically scanned the subjects and recorded their reactions to the film. He observed each subject once every 10 seconds, so that over the course of the film 88 units of each subject's behavior were categorized. The observer simply recorded each subject's reaction to the film according to the following scheme.

1. Neutral. Straight-faced watching of film with no indication of amusement.

2. Smile.

3. Grin. A smile with teeth showing.

4. Laugh. A smile or grin accompanied by bodily movements usually associated with laughter, e.g., shaking shoulders, moving head, etc.

5. Big laugh. Belly laugh—a laugh accompanied by violent body movement such as doubling up, throwing up hands, etc.

In a minute by minute comparison, two independent observers agree in their categorization of 90 percent of the 528 units recorded in six different reliability trials. Lumping Categories 2 through 5 together, the two obervers agreed on 93 percent of the units jointly recorded.

The observer, of course, never knew which subject had received which injection.

Evaluation of the film

The moment the movie ended the lights were turned on and the experimenter proceeded:

Before beginning the visual tests, we want your eyes to recover somewhat from the constant stimulation they've just received. The rate of neuro-limnal recovery under conditions of perfectly normal lighting and coloring is of major interest to us. The recovery will have begun in about 12 minutes, and after that time, Dr. Mena will give you the more precise visual examination.

In the meantime, I'd like to ask your help. As I told you, we need about 15 minutes of retinal stimulation, for which purpose we use a movie. Obviously, it doesn't matter at all to us which movie we use, so long as it is black and white. We can use one movie just as easily as another, but we do want to use a film that you like. I'm sure that you can see the necessity of using a film which our subjects will like. Of course, the only way to find out if you like it is to ask you. We're just beginning this experiment and will have many more subjects like you. Since you are one of the first groups, it will be a big help if you will give us

your personal reactions to the film. If you like it, we'll keep it and if you don't like it, we can just as easily get another. If you'll use these mimeographed questionnaires, it will make it easier for us.

The experimenter then handed out a questionnaire whose chief items, for present purposes, were the following:

1. How funny did you find this film?
   (1) Extremely dull
   (2) Very dull
   (3) Somewhat dull
   (4) Mildly funny
   (5) Very funny
   (6) Extremely funny

2. All in all, how much did you enjoy this film?
   (1) Disliked it intensely
   (2) Disliked it very much
   (3) Disliked it a little
   (4) Enjoyed it a little
   (5) Enjoyed it very much
   (6) Enjoyed it enormously

The figures in brackets represent the values used in computing the means presented in later tables.

3. Would you recommend that we should show this particular film to our future subjects?
   (3) Strongly recommend keeping this film.
   (2) Moderately recommend keeping this film.
   (1) Recommend you get another film.

Physical condition

In order to check on whether or not the drugs were having the desired effect on the subject's internal state, after the subjects had evaluated the film, the experimenter continued with the following spiel:

Before we begin the eye tests, we need a bit more information about you. Earlier studies on the visual processes have shown that a person's physical and emotional states influence the visual process. Because of this it is necessary to know how you feel physically and emotionally at this time. We know, for example, that certain states such as hunger, or fatigue, or boredom, do have a noticeable effect on these processes. Naturally, we have to know these things about you in order to interpret the results we will obtain from each of you, and the only way we can find out such things is to ask you.

A bit more on this line and the experimenter then handed round a questionnaire whose chief items were the following:

A. For evaluation of the effects of epinephrine:

1. Have you experienced any palpitation (consciousness of your own heartbeat) during the last half hour or so?

   (0) Not at all
   (1) A slight amount
   (2) A moderate amount
   (3) An intense amount

2. Have you felt any tremor (involuntary shaking of the hands, arms, or legs) during the last half hour or so?

   (0) Not at all
   (1) A slight amount
   (2) A moderate amount
   (3) An intense amount

B. For evaluation of the effects of chlorpromazine: Any direct measure (such as blood pressure) of the effects of the chlorpromazine injection on each subject was pretty much out of the question owing to limitations of time and personnel. It is known, however, that chlorpromazine does have somewhat of a dehydrating effect. As some indication that within the experimental time interval the chlorpromazine had been absorbed, the following questions were asked:

1. Does your mouth feel dry?

   (0) Not at all dry
   (1) A little dry
   (2) Somewhat dry
   (3) Very dry
   (4) Extremely dry

2. Does your nose feel stuffy?

   (0) Not at all stuffy
   (1) A little stuffy
   (2) Somewhat stuffy
   (3) Very stuffy
   (4) Extremely stuffy

Film detail questionnaire

Since it is known that chlorpromazine produces drowsiness, it seemed possible that experimental differences might be due to the fact that subjects had simply not watched the film. In order to check on this, a 10-item multiple-choice test concerned with small details of the film was administered. This test was rationalized to the subjects as a means of measuring the amount of time they had watched the movie, therefore, the amount of retinal stimulation received. Presumably the more they had watched the screen the more details they would remember.

Following this test the purpose of the experiment was disclosed, the deception was explained in detail, and the subjects were sworn to secrecy. Finally, the subjects filled out a brief questionnaire concerned with their past experiences with adrenalin and tranquilizers and with their suspicion, if any, of the experiment.

RESULTS

Physical effects of the injections

Evaluating, first, the effects of the injections, it can be seen in Table 1 that there are good indications that epinephrine has produced the required pattern of sympathetic activation. On self-reports of palpitation and tremor, subjects in the epinephrine condition report considerably more disturbance than subjects in either the placebo or chlorpromazine condition. On pulse measures, epinephrine subjects increase significantly when compared with placebo subjects. A subject's pulse was measured immediately before the injection and shortly after the movie. Pulse increased for some 63 percent of the epinephrine subjects and for 28 percent of the placebo subjects.

TABLE 1. PHYSICAL EFFECTS OF THE INJECTIONS

Condition	N	Pulse Pre-injection	Pulse Post-injection	Palpita-tion	Tremor	Mouth Dry	Nose Stuffy
Epinephrine	44	81.4	87.3	2.00	1.86	0.72	0.39
Placebo	42	78.7	75.5	0.30	0.12	0.30	0.68
Chlorpromazine	46	81.4	86.0	0.52	0.26	1.12	2.16
p value							
Epinephrine versus Placebo				<.001	<.001	<.01	ns
Epinephrine versus Chlorpromazine				<.001	<.001	<.07	<.001
Placebo versus Chlorprom-azine				ns	ns	<.001	<.001

As to the effects of chlorpromazine, it can be seen in Table 1 that subjects in this condition report considerably more nose stuffiness and mouth dryness than subjects in the placebo or epinephrine conditions. This may be taken as indirect evidence that within the time limits of the experiment, chlorpromazine was taking effect. The increase in pulse rate (61 percent of chlorpromazine subjects increase) is a standard reaction to chlorpromazine and appears to be compensatory for the decreased blood pressure caused by this agent. It should be noted, however, that unlike epinephrine subjects the chlorpromazine subjects were unaware of this increased heart rate, for on the palpitation scale they are quite similar to subjects in the placebo condition.

Six subjects (included in Table 1) in the epinephrine condition were unaffected by the injection. They reported virtually no palpitation or tremor and their pulses were not markedly affected. Since for these subjects the necessary experimental state was not produced, they are not included in any further presentation of data.

Effects of drowsiness

It is known that chlorpromazine produces drowsiness, a state which in this experimental context might mean that the subjects paid less attention to the movie. Differences between chlorpromazine subjects and those in the other two conditions in reaction to the film could then be due to differential attention rather than to the factors presumably being tested. In order to check for this, the film details questionnaire, described earlier, was administered shortly after the movie. The results of this questionnaire are presented in Table 2 where the figures represent the mean number of correct answers in each of the conditions. It can be immediately seen that the three conditions are virtually identical. None of these figures is significantly different from one another and any differences in reaction to the film cannot, then, be attributed to differences in attention.

TABLE 2. MEAN NUMBER OF CORRECT ANSWERS ON THE FILM DETAILS QUESTIONNAIRE

Condition	N[a]	Mean Number Correct
Epinephrine	38	9.29
Placebo	41	9.15
Chlorpromazine	45	9.38

[a]One subject in the placebo and one in the chlorpromazine condition did not answer the questionnaire.

TABLE 3. THE EFFECTS OF EPINEPHRINE, PLACEBO, AND CHLORPROMAZINE ON AMUSEMENT

Condition	N	Mean Amusement Index
Epinephrine	38	17.79
Placebo	42	14.31
Chlorpromazine	46	10.41
p value		
Epinephrine versus placebo		ns
Epinephrine versus chlorpromazine		.01
Placebo versus chlorpromazine		.05

Overt reactions to the film

The observation record provides a continuous record of each subject's reaction to the film. As an overall index of amusement, the number of units in which a subject's behavior was recorded in the categories Smile, Grin, Laugh, and Big Laugh are summed together. The means of this amusement index are presented in Table 3. The larger the figure, the more amusement was manifest. Differences are in the anticipated direction. Epinephrine subjects gave indications of greater amusement than did placebo subjects who, in turn, were more amused than chlorpromazine subjects. The U test was used to test for significance of differences since the variance in the epinephrine condition was significantly greater than that in either the placebo or chlorpromazine condition. The means of both the epinephrine and the placebo conditions are significantly greater than the mean of the chlorpromazine condition.

Though the trend is clearly in the predicted direction, epinephrine and placebo subjects do not differ significantly in this overall index. The difference between these two groups, however, becomes apparent when we examine strong reactions to the film. Considering just the categories Laugh and Big Laugh, as indicating strong reactions to the film, we find an average of 4.84 such units among the epinephrine subjects and of only 1.83 such units among placebo subjects. This difference is significant at better than the .05 level of significance. Epinephrine subjects tend to be openly amused at the film, placebo subjects to be quietly amused. Some 16 percent of epinephrine subjects reacted at some point with belly laughs while not a single placebo subject did so. It should be noted that this is much the state of affairs one would expect from the disguised injection of epinephrine—a manipulation which, as Schachter and Singer (1962) have suggested, creates a bodily state "in search of" an appropriate cognition. Certainly laughter can be considered a more appropriate accompaniment to the state of sympathetic arousal than can quietly smiling.

It would appear, then, that degree of overt amusement is directly related to the degree of manipulated sympathetic activation.

Evaluation of the film

Responses to the post-movie questionnaire in which the subjects evaluated the film are presented in Table 4. The

TABLE 4. EVALUATION OF THE FILM

Condition	N	Funny	Enjoy	Recommend
Epinephrine	38	4.09	3.99	2.04
Placebo	42	4.01	3.95	1.93
Chlorpromazine	46	3.85	3.85	1.85

column heading Funny includes answers to the question "How funny did you find this film?"; the heading Enjoy includes answers to the question "All in all, how much did you enjoy the film?"; and the heading Recommend presents answers to the question, "Would you recommend that we show this particular film to our future subjects?"

For all three questions, the trend is in precisely the same direction, epinephrine subjects like the film slightly more than do placebo subjects who like it more than do chlorpromazine subjects. On all questions, however, the differences between conditions are small and, at best, significant at only borderline probability levels.

The fact that between-condition differences are large on the behavioral measure and quite small on the attitude scales administered after the film is an intriguing one. The most reasonable explanation comes from the subjects themselves. For example, after the experiment an epinephrine subject said,

> I just couldn't understand why I was laughing during the movie. Usually, I hate Jack Carson and this kind of nonsense and that's the way I checked the scales.

For this subject, then, his long time preferences determined his answers to the questions whereas his immediate bodily state seems to have determined his reaction while watching the movie. If this is widespread, it should be anticipated that there will be relatively little relationship between past preferences and overt behavior in the epinephrine condition and a considerable stronger relationship in the placebo condition. For chlorpromazine, too, one should anticipate slight relationship between past preferences and behavior. No matter what the long time feeling about such films the immediate reaction to the movie should be restrained owing to lack of sympathetic activity. However, as pointed out earlier, chlorpromazine is a weak blocker and, most reasonably, one should expect a somewhat weaker relationship with this drug than with the placebo.

As a measure of general attitude toward the sort of film shown, at the time that they were evaluating the film the subjects also answered the question, "In general, how well do you like this kind of slapstick film?" by checking one of five points along a scale ranging from "Slapstick is the kind of film I like least" to "Slapstick is my favorite kind of film." The relationship of attitude to this sort of film to reactions to this particular film in each of the drug conditions is presented in Table 5. The subjects are divided into two groups—those who dislike slapstick and those who like it as much as or more than they do other kinds of films. The entries in the table are the mean laugh indices for each of the breakdowns.

TABLE 5. RELATIONSHIP BETWEEN LAUGHTER AND PREVIOUS ATTITUDE TOWARD SLAPSTICK FILMS

Attitude to slapstick	Epinephrine		Placebo		Chlorpromazine	
	N^a	Laugh Index	N^a	Laugh Index	N^a	Laugh Index
Dislike	25	15.12	29	10.52	29	7.34
Like	12	21.75	12	23.25	16	14.69
t		1.18		3.40		2.04
p		ns		.001		.05

[a]One subject in each condition did not answer the question concerned with general attitude to such films.

It is evident that there is a very strong relationship between general attitude toward such films and laughter in the placebo condition, a considerably weaker relationship in the chlorpromazine condition, and the weakest relationship of all in the epinephrine condition.

DISCUSSION

The overall pattern of experimental results of this study and the Schachter and Singer (1962) experiment gives consistent support to a general formulation of emotion as a function of a state of physiological arousal and of an appropriate cognition. The fact that the epinephrine-placebo difference in this study, though in the proper direction, was not larger must be considered within the context of other relevant studies. As noted earlier, Schachter and Singer obtained similar results in their tests of the effects of epinephrine on euphoria and anger. In their attempt to account for their results, they identify two factors which could attenuate the differences between subjects injected with epinephrine and those receiving a placebo. One of these factors—the self-arousal of placebo subjects—has been tested in the present study. The second factor they identify is what they call the "self-informing" tendency of epinephrine subjects. To understand this notion will require a brief review of the formulation proposed by Schachter (1959) who has suggested that an emotion be considered a joint function of a state of physiological arousal and of a cognition appropriate to this state. Given a state of physiological arousal for which an individual has no immediate explanation, he will "label" this state and describe his feelings in terms of the cognitions available to him. Given a state of arousal for which an individual has a completely appropriate explanation (e.g., "I feel this way because I have just received an injection of adrenalin.") no evaluative needs will arise and he is unlikely to label his feel-ings in terms of the alternative cognitions available. These propositions are strongly supported in the Schachter-Singer study where subjects, injected with epinephrine and told precisely what they would feel and why, were considerably less emotional (either angry or euphoric) than were subjects injected with epinephrine and told simply that they would experience no side effects. Inevitably, however, some of the subjects in this latter condition were self-informed; that is, on their own, they attributed their states of arousal to the injection. Consistent with expectations, such "self-informed" subjects proved to be considerably less emotional than subjects in the same condition who were not self-informed. To the extent, however, that this self-informing tendency operates, the differences between placebo and epinephrine conditions will, then, be attenuated. There is little question that such a tendency also operated in the present study and we suggest, of course, that this is one of the chief factors limiting the magnitude of differences between the epinephrine and the placebo conditions. Such a self-informing tendency will probably operate in any experiment on humans which employs an injection technique.

In order to make the epinephrine-placebo comparison under conditions which would rule out the operation of any "self-informing" tendency, two experiments were conducted on rats. In one of these, Singer (1961) demonstrated that under fear-inducing conditions, rats injected with epinephrine were considerably more frightened than rats injected with a placebo. In another study, Latane and Schachter (1962) demonstrated that rats injected with epinephrine were notably more capable of avoidance learning than were rats injected with a placebo. Viewed together, this series of experiments on rats and humans give clear support to the hypothesis that "emotionality" is, in part, a function of degree of sympathetic excitation.

The identification of the "self-informing" tendency does permit us to consider one alternative interpretation of the results of the experiment presented in this paper. One might consider that the effects of the several injections have been to vary "level of activation" in the sense employed by Lindsley (1951) and Woodworth and Schlosberg (1958). This would imply that no matter what the state or activity, epinephrine subjects would react more extremely than either placebo or chlorpromazine subjects. If correct, this would negate the cognitive component of this formulation of emotion. It must be remembered, however, that this experiment was planned hand in hand with the Schachter and Singer (1962) study. In this prior study the "epinephrine informed" conditions were deliberately built into the experiment to test for this possibility. Subjects who were injected with epinephrine and told precisely what they would feel and why did not "catch" the induced emotional state at all. It seems safe to generalize from these results to the present study and conclude that the level of activation notion alone cannot explain the results of these two studies.

SUMMARY

An experiment is described which was designed to test the proposition that "emotionality" is, in part, a function of the degree of excitation of the sympathetic nervous system. The degree of sympathetic activation was manipulated by injections of (a) the sympathomimetic agent—epinephrine, (b) a placebo, and (c) the sympatholytic drug—chlorpromazine. The effects of these drugs on amusement were tested by exposing subjects to a slapstick film. Epinephrine subjects were more amused than were placebo subjects who, in turn, were more amused than chlorpromazine subjects.

References

1. Killam, Eva K. The pharmacological aspects of certain drugs useful in psychiatry. In *Psychopharmacology: Problems in evaluation.* Washington, D.C.: National Academy of Sciences, National Research Council, 1959. (NASNRC Publ. No. 583.)

2. Latane, B., and Schachter, S. Adrenalin and avoidance learning. *J. comp. physiol. Psychol.*, 1962, **55**, 369–372.

3. Lindsley, D. B. Emotion. In S. S. Stevens (Ed.), *Handbook of experimental psychology.* New York: Wiley, 1951. Pp. 473–516.

4. Schachter, S. *The psychology of affiliation.* Stanford, Calif.: Stanford Univ. Press, 1959.

5. Schachter, S., and Singer, J. E. Cognitive, social, and physiological determinants of emotional state. *Psychol. Rev.*, 1962. In press.

6. Singer, J. E. The effects of epinephrine, chlorpromazine and dibenzyline upon the fright responses of rats under stress and nonstress conditions. Unpublished doctoral dissertation, University of Minnesota, 1961.

7. Woodworth, R. S., and Schlosberg, H. *Experimental psychology.* New York: Holt, Rinehart & Winston, 1958.

Cognitive effects on bodily functioning: studies of obesity and eating
stanley schachter

Although we rarely bother to make the matter explicit, the assumption of an identity between a physiological state and a psychological or behavioral event is implicit in much contemporary work in such areas as psychopharmacology, psychophysiology, or any domain concerned with the relationship of bodily state to emotion or to behavior. Simply put, much of this work seems to proceed on the assumption that there is a simple, one-to-one relationship between a biochemical change or a physiological process and a specific behavior. It is as if we assumed that physiological state is an "unconditionally sufficient condition" to account for a psychological event.

Such an assumption has, of course, been enormously fruitful in many areas of purely biological and medical research. Spirochetes cause syphilis. Kill the spirochete and cure syphilis. An iodine-deficient diet leads to colloid goiters; repair the deficiency, repair the goiter. As one moves from the world of purely medical and physiological research, however, the assumption of such an "identity" seems to become more and more troublesome. It is this assumption, for example, which is the crux of the James-Cannon difficulties. James' view of emotion rested squarely on the assumption of an identity between physiological and emotional state, and Cannon's brilliant critique of the James-Lange theory was, in essence, an attack on this assumption. It is this implicit assumption which is, I suspect, responsible for the

From *Neurophysiology and Emotion* by Stanley Schachter. Used by permission of the author and publisher, Rockefeller University Press and Russell Sage Foundation.

impression of utter confusion in an area such as psychopharmacology, where it sometimes seems the rule rather than the exception to find a single drug proved in a variety of studies to have blatantly opposite behavioral effects. LSD, for example, has been proved to be a hallucinogenic and a nonhallucinogenic, to be a euphoriant, a depressant, and to have no effects on mood at all. This nightmarish pattern of conflicting and nonreplicable results is familiar to anyone who has delved into the literature on behavioral or "emotional" effects of many of the so-called psychotropic drugs. The pattern, however, is not limited only to the exotic drugs; even as familiar an agent as adrenalin has a similarly depressing history. Many years ago the endocrinologist Marañon injected several hundred of his patients with adrenalin and then asked them to introspect. Some of his subjects simply described their physical symptoms and reported no emotional effects at all; others described their feelings in a fashion that Marañon labeled the "cold," or "as if," emotions; that is, they made statements such as "I feel *as if* I were afraid," or "*as if* I were awaiting a great happiness." Still other subjects described themselves as feeling genuine emotions. Of those who noted any emotional effects at all, some described themselves as feeling anxious, some as angry, some as euphoric. In short, adrenalin, producing almost identical and typical physiological effects in most of these subjects, produced a wide diversity of self-reports of feeling states. This situation is, I suspect, inevitable and will remain puzzling and discouraging as long as we persist in the assumption of an identity between the physiological and the psychological effects of a drug. If we do, my guess is that we will be just about as successful at deriving predictions about complex behavior from a knowledge of bio-chemical and physiological conditions as we would be at predicting the destina-tion of a moving automobile from an exquisite knowledge of the workings of the internal combustion engine and of petroleum chemistry.

If we are eventually to make sense of this area, I believe we will be forced to adopt a set of concepts with which most physiologically inclined scientists feel somewhat uncomfortable and ill-at-ease, for they are concepts which are, at pres-ent, difficult to physiologize about or to reify. We will be forced to examine a subject's perception of his bodily state and his interpretation of it in terms of his immediate situation and his past expe-rience. We will be forced to deal with concepts about perception, about cognition, about learning, and about the social situation.

In order to avoid any misunderstand-ing, let me make completely explicit that I am most certainly not suggesting that such notions as perception and cogni-tion do not have physiological correlates. I am suggesting that at present we know virtually nothing about these physio-logical correlates, but that we can and must use nonphysiologically anchored concepts if we are to make headway in understanding the relations of complex behavioral patterns to physiological and biochemical processes.

To move from generalities, let us con-sider the effects of adrenalin or epi-nephrine. We know that an injection of $\frac{1}{2}$ cc of 1:1000 solution of epinephrine causes an increase in heart rate, a marked increase in systolic blood pressure, a redistribution of blood with a cutaneous decrease, and a muscle and cerebral blood-flow increase. Blood sugar and lactic acid concentrations increase and respiration rate increases slightly. As far as the human subject is concerned, the major subjective symptoms are palpi-tation, slight tremor, and sometimes a feeling of flushing and accelerated breathing.

These are some of the measured phys-iological effects of an injection of epinephrine. In and of themselves are such bodily changes pleasant or un-pleasant? Given these symptoms, should the subject describe himself as angry, or as anxious, or as manic or euphoric, or simply as sick? From the results of the Marañon study, any of these self-descriptions are possible. How can we make coherent sense of such findings?

Several years ago, bemused by such results, my colleagues and I undertook a program of research on the interaction of physiological and cognitive determi-nants of emotional state. This program was based on speculation about what was, at that time, a hypothetical event. Imagine a subject whom one somehow managed to inject covertly with adren-alin, or to feed a sympathomimetic agent, such as ephedrine. Such a subject would become aware of palpitations, tremor, etc., and at the same time be utterly un-aware of why he felt this way. What would be the consequences of such a state?

In other contexts, I have suggested that precisely this condition would lead to the arousal of evaluative needs; that is, pressures would operate on such an individual to understand and evaluate his bodily feelings. His bodily state roughly resembles the condition in which it has been at times of emotional excitement. How would he label his present feelings? I would suggest that such an individual would label his bodily feelings in terms of the situation in which he finds himself. Should he at the time be watching a horror film, he would probably decide that he was badly fright-ened. Should he be with a beautiful woman, he might decide that he was wildly in love or sexually excited. Should he be in an argument, he might explode in fury and hatred. Or, should the situation be completely inappropriate, he could decide that he was excited or upset by something that had recently happened. In any case, it is my basic assumption that the labels one attaches to a bodily state, how one describes his feelings, are a joint function of such cognitive factors and of a state of physiological arousal.

This line of thought, then, leads to the following propositions:

Given a state of physiological arousal for which an individual has no immediate explanation, he will "label" this state and describe his feelings in terms of the cognitions available to him. To the extent the cognitive factors are potent determiners of emotional states, it could be anticipated that precisely the same state of physiological arousal could be called "joy" or "fury" or any of a great diversity of emotional labels, depending on the cognitive aspects of the situation.

Given a state of physiological arousal for which an individual has a completely appropriate explanation (e.g., "I feel this way because I have just received an injection of adrenalin"), no evaluative needs will arise and the individual is unlikely to label his feelings in terms of the alternative cognitions available.

Given the same cognitive circumstances, the individual will react emotionally or describe his feelings as emotions only to the extent that he experiences a state of physiological arousal.

The experimental test of these propositions requires, first, the experimental manipulation of a state of physiological arousal or sympathetic activation; second, the manipulation of the extent to which the subject has an appropriate or proper explanation of his bodily state; and third, the creation of situations from which explanatory cognitions may be derived.

In order to satisfy these requirements, Jerome Singer and I constructed an ex-periment that was cast in the framework of a study of the effects of vitamin supplements on vision. As soon as a subject arrived, he was told: "In this experiment we would like to make various tests of your vision. We are particularly interested in how a vitamin compound called Suproxin affects the visual skills. If you agree to take part in the experiment we would like to give you an injection of Suproxin."

If a subject agreed (and all but one of the 185 subjects did), he received an injection of one of two forms of Suproxin— placebo or epinephrine. We have, then, two groups of subjects—placebo subjects on whom the injection can have no possible effects, and epinephrine subjects who, within a few minutes after injection, will become aware of the full battery of sympathomimetic symptoms.

In order to manipulate the extent to which subjects had a proper explanation of their bodily state, those who received epinephrine received one of two types of instructions.

Informed subjects. Before receiving the injections, such subjects were told, "I should also tell you that some of our subjects have experienced side effects from the Suproxin. These side effects will only last for 15 or 20 minutes. Probably your hands will start to shake, your heart will start to pound, and your face may get warm and flushed."

These subjects, then are told precisely what they feel and why they will feel it. For such subjects, the evaluative needs are low. They have an exact explanation for their bodily feelings, and cognitive or situational factors should have no effects on how the subject labels his feelings.

Uninformed subjects. Such subjects are told that the injection will have no side effects at all. These subjects, then, will experience a state of sympathetic arousal, but the experimenter has given them no explanation for why they feel as they do. Evaluative needs then should be high, and cognitive-situational factors should have maximal effect on the way such a subject labels his bodily state.[1]

Finally, in order to expose subjects to situations from which they might derive explanatory cognitions relevant to their bodily state, they were placed in one of two situations immediately after injection:

Euphoria. A subject was placed alone in a room with a stooge who had been introduced as a fellow subject and who, following a completely standardized routine, acted in a euphoric-manic fashion, doing such things as flying paper airplanes, hula-hooping, and the like, all the while keeping up a standard patter and occasionally attempting to induce the subject to join in.

Anger. A subject was asked to fill out a long, infuriating personal questionnaire that asked such questions as:

"With how many men (other than your father) has your mother had extramarital relationships?"
4 and under——: 5–9——: 10 and over——."

Filling in the questionnaire alongside the subject was a stooge, again presumably a follow subject, who openly grew more and more irritated at the questionnaire and who finally ripped the thing up in a rage, slammed it to the floor while biting out, "I'm not wasting any more time; I'm getting my books and leaving," and stamped out of the room.

In both situations, an observer, watching through a one-way mirror, systematically recorded the behavior of the

[1] For purposes of brevity, the description of this experiment does not include details of all the conditions in this study. The chief omission is a description of a control condition introduced to evaluate alternative interpretations of the data. The interested reader is referred to the original paper by Schachter and Singer (1962).

subject in order to provide indexes of the extent to which the subject joined in the stooge's mood. Once these rigged situations had run their course, the experimenter returned and, with a plausible pretext, asked the subject to fill out a series of standardized scales to measure the intensity of anger or euphoria.

We have, then, a set of experimental conditions in which we are simultaneously manipulating the degree of sympathetic arousal and the extent to which subjects understand why they feel as they do, and measuring the impact of these variations on the extent to which the subject catches the mood of a situation rigged to induce euphoria in one set of conditions and to induce anger in another. From the line of thought that generated this study, it should be anticipated that subjects injected with epinephrine and told that there would be no side effects should catch the mood of the rigged situation of a greater extent than subjects who had been injected with a placebo or those who had been injected with epinephrine and given a completely appropriate explanation of what they would feel and why.

Examining first the results of the euphoria conditions, we find that this is exactly the case. The uninformed epinephrine subjects—those who had been told that there would be no side effects—tend to catch the stooge's mood with alacrity; they join the stooge's whirl of activity and invent new manic activities of their own. In marked contrast, the informed epinephrine subjects and the placebo subjects who give no indication of autonomic arousal tend simply to sit and stare at the stooge in mild disbelief. The relevant data are reported in detail elsewhere. For present purposes it should suffice to note that these differences between conditions are large and statistically significant on both observational and self-report measures of mood.

In the anger conditions, the pattern of results is precisely the same. Uninformed epinephrine subjects grow openly annoyed and irritated, while placebo and informed epinephrine subjects maintain their equanimity. The evidence is good, then, in support of our basic propositions. Given a state of physiological arousal for which a subject has no easy explanation, he proves readily manipulable into the disparate states of euphoria and anger. Given an identical physiological state for which the subject has an appropriate explanation, his mood is almost untouched by the rigged situation.

Such results are not limited to the states of anger and euphoria. In still other experiments in which similar techniques and comparisons were employed, we have been readily able to manipulate uninformed epinephrine subjects into amusement, as measured by laughter at a slapstick movie, and into fearful or anxious states.

In sum, precisely the same physiological state—an epinephrine-induced state of sympathetic arousal—can be manifested as anger, euphoria, amusement, fear, or, as in the informed subjects, as no mood or emotion at all. Such results are virtually incomprehensible if we persist in the assumption of an identity between physiological and psychological states, but they fall neatly into place if we specify the fashion in which cognitive and physiological factors interact. With the addition of cognitive propositions, we are able to specify and manipulate the conditions under which an injection of epinephrine will or will not lead to an emotional state and to predict what emotion will result.

These demonstrations of the plasticity of interpretation of bodily state have depended upon the experimental trick of manipulating physiological and cognitive factors simultaneously and independently. In nature, of course, cognitive or situational factors trigger physiological processes, and the triggering stimulus usually imposes the label we attach to our feelings. We see the threatening object; this perception-

cognition initiates a state of sympathetic arousal and the joint cognitive-physiological experience is labeled "fear."

Several considerations suggest that the line of reasoning guiding these experimental studies of emotion may be extended to such naturally occurring states, and that the intensity of such states may be as modifiable as are experimentally induced states of arousal. As an example of this possibility, consider pain. Broadly, we can conceive of the intensity of experienced pain and of one's willingness to tolerate pain as a function of the intensity of stimulation of the pain receptors, of the autonomic correlates of such stimulation, and of a host of cognitive and situational factors. To the extent that we can convince a subject undergoing electric shock that his shock-produced symptoms and arousal state are caused not by shock but by some outside agent such as a drug, he should, following the above considerations, experience less pain and be willing to tolerate more shock. Such an individual would, of course, regard his arousal as a drug-produced state, rather than as an indicator of pain or fear.

In an experiment designed to evaluate these expectations, Nisbett and Schachter tested subjects' tolerance for a graded series of electric shocks. There were, in essence, two conditions. In one, the subjects took a placebo pill and were told that the side effects of the pill would be palpitations, hand tremor, breathing rate changes, and a sinking feeling in the pit of the stomach—all symptoms which pretests had shown actually accompanied anticipation and receipt of shock. In a second condition, the subjects also received a pill, but the side effects described (e.g., itching skin, numb feet, etc.) had nothing in common with the physiological symptoms accompanying shock. Ten minutes after taking the pill, both groups of subjects were given a series of brief shocks that systematically increased in intensity. They were told to tell the experimenter when the shock was too painful to endure and they wanted to stop. This point was reached at an average of only 350 microamperes by subjects who had been given the list of irrelevant symptoms and therefore attributed their feelings to the shock proper. In sharp contrast, it required an average of 1450 microamperes before this point was reached by subjects who attributed their symptoms to the pill rather than to the shock. Obviously, the attribution of symptoms has a major impact on the pain experience.

Because pain is notoriously manipulable, differences, even of this magnitude, may not be completely surprising. More revealing, perhaps, is some of the recent Russian work on interoceptive conditioning which has demonstrated that even such presumably nonmalleable states as the feelings associated with micturition are astonishingly manipulable. Working with patients with urinary bladder fistulas, investigators have, by essentially cognitive procedures, been able to induce subjects with almost empty bladders to report an intense need to urinate, as well as to induce subjects with full bladders to report no particular urge to do so.

I trust that it is by now tediously clear that cognitive factors are, indeed, major determiners of the labels we attach to bodily states and to the affective tone we attribute to these states. There seems little need to elaborate or belabor the point further. For the remainder of this paper, I want to examine some of the implications of this way of thinking about bodily states, and to see how some very old biological phenomena look if we explicitly abandon the assumption of identity. Specifically, I would like to look into just one question: what happens if an individual makes a mistake; if, in the socially defined sense, he does not label a bodily state as most other people do.

If it is correct that the labels attached to feeling states are cognitively, situationally, or socially determined, it becomes a distinct possibility that an uncommon or inappropriate label can be attached to a feeling state. Where such is the case, we may anticipate behavior that appears bizarre and pathological. As an example of this possibility, consider the state of hunger. We are so accustomed to think of hunger as a primary motive, wired into the animal, and unmistakable in its cues, that even the possibility that an organism would be incapable of correctly labeling the state seems too far-fetched to credit. The physiological changes accompanying food deprivation seem distinct, identifiable, and invariant. Yet even a moment's consideration will make it clear that attaching the label "hunger" to this set of bodily feelings and behaving accordingly, is a learned, socially determined, cognitive act. Consider the neonate. Wholly at the mercy of its feelings, it screams when it is uncomfortable or in pain or frightened or hungry. Whether it is comforted, soothed, fondled, or fed has little to do with the state of its feelings, but depends entirely on the ability and willingness of its mother or nurse to recognize the proper cues. If she is experienced, she will comfort when the baby is frightened, soothe him when he is chafed, feed him when he is hungry, and so on. If inexperienced, her behavior may be completely inappropriate to the child's state. Most commonly, perhaps, the compassionate but bewildered mother will feed her child at any sign of distress.

It is precisely this state of affairs that the analyst Hilde Bruch suggests is at the heart of chronic obesity. She describes such cases as characterized by confusion between intense emotional states and hunger. During childhood, she presumes, these patients have not been taught to discriminate between hunger and such states as fear, anger, and anxiety. If this is so, the patients may be labeling almost any state of arousal as hunger or, alternatively, labeling no internal state as hunger.

If Bruch's speculation is correct, it might be anticipated that the set of physiological symptoms considered characteristic of food deprivation are not labeled as "hunger" by the obese. In other words, the obese literally may not know when they are physiologically hungry. This may seem to be a remote possibility, but it appears to be the case. In an absorbing study, Stunkard has related gastric motility to self-reports of hunger in 37 obese and 37 normal-sized subjects. His experiment was simple and clear-cut. Subjects who had eaten no breakfast came to the laboratory at 9 A.M. and swallowed a gastric balloon. For the next four hours Stunkard continuously recorded gastric motility. Every fifteen minutes the subject was asked if he was hungry. He answered "yes" or "no" and that was all there was to the study. We have, then, a record of the extent to which a subject's self-report of hunger corresponds to his gastric motility. Let us note first that the two groups do not differ significantly in the extent of gastric motility, and second, that when the stomach is not contracting, obese and normal subjects are quite similar, both groups reporting hunger roughly 38 percent of the time. When the stomach is contracting, however, the two groups differ markedly. For normals, self-report of hunger coincides with motility an average of 71 percent of the time. For the obese, the coincidence is only 47.6 percent. This difference is significant at considerably better than the .01 level of confidence.

Stunkard's work, then, would seem to indicate that obese and normal subjects do not refer to the same bodily state when they use the term hunger. Whether to interpret Stunkard's results as an instance of mislabeling, however, is still an open question. Stunkard himself tends to interpret his results in more psychodynamic terms, for he suggests denial mechanisms to account for at least some of his findings. In any case, it does seem that for the obese there is

little correspondence between the bodily states commonly associated with hunger and the statement "I am hungry."

If all of this is correct, we should anticipate that if we were to directly manipulate gastric motility and the other symptoms that we associate with hunger, we should, for normals, directly manipulate feelings of hunger and eating behavior. For the obese, on the other hand, there should be no correspondence between the manipulated internal state and eating behavior. In order to test these expectations, Schachter, Goldman, and Gordon did an experiment in which bodily state was manipulated by two means: first, by manipulating food deprivation so that some subjects entered an experimental eating situation with empty stomachs and others with full stomachs; second, by manipulating fear so that some subjects entered the eating situation badly frightened and others quite calm. Carlson has indicated that fear inhibits gastric motility; Cannon has demonstrated that the state of fear leads to the suppression of gastric movement and the liberation from the liver of sugar into the blood. Hypoglycemia and gastric contractions are generally considered the chief peripheral physiological correlates of food deprivation.

Our experiment was conducted within the framework of a study of taste. Subjects, all male undergraduates at Columbia, came to the laboratory in mid-afternoon or evening. On the previous evening they had all been asked not to eat the meal (lunch or dinner) preceding their experimental appointment. The experimenter's introductory patter was an expanded version of the following:

A subject of considerable importance in psychology today is the interdependence of the basic human senses, that is, the way the stimulation of one sense affects another. To take a recent example, research has discovered that certain sounds act as very effective pain killers. Some dentists are, in fact, using these sounds instead of Novocain to "block out" pain when they work on your teeth. Some psychologists believe that similar relationships exist for all the senses. The experiment we are working on now concerns the effect of tactile stimulation on the way things taste.

The reason we asked you not to eat before coming here is that in any scientific experiment it is necessary that the subjects be as similar as possible in all relevant ways. As you probably know from your own experience, an important factor in determining how things taste is what you have recently eaten. For example, after eating any richly spiced food such as pizza almost everything else tastes pretty bland.

The experimenter then manipulated pre-loading as follows:

To the Full Stomach subjects he said, "In order to guarantee that your recent taste experiences are entirely similar, we should now like you each to eat exactly the same thing. Just help yourself to the roast beef sandwiches on the table. Eat as much as you want—until you're full." The subjects spent about 15 minutes eating, and filled out a long food-preference questionnaire while they ate.

In the Empty Stomach condition, of course, the subjects were not fed. They simply spent the 15-minute period filling out the questionnaire about food.

Next, the subject was seated in front of five bowls of crackers and told, "Now that we are through with the preliminaries we can get to the main part of the experiment. We are going to have each of you taste five different kinds of crackers and tell us how they taste to you. These are very low-calorie crackers designed to resemble commercial products." The experimenter then presented the subject with a long set of rating scales and said, "We would like

you to judge each cracker on each of the dimensions (salty, cheesy, garlicky, etc.) listed on this sheet. Taste as many or as few of the crackers of each type as you want in making your judgments; the important thing is that your ratings be as accurate as possible."

Before permitting the subjects to eat, the experimenter continued with the final stage of the experiment—the manipulation of fear. "As I mentioned before, our primary interest in this experiment is the effect of tactile stimulation on taste. Electric stimulation is the means we have chosen to excite your skin receptors. We use this method so that we can carefully control the amount of stimulation you receive."

For Low Fear, the subject was told, "In order to create the effect that we are interested in we need to use only the lowest level possible. At most, you will feel a slight tingle in your skin. Probably you will feel nothing at all. We are only interested in the effect of very weak stimulation."

For High Fear, the experimenter pointed to an eight-foot high, jet-black console loaded with electrical junk and said, "That machine is the one we will be using. I am afraid that these shocks will be painful. In order for them to have any effect on your taste sensations, they must be of a rather high voltage. There will, of course, be no permanent damage. Do you have a heart condition?" The subject was then connected to the console by attaching a very large electrode to each ankle, and the experimenter concluded with, "The best way for us to test the effect of the tactile stimulation is to have you rate the crackers now, before the electric shock, to see how the crackers taste under normal circumstances, and then rate them again after the shock to see what changes in your ratings the shock has made."

The subject then proceeded to taste and rate crackers for 15 minutes. He was under the impression that he was tasting and, of course, we were simply counting the number of crackers he ate.[2] In this way we have a measure of the eating behavior of subjects who were empty or full and who were frightened or calm. Finally, of course, there were two groups of subjects—the obese, ranging from 14 percent to 75 percent overweight, and normals, ranging from 8 percent underweight to 9 percent overweight. We are co-varying three variables—pre-loading, fear, and obesity—in an eight-condition experiment. For expositional simplicity, I will present here only the main effects of this study, and will not give the data for all eight conditions.

To review expectations briefly: if it is correct that the obese do not label as hunger the bodily states of gastric motility and hypoglycemia, our several experimental manipulations should have no effects on the amount eaten by obese subjects. In sharp contrast, the eating behavior of normal subjects should directly parallel the effects of the manipulations on bodily state.

Let us examine first the effects of pre-loading on the eating behavior of the two groups of subjects. From Figure 1 it will be a surprise to no one to learn that normals eat considerably fewer crackers when their stomachs are full than when they are empty. Fats stand in fascinating contrast. They eat as much—in fact slightly more—when their stomachs are full, as when they are empty (interaction p < .05). Obviously, the actual state of the stomach has nothing to do with the eating behavior of the obese.

Turning to fear in Figure 2, we see much the same picture. High fear markedly decreases the number of crackers normal subjects eat and has no effect on the amount eaten by the obese (interaction p < .01). Again, there is a small,

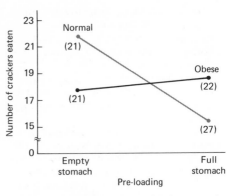

Figure 1. Effects of pre-loading on the eating behavior of normal and obese subjects. ( ) = number of subjects.

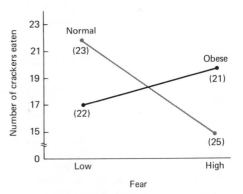

Figure 2. Effects of fear on the eating behavior of normal and obese subjects. ( ) = number of subjects.

although nonsignificant, reversal. The fearful obese eat slightly more than the calm obese.

There appears, then, to be little question that the obese do not label as "hunger" the same set of bodily symptoms as do normals. Whether we measure gastric motility, as in Stunkard's studies, or manipulate it, as I assume we have done in my studies, there is a high degree of correspondence between the state of the gut and the eating behavior of normals, and virtually no correspondence for the fat subjects.

---

[2]It is a common belief among researchers in obesity that the sensitivity of their fat subjects makes it almost impossible to study their eating behavior experimentally—hence this roundabout way of measuring eating; the subjects in this study are taking a taste test, not eating.

Another way of summarizing these data would be: while almost anything we have manipulated experimentally has had a major effect on the amount eaten by normal subjects, apparently virtually nothing we have done has any substantial effect on the amount eaten by obese subjects. Still other indications of our complete inability to affect the eating behavior of obese subjects come from a small number of case studies I have been doing in order to compare the effects of injections of adrenalin and placebo on the eating behavior of hospitalized obese and normal patients. These studies are attempts to test the hypothesis offered some years ago that the obese label the state of sympathetic activation as hunger—a suggestion that would lead to the expectation that the obese would eat considerably more when injected with adrenalin. This is not what we have found so far. Our obese subjects tend to eat very slightly more under adrenalin than under placebo (much as with the high and low fear comparison in Figure 2), while our normals tend to eat less with adrenalin in them. Again, in the work described so far, there is nothing that we have been able to do—from feeding to frightening to injecting with adrenalin— that has any effect on the eating behavior of the obese subject or that fails to have an effect on the eating behavior of the normal subject.

Keeping this in mind, let us turn to the work of the members of the Nutrition Clinic in St. Luke's Hospital in New York, chiefly Drs. Hashim and Van Itallie. Summarizing their findings, virtually everything they do seems to have a major effect on the eating behavior of the obese and almost no effect on the eating behavior of the normal subject.

These researchers have prepared a bland and homogenized liquid diet, similar in taste and composition to the vanilla flavors of such commercial preparations as Nutrament or Metrecal, to which the subjects are restricted. They can eat as much or as little as they want

of this relatively tasteless and uninteresting pap, but this and this alone is all they can eat for periods ranging from a week to several months. Some of their subjects get a large pitcher full of the stuff and can pour themselves a meal anytime they are so inclined. Other subjects are fed by a machine, which delivers a mouthful of the food every time the subject presses a button. Whichever feeding technique is used, the eating situation is characterized by three properties. First, the food itself is dull and unappealing. Second, eating is entirely self-determined— whether the subject eats, how much and when he eats is up to the subject and no one else. It should be specifically noted that absolutely no pressure is put on the subject to limit his consumption. Third, the eating situation is totally devoid of any social or domestic trappings. It is simply basic eating; it will keep the subject alive, but it's not much fun.

To date, six grossly obese and five normal subjects have been run in this setup. Figure 3 plots the eating curves for a typical pair of subjects over a 21-day period. Both subjects were healthy, normal people who lived in and did not leave the hospital during the entire period of the study. The obese subject in this figure was a 52-year-old woman, 5' 3" tall, who weighed 307 pounds on admission. The normal subject was a 30-year-old male, 5' 7" tall, who weighed 132 pounds.

On the left of the figure is shown the estimated daily caloric intake for each subject before entering the hospital— estimates based on detailed interviews. While in the hospital, but before entering the experimental regime, each subject was placed on a general hospital diet served on a tray. The obese subject placed on a 2400-calorie general hospital diet for seven days and a 1200-calorie diet for the next eight days. As can be seen on the figure, she consumed everything on her tray during this 15-day period. The normal subject was placed on a 2400-calorie general hospital diet

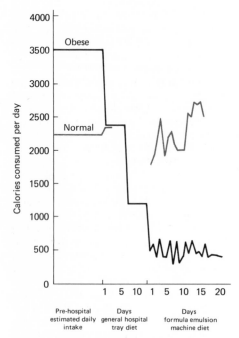

Figure 3. The effects of a formula emulsion diet on the eating behavior of an obese and a normal subject.

for two days and he, too, ate everything on his tray.

With the beginning of the experiment proper, the difference in the amounts eaten by the two subjects becomes dramatic and startling. You will note immediately that the food consumed by the obese subject drops precipitously the moment she enters on the regime and remains at this incredibly low level for the duration of the experiment. This effect is so dramatic that one of the obese subjects who remained in the experiment for eight months dropped from 410 pounds to 190 pounds. The normal subject, on the other hand, drops slightly on the first two days, then returns to a fairly steady 2300 grams or so of food a day. These are typical curves. Every one of the six fat subjects has been characterized by this marked and persistent decrease in food consumption. Every one of

the normal subjects has fairly steadily consumed about his normal amount of food.

Before worrying through possible interpretations of this data, I must note that there are certain marked differences between the two groups of subjects. Most important, the obese subjects have come to the clinic for help in their weight problems and are, of course, motivated to lose weight. The normal subjects are simply volunteers for an experiment. Without question, this difference could account for the effect, and until a group of obese volunteers who are unconcerned with their weight are run through the procedure we cannot be completely sure of the phenomenon. However, I would like to be sure that we do not, only on the grounds of methodological fastidiousness, dismiss these findings. As we have said, every obese subject was motivated to lose weight before entering the hospital, and certainly while in the hospital and before going on the formula emulsion diet. Yet, despite this motivation, not one of these subjects was capable of restricting his *home* diet successfully. When placed on the general hospital tray diet, motivated or not, every one of the obese subjects polished off his tray. Only when the food is dull and the act of eating self-initiated and devoid of any ritual trappings does the obese subject, motivated or not, severely limit his consumption.

On the one hand, then, we have a series of experiments that indicate virtually no relation between internal state and the eating behavior of the obese subject; on the other hand, this series of case studies seems to indicate a very close tie-up between the eating behavior of the obese and what might be called the circumstances of eating. When the food is uninspired and the eating situation uninteresting, the fat subject eats virtually nothing. The relationships are quite the reverse for the normal subject; his eating behavior seems directly linked to internal state but relatively unaffected by the external circumstances surrounding the eating routine and ritual.

Given this set of facts, it seems eminently clear that the eating behavior of obese and normal subjects is not triggered by the same set of bodily symptoms. Indeed, there is growing reason to suspect that the eating behavior of the obese is relatively unrelated to any internal gut state but is, in large part, under external control; that is, eating behavior is initiated and terminated by stimuli external to the organism.

Let me try to convey by a few examples what I mean by external control. A person whose eating behavior is under external control will stroll by a pastry shop, find the window irresistible and, whether or not he has recently eaten, will buy a goody. He will wander by a hamburger stand, smell and see the broiling meat, and although he may have eaten recently, he will buy a hamburger. Obviously, such external factors—smell, sight, taste, what other people are doing, and so on—affect anyone's eating behavior to some extent. However, for normals such external factors clearly interact with internal state. They may affect what, where, and how much the normal eats, but do so chiefly when he is in a state of physiological hunger. For the obese, I suggest, internal state is irrelevant and eating is determined largely by external factors.

Obviously, this hypothesis fits beautifully with the various data presented— as well it should, since it is an *ad hoc* construction specifically designed to fit the data. Let us see what independent support there is for the hypothesis and where it leads.

The essence of this notion of the external control of eating behavior is this: stimuli outside of the organism trigger eating behavior. In effect, since such internal states as gastric motility and hypoglycemia are not labeled as hunger, some cue outside the organism must tell it when it is hungry and when to eat. Of course, such cues are multiple, but one

of the most intriguing is simply the passage of time. Everyone "knows" that four to six hours after eating his last meal he should eat his next one. Everyone "knows" that within narrow limits there are set times to eat regular meals. In the absence of alternative cues, in the absence of competing alternatives to eating, the eating behavior of the externally controlled person should be time-bound. We should expect that if we manipulate time we should be able to manipulate the eating behavior of the obese subject. In order to do this, we have simply taken two clocks and so gimmicked them that one runs at half normal speed and the other at roughly twice normal speed. A subject arrives at five in the afternoon, presumably to take part in an experiment on the relationship of base levels of autonomic reactivity to personality factors. He is ushered into a windowless room containing nothing but electronic equipment and a clock. Electrodes are put on the subject's wrists, his watch is removed so it will not be gummed up with electrode jelly, and he is connected to a polygraph. This consumes five minutes, and at 5:05 he is left completely alone with nothing to do for a true thirty minutes while presumably we are getting a record of resting-level rate of such autonomic indicators as galvanic skin response, cardiac rate, and so on. There are two conditions. In one the experimenter returns after a true thirty minutes and the clock reads 5:20. In the other, the clock reads 6:05 when the experimenter returns. In both cases, the experimenter is nibbling at crackers from a box as he comes into the room; he puts the box down, invites the subject to help himself, removes the subject's electrodes, and proceeds with the personality-testing phase of the study. For five minutes he administers a short version of the Embedded Figures Test. He then gives the subject a self-administering personality inventory and leaves him alone with the box of crackers for another true ten minutes. There are two groups of subjects—normal and obese —and of course the only datum we collect is the weight of the box of crackers before and after the subject has had a chance at it. If these ideas on internal and external controls of eating behavior are correct, we should anticipate the following pattern of results. Normal subjects, whose eating behavior is presumably linked to internal state, should be relatively unaffected by the manipulation and should eat roughly the same number of crackers whether the clock reads 5:20 or 6:05. The obese, on the other hand, if indeed they are under external control, should eat very few crackers when the clock reads 5:20 and a great many crackers when it reads 6:05.

The data of the experiment are presented in Figure 4, and indeed we do find that the obese eat almost twice as much when they think the time is 6:05 as they do when they believe it to be 5:20. For normal subjects, there is a distinct reverse trend (interaction p = .002)—a finding we had not originally anticipated, but one that seems embarrassingly simple to explain, as witness the several 6:05 normal subjects who politely refused the crackers, saying, "No, thanks, I don't want to spoil my dinner." Obviously, cognitive factors have affected the eating behavior of both normal and obese subjects with, however, a vast difference. While this cognitive manipulation of time serves to trigger or stimulate eating among the obese, it has the opposite effect on normal subjects, most of whom are at this hour, we presume, physiologically hungry, aware in the 6:05 condition that they will eat dinner very shortly, and unwilling to ruin their appetites by filling up on crackers.

In another study, Nisbett has examined the effects of taste on eating behavior. He reasons that taste, like the sight or smell of food, is essentially an external stimulus to eating. His experiment also extends the range of weight deviation by including a group of very skinny subjects, as well as obese and normal subjects. His purpose in so doing was to examine the hypothesis that the relative potency of external versus internal controls is a dimension directly related to the degree of overweight. If this is correct, it should be anticipated that the taste of food will have the greatest impact on the amount eaten by obese subjects and the least effect on skinny subjects. To test this, Nisbett had his subjects eat as much vanilla ice cream as they wanted. He gave them either a creamy and delicious, extremely expensive, preparation or an acrid brew of cheap vanilla ice cream and quinine, which he called "vanilla bitters." The effects of taste are presented in Figure 5, which plots the relation of a subject's ratings of how good or bad the ice cream was to the amount eaten. Obviously, when the ice cream is rated as "fairly good" or better, obese subjects eat considerably more than do normal subjects, who, in turn, eat more than skinny subjects. When the ice cream is rated as "not very good" or worse, this ordering tends to reverse, with skinny subjects eating more than either normal or obese subjects. This experiment indicates that the external or, at least, the nonvisceral taste cue does indeed have differential effects on the eating behavior of skinny, normal, and obese subjects.

The indications in this experiment—

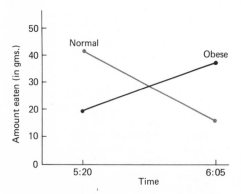

Figure 4. The effects of manipulated time on eating.

that the degree of dependence on external versus internal cues is a dimension covarying with weight deviation—is a particularly fascinating finding, for if further work supports this hypothesis we do have the beginnings of a plausible explanation of why skinnies are skinny and fats are fat. We know from work such as that of Carlson that gastric contractions cease after the introduction of only a small amount of food into the stomach. To the extent that such contractions are directly related to the hunger "experience," to the extent that a person is under internal control, he should literally "eat like a bird"—only enough to stop the contractions. Eating beyond this point should be a function of external cues—the taste, sight, and smell of food, perhaps the sheer joy of mastication. Externally controlled individuals, then, should have difficulty in stopping eating—a suggestion that may account for the notorious "binge" eating of the obese or monumental meals lovingly detailed by students (e.g., Beebe) of the great, fat, gastronomic magnificos.

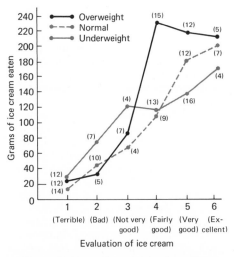

Figure 5. The effects of food quality on the amounts eaten by obese, normal, and skinny subjects. ( ) = number of subjects.

This last, loose attempt to account for why the obese are obese does in itself raise intriguing questions. For example, does the external control of eating behavior inevitably lead to obesity? I assume it is evident that logically such a link is not inevitable and that the condition of external control of eating behavior can indeed lead to the state of emaciation. An externally controlled person should eat and grow fat when food-related cues are abundant and when the person is fully aware of them. However, when such cues are absent or, for some reason, such as withdrawal or depression, the person is unaware of these cues, the person under external control should not eat, and if the condition persists, grow concentration-camp thin. If you go through the clinical literature you receive the impression that there is an odd but distinct relationship between extreme obesity and extreme emaciation. For example, 11 of 21 case studies in Bliss and Branch's book on anorexia nervosa were at some point in their lives obese. In 8 of these 11 cases, anorexia was preceded and accompanied either by marked withdrawal or by an intense depression. In contrast, intense attacks of anxiety or nervousness (states that the experiment by Schachter, Goldman, and Gordon would suggest inhibited eating in normal subjects) seem to characterize the development of anorexia among most of the cases who were originally normal size.

At this point, obviously, these speculations are simply idea spinning—fun, but ephemeral. Let us return to the facts of the studies described so far. The results can be summarized quickly as follows:

1. Physiological correlates of food deprivation, such as gastric motility and hypoglycemia, are directly related to eating behavior and to the reported experience of hunger in normal-sized subjects but unrelated in obese subjects.

2. External or nonvisceral cues, such as smell, taste, the sight of other people eating, the passage of time, and so forth,

affect eating behavior in obese subjects to a greater extent than in normal subjects.

Given these basic facts, their implications ramify to almost any area involved in food and eating, and some of our recent studies have been concerned with the implications of these experimentally derived relationships for eating behavior in a variety of nonlaboratory settings. Thus, Goldman, Jaffa, and Schachter have studied the relationship of obesity to fasting on Yom Kippur, the Jewish Day of Atonement, which requires of the traditional Jew that he do without food or water for 24 hours. Reasoning that this occasion is one in which food-relevant external cues are particularly scarce, it seemed logical to expect that fat Jews would be more likely to fast than would normal Jews. In a study of 296 religious (defined as anyone who has been to a synagogue at least once during the past year for some reason other than a wedding or a bar mitzvah) Jewish college students, this does prove to be the case, for 83.3 percent of fat Jews fasted as compared with 68.8 percent of normal Jews who did so (p < .05).

Further, this external-internal control schema leads to the prediction that fat, fasting Jews who spend a great deal of time in synagogue on Yom Kippur will suffer less from fasting than fat, fasting Jews who spend little time in synagogue, and that there will be no such relationship for normal fasting Jews. It is apparent there will be far fewer food-related cues in the synagogue than on the street or at home. Therefore, the likelihood that the impulse for obese Jews to eat will be triggered is greater out of synagogue than in it. For normal Jews, this distinction is of less importance. In or out of synagogue, stomach pangs are stomach pangs. Again, the data support the expectation. Correlating the number of hours in synagogue against self ratings of fasting unpleasantness, there is, for obese subjects, a correlation of −.50, while for normal subjects the correlation

is only −.18. Testing the difference between these correlations, z = 2.19, which is significant at the .03 level. Obviously, for the obese, the more time in synagogue the less an ordeal is fasting. In contrast, for normals, the number of hours in synagogue has little to do with the difficulty of the fast.

In another study, Goldman, Jaffa, and Schachter examined the relationship of obesity to choice of eating places. Generalizing from Nisbett's findings on taste, it seemed a plausible guess that the obese would be more drawn to good restaurants and more repelled by bad ones than would normal subjects. At Columbia, students have the option of eating in the University dining halls or in any of the swarm of more or less exotic restaurants, lunch counters, and delicatessens that surround this metropolitan campus. At this university, as probably at every similar place in the United States, student opinion of the institution's food is low. If a freshman elects to eat in a dormitory dining hall, he may, if he chooses, join in a prepay food plan at the beginning of the school year. In so-doing, he prepays, at the rate of $16.25 a week for all of his meals. Any time after November 1, by paying a penalty of $15.00, the student may cancel his food contract. If we accept prevailing campus opinion as at all realistically based, we should anticipate that those for whom taste or food quality is most important will be most likely to let their food contracts expire. Obese freshmen, then, should be more likely to drop out of the food plan than normal freshmen. Again, the data support expectations, for 86.5 percent of fat freshmen let their contracts drop as compared with the 67.1 percent of normal students who did so (p < .05). Obesity does to some extent predict who chooses to subsist on institutional food.

In the final study in this series, Goldman et al., examined the relationship of obesity to the difficulty involved in adjusting to new eating schedules imposed by time-zone changes. Thanks to the generosity of the Medical Department of Air France, it was possible to examine data of a study conducted by this department on medical effects of time-zone changes on 236 flight personnel regularly assigned to the Paris-New York and Paris-Montreal flights. This investigation was concerned largely with the effects of the east-to-west journey. Most of these flights are scheduled to leave Paris around noon, French time, fly for approximately eight hours, and land in North America sometime between 2:00 and 3:00 P.M., Eastern Standard Time. Flight-crew members all eat lunch shortly after takeoff and, being occupied with landing preparations and serving passenger needs, are not served another meal during the flight. They land in North America, then, some seven hours after their last meal, at a time that is past the local lunch hour and before the local dinner time.

The Air France study was not directly concerned with reports of hunger or eating behavior, but the interviews systematically noted all individuals who volunteered that they "suffered from the discordance between their physiological state and meal time in America." (Quotation from letter from Dr. Lavernhe.) The interpretation of this coding is not completely clear-cut, but it appears to apply chiefly to fliers who complain that they either do without food or make do with a snack until local dinner time. Probably some complainers are those who eat a full meal on landing, are then sated at local dinner time, and are again physiologically hungry at a time long past local dinner time. In either case, it should be anticipated that the fatter fliers, sensitive to external rather than internal cues, should most readily adapt to local eating schedules and be least likely to complain of the discrepancy between American meal times and physiological state.

Given the rigorous physical requirements involved in air crew selection, there are, of course, relatively few really obese people in this sample. Nisbett's experiment, however, has indicated that the relative reliance on external versus internal cues may well be a dimension covarying with the degree of weight deviation. It seems at least reasonable, then, to anticipate that even within a restricted sample there should be differences between the heavier and lighter members of the sample. This is the case. Comparing the 101 flying personnel who are overweight (0.1 percent to 29 percent overweight) with those 135 fliers who are not overweight (0 percent to 25 percent underweight) we find that 11.9 percent of the overweight complain as compared with 25.3 percent of the nonoverweight ($p < .01$). It does appear that fatter flying Frenchmen are less likely to be troubled by the effects of time changes on eating.

Obviously, I make no pretense that the *only* explanation of the results of these last three studies lies in this external-internal control formulation of eating behavior. These studies were deliberately designed to test implications of the general schema in field settings. As with any field research, alternative explanations are legion, and within the context of any specific study are simply impossible to overrule. At the very least, however, these results are nonobvious and are consistent with this formulation.

The studies of Yom Kippur and of the eating behavior of Columbia freshmen and French fliers may at this point seem wildly remote from my introductory remarks, but they derive ultimately from this skepticism about the assumption of an identity between a physiological state and a psychological or behavioral event. The physiological correlates of food deprivation may or may not be associated with "hunger," may or may not be associated with eating. Explicitly abandoning the assumption of identity has for "hunger" proved experimentally worthwhile. I suspect that doing so for many of the other feeling states that are presumably physiologically well anchored may prove equally rewarding.

Stages of recovery and development of lateral hypothalamic control of food and water intake

philip teitelbaum
mei-fang cheng
and
paul rozin

In 1951 Anand and Brobeck[2] observed that destruction of a small area in the lateral hypothalamus in rats and cats led to loss of eating and death from starvation. In 1954 Teitelbaum and Stellar[16] found that rats with lateral hypothalamic damage not only starved but also refused to drink. However, if such rats were kept alive by tube-feeding and were offered a variety of wet and palatable foods in addition to the ordinary diet of dry Purina and water, they eventually recovered both feeding and drinking in a regular sequence.

Such a gradual recovery of hypothalamic function through qualitatively discrete stages offers a remarkable opportunity for experimental fractionation of the multiple controls that ordinarily interact simultaneously to maintain normal intake. Even after the lateral hypothalamic animal eats and drinks again, thereby adjusting caloric intake and maintaining his body weight, recovery is not complete[6,7,15] suggesting that some normal controls are permanently lost.

In the first part of this paper, we will review our knowledge of the mechanisms of the lateral hypothalamic control of food and water intake, based on a detailed analysis of the pattern of deficits seen in various stages of recovery. Then, in the second part of the paper, we will present new findings which suggest that a parallel to adult recovery is seen in the pattern of infantile development of control of feeding and drinking.

From *Annals* of The New York Academy of Sciences, Vol. 157, Art. 2, P. Teitelbaum et al., pp. 849–858, © 1969.

THE LATERAL HYPOTHALAMIC SYNDROME

In a detailed analysis, Teitelbaum and Epstein[15] identified four clear-cut stages in the recovery from lateral hypothalamic lesions. The animal whose record is graphed in Figure 1 had large symmetrical lesions (see Figure 2), engendering an extremely slow recovery, and thus making it possible to see the events in each stage quite clearly.

The stage of aphagia and adipsia occurs first. The animal refuses all food, wet or dry, and drinks no water. It would die if not maintained by tube-feeding. The animal whose data are shown in Figure 1 neither ate nor drank for 19 days, steadily lost weight, and had to be kept alive from the seventh day on by gastric intubation with a liquid diet. Such a rat can lick, chew, and swallow reflexively if milk is placed in its mouth with a medicine dropper, but after a short time it will avoid food by turning its head away or by letting milk placed in its mouth dribble over the side without swallowing it. The rat is alert and moves around readily, but it ignores food and will actively push away food that is forced upon it.

A stage of anorexia and adipsia appears next. The animal becomes increasingly attracted to palatable wet foods. It ingests appreciable quantities but still does not regulate its caloric intake or maintain its body weight. (The rat represented in Figure 1 nibbled at milk chocolate and ate small amounts of a liquid diet beginning on the 20th day, but for an additional 19 days it did not eat enough to maintain its weight without tube-feeding.) Therefore, eating does not necessarily imply regulation. Eating in

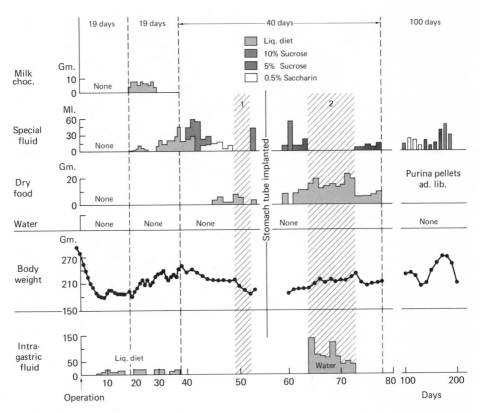

Figure 1. Recovery of food intake with permanent adipsia after large lateral hypothalamic lesions. (The first two dashed vertical lines set off stages of recovery. First, for 19 days, the animal neither eats nor drinks; second, for 19 more days, it eats wet and palatable foods but still has to be tube-fed; and third, for the rest of its life, it regulates its food intake but does not drink water. The rat was weaned to sweet nonnutritive fluid and then ate dry food. When offered only water (shaded area 1), it did not drink and then stopped eating. Gastric hydration (shaded area 2) allowed normal feeding. Thereafter, the animal ingested sweet fluid and survived on dry food. [From (15) Teitelbaum and Epstein]

this stage of recovery seems to be evoked by the sight, smell, and taste of the food, but there is no maintained (internally driven) character to the eating.

However, the urge to eat returns, often abruptly. Sooner or later, depending on the size and accuracy of placement of the lesions, the animal may suddenly eat a large quantity of wet, palatable food and will gain weight sharply (the 39th day after operation for the rat whose recovery is graphed in Figure 1). This defines the onset of the third stage of recovery: adip-

sia. The rat is no longer anorexic, and no longer needs to be tube-fed. It now adjusts its volume intake when the caloric content of food is varied.[15,17] A new control has reappeared, enabling the animal to regulate its caloric intake. However, adipsia still persists. It can mask caloric regulation if only dry food and water are available. The animal refuses to drink water, becomes dehydrated, will not eat dry food, and eventually will die. It does not drink water in response to bodily dehydration (produced by fluid depriva-

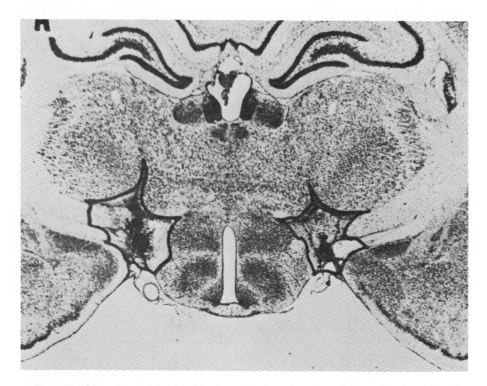

Figure 2. Photomicrograph of a thionine-stained section through the tuberal region of the hypothalamus from the brain of the animal whose recovery after lateral hypothalamic lesions is graphed in Figure 1. (The damaged tissue is outlined in black.) [From Teitelbaum and Epstein]

tion, injection with hypertonic saline, or exposure to heat).[7,15] It can, however, by gradual weaning from its liquid diet, be induced to ingest saccharin solutions (it responds to the sweet taste of saccharin as though it were food), thereby unwittingly hydrating itself sufficiently to allow it to eat dry pellets.[15]

Eventually, most animals will drink water and will accept dry food. They maintain themselves adequately on dry food and water and enter a final stage, recovery. But more subtle tests reveal that recovery of feeding and drinking is not yet complete, and indeed, may never be. Many of these animals still drink quite abnormally. They still do not respond to bodily dehydration, but instead, drink only when they eat. For example, in contrast to normal rats, they drink practically no water during 24 hours of food deprivation. This form of drinking has been called prandial drinking[7,15] and appears to be controlled by peripheral stimuli arising from a dry mouth.[5]

Their feeding is also still abnormal. A normal animal will eat more in response to low blood sugar produced by insulin injection ("glucostatic" regulation?). It will also eat more in a cold and less in a warm environment ("thermostatic" regulation?). As shown in Figure 3, recovered lateral hypothalamic rats respond normally to environmental temperature, eating more in the cold and less when it is warm. But they do not eat more in response to lowered blood sugar (see Table 1), even when their hypoglycemia is severe enough to be fatal. Finally, although they do accept the ordinary

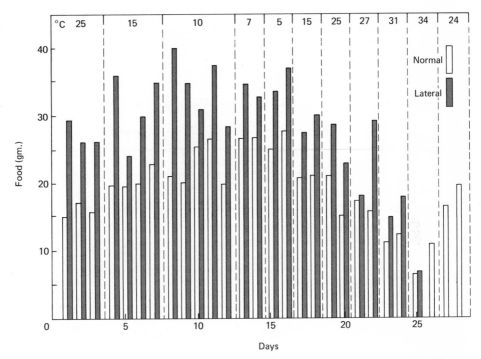

Figure 3. Increased food intake in cold and decreased intake in heat in normal (open, stippled bars) and recovered lateral hypothalamic (solid bars) animals.

diet, they are still quite finicky, rejecting the food if it is made even slightly bitter with quinine.[15]

On the basis of these results, we can tentatively suggest an explanation for the loss of caloric regulation after lateral hypothalamic lesions. Perhaps, even when the capacity to eat is clearly present (recall the anorexia of the second stage), both "thermostatic" and "glucostatic"[5] regulation of food intake are still lacking. The animal recovers its ability to regulate caloric intake and to maintain its weight in the third stage of recovery when "thermostatic" regulation returns.[7,13,15] "Glucostatic" regulation, however, may never recover. It is conceivable, therefore, that "thermostatic" regulation is sufficient for the regulation of caloric intake.

The converse may also hold.[13] With appropriate brain damage,[8] it might be possible to demonstrate that "glucostatic" regulation may be sufficient for caloric regulation, even when "thermostatic" regulation is lacking. It is also possible that elements of regulation other than "thermostatic," but still unidentified, may reappear with it to produce the recovery of caloric and body weight regulation in the lateral hypothalamic syndrome.[13]

DEVELOPMENT IN
INFANCY PARALLELS ADULT RECOVERY

Every animal follows the same sequence of recovery from lateral hypothalamic damage. The sequence is shown diagrammatically in Table 2. This striking invariability suggests that recovery of hypothalamic control of food and water intake occurs according to some fundamental principle of neural reorganiza-

TABLE 1. ABSENCE OF INSULIN-INDUCED FEEDING IN RATS RECOVERED FROM LATERAL HYPOTHALAMIC APHAGIA

	Food	N	Insulin	Extra Intake Elicited	Died
Normal	Purina Chow	12	Crystalline	All	0
		7	Protamine Zinc	All	0
	Liquid Diets	2	Crystalline	All	0
		6	Protamine Zinc	All	0
Recovered Lateral	Purina Chow	6	Crystalline	None	5
		4	Protamine Zinc	None	4
	Liquid Diets	4	Crystalline	1	3
Medial	Purina Chow	5	Crystalline	4	1
	Liquid Diets	2	Crystalline	All	0

tion. Is there any clue to its nature?

A newborn suckling rat ingests a liquid diet but does not drink water. It is adipsic but not aphagic. Later, when it eats ordinary dry food and drinks water, it does not respond fully to dehydration. This is quite similar to the later stages of the lateral hypothalamic syndrome. A rat in the third stage is adipsic but not aphagic. Later it eats and drinks ordinary food and water, but is still abnormal in subtle aspects of its eating and drinking. In a sense, with respect to its feeding and drinking, the lateral hypothalamic rat is more like an infant than like an adult. Is this merely a coincidence, or is there really a parallel between normal infant development and adult recovery of the control of food and water intake?

The simplest approach to this problem is to test the regulatory capacity of the normal rat at weaning. If development is not yet complete at weaning, we might expect that deficits in feeding and drinking characteristic of the adult recovered lateral hypothalamic rat in the fourth stage might be evident. However, in preliminary experiments we found that albino Sprague-Dawley rats of the Charles River strain appeared relatively normal at weaning or shortly thereafter. They regulated their caloric intake normally when their diet was diluted and did not seem selective in their response to less palatable food. They drank water in response to dehydration by injection of hypertonic saline. Therefore, to discover possible deficits in regulation, we decided to test rats earlier in their development.

But here we faced a problem. The earliest we can meaningfully test the food intake of an infant rat isolated from its mother is at the age of 14 days. The various tests for regulation ordinarily require a few days each, and development

TABLE 2. STAGES OF RECOVERY SEEN IN THE LATERAL HYPOTHALAMIC SYNDROME*

	STAGE I Adipsia, Aphagia	STAGE II Adipsia, Anorexia	STAGE III Adipsia, Dehydration- Aphagia	STAGE IV Recovery
Eats Wet Palatable Foods	NO	YES	YES	YES
Regulates Food Intake and Body Weight on Wet Palatable Foods	NO	NO	YES	YES
Eats Dry Foods (If Hydrated)	NO	NO	YES	YES
Drinks Water Survives on Dry Food and Water	NO	NO	NO	YES

*The critical behavioral event defining the stages are listed on the left. (From reference 15.)

proceeds so rapidly that a symptom may disappear before we can reliably demonstrate its presence. To solve this problem, we decided to try to slow down the course of infantile development. If successful, we might reveal the development of elements of regulation in the same way that the slow course of recovery reveals the elements of regulation in the lateral hypothalamic syndrome.

Thyroidectomy slows development. We exposed the trachea of rats one or two days after birth and surgically removed the thyroid glands. Normal littermate controls were subjected to the same surgical procedures, except that the thyroid was not removed. The success of thyroidectomy was clearly evident within a few days. Weight gain and growth were drastically retarded, so that at one week of age, thyroidectomized rats were much smaller than normal. At two weeks,

in contrast to normal animals, their eyes had not yet opened, their heads were still infantile in shape and their fur was still typical of young infants. At three weeks, the normal weaning age, they looked like normal animals, but were smaller in length and were markedly underweight (apparently in direct proportion to how successfully the thyroid was removed). For example, 35 thyroidectomized animals at 21 days of age weighed from 10–62 g, in contrast to 13 normal animals which ranged from 51–68 g.

At 21 days of age, all the animals were weaned. They were separated from their mothers, housed in individual living cages, and offered dry Purina chow pellets strewn on the floor of the cage and water in a Richter tube. If they did not accept dry food and water, they were also offered wet and palatable foods, and subjected to the same tests of regulation which were sufficient to establish the presence or absence of deficits in the eating and drinking behavior of lateral hypothalamic rats. When tested at 21 days of age (the normal weaning age), thyroidectomized weanling rats displayed every stage of the lateral hypothalamic syndrome. If greatly retarded in development (as measured by their body weight at weaning), some weanlings were completely aphagic and adipsic when offered wet palatable foods or ordinary food and water. They nursed reflexively (recall that aphagic adult lateral hypothalamic rats lick and swallow milk reflexively from a dropper), but did not voluntarily ingest food or water, no matter how palatable. Others, more fully developed at weaning, accepted wet palatable foods but did not eat enough to maintain their weight. If this stage lasted too long, they died. Other weanlings, even less retarded, gained weight and regulated their caloric intake of a liquid diet (they at least doubled their caloric intake when the caloric content was one-third as great), but were still adipsic and would die if offered only dry food and water. Finally, the least retarded weanlings accepted dry food and water, but drank only when they ate, thus being prandial drinkers and not drinking in response to bodily

TABLE 3. DEVELOPMENT OF EATING AND DRINKING PARALLELING RECOVERY*

Decrease in Lesion Size Increase in Weight at Weaning	Stage I Adipsia Aphagia	Stage II Adipsia Anorexia	Stage III Adipsia	Stage IV Partial Recovery
Eats Wet Palatable Foods (Voluntary Eating)	NO / NO	YES / YES	YES / YES	YES / YES
Regulates Food Intake & Body Weight on Wet Palatable Foods	NO / NO	NO / NO	YES / YES	YES / YES
Drinks Water. Survives on Dry Food & Water.	NO / NO	NO / NO	NO / NO	YES / YES

Drinking		Eating		
Prandial Drinking	Osmotic Regulation	Finickiness	Glucostatic Regulation	Thermostatic Regulation
NO / NO	NO / NO	NO / NO	NO / NO	YES / YES

*The upper half of each box represents the stages of recovery from lateral hypothalamic lesions (as diagrammed in Table 2, except that stage 4, the stage of partial recovery, has been expanded to illustrate the residual defects in eating and drinking). The bottom half of each box represents the stages of development seen in thyroidectomized weanling rats.

dehydration. They were very finicky and although they ate more in the cold, they did not eat more in response to hypoglycemia. Thus, depending on the degree of retardation, every stage of the lateral hypothalamic syndrome was seen in thyroidectomized rats at weaning. Indeed, many individual thyroidectomized infant rats, in the course of their development after weaning, progressed slowly and in exactly the same sequence through several of the stages of the lateral hypothalamic syndrome. As summarized diagrammatically in Table 3, the parallel is perfect—recovery of feeding and drinking recapitulates its ontogeny.

RECOVERY OF SUBCORTICAL FUNCTION PARALLELS ITS ENCEPHALIZATION

Why does recovery of lateral hypothalamic control of feeding and drinking parallel the development of such controls in infancy? Does the same basic process underlie infantile development of the nervous system and recovery of function in the brain-damaged adult? A human infant at birth is very much like a decerebrate animal.[12] Its behavior consists almost entirely of automatic reflexes of approach and withdrawal. Thus, we find rooting, sucking, and grasping—approach reflexes of head, mouth, hands, and feet. Painful stimuli elicit withdrawal reflexes in these parts of the body. The same reflexes are seen in anencephalic human infants. Rhombencephalic or mesencephalic infants nurse reflexively, but do not ingest enough, and will die unless maintained by tube-feeding.[10,14] The same is true of decerebrate adult rats,[18] and as we have mentioned before, of lateral hypothalamic rats. But with increasing encephalization during development, the normal infant develops the capacity for motivated homeostatic control of food and water intake.

Perhaps the process of recovery in the adult rat with lateral hypothalamic lesions is essentially a process of reen-cephalization. If so, then functional decortication (spreading cortical depression) should reinstate the lateral hypothalamic syndrome in animals that have previously recovered from it. As shown by Teitelbaum and Cytawa[14] and as illustrated in Figure 4, this is exactly what happens. Indeed, other subcortical syndromes (the hyperemotionality produced by septal lesions and the temperature impairment produced by anterior hypothalamic lesions), in which recovery also occurs, are also reinstated by spreading cortical depression.[4]

In summary, we have used the process of recovery from lateral hypothalamic lesions to reveal some of the elements involved in the normal control of eating and drinking. The sequence of stages of recovery in the adult brain-damaged animal is an exact parallel to the sequence of development in infancy. We suggest that lateral hypothalamic recovery is essentially a process of reencephalization of function. In other words, recovery recapitulates ontogeny.

DISCUSSION

Dr. Gold. You have demonstrated that spreading cortical depression can reinstate aphagia and adipsia in rats that have recovered from lateral hypothalamic lesions. Have you been able to localize the effect within the cortex?

Dr. Teitelbaum. Dr. Cytawa and I tried to localize the effect of spreading cortical depression to either the anterior or posterior half of the cortex by using magnesium chloride to protect parts of the cortex from KCl-induced spreading depression. Our preliminary findings suggested that frontal cortex depression was as effective as total cortical depression and more effective than posterior cortical depression. However, these findings were quite fragmentary and do not allow me to make more than a tentative suggestion to this effect at the present time.

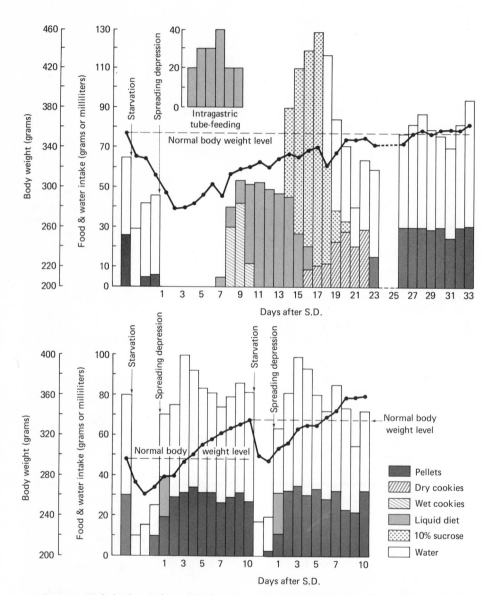

Figure 4. Daily body weight and food and water intake after the onset of spreading cortical depression. The height of each bar on any day represents the cumulative intake of all substances on that day (30 g of food plus 50 ml of water equals a total height of 80). (Top) Prolonged aphagia and adipsia reinstated in a rat recovered from lateral hypothalamic lesions. During recovery, the rat was weaned from wet cookies to the liquid diet, and from a liquid diet to pellets and water. (Bottom) In a control rat, on two occasions, spreading depression had little effect on the food and water intake. [From Teitelbaum and Cytawa (14)]

E. M. Gurowitz. How do you reconcile your results relating to early neodecortication with those of Kling, who finds a very different syndrome both in cats and in monkeys subjected to decortication soon after birth?

Dr. Teitelbaum. Loss of function after brain damage is generally of two types: (1) absence of excitatory function, as in paralysis or loss of sensory capacity; and (2) release phenomena, in which normal functions are apparently exaggerated, due to loss of inhibitory controls.

Release phenomena, such as the hyperactivity seen after frontal pole removal, or the hypersexuality seen after amygdalectomy, are not seen after such damage in infancy, probably because the tissue removed has not yet developed its inhibitory control function.

Although, in the experiments reported here, we did not actually do neo-decortication in infancy, if such tissue is necessary to maintain feeding, we would expect its loss in infancy to prevent full development of normal regulation of food intake later in life as well.

Dr. Fleming. I find that you are able to observe both physiological and behavioral changes in the young rats following thyroidectomy, and that these changes constituted a close parallel to those seen in the lateral hypothalamic animals. The question I pose is whether these changes may be reversed with thyroxin replacement therapy. If the answer is in the negative, then at what point do these changes become embedded in the animal's behavior? In other words, if replacement therapy is initiated at progressively earlier stages after the extirpation, at what point do you see no physiological or behavioral changes? The implications of your data extend far beyond the experiment itself, for you may have a technique that would make it possible to manipulate the appearance of age-locked physiological and behavioral responses.

Dr. Teitelbaum. The problem you raise is one of critical periods in development. It is important, as you point out, and we have thought about it, but have not begun to work on it. However, there are some facts which are relevant. Thyroidectomy in adult rats does not produce the symptoms seen in rats thyroidectomized at birth. Therefore, the syndrome is related to impairment of development. Replacement therapy in infant thyroidectomized rats, initiated at the same time as the removal of the thyroid, is reported to counteract the effects of thyroidectomy completely, as measured by rate of growth and weight gain.

From this I would guess that feeding also develops normally with adequate replacement therapy. Replacement therapy in the adult cannot reverse impairment in infantile development (witness cretinism in humans) and, therefore, there must be a critical period of development. Since five to seven days of age seems critical for sexual differentiation in the rat, this would be my best guess of the critical period for feeding.

J. Mendelson. I should like to make a brief informative statement that does not require an answer from Dr. Teitelbaum. Dr. Juan Roig in Dr. James Olds' laboratory has recorded from many cells in the lateral hypothalamus whose rate of firing greatly *increases* (by a factor of 3–8) with intracarotid glucose injections (latency of increase is about five seconds after the beginning of an injection of 0.15 cc of 5–50 percent glucose at 0.007 cc/sec). Control injections of saline and mannose failed to produce any significant increase in firing rate.

I referred to these cells as "gluco-receptors," not to imply that they are the "detectors" of glucose (in the sense that rods and cones are the "detectors" of light), but simply to indicate that they are responsive to changes in blood glucose concentration (in the same sense that cells of the visual cortex are responsive to light on the retina). I mentioned Dr.

Roig's data because they are in contrast to that of other workers who report tonic decreases in lateral hypothalamic unit activity in response to increases in blood glucose concentration.

L. Stein. I was impressed by your demonstration that the development of feeding in the infant rat parallels the recovery of feeding in the hypothalamic adult, and intrigued by your idea that the parallel depends on the fact that a process of encephalization underlies both. Do you assume that the hypothalamic lesion causes a loss of cortical control and, if so, can you duplicate the hypothalamic syndrome with lesions at higher levels?

Dr. Teitelbaum. Our assumption is that hypothalamic function as we know it is normal by virtue of its connections with the cortex. Thus, as you suggest, lesions at higher levels should indeed duplicate the symptoms of lateral hypothalamic damage. This is actually so. Frontal pole removal, as reported by Richter and Hawkes in 1938, produces aphagia and adipsia, from which rats recover in about ten days. During part of this time they will accept a little bread soaked in milk—like our anorexic animals.

Also, Harrison, in work on rats with septal lesions has reported temporary aphagia and adipsia. These animals also accept wet palatable foods before they eat normally.

J. W. Greenfield. I have found evidence that weanling albino rats seem to be hyperphagic rather than show signs of having been aphagic. Not only are their ratios of food intake to weight proportional to that of the dynamic hyperphagic rat (13–16 g/100 g body weight), but they also display finickiness to quinine dilution of rat chow. They overeat on highly palatable fat diets. Yet they regulate to caloric dilution when placed on a 40 percent cellulose, 60 percent rat chow mixture. My data on normal weanling, 21-day-old rats, do not suggest recovery from aphagia, but rather, a tendency towards hyperphagia.

Dr. Teitelbaum. Kennedy has pointed out that young, growing rats overeat as much as ventromedial-damaged animals of the same age. We have verified this in our own laboratory, and also the fact that they adjust very well to caloric dilution of the diet.

The problem you raise is one of evaluating the stage of development in young rats. The maturity of development at weaning (21 days) depends on strain, litter size, and adequacy of care and nourishment provided by the mother. Your data suggest that your animals are relatively well-developed at 21 days of age, except for your finding that they are finicky. But finickiness is quite relative. Our normal animals at weaning seem less finicky than adult animals of the same strain, and are clearly much less finicky than thyroidectomized weanlings. But if switched from a palatable food to a quinine-adulterated diet, they would undoubtedly display finickiness, in the sense of a heightened negative response to the diet produced by its contrast with the preceding highly palatable one. All that I can suggest is that you compare your normal weanlings with under-developed ones, and with animals of the same age subjected to ventromedial damage, to try to interpret the meaning of finickiness as a symptom in these animals.

References

1. Adolph, E. F. Ontogeny of physiological regulations in the rat. *Quart. Rev. Biol.,* 1957, **32**, 89.

2. Anand, B. K., and Brobeck, J. R. Hypothalamic control of food intake. *Yale J. Biol. Med.,* 1951, **24**, 123.

3. Brobeck, J. R. Food and temperature. *Recent Progress in Hormone Research*, 1960, **16**, 439.

4. Cytawa, J., and Teitelbaum, P. Spreading cortical depression and recovery from subcortical damage. XXIII International Congress of Physiol. Sciences, Tokyo, Japan. No. 1141, 1965.

5. Epstein, A. N., Spector, D., Samman, A., and Goldblum, K. 1964. Exaggerated prandial drinking in the rat without salivary glands. *Nature*, 1964, **201**, 1342.

6. Epstein, A. N., and Teitelbaum, P. 1962. Lateral hypothalamic control of insulin-induced feeding. *Proc. Intern. Congr. Physiol. Sci. 22nd*, Leiden, 1962, Abstr. 361.

7. Epstein, A. N., and Teitelbaum, P. Severe and persistent deficits in thirst produced by lateral hypothalamic damage. In M. J. Wayner (Ed.), *Thirst*. P. 395. (First Florida State University Symposium, Tallahassee, 1963.) Oxford: Pergamon Press, 1964.

8. Hamilton, C. L. Interactions of food intake and temperature regulation in the rat. *J. comp. physiol. Psychol.*, 1963, **56**, 476.

9. Mayer, J. Regulation of energy intake and the body weight: the glucostatic theory and the lipostatic hypothesis. *Ann. N. Y. Acad. Sci.*, 1955, **63**, 15.

10. Monnier, M., and Willi, H. Die integrative Tätigkeit des Nervensystems beim normalen Säugling und beim bulbo-spinalen Anencephalen (Rautenhirnwesen). *Ann. Pacdiatrici (Basel)*, 1947, **168**, 289.

11. Monnier, M., and Willi, H. Die integrative Tätigkeit des Nervensystems beim mesorhombo-spinalen Anencephalus (Mittelhirnwesen). *Mschr. Psychiat. Neurol.*, 1953, **126**, 239.

12. Peiper, A. Cerebral function in infancy and childhood. New York: Consultants Bureau, 1963.

13. Teitelbaum, P. 1967. Motivation and the control of food intake. In C. F. Code et al. (Eds.), *Handbook of physiology*, Section 6, Alimentary canal. Washington, D.C.: American Physiological Society. Vol. I, Chap. 24.

14. Teitelbaum, P., and Cytawa, J. Spreading depression and recovery from lateral hypothalamic damage. *Science*, 1965, **147**, 61.

15. Teitelbaum, P., and Epstein, A. N. The lateral hypothalamic syndrome: recovery of feeding and drinking after lateral hypothalamic lesions. *Psychol. Rev.*, 1962, **69**, 74.

16. Teitelbaum, P., and Stellar, E. Recovery from the failure to eat produced by hypothalamic lesions. *Science*, 1954, **120**, 894.

17. Williams, D. R., and Teitelbaum, P. Some observations on the starvation resulting from lateral hypothalamic lesions. *J. comp. physiol. Psychol.*, 1959, **52**, 458.

18. Woods, J. W. Behavior of chronic decerebrate rats. *J. Neurophysiol.*, 1964, **27**, 634.

Chemical coding of behavior in the brain
neal e. miller

Two classical methods for studying how the brain controls behavior have been to study the effects of destroying specified areas and to study the effects of stimulating specific sites. These methods, which have led to a great increase in our knowledge, can be illustrated by work on the hypothalamus. This is a primitive structure deep in the base of the brain, which first appears in vertebrates, such as primitive fish, and has quite similar structure in mammals from the rat to man.

If a certain small area is destroyed on both sides of the hypothalamus, the animal will stop eating and will starve to death (1). Conversely, electrical stimulation in this same lateral area will cause an animal which has just eaten to satiation to eat voraciously (2). Various studies have shown that such stimulation does not elicit mere reflex gnawing, but that it also can elicit learned food-seeking habits, and that it has many, and perhaps all, of the properties of the strong hunger that normally develops during a fast (3). The results of destruction and of stimulation agree in showing that the lateral hypothalamus is significantly involved in food-seeking behavior.

Additional studies, however, have shown that the effects of lesions and of stimulation in the lateral hypothalamus are not as simple as was originally supposed. Lesions in this area cause animals to stop drinking water as well as to stop eating food. Tests in which water is tubed directly into the stomach show

From *Science*, 1965, 148 (3668), 328–338. Copyright 1965 by the American Association for the Advancement of Science.

that the interference with eating is not secondary to dehydration produced by failure to drink (4). Furthermore, electrical stimulation of certain sites in the lateral hypothalamus will cause animals which have just drunk water to satiation to resume drinking. Also, stimulation of this area can evoke sexual responses, such as penile erection and ejaculation (5). It can serve, also, as a reward: animals learn to press a bar to get a few moments of electrical stimulation in this area (6); yet, paradoxically, if exactly the same stimulation is provided for too long, the same animals learn to press a bar to turn it off (7). Lesions in the lateral hypothalamus will abolish the rewarding effect of electrical stimulation in another region of the brain, and will abolish the appetitive response to a deficiency of salt (8). Thus, it becomes painfully obvious that a number of diverse motivational and emotional functions all involve this tiny area of the brain, and that the techniques of making lesions or of providing electrical stimulation are relatively crude and indiscriminate in that they are likely to affect all of these diverse functions.

When diverse effects are produced from the same site, one may obscure the other. For example, stimulating the lateral hypothalamus with electric current at higher voltages produces frantic, escape-like activity which precludes the possibility of observing anything else. Perhaps we are observing only a few of of the most dominant functions.

We first attempted to deal with these difficulties by using electrodes with tinier bare tips for stimulating smaller regions of the lateral hypothalamus of rats. Instead of getting more specific, better effects, we got almost none at all, and we tentatively concluded that one must stimulate a fairly large population of cells or fibers in order to produce observable behavioral effects.

Other investigators have thought it might be easier to isolate functions in the larger brain of the monkey. However, it appears that the probability of getting a given specific effect from electrical stimulation via an electrode in the hypothalamus is lower in the monkey than it is in the rat. Furthermore, stimulation of a site in the hypothalamus may elicit several effects in relatively unpredictable combinations (9). The picture is one of networks that are spread out and interlaced, rather than of functions that are completely separated into distinctive areas. While this diffusion of function is adaptive in preventing a small lesion produced by a tiny blood clot or infection from completely interrupting any vital function, it necessarily makes investigation of the organization of the brain more difficult.

Yet another difficulty arises from the fact that lesions and electrical stimulation both affect fibers that are merely passing through an area, as well as the synapses of neurons, at which information from various fibers is brought together and processed. To use a loose analogy, they affect the telephone cables as well as the switchboard.

The foregoing difficulties have caused workers at our laboratory, among others, recently to explore the possibility that chemical stimulation may produce effects which are more specific to given functional systems than effects produced by electrical stimulation, and may act on synapses or cells without affecting fibers of passage.

EARLY EVIDENCE
FOR CHEMICAL SPECIFICITY

Some early behavioral evidence for "chemical" specificity came from the work of Andersson, who anesthetized goats and cemented needles into place through their skulls, by means of which minute injections could later be made into the brain of the recovered, normal, unanesthetized animal (10). He found that injection into the medial anterior region of the hypothalamus of goats of a solution of sodium chloride which had slightly higher osmotic pressure than body fluids have would cause an animal that had just drunk to satiation to resume drinking. We obtained similar results with cats; we showed that such an injection would elicit not only drinking but also the performance of a learned response of working for water, and that an injection of pure water would have the opposite effect, that of stopping either drinking or working for water (5). These specific behavioral effects, which are not elicited from other regions of the brain, presumably are due to the osmotic, rather than the chemical, action of the solution and are mediated by specialized sense organs or osmoreceptors in the brain.

Alan Fisher used a similar technique to test the effects of a soluble form of a male hormone, sodium testosterone sulfate, on different parts of the rat's brain (11). He thought that this hormone might elicit male sexual behavior. What he first observed, however, in both male and female rats, was the maternal behavior of nest-building and retrieving infant rats, activities that male rats ordinarily do not engage in. In an extensive series of subsequent investigations he has found that when this hormone is applied to the medial preoptic region of the hypothalamus it can elicit the maternal-like behavior of nest-building and of carrying infants to the nest in either male or female rats (12). When the same hormone is applied to a slightly different area, the lateral preoptic region, it can elicit male sexual behavior in either male or female rats. Such injections can cause male rats to mount nonreceptive females and even other males or infant rats, going through as much as is physically possible of the complete sex pattern, including ejaculation. It can cause similar behavior in female rats, with the exception, of course, of intromission and ejaculation.

When the needle delivers the hormone to a site between these two areas, mixed behavior may result; a male, for example, may alternatively mate with a female and carry strips of paper to build a nest, his responses apparently being determined by the type of object that happens to fall in his sensory field.

These effects occur within from 20 seconds to 5 minutes after injection of the hormone. They are not produced by injections in other parts of the brain. Interestingly enough, the female hormone, estrogen, which has a related chemical structure, produces similar effects but is apparently less potent. These effects are produced by from 1 to 4 micrograms of either hormone, irrespective of whether it is administered in the form of crystals or as a liquid in 1-microliter amounts.

Many other chemical substances, ranging widely in osmotic pressure and pH, have been tried, with negative results. So far, the only substance that has been found to produce similar behavior is the chelating agent sodium versenate. The behavioral effects of this agent are highly similar to those of sex hormones and occur after approximately the same delay. In line with previous notions about the normal action of endogenous sex hormones, Fisher interprets their effect as being that of lowering thresholds, so that external cues will be more likely to elicit sexual responses. He does not believe that the hormone is itself a direct excitant of the brain. He advances the tentative hypothesis that a chelating agent may produce its effect of lowering threshold, or reducing inhibition, by removing calcium ions from the nerve cells.

One perplexing aspect of these experiments is the fact that in only about 10 percent of the implants does Fisher get any effect. Once he finds an animal which shows an effect, however, he often is able to reproduce this effect many times, sometimes over a period of weeks. Thus far he has been unable to determine the cause of this low percentage of effective placements—to learn whether it is due to individual differences in the degree to which cells responsible for such behavior are concentrated in one location or to other factors. The very rareness of the effect has prevented detailed analysis.

Fisher's experiments have shown that the neural circuits necessary for complex patterns of distinctively male or female behavior are present in the brains of both male and female rats. He has also shown that these patterns can be activated by the presence of sex hormones. But the fact that both of these distinctively different types of behavior can be activated by the same hormone is puzzling. What, under normal circumstances, causes activation of characteristically male responses in the brain of the male and of characteristically maternal responses in the brain of the female? It may be that the threshold is lower for the pattern appropriate to the sex of the animal in question, or that two different hormones are normally involved. In either case, since hormones, especially the steroids, frequently are not completely specific, it is entirely possible that a local application of an abnormally high dose activates a response not normally governed by the particular hormone applied. Thus, testosterone might be the normal hormone for eliciting male sexual behavior and some other, as yet untested, hormone might change the normal one for eliciting maternal behavior.

Somewhat similar experiments have been performed by Harris and Michael on cats previously subjected to ovariectomy and hence not sexually receptive (13). These workers made up a tiny pellet of paraffin containing a synthetic female hormone, stilbestrol; when this was implanted in the hypothalamus the stilbestrol would slowly diffuse into the body. They found that when large pellets were implanted outside the brain or in inactive sites in the brain, changes in vaginal cells always occurred at doses smaller than those required to restore sexual receptivity.

When pellets were implanted in the hypothalamus, however, doses too small to produce changes in vaginal cells restored complete receptivity. In fact, the cats could be described as hypersexual; they would repeatedly accept successive males at any time of the day or night, without showing any signs of the refractoriness which normally follows mating. These effects first appeared only several days after implantation of the pellets containing the slowly diffusing form of the hormone. However, the proportion of cases in which the effects occurred was much higher than the proportion of cases in which the male sexual behavior or the maternal behavior was elicited in rats by the soluble hormones which Fisher used.

DIFFERENTIAL EFFECTS OF PRESUMPTIVE TRANSMITTER AGENTS

The results just described show that specific forms of behavior can be produced by applying directly to the proper part of the brain certain chemical substances that are normally found in the body. The experiments described below differ in that they involve use of a special class of substances believed to act as transmitters in the synapses of the more readily accessible and more thoroughly studied peripheral nerves. Transmission in the synapses of the parasympathetic nervous system is via acetylcholine. Chemicals having this effect are called cholinergic. Similarly, norepinephrine seems to be the transmitter for at least some of the synapses in the sympathetic nervous system. Chemicals having this effect are called adrenergic. Does similar chemical coding of transmission occur in the brain, and if it

does, is it related to specific forms of behavior? Biochemists have shown that the hypothalamus is especially rich in both acetylcholine and norepinephrine. What are they doing there?

Effects of same agent in different sites

Investigators such as Delgado, Feldberg, and MacLean have shown that injection of acetylcholine into the brain of a cat can evoke a variety of responses (14). When injected at one site it produced motor responses such as circling. When injected at another it produced catatonic-like postures; at another, rage; and at yet another, convulsions, followed by purring and other apparent manifestations of pleasure. In addition to the naturally occurring substance acetylcholine, these investigators used a synthetic substance, carbachol, which is similar in structure and in cholinergic effects. Because of a slight difference in its molecule, carbachol is not disposed of by the deactivating enzymes as rapidly as acetylcholine is, hence its effects last longer.

Effects of different agents in the same site

Encouraged by these results, Grossman, in our laboratory, tried implanting, in the "feeding-drinking" area of the lateral hypothalamus, minute crystals (weighing from 1 to 4 μg) of various substances thought likely to act as transmitter agents (15). An anesthetized rat was placed in a stereotaxic instrument with its head at the proper angle for insertion of a tiny cannula through a hole drilled in the skull. When the tip of this cannula was in the desired location the cannula was cemented into place and the skin was sewed together; the rat recovered and appeared perfectly normal and healthy. Figure 1 (top) shows photographs of the cannula. It consisted of a tiny hypodermic needle fitting snugly inside a slightly larger one; the two tips were cut off flush and the hubs were machined down so that the inner needle

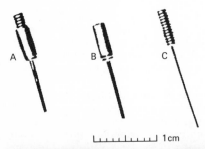

Figure 1. Double cannula system for chemostimulation: (A) the complete implant; (B) the outer cannula; (C) the inner cannula; (D) rat with double cannula implant and three additional pins for electrical stimulation and recording. [From Grossman (38)]

could screw into the outer one. After the rat had completely recovered, the inner cannula was withdrawn, tiny crystals were tapped into the tip, and the cannula was reinserted.

By this means Grossman found that either acetylcholine (mixed with eserine to delay its destruction by enzymes in the brain) or carbachol would cause rats that had just eaten or drunk to satiation to start drinking again within 5 to 10 minutes after implantation of the cholinergic agent and to consume an average of 12 milliliters of water during the next hour. These cholinergic agents would also cause satiated rats to work at the learned response of pressing a bar to get water. Subsequent implantation of tiny crystals of the adrenergic substances epinephrine or norepinephrine into the brains of the same satiated rats, at exactly the site where

the cholinergic agent had been implanted, via the same cannulas, elicited a different response—eating, or pressing a different bar, one that delivered food.

When carbachol was implanted in the brains of thirsty rats, the amount of water drunk was increased and the amount of food eaten was decreased, relative to the results for nonthirsty rats. Implantation of norepinephrine in the brains of hungry rats had the opposite effect, that of decreasing water consumption and increasing food consumption.

Whereas in previous studies different types of behavior were induced by implanting the same substance at different sites, in Grossman's study different types of behavior were induced by implanting different substances at the same site. These results clearly showed that systems located in the same region of the brain but controlling different types of behavior can be selectively affected by cholinergic or adrenergic substances.

Effects of blocking agents

It is conceivable that the different behaviors induced by the administration of different transmitter agents to the brain could be due to some differential side effects, rather than to the transmitter, or even due to a disinhibitory or modulating effect in the brain. Therefore, a number of control studies were made; these ruled out osmotic pressure, pH, and vasoconstriction or vasodilation as factors in the behavioral effects observed.

The most convincing control studies, however, were of a different nature. Studies on more easily isolated and manipulated peripheral nerves have shown that atropine blocks only the transmitting effect of carbachol or acetylcholine in such nerves and fails to block that of norepinephrine; conversely, ethomoxane blocks the effect of epinephrine or norepinephrine without affecting that of acetylcholine or carbachol. Therefore, Grossman investigated the effects of these blocking agents on the behavioral effects of chemostimulation in the brain (16). He injected the blocking agent into the peritoneal cavity so that it was circulating throughout the body before the crystals were applied to the brain.

He found that either blocking agent, if administered at sufficiently high dosage, would prostrate the rat and eliminate all behavior. But at an intermediate dose, results were differential. Results for such a dose are summarized in Figure 2. It may be seen that the cholinergic blocking agent atropine produced little reduction in the eating elicited by norepinephrine, while completely

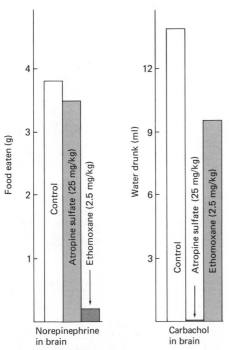

Figure 2. Differential effects of blocking agents on eating and drinking elicited by application of norepinephrine and carbachol, respectively, in the lateral hypothalamus of the rat. First, blocking agent is injected systemically, then crystals of norepinephrine or carbachol are implanted in the brain. [Data from Grossman (16)]

eliminating the drinking elicited by carbachol. Conversely, the adrenergic blocking agent ethomoxane produced only a moderate reduction in the drinking elicited by carbachol but a much larger reduction in the eating elicited by norepinephrine. These results strongly indicate that the differential behavioral effects are indeed due to the cholinergic and adrenergic properties, respectively, of the implanted substances.

While these results make it clear that the systems responsible for the eating and drinking are differentially susceptible to acetylcholine and norepinephrine, it is possible that these drugs produce their effects in some abnormal way and are not the normal transmitter substances for these systems. If they are indeed the normal transmitters, we would expect the blocking agents to have differential effects on normally elicited hunger and thirst analogous to their effects on hunger elicited by norepinephrine and their effects on thirst elicited by carbachol. And, indeed, Grossman found that such differential effects on normally elicited hunger and thirst could be induced either by systemic injection of the blocking agent or by direct introduction of the blocking agent into the lateral, or feeding-drinking, area of the hypothalamus. While these differential effects were not as complete as those illustrated in Figure 2, the differences were statistically highly reliable.

Furthermore, Coons and I have found that an injection, into the body, of atropine methyl nitrate, which does not readily cross the blood-brain barrier, produces much less reduction in drinking by water-deprived rats than does an injection of atropine sulfate, the form of atropine used by Grossman, which readily gets into the brain (17). This shows that the interference with thirst is primarily due to the action of atropine in the brain, rather than to its action on peripheral structures.

Effect of enzyme inhibitor

It is known that eserine inhibits the action of the cholinesterases, the enzymes that normally deactivate acetylcholine soon after it is released at the synapse. Therefore, if acetylcholine is indeed the transmitter normally involved in the thirst system, one would expect an injection of eserine into a synaptic region of this system to cause the normal acetylcholine to last longer, so that it would stimulate more transmission and thus cause more drinking. And indeed Chun-Wuei Chien and I have recently found that an injection of 3×10^{-8} mole of eserine into the preoptic area of the brain of a rat very slightly deprived of water will increase the amount it drinks during the next 30 minutes from an average of 0.3 milliliter to 10.5 milliliters. In addition to being an independent test of our conclusions, this is a more powerful test than that of injecting a cholinergic substance for demonstrating the normal participation of such a substance in thirst.

Dose-response curves

A dose-response curve is useful in determining whether an apparent differential effect is an artifact of a particular dose-threshold interaction and whether the amount of substance needed to produce an effect is of the order of magnitude one might reasonably expect for the normal process.

While Grossman's use of crystals prevents spread up the needle shaft, with crystals the concentration is highly abnormal and it is impossible accurately to control the dose. Therefore, in the dose-response study performed in our laboratory, aqueous solutions were used (18). The results are presented in Figures 3 and 4. It may be seen that there is a marked differential effect of all active doses of the carbachol and norepinephrine. Increasing the dose of carbachol produces marked increases in drinking but not in eating, while increasing the dose of norepinephrine produces marked increases in eating but not in

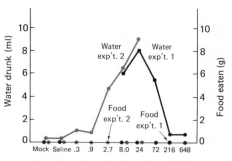

Figure 3. Dose-response curve for drinking elicited by injections of carbachol into the lateral hypothalamus of rats that had eaten and drunk to satiation. No eating is elicited. [From Miller et al. (18)]

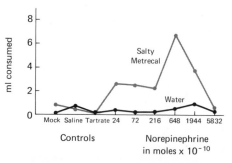

Figure 4. Dose-response curve for consumption of a liquid food (salty Metrecal) elicited by injection of norepinephrine into the lateral hypothalamus of rats that had eaten and drunk to satiation. Negligible amounts of water are consumed. [From Miller et al. (18)]

drinking. With either substance, the highest doses produce side effects, such as convulsions, which interfere with eating and drinking.

The carbachol elicits drinking at doses as low as 2.7×10^{-10} mole (0.047 μg); the smallest dose of norepinephrine that elicits eating is 24×10^{-10} mole (0.8 μg). The effective dose for carbachol seems to be somewhere near the content of the normal substance, acetylcholine, in the volume of tissue probably reached by our injections. The norepinephrine content of this part of the brain probably is no higher (in micrograms) than the acetylcholine content, but our effective dose of norepinephrine is approximately 20 times as high. This seems to be a high dose, but in our present state of considerable ignorance we cannot be sure that more of the norepinephrine reaches the receptor sites after an injection than is involved in normal transmission.

It should be noted that both dose-response curves cover the whole range, from the dose producing no effect to that producing prostrating side effects. In neither case is there any suggestion that low doses activate one behavioral system while higher doses cause the other system to be dominant. Thus, these results agree with those of the previous experiments in indicating that the difference between the systems is indeed a qualitative one, rather than the product of a mere quantitative interaction of the thresholds and the dominance of the systems with a nonspecific difference in the potency of the cholinergic and adrenergic compounds used.

Central versus peripheral effects

Dextroamphetamine is a compound closely resembling norepinephrine in its general structure and many of its physiological effects. But extensive clinical experience with people and careful experimental work with animals consistently show that dextroamphetamine lessens appetite. Why should these effects be opposite to those just described for norepinephrine?

There are two plausible possibilities. One is that the dextroamphetamine molecule is similar enough to the norepinephrine molecule to attach itself to the same receptor sites in the brain, but not similar enough to excite them. According to this hypothesis, dextroamphetamine acts like a bad key which jams in a lock without opening it. The fact that dextroamphetamine is administered peripherally, either by mouth or by injection, suggests the other major

possibility: the peripheral action of substances of this class may be opposite to, and may occur at lower thresholds or be stronger than, their action in the feeding-drinking area of the brain; thus, when the substance is administered to the whole body, the peripheral effects may override the effects of the substance diffusing from the blood to the brain.

In order to test these hypotheses, Coons, Quartermain, and I used the dose of norepinephrine (22 μg) that had been shown by the dose-response study to be optimum for eliciting eating when injected into the lateral hypothalamus. We injected exactly this dose into the jugular vein, via a permanently implanted catheter, and washed it down with isotonic saline. This injection caused hungry rats to stop eating, or to stop pressing a bar for food. These results demonstrate that the central and the peripheral effects of the same dose of norepinephrine are indeed antagonistic. They fit in with previous unpublished results, obtained by Coons in our laboratory, which show that peripheral administration of another adrenergic compound, epinephrine, raises the threshold for eating elicited by electrical stimulation of the lateral hypothalamus, and with results of Russek and Tina which show that peripheral administration of epinephrine will stop eating (19). Since we found that the same peripheral dose of norepinephrine stopped drinking as well as eating, it seems likely that it produces some general disturbance, perhaps as a result of a sudden increase in blood pressure, rather than a specific inhibition of a drive.

The norepinephrine injected into the blood stream becomes vastly more diluted than that affecting the cells adjacent to the cannula in the brain. Thus, the fact that the same dose is quite effective by either route is surprising. Perhaps the peripheral receptors are much more sensitive than the central ones, or the central receptors may be so well protected that only a minute fraction of the chemicals in the surrounding tissue reaches them. We must also consider the possibility that the consistent pattern of central-nervous-system results we have described is only an effect of a dose that is abnormally high, and thus does not necessarily mean that norepinephrine is involved in normal transmission in this part of the brain.

If norepinephrine does indeed act as a normal neural transmitter in the brain, its natural release should be limited to the active sites and not be diffused widely. Some of the norepinephrine which we inject into the lateral hypothalamus must diffuse into the bloodstream, where, presumably, it produces appetite-inhibiting peripheral effects. These effects may well mask some of the central hunger-arousing effects of the norepinephrine injected into the brain. If we could eliminate the peripheral effects by administering to the body a blocking agent for norepinephrine that would have difficulty in getting into the brain across the blood-brain barrier, we could eliminate or greatly reduce the antagonistic peripheral effects and might get a clearer picture of how norepinephrine works in the brain. To date, we have been unable to find such an agent, but it seems likely that side chains could be attached to the molecule of a suitable adrenergic blocking agent to produce a drug that would have difficulty in diffusing through the blood-brain barrier.

ACTIVATING VARIOUS ELEMENTS OF A GENERAL HOMEOSTATIC SYSTEM

Although carbachol in the brain elicits drinking and norepinephrine elicits eating, it is conceivable that these drugs do not directly stimulate thirst and hunger systems in the brain but, instead, produce their effects indirectly. For example, carbachol could stimulate nuclei in the brain which, in turn, stimulate a sudden water loss via the kidney,

the subsequent thirst and drinking being a by-product of the normal reaction of the body to the rapid dehydration. Similarly, norepinephrine could stimulate nuclei to send neural impulses that would cause the pancreas to secrete insulin; this would produce a drop in blood sugar and elicit eating. It is known that a peripheral injection of insulin can cause rats just fed to satiation to eat. Thus, it is possible that the thirst and hunger mechanisms are not themselves chemically coded, but that the differential effect of these chemicals is on some completely different systems which activate the thirst and hunger mechanisms in some indirect way. In the examples cited, which are the most plausible ones, we would expect the carbachol in the brain to produce a sudden excessive secretion of urine (in other words, diuresis), and the norepinephrine to produce a drop in the blood sugar, or glucose.

There is another possibility, however, from which one would predict the opposite results. Perhaps we are activating general homeostatic systems, which regulate food and water balance by activating a variety of mechanisms, some physiological and some behavioral, to deal with any deficit. If we are activating the entire system that normally responds to water deficit, we would expect one corrective measure to be stimulation of the secretion of the antidiuretic hormone which causes the kidney to reabsorb water from the urine, so that a smaller volume of more concentrated urine is lost. While thus conserving water, the animal would also go out looking for water to drink to replenish its supply. Similarly, the activation of an entire system for responding to a nutritional deficit would mobilize stores, such as those in the liver and fat, pouring them out as glucose into the blood, and at the same time would elicit hunger which would motivate the animal to find and eat food as a new source of nutrition. While the hypothesis given in the preceding paragraph predicts increased secretion of urine and a drop in blood sugar in response to stimulation of the brain by carbachol and norepinephrine, respectively, this second hypothesis predicts the opposite results.

Effects on secretion of urine

Chun-Wuei Chien and I have recently tested the effects on urine secretion of injecting into the lateral hypothalamus the optimum dose of carbachol (0.43 μg) for eliciting drinking. First, we briefly anesthetized water-satiated rats with ether and gently squeezed them to remove the residual urine from their bladders; we then administered, via stomach tube, 15 milliliters of water and injected into the hypothalamus either 1 microliter of carbachol solution or, as a control, the isotonic saline used as the vehicle. After this the rats were put in metabolism cages without food or water, and the urine was collected via stainless steel funnels underneath the cages.

We found that the carbachol greatly reduced the volume of urine. It also increased the concentration, as measured by the freezing-point-depression test of osmolarity; this increase in turn showed that the decrease in volume was caused by reabsorption stimulated by the secretion of the antidiuretic hormone normally released in response to water deprivation (20). If the carbachol had merely caused some interference with kidney function—for example, by producing a drop in blood pressure that interfered with the initial secretion by the kidneys—the decrease in volume would not have been accompanied by an increase in concentration.

Similar results were obtained from another part of the brain, the preoptic area; carbachol in this area, too, elicits drinking. Injection into the jugular vein (via an implanted cannula) of exactly the same dose as that given in the earlier studies (the optimum dose for eliciting drinking when injected into the brain) neither appreciably elicited drinking in

water-satiated rats nor decreased the volume and increased the concentration of urine of water-satiated rats that had been given additional water by stomach tube. Administration of this same dose to thirsty rats produced no obvious lessening of drinking. Thus, with carbachol, at least at this dose level, we do not find the marked differences in the behavioral effects of central and peripheral administration that we observed with norepinephrine.

To return to the antidiuretic effect of carbachol injected into the brain, if this is indeed a cholinergic effect, it should be blocked by atropine but not by ethomoxane. Chun-Wuei Chien and I tested these expectations. First we injected intraperitoneally either the blocking agent or isotonic saline as a control. We used the doses that had produced the greatest differential effects on drinking and eating. Then, 20 minutes later, after the agent had time to diffuse through the body, we gave the water-satiated rats additional water by stomach tube and injected into the lateral hypothalamus either the optimum dose of carbachol or a control dose of the isotonic saline used as the vehicle.

The results are shown in Figure 5. It may be seen that, as compared with the injection of saline, both intraperitoneally and into the brain, injection of carbachol into the brain (preceded by a control injection of saline) greatly reduced the volume and increased the concentration of the urine. Previous injection of the adrenergic blocking agent ethomoxane did not interfere with this antidiuretic effect, but previous injection of the cholinergic blocking agent atropine markedly reduced it. In another experiment we injected these two agents into water-satiated rats given additional water by stomach tube but not injected with carbachol. Neither agent produced a marked effect. Thus, the effects observed in the preceding experiment presumably were due to differential blocking of the effects of carbachol

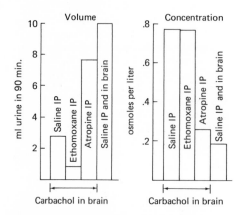

Figure 5. Effects of injecting carbachol into the lateral hypothalamus of unanesthetized rats. Such injection reduces the volume and increases the concentration of urine. Prior intraperitoneal (IP) injection of the cholinergic blocker atropine reduces these effects, but injection of the adrenergic blocker ethomoxane does not. Injections of the isotonic saline used as the vehicle serve as controls. [Unpublished recent data of Miller and Chien]

rather than to any other direct effects of these agents.

Our results confirm those of previous investigators who have concluded, from work on anesthetized dogs, that secretion of the antidiuretic hormone is mediated by a cholinergic link in the preoptic area (21). Our results show that such links exist in at least two areas— the lateral hypothalamus and the preoptic area—in which carbachol can elicit drinking and that they are strongly stimulated by the dose that elicits the most drinking. The results show that the carbachol does not produce behavioral manifestations of thirst in some indirect way, but that it activates a general water-conserving mechanism, one aspect of which is conservation of water by reabsorption in the kidneys and another aspect of which is motivation of animals to perform learned water-seeking habits.

As an extension of the foregoing study we injected norepinephrine into

the lateral hypothalamus of a number of rats at the dosage (22 μg) that we had found optimum for producing eating. While the major response of the rats was eating, to our surprise some of them drank a few milliliters of water before starting to eat. When we investigated the effects of norepinephrine on the secretion of urine, we found in general little, if any, effect in the animals whose first response had been eating but some reduction in the volume, and some increase in the concentration, of urine in the rats which had done a little preliminary drinking. These antidiuretic effects observed to date have been considerably less than those elicited in our experiments with carbachol, but we cannot draw any definitive conclusions until we have completed dose-response studies. We must also determine the action of blocking agents on these effects. When stained slides of these rats' brains are completed, it will be interesting to see whether or not the location of the implants differs slightly for the animals which showed only an eating effect and for those which showed also a slight drinking effect.

Effects on blood sugar

Coons, Booth, Pitt, and I have shown recently that the same electrical stimulation in the hypothalamus that causes satiated rats to eat produces a marked elevation in blood sugar during tests in which no food is present. This result suggests that stimulation in that area of the brain activates a general homeostatic mechanism which deals with a nutritional deficit both by increasing blood sugar and by motivating the animal to get food to replenish the deficit.

We are using chemostimulation to further investigate this problem. Some recent results are shown in Figure 6. In these tests, no food is present. Samples of blood are taken from the tip of the animal's tail at specified intervals and analyzed by the glucose oxidase method. The portions of the curve for time prior

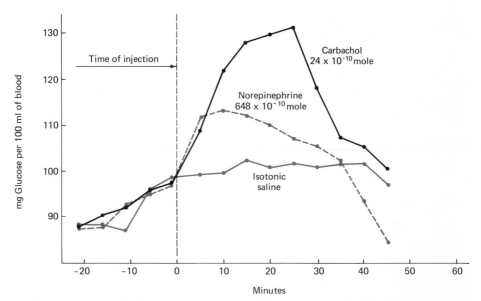

Figure 6. Effects on blood glucose of injecting norepinephrine and carbachol into the lateral hypothalamus of rats. As compared with an injection of isotonic saline, an injection of the dose of norepinephrine that is optimum for eliciting eating produces an increase in blood glucose, but an injection of the dose of carbachol that is optimum for eliciting drinking produces an even greater increase. No food and water are given during these tests. [Unpublished recent data of Coons, Booth, Pitt, and Miller]

to injection of substances into the lateral hypothalamus show a gradual rise; this rise continues with negative acceleration following the injection of isotonic saline into the brain, suggesting that the stress of handling and the taking of successive samples of blood produces some increase in the level of blood glucose. This increase, however, is definitely less than that which follows injection of the norepinephrine into the brain, a finding which shows that the mechanism by which the norepinephrine injection elicits eating is not that of stimulating insulin secretion and thus producing a drop in blood sugar. The results obtained thus far are symmetrical and esthetically satisfying and favor the hypothesis that norepinephrine activates a general mechanism for correcting nutritional deficits.

From such an hypothesis, one would

not expect carbachol to produce an increase in blood sugar. But, as Figure 6 clearly shows, the carbachol produces a considerably greater increase than the norepinephrine does. This unexpected result shows that our understanding of what is going on is still far from complete; it presents us with a puzzle that we would not have discovered had we confined our studies to electrical stimulation.

When the same dose of carbachol or of norepinephrine that was injected into the brain is injected into the jugular vein by means of an implanted cannula, the carbachol has no measurable effect, but the norepinephrine has approximately the same effect that it has when injected into the brain; the latter result suggests that at least some of the increase in blood sugar following the injection of norepinephrine into the brain could be caused by peripheral effects after it has been absorbed into the blood.

Effects on shivering and temperature

Feldberg and Myers recently have shown that both shivering and an increase in body temperature are elicited by the injection into the anterior hypothalamus of a cat of a few micrograms of serotonin, an amine normally found in this area (22). Conversely, injections of either epinephrine or norepinephrine inhibit such shivering and reduce the fever. They also cause a drop in the temperature of normal cats. Injections outside this general area of the brain do not produce such effects.

Evidence that serotonin is indeed involved in normal temperature regulation comes from a study in which Canal and Ornesi showed that cyproheptadine, an agent that blocks serotonin, inhibits a fever induced by injecting typhoid vaccine into the ventricles of the brain (23). These studies suggest that the central mechanisms controlling shivering and temperature regulation may be chemically coded, and the results add a new substance, serotonin, to the list of substances known to produce differential effects.

But there is an intimate relationship between temperature, on the one hand, and food and water regulation on the other. For example, Andersson and Larsson found in the goat that local cooling in the preoptic area, which is adjacent to the anterior hypothalamus, will elicit eating and shivering, while heating will stop eating and elicit panting and drinking (24).

These facts suggested to us the desirability of studying, in the rat, the effects on body temperature of injecting carbachol and norepinephrine into the lateral hypothalamus in the doses that are optimum for eliciting drinking and eating, respectively. Coons, Levak, Wechsler, and I found that the norepinephrine produces a drop in temperature of approximately 0.5°C, while the carb-

achol produces approximately twice this drop in temperature. Except for the fact that the effect is a drop instead of a rise, the curves look strikingly like those of Figure 6. Furthermore, as was found for blood sugar, the effects of this dose of norepinephrine are much the same regardless of whether it is injected in the vein or in the brain, but injection of this dose of carbachol by vein has no measureable effect.

To summarize, the effects on body temperature of injecting norepinephrine in the vein, norepinephrine in the brain, and carbachol in the brain are similar to each other and opposite to those of injecting serotonin in the brain. The effects on blood sugar of injecting carbachol in the brain and nonepinephrine in the brain and in the vein are also similar to each other. But the effects on food intake of injecting norepinephrine in the vein and in the brain are opposite. Injection of norepinephrine in the lateral hypothalamus typically increases food intake and decreases water intake, while such injection of carbachol typically has the opposite effects.

It seems unlikely that the drinking elicited by injection of carbachol in the lateral hypothalamus and the eating elicited by injection of norepinephrine are secondary to temperature changes, since these two substances change temperature in the same direction, while a given change in temperature has opposite effects on eating and drinking. The fact that norepinephrine in the central system and norepinephrine in the peripheral system produce similar effects on body temperature but opposite ones on eating also argues against the hypothesis that the effect of this substance on temperature produces its effect on eating.

USE OF CHEMOSTIMULATION FOR TRACING NEURAL CIRCUITS

Since Grossman's initial demonstration, a number of investigators have been using the selectivity of chemostimulation to trace the circuits involved in various behavioral effects.

The thirst system

Fisher and Coury have found that injection of carbachol into any of the 10 different structures they have investigated throughout the limbic system will elicit drinking (25). This is a system that extends beyond the hypothalamus and is characterized by a number of closed loops and other intricate interconnections which seem to provide the anatomical basis for sustaining activity by central positive feedback, as well as providing alternate pathways and intimate intercorrelations between various functions. They have also found that carbachol in any of 10 nearby areas outside this circuit does not elicit appreciable drinking.

While Fisher and Coury found that the relationship between cholinergic stimulation and drinking throughout the limbic system was remarkably specific, they did find a few cases in which carbachol increased both eating and drinking. And we have noted instances in which norepinephrine elicited some slight drinking. Myers has noted even more drinking elicited by norepinephrine (26). Also, as discussed earlier, the effects of carbachol and norepinephrine on blood sugar are similar. These exceptions are puzzling. The effects of blocking agents on these exceptional effects have not yet been investigated. These exceptions may indicate that the same system changes its chemical coding in different parts of the brain: they could be produced by interactions between different systems that are differently coded, or they might have still other implications. We do not yet know the answer.

The reward system

It has long been known that the limbic system is involved in emotional behavior. As Fisher and Coury point out, there is a remarkable parallelism between the brain structures from which they can elicit drinking by injection of carbachol and those from which MacLean and Ploog, by electrical stimulation, have elicited penile erection (27, 28). Furthermore, these are the same structures in which electrical stimulation has been shown, by Olds, to act as a reward to reinforce learning and maintain the performance of learned habits (6).

In addition to investigating the rewarding effects of electrical stimulation of the brain, Olds has recently tested the rewarding effects of various chemicals applied in minute amounts to different sites in the brain (29). In these studies the rat is in a small cage containing a bar. Every time the rat presses the bar he activates a device which injects approximately 3 millimicroliters of solution via a thin polyethylene tube leading to a special needle permanently implanted in the skull. If the injection is rewarding, the rat learns to press the bar and works to give itself injections. Olds gets rewarding effects from injecting acetylcholine or carbachol in certain brain areas, while norepinephrine, epinephrine, and serotonin have the opposite effect of reducing the rewarding effect of another solution. He also gets good rewarding effects with chelating agents, and the best of all with testosterone sulfate. It is interesting to note that these two latter agents are the only ones with which Fisher could elicit either male sexual or maternal nest-building and infant-retrieving behavior in the rat.

Specificity of responsiveness of overlapping systems

As further evidence for the specificity of response to chemostimulation of overlapping systems, Fisher and Coury have found one animal that consistently responded to injections of carbachol by drinking, to injections of norepinephrine by eating, and to injection of a soluble sex hormone by building nests (25). All three chemicals were applied to the same site at the junction of the area of the diagonal band of Broca and the medial preoptic region, and all three effects were specific.

Variety of tests required

Certain studies which Grossman has made since he left our laboratory have indicated further lines of fruitful work on chemical stimulation and, at the same time, the difficulty of the survey that is needed to give us a more adequate picture of the brain (30). He found that carbachol in the medial septal area elicited drinking in water-satiated rats and increased the water consumption of thirsty ones. It also depressed the food intake of hungry rats and impaired the learning and the performance of responses which allowed the rat to avoid electric shocks.

Implantation of the cholinergic blocking agent atropine into this area of the brain reduced the water consumption of thirsty rats and improved the performance of a previously acquired avoidance response. Implantation of noradrenaline had no effect on intake of food or water but improved the avoidance response; hence, in this respect, noradrenaline acted oppositely to carbachol. Thus the inclusion of an avoidance-learning situation, presumably measuring fear-motivated behavior, proved to be a useful addition to the tests.

Grossman observed no marked or consistent effects of chemostimulation of the ventral amygdala of satiated rats (31). From this one might conclude that there were little, if any, effects of chemostimulation in this area on hunger or thirst. But when he tested animals that had been deprived of food and water, he found that norepinephrine increased the food intake and decreased the water intake, while administration of an adrenergic blocking agent, dibenzyline, in the same area of the brain had the opposite effect of decreasing food intake and increasing water intake. Cholinergic

agents produced symmetrically opposite results; carbachol decreased food intake and increased water intake, while the blocking agent atropine tended to increase food intake but decrease water intake.

A number of other agents and control substances had no observable effects. Gamma-amino butyric acid, however, produced results similar to those produced by carbachol. This substance, which is normally found in the brain, is believed not to have any cholinergic effect. Thus, it is possible that it acted by blocking an inhibitory system. Recent results by Booth at Yale fit in with such an interpretation of the effects of gamma-amino butyric acid. Booth injected this substance into the ventromedial nucleus of the hypothalamus, an area known to exert an inhibitory effect on hunger. He found that such injections markedly increased the rate at which rats pressed a bar to get food without producing comparable increases in rates of pressing other bars to get water or to avoid an electric shock.

To return to Grossman's experiments on the amygdala, the fact that the effective chemicals did not elicit any appreciable results with satiated animals, but only with animals deprived of food and water, suggests that the function of the sites he stimulated is to modulate ongoing activity rather than to initiate activity.

Even when one is investigating a limited aspect of behavior, such as motivation, there are various different types of tests which are needed in initial screening investigations. Such tests should be made not only when the appropriate motive is initially absent but also when it is present. After an effect is discovered, additional tests are often needed to check alternative interpretations of the results. We have illustrated in detail elsewhere (32) the desirability of using a variety of behavioral tests to cross-check all conclusions.

In each of these behavioral tests one

must try the effects of a number of different presumptive transmitters, and also blocking agents. Each of these must be tested at a number of dosages, since our inverted U-shaped dose-response curves in Figure 3 and 4 show that one can fail to get results by using either too high or too low a dose. Furthermore, this process must be carried out for a great number of different points in the brain, sometimes separated by as little as 1 millimeter. It is obvious that a thorough survey will involve an enormous amount of work, and also that there are many opportunities for significant discoveries.

COMBINATION OF CLASSICAL AND CHEMOSTIMULATION TECHNIQUES

The classical technique of destroying a certain part of a pathway can be combined with the technique of chemostimulation to determine the direction of the pathway, or to indicate what are the most critical parts of the system. Thus, Wolf and I have shown (33) that a lesion in the feeding-drinking area of the lateral hypothalamus eliminates drinking elicited by chemostimulation at sites anterior or posterior to this location, while lesions in the anterior or posterior sites do not eliminate drinking elicited by chemostimulation in the lateral hypothalamus. Such results show the special importance of the lateral hypothalamic area.

Similarly, Paolino and I are combining the technique of electrical stimulation of brain areas in reward and punishment experiments with the use of reversible biochemical lesions. When a general blocking agent, such as the local anesthetic Xylocaine, is used to make such a lesion in the lateral hypothalamus, it greatly reduces the rewarding effects of electrically stimulating the anterior part of the medial forebrain bundle but seems to have less effect on the punishing effects. Having used a general blockade by a local anesthetic to confirm the location of a crucial point

in the system, we are now exploring the effects of specific blocking agents to produce biochemical lesions that are not only reversible but also selective, and to throw light on the chemical coding of the system.

Additional combinations of classical and chemostimulation techniques are used in studies of the sleep and arousal systems.

Sleep versus arousal in the cat

Hernandez-Peon and his colleagues have demonstrated the usefulness of chemostimulation for dissecting out, in more detail than had been possible in work with electrical stimulation, the brain circuits involved in sleep and in arousal (34, 35). At the same time his work demonstrates a puzzling species difference between effects on the rat, the animal used for most of the studies so far described, and the cat, which he used. Thus, these results provide still further evidence for both the fruitfulness of work with chemostimulation and the magnitude of the task.

Hernandez-Peon and his co-workers found that the sleep system involves a number of pathways descending from the cortex through the limbic midbrain circuit, and also an ascending component coming up from the spinal cord through the medulla and pons to the midbrain. Along the pathways of this circuit, stimulation with acetylcholine or carbachol elicits sleep. As might be expected, if the normal transmitter is cholinergic, injection into this system of eserine, which is known to inhibit the enzymes that destroy natural acetylcholine, will elict sleep. By preventing the destruction of the transmitter, presumably the eserine potentiates impulses that are a part of the normal background activity of this system, and thus tips in the direction of sleep the balance between such impulses and those of arousal.

Additional evidence that the chemostimulation is indeed cholinergic comes from the finding that it can be blocked by atropine. If one point in a circuit is stimulated by an injection of acetylcholine and a crystal of atropine is placed downstream, the atropine blocks the induction of sleep. But if the location of the injections of the two substances is reversed, no blockade occurs. Test involving the use of atropine, production of temporary chemical lesions by a local anesthetic, or permanent destruction of the path by an electrolytic lesion have yielded similar results, confirming earlier findings concerning the directions of the pathways.

An arousal system that runs roughly parallel to the sleep system at some levels and overlaps it at others responds to injections of norepinephrine. At some levels of the brain, acetylcholine and norepinephrine elicit their effects from different sites. At these sites, presumably, the two systems do not overlap. At other brain levels both substances produce an effect from the same site; the nature of the effect is determined by the type of substance. Here, presumably, the two systems overlap. One such point of overlap is the preoptic area, where the application of noradrenaline elicits alertness, while application of acetylcholine via the same cannula into the same site elicits sleep. Another site where injection of one and then the other substance via the same cannula produces opposite results is the central gray matter of the spinal cord at the level of the 8th cervical vertebra.

A number of investigators have elicited sleep through electrical stimulation of some of these same parts of the brain (2, 36). In some sites, long slow pulses have elicited sleep while short rapid ones have produced arousal. In other sites, Hernandez-Peon and his collaborators have found it easy to elicit sleep by chemostimulation but difficult or perhaps impossible to do so by electrical stimulation. Furthermore, while studies with electrical stimulation have seemed to indicate that there is an anterior center for light sleep and a posterior center for deep sleep (37). Hernandez-Peon and his colleagues have found it possible to elicit light sleep from either location by weak doses of acetylcholine or carbachol, and deep sleep from either location by stronger doses. Thus, it appears that the depth of sleep is a function of the strength of stimulation of the sleep system, and that the earlier apparent finding of two different centers for these two types of sleep probably was an artifact of a difference in the degree of separation of the sleep system and the arousal system, which allowed electrical stimulation to produce a stronger differential effect in one case than in the other.

Although cholinergic stimulation of certain brain areas in the cat produces sleep, stimulation of other areas, some of them quite close to the sleep circuits, elicits a spectacular attack response: the cat growls, hisses, flattens back its ears, arches its back, raises its hair, strikes out with its claws, and bites. Similar manifestations of rage had previously been elicited by electrical stimulation of these areas. These results further illustrate that the response elicited depends on the area stimulated as well as on the "transmitter" used.

Species differences

Some of the sites at which injection of carbachol or acetylcholine elicits either sleep or rage in the cat correspond to sites at which injection of these substances elicits drinking in the rat. Nevertheless, in investigating these and many other sites in the cat's brain, Hernandez-Peon and other workers have not observed a single instance of elicited drinking (27, 35). The fact that drinking can be elicited easily by application of cholinergic substances at any of a wide variety of brain sites in the rat but has not yet been elicited by these substances in the cat is puzzling. It could be (1) that carbachol and acetylcholine, although somewhat more differential in their effects than electrical stimulation, nevertheless stimulate a number of over-lapping systems, the effect on thirst being dominant in the highly domes-ticated albino rat and effects on rage, sleep, and other systems being dominant in the cat. Perhaps stimulation of the remnants of the rage system in the domesticated rat was the basis for the unexpected rise in blood sugar that accompanied the dominant drinking elicited by carbachol. If species dif-ferences are merely a matter of the rela-tive dominance of systems in different animals, one might expect different results from the wild cousins of labora-tory rats, which show much more fear and aggression, or from certain desert rats that apparently can get along with-out any water. On the other hand (2), it is conceivable that there are genuine dif-ferences in the chemical coding of the brains of different species of mammals, or that (3) we are not yet using quite the right substances in the right way to exploit the subtleties of the chemical code.

SUMMARY

Distinctive patterns of behavior can be elicited by directly stimulating the brain and substances that are normally found in it, or with synthetic com-pounds resembling these substances. Recent research shows that the response elicited depends on both the site stim-ulated and the type of chemical used. Compounds of different classes, applied via the same cannula to exactly the same site in the brain, can elicit dif-ferent kinds of behavior, or opposite effects on the same kind of behavior. This differential sensitivity is useful in tracing the circuits in the brain that control different types of behavior, especially since some of these circuits are intimately interlaced in certain places. A better understanding of the chemical coding of behavioral systems in the brain may also help ultimately to pro-vide a more rational foundation for the discovery of new drugs to treat certain forms of mental disorder.

Evidence is accumulating that a gen-eral homeostatic system, with both overt behavioral and internal physio-logical components, may use neural circuits that are chemically coded in the same way in at least certain different regions of the brain. Stimulation of any of a number of areas of the rat brain by the cholinergic substances acetyl-choline or carbachol causes water-satiated rats to drink and to perform thirst-motivated learned behavior, at the same time conserving water by stim-ulating the reabsorption of water by the kidneys. Cholinergic stimulation also causes water- and food-deprived rats to drink more and to eat less. On the other hand, stimulation of some of these sites by the adrenergic substances epineph-rine and norepinephrine has the op-posite effect of causing rats that have eaten and drunk to satiation to eat, or rats that have been deprived of food and water to eat more and to drink less.

In the cat a similar antagonism has been found between the effects of cho-linergic and adrenergic substances, only in this case the cholinergic effect is sleep and the adrenergic one arousal. While cholinergic stimulation of certain areas of the cat brain elicits sleep, cholinergic stimulation of other areas elicits a spec-tacular rage response: the cat hisses, arches its back, raises its hair, flattens its ears, and makes an accurately directed attack.

The finding that some of the brain structures in which cholinergic stimula-tion elicits drinking in the rat are anal-ogous to structures in which it elicits sleep or attack in the cat is an unsolved puzzle.

Agents that are known to block the effects of certain transmitter substances, or to have the opposite effect of in-hibiting the enzymes that destroy these substances, provide a means of rigor-ously cross-checking conclusions. Such cross checks have provided data that are consistent with, and strongly support, the conclusions drawn from the studies described.

Although the new method of chemostimulation has revealed some esthetically satisfying symmetrical patterns of lawful relationships, it has also turned up some unexpected, apparently discordant, and tantalizing results. It is becoming increasingly clear that we need to use a variety of behavioral tests to determine the effects of different doses of a considerable number of possible transmitting, inhibitory, modulating, or blocking agents at a vast number of different sites in the brain. The chemical methods should be combined, also, with other approaches, such as electrical stimulation, the recording of evoked potentials, and the destroying of discrete pathways or nuclei by lesions. The task before us is enormous, but, by the same token, so is the opportunity for making new discoveries about one of the most miraculous products of nature—the brain.

References and notes

1. Anand, B. K., and Brobeck, J. R. *Yale J. Biol. Med.*, 1951, **24**, 123.
2. Hess, W. R. *Das Zwischenhirn: Syndrome, localisationem junctionem.* Basel: Schwabe, 1949.
3. Miller, N. E. *Bull. Brit. Psychol. Soc.*, 1964, **17**, 1.
4. Teitelbaum, P., and Epstein, A. N. *Psychol. Rev.*, 1962, **69**, 74.
5. Miller, N. E. In D. Sheer (Ed.), *Electrical stimulation of the brain.* Austin: Univ. of Texas Press, 1961. P. 387.
6. Olds, J. *Physiol. Rev.*, 1962, **42**, 554.
7. Roberts, W. W. *J. comp. physiol. Psychol.*, 1958, **51**, 400; Bower, G. H., and Miller, N. E. *J. comp. physiol. Psychol.*, p. 669.
8. Miller, N. E. *Electroencephalog. Clin. Neurophysiol.*, 1963, **24**, suppl., 247; Wolf, G. *Psychonomic Sci.*, 1964, **1**, 211.
9. Robinson, B. W. In M. J. Wayner (Ed.), *Thirst.* New York: Pergamon, 1964. P. 411.
10. Andersson, B. *Acta Physiol. Scand.*, 1953, **28**, 188.
11. Fisher, A. E. *Science*, 1956, **124**, 228.
12. Fisher, A. E. In Hull and Brazier (Eds.), *Brain and the gonadal function.* Washington, D.C.: American Institute. In press.
13. Harris, G. W., and Michael, R. P. *J. Physiol. London*, 1964, **171**, 275.
14. Delgado, J. M. R. *J. Neurophysiol.*, 1955, **18**, 261; Feldberg, W. S. *Proc. Assoc. Res. nerv. ment. Dis.*, 1958, **36**, 401; MacLean, P. D. *Arch. Neurol. Psychiat.*, 1957, **78**, 128.
15. Grossman, S. P. *Science*, 1960, **132**, 301; *Am. J. Physiol.*, 1962, **202**, 872.
16. Grossman, S. P. *Am. J. Physiol.*, 1962, **202**, 1230.
17. Where names but no references are given, the results are from recent unpublished studies in this laboratory.
18. Miller, N. E., Gottesman, K. S., and Emery, N. *Am. J. Physiol.*, 1964, **206**, 1384.
19. Russek, M., and Tina, S. *Nature*, 1962, **193**, 1296.
20. I wish to thank Dr. Howard Levitin and Mrs. Nadia T. Myketey of the Yale School of Medicine for supplying the measures of osmolarity.
21. Pickford, M. *J. Physiol. London*, 1947, **106**, 264.
22. Feldberg, W., and Myers, R. D. *J. Physiol. London.* In press.
23. Canal, N., and Ornesi, A. *Atti Accad. Med. Lombarda*, 1961, **16**, 69.
24. Andersson, B., and Larsson, B. *Acta Physiol. Scand.*, 1961, **52**, 75.
25. Fisher, A. E., and Coury, J. N. *Science*, 1962, **138**, 691.
26. Myers, R. D. In M. J. Wayner (Ed.), *Thirst.* New York: Pergamon, 1964. P. 533.
27. Fisher, A. E., and Coury, J. N. In *Thirst*, p. 515.
28. MacLean, P. D., and Ploog, D. W. *J. Neurophysiol.*, 1962, **25**, 29.
29. Olds, J. "The induction and suppression of hypothalammic self-stimulation behavior by micro-injection of endogenous substances at the self-stimulation site." *Proc. Intern. Congr. Endocrinol., 2nd, London*, 1964. Excerpta Med. Intern. Congr. Ser. No. 83 1965. Pp. 426–434.

30. Grossman, S. P. *J. comp. physiol. Psychol.*, 1964, **58**, 194.

31. Grossman, S. P. *J. comp. physiol. Psychol.*, 1964, **57**, 29.

32. Miller, N. E., and Barry, H., Ill. *Psychopharmacologia*, 1960, **1**, 169; Miller, N. E. In H. Steinberg (Ed.), *Animal behaviour and drug action*. London: Churchill, 1964. P. 1.

33. Wolf, G., and Miller, N. E. *Science*, 1964, **143**, 585.

34. Hernandez-Peon, R., Chavez-Ibarra, G., Morgane, P. J., and Timo-Iaria, C. *Exptl. Neurol.*, 1963, **8**, 93.

35. Hernandez-Peon, R. In *Progress in brain research*. Amsterdam: Elsevier. In press.

36. Magoun H. W. In M. R. Jones, (Ed.), *Nebraska symposium on motivation*. Univ. of Nebraska Press, Lincoln: 1963. P. 161.

37. Jouvet, M. In G. E. W. Wolstenholme and C. M. O'Connor (Eds.), *The nature of sleep*. London: Churchill, 1961. P. 188.

38. Grossman, S. P. Thesis, Yale University, 1961.

Rhinencephalic lesions
and
behavior in cats
j. d. green
c. d. clemente
and
j. de groot

INTRODUCTION

Since the latter part of the nineteenth century, bilateral temporal lobe lesions have been known to produce various behavioral changes (Brown and Schäfer, 1888). Klüver and Bucy (1939), Gastaut (1952) and Schreiner and Kling (1953, 1954, 1956) have observed aberrations in male sexual behavior in the monkey, cat, lynx, and agouti. Similar manifestations following temporal lobectomy have been reported in the human male (Terzian and Dalle Ore, 1955). Changes in female sexual behavior have been described by a few authors. Schreiner and Kling (1953) reported persistent estrus in the cat, and Klüver and Bartelmez (1951) reported one case of a monkey which showed a condition resembling metropathia hemorrhagica following lesions of the frontal and temporal lobes. Other behavioral changes described following the ablation of the temporal lobe and subjacent amygdala-pyriform area have been: relative docility (Brown and Schäfer, 1888; Gastaut, 1952; Schreiner and Kling, 1954, 1956) with generally an increase in range threshold; psychic blindness (Klüver and Bucy, 1937, 1938, 1939) similar, possibly, to the state of idiocy described by Brown and Schäfer (1888); hyperphagia (Brown and Schäfer, 1888); a lowered rage threshold (Bard and Mountcastle, 1948); exaggerated oral and vocal behavior (Brown and Schäfer, 1888; Klüver and Bucy, 1939; Schreiner and Kling, 1953). Recently Koikegami, Fuse, Kimoto and their collaborators

From *Journal of Comparative Neurology*, 1957, **108**, 505–545. By permission.

have observed ovulation in the rabbit and a variety of other effects following stimulation of the amygdala (1952, 1953, 1954, 1955).

Since the amygdala is a large structure and has generally been destroyed only after injury to the overlying cortex, an attempt has been made in our studies to delimit more precisely the nuclear masses involved, to try to analyze the syndrome into its component parts, and to correlate the behavioral changes with selective partial destruction of the amygdala and adjacent areas.

Since the amygdala seems to be associated functionally with many other rhinencephalic structures (Adrian, 1942; Fox, McKinley, and Magoun, 1944; Gloor, 1955a 1955b; Green, 1956; Green and Adey, 1956), it was decided to determine the effects of lesions in other parts of the rhinencephalon as well. Our attention has been directed primarily to changes in sexual behavior, with secondary interest in the other phenomena.

In order to control the changes observed, studies of normal cat sex behavior were made, and the extreme variations of sexuality which could be induced by castration or gonadal steroid administration were also studied. This account falls into four general subdivisions:

1. Observations on normal sex behavior.
2. Observations on behavior following castration and/or steroid hormones.
3. Observations of the effects of lesions in the amygdala and other rhinencephalic structures on nonsexual behavior.

4. Observations on sexual behavior under the same circumstances.

METHODS

Healthy cats, obtained from the city pound, were maintained in individual cages on a diet of prepared cat food and milk with an occasional horse-meat ration. The amounts of food offered were such that control cats failed to consume it all. Operations were carried out under nembutal anesthesia using the Horsley-Clark stereotaxic apparatus and a D. C. lesion-maker, or by surgical methods. The procedures carried out on the cats in this group of experiments were as follows:

All cats were observed for at least one week preoperatively, and some up to several months, with observation of adaptation to territory. A total of 122 cats was studied. Lesions were placed in 82 animals (22 females and 60 males). They were placed primarily in the region of the amygdala and pyriform cortex in 71 and in other rhinencephalic areas in 11. Of the major behavioral changes seen following these lesions, there were 20 male cats with hypersexuality and three females with doubtful changes, possibly related to sexuality. Fourteen animals were definitely hyperphagic and probably more would have shown changes had data been complete. Seventeen showed cataleptic changes. Fifteen cats had major motor convulsions, and eight additional cats showed symptoms suggestive of sensory seizures. In the male hypersexual cats, additional changes were seen in eight (four with hyperphagia, two with seizures and two with transitory cataleptic changes). Twenty-four animals were observed not to change.

Controls included the 40 control cats which were subjected to essentially the same testing procedures, and the preoperative observation of all cats, as well as of the 24 animals which showed no change following lesions. In attempts

to influence behavior, a variety of procedures were carried out both on experimental and control animals, including the administration of hormones before and after puberty (testosterone, estradiol, stilbestrol, progesterone, desoxycorticosterone acetate, cortisone), castration, etc. The conditions for these procedures will be dealt with in the appropriate sections of the results.

RESULTS

1. "Normal animals"

The term "normal" is used to indicate a concept of the behavior of control animals maintained under our particular laboratory conditions. Since sexual behavior is greatly influenced by environmental conditions it is not intended to imply that the sort of behavior seen by us in "normal" animals would resemble that of domestic or semi-wild animals, for example.

(a) Females. The posturing, treading, tail deviation, low growling cries, rolling and rubbing behavior patterns of the estrus female cat have been described in detail by Bard (1939). Under the conditions in which our animals were kept, these reactions were seen not only in the presence of the male, as described by Scott (1955) and Scott and Lloyd-Jacob (1955), but also spontaneously, as found also by Bard (1939).

The degree of activity of the male was found to be an important factor in determining female receptivity. Thus, a virile animal may attack a resisting female while a less vigorous partner may easily be rebuffed by a female showing many signs of heat.

Treading and tail deviation may sometimes be seen in males when the animal is held firmly and the perineal region stimulated. This reaction pattern, however, can readily be distinguished from the treading of the fully estrus cat. After such stimulation, the estrus female continues to tread and maintain the characteristic position, while the male shows indication that his reaction was an attempt to escape. Unrestrained posturing and treading we regard as a certain indication that the cat is receptive. When the female treads and postures while held and makes no attempt to escape, adapted male cats mate with her, but if she struggles or snarls, successful copulation is unlikely, except with a vigorous partner.

Individual females vary widely in their general disposition during heat. Some are extremely docile, while at the other extreme, others are vicious. Although the latter are more difficult for the male to manage, once grasped they are frequently quite receptive. These females commonly exhibit wild after-reactions and may attack the male or the investigator. The fully estrus female sometimes snarls, spits and strikes at a male introduced into her own cage, even though she has been posturing expectantly just before. When she is introduced into the male's cage, she is much more receptive.

(b) Males. The behavior of the male has not received much attention in the past, although Scott and Lloyd-Jacob (1955) have given a good account of male behavior in the colony at the Royal Free Hospital in London, and one of us (J.D.G.) has had the opportunity to see these animals. As Bard (1939) and Scott and Lloyd-Jacob (1955) have shown, in the laboratory the male cat will not mate unless he is familiar with his surroundings. Adapting a male to his environment usually takes about a week, with a good deal of individual variation (48 hours to several weeks). The male must be placed in a quiet room and allowed to investigate it thoroughly by giving him a daily exercise period, during which he inspects and sniffs everything unfamiliar. All objects, including other animals, are scrutinized and when frequent environmental changes occur, adaptation is delayed. After the male has familiarized himself, an estrus female is presented. He will usually walk up to her, sniff her genitalia and then retire to some point where he can watch her. In a day or two he may seem completely indifferent and reject her if she advances too closely, even though she postures and rubs. Nevertheless, he exhibits more interest as time goes by and eventually, usually after a rather prolonged period of investigation, he seizes the female by the neck and mounts her, achieving intromission following a somewhat long coitus.

When the male is next tested, it is found that an abrupt change in behavior has ensued. On being allowed into his territory, he clamors with short cries. If no female is presented, he commonly goes to a dark corner to lie down. Occasionally, he may snarl when approached or seize the investigator's clothes and show other signs of apparent displeasure.

If another cat of either sex is now brought into the room, he runs at once to the place where he previously had coitus and again vocalizes with short staccato cries. If the other cat is hidden behind a cardboard partition, he does not exhibit this behavior so that the cue for the actions appears to be visual rather than olfactory or auditory. If a posturing estrus female is placed under a bell jar, an adapted male brought into the room will attempt to free her.

When another animal is put with an adapted male, he seizes it at once, often before it can be placed on the floor, and then attempts copulation regardless of its sex. With an estrus female, intromission is quickly achieved and, although he refrains during the after-reaction, he seizes her again at the first opportunity. The estrus female, recovering her receptivity much more rapidly than is suggested in the literature (Eckstein and Zuckerman, 1956), usually accepts the male a second time immediately following the after-reaction, i.e., in 5 minutes or less. In a few cases, active males achieve intromission with females which do not appear to be receptive, but females which are really anestrus usually evade the male by rolling on their sides, sometimes snarling, striking or hissing. An active adapted male will mount a second estrus female immediately after coitus and shows prodigious vigor in carrying out many successful copulations. In casual observations, 4 intromissions were seen within three minutes in one example and 15 intromissions in 30 minutes in another.

More than one male may be adapted to the same territory. Unlike Scott's cats, ours did not fight under such circumstances, possibly because our males were about the same size and weight. They would mount each other without any particular dominance being displayed. In any event, dominance, if present, appeared to vary from day to day. In only one instance did we observe a fight among adapted males, and in this case one animal, the aggressor, had been given a large dose of testosterone. Growling and slapping, however, were not uncommon.

Territory is difficult to define precisely. Cats became adapted to large spacious cages quite readily, but usually failed to adopt to small ones. If a female was introduced to a male waiting in his territory, he usually seized her instantly. On the other hand, if the female was placed in the area first, the male's approach was more wary. Under these circumstances, the male often eyed the female for a period of a few seconds to minutes. The pupils, at first dilated, gradually constricted and he would vocalize and pounce suddenly.

The area of territory also seemed to expand gradually. Cats which at first copulated only in their cages soon began to do so elsewhere in the room. Eventually, they began to follow the investigator when he went to get a female and they would attempt to copulate in the corridor or animal house. In completely unfamiliar surroundings, however, attempts at copulation were never seen.

We have the impression that repeated copulations seem to increase the vigor of the normal male and that the sight of mating animals shortens the time of adaptation. While our cats behaved indifferently to laboratory procedures carried out by the investigator on other cats, they seemed to be very much interested in feline sex behavior. Kittens, on seeing copulation for the first time, would arch their backs and run away, only to creep back a few moments later as if fascinated by the performance.

Males would sometimes vocalize while other cats were copulating, especially at the moment of intromission or during the after-reaction. Individual variations seemed more frequent in the male than in the female, and strain variations are also probable. Limits of normal male behavior observed by us are indicated in columns one and two of Table 1.

The normal males, once adapted to territory, copulated heterosexually or homosexually. When two males were allowed to roam in common territory, one usually mounted the other. If an estrus female was now introduced, the mounting cat continued to try to copulate with the male and, if separated, returned at once to the male. If the mounted male could, he would try to mount the female, so that a tandem arrangement occurred. In situations where choice between male and female was apparently free, both males would attempt to mount the female. The unsuccessful one then frequently mounted the copulating male. During the period of adaptation to territory, attempts to mount kittens and docile males were seen before a female had been mounted, but adapted cats showed little or no interest in kittens. In our experience, normal males refused to mount inanimate objects, did not masturbate and did not attempt to copulate with other species.

2. Effects of hormones

(a) Males. Castration of adult male cats after adaptation to territory resulted

TABLE 1.

	Normals			Hormones		Lesions	
	Un-adapted	Adapt-ing	Adapted	Un-adapted	Adapted	Un-adapted	Adapted
Heterosexuality	—	—	+	—	+	+	+
Homosexuality	—	±	+	—	+	+	+
Pederasty	—	±	—	—	+	+	+
Plural coitus	—	—	+	—	+	+	+
Other species	—	—	—	—	+	+	+
Anesthetized animals	—	—	—	—	+	+	+
Inanimate objects	—	—	—	—	+	+	+
Masturbation	—	—	—	—	+	+	+

in a rapid change in their sex behavior. Within the first one or two days after castration, their activity appeared unchanged, but within a week there was an obvious loss of drive, and in about 10 days intromission seemed no longer possible. Nevertheless, the castrated male continued to mount for several months following the operation when a female was presented. These males would take a neck grip, make a few tentative thrusts and then release the female. Usually, no further attempts at copulation were made for a considerable time. Thus, the effect of castration on the male cat was a very obvious loss of drive. The drive could be restored with testosterone (2.5 mg or less, intramuscularly) and would return in 24 to 48 hours. It then waned once more and in one week to 10 days was lost. Surprisingly, the female hormones, estradiol (6000 rat units) or stilbestrol (1 to 5 mg), had similar effects in restoring drive.

These observations apply only to acutely castrated animals. Possibly after a long period of castration, genital atrophy would prevent restoration of drive following the administration of estrogens. In one case, the implantation of a testosterone propionate tablet (75 mg) in an old animal which had been castrated was followed by the most violent sex behavior of any animal except those with lesions. This cat would attempt copulation with a teddy bear (providing he was first teased with it) as well as with males, females and kittens. He would do this only in his own cage, however, and would make no attempt whatever when outside his territory. This was the only case in which we observed any increase in male sex behavior in castrates. It may be argued that since he would only copulate in his cage, he was adapted there.

Although testosterone readily restored the drive to animals first adapted and then castrated, it did not accelerate as much as delay the rate of adaptation to territory. Desoxycorticosterone acetate (5 mg), cortisone (25 mg) and progesterone (5 mg) failed to restore the male drive.

Although testosterone propionate, estradiol and stilbestrol all restored the sex drive in castrates, testosterone had an entirely opposite effect from the female hormones on the hairs of the coat. Testosterone increased the growth of the guard hairs, which are longer and paler than the underlying hair. As a result, the cat tended to have a rough and dry looking coat; its appearance was shaggy and the fur felt rough. Estrogen administration was associated with the appearance of soft and sleek fur, and the long guard hairs were less conspicuous. Active normal males and females given testosterone were noticed to be shedding continuously.

We were surprised to find that the sex hormones had somewhat contrary effects in prepubertal males. The effects on the coat were the same, and after testosterone the animals became more aggressive and played in a rather wild fashion, freely slapping and biting at each other. We could not adapt them to a territory. In three young male animals given estrogen in doses up to 25 mg stilbesterol intramuscularly, however, there resulted a behavior pattern resembling that of estrus. Two of the three began to show treading and tail deviation but were never receptive. The third, a slightly older animal, not only did this, but also assumed the characteristic crouched position spontaneously, allowed another male to mount him, trod vigorously, elevated the pelvis like a female and when the male was withdrawn, exhibited a typical after-reaction. This behavior continued for a period of six weeks. The stilbestrol tablets were then removed and replaced with testosterone pellets. After about a week the behavior exhibited was indistinguishable from that of intact prepubertal males given testosterone. Attempts to adapt these animals to territories were not successful. The animal which had shown the most markedly feminine behavior became very aggressive when adult, and sometimes behaved wildly in the presence of a female, jumping, pouncing, playfully attacking her tail and slapping her vigorously. This behavior differed only in degree from that of other animals given testosterone, however, and may perhaps represent the usual difficulty in adapting animals given male sex hormone. When given estrogen after maturity, this animal resumed the posturing pattern of reaction.

(b) Females. The effects of spaying and stilbestrol administration on females are well known. We found that in the adult cat, testosterone may induce estrus behavior as in the rabbit (Klein, 1947). Testosterone has the same effect prepubertally on either sex as described above, i.e., an increase in aggressiveness, playful biting and slapping, and sudden pounces were seen. These attacks commonly took the form of seizing the other animal by the neck as if to mount; partial mounting always ended in skittish wrestling. In adult females, testosterone administration caused marked estrus behavior in seven animals before and after spaying. Two other animals showed little or no signs of estrus, but this could possibly be attributed to intercurrent disease which may prevent the appearance of estrus behavior even after stilbestrol. The estrus behavior was not associated with an estrus condition in the uterus, but the uterus was not atrophic. Repeated copulation in these animals was never followed by pregnancy. The ovaries were small, contained many follicles, 0.5 mm to 1 mm in diameter, and showed no evidence of corpora lutea. There was no indication that ovulation occurred. After ovariectomy, the uterus became atrophic but estrus behavior persisted.

Thus, a clear distinction between the development of sex behavior and the development of the reproductive organs or secondary sex characteristics seemed possible both in males and females.

3. Lesions

Since a rather large complex of general changes was found, it seems appropriate to detail the effects which were seen and in each case try to delimit the areas of the brain concerned. The general recovery from operation was excellent. Major disturbances usually did not appear until about 24 hours post-operatively, sometimes considerably later.

(a) Seizures. Lesions in the amygdala and in the dorsal or ventral hippocampus were followed by seizures in about 20 percent of the animals. These were rather uniformly associated with primary or secondary hippocampal injury. They

followed both secondary vascular damage and direct lesions limited to the hippocampus. A full description will be given
elsewhere (Green, Clemente, and de
Groot, 1957).

(b) Hyperthermia. Was seen in some
animals and was related to the seizures,
subsiding along with them. It was noted
that a motor fit often raised the body
temperature 0.5 to 1.0°F. The highest
temperature recorded was 109.2°F, the
temperature of the body of a cat found
in rigor mortis on a day during which six
generalized seizures had been observed
and doubtless others had occurred. The
control mean body temperature of our
animals was 101.4 ± 0.2.

(c) Hyperphagia and hypophagia. Were
seen in some cases. No special attempts
were made to study these phenomena
since we were primarily interested in
sex behavior, but the data collected
proved unexpectedly interesting. The
cats were given enough food so that
normal cats almost invariably left about
50 percent of the solids given them. On
inspection of the routine weighings it
was found that 14 cats had shown abnormally large increases in weight in the
first month postoperatively. Since these
animals all had lesions at the same anteroposterior level (though at slightly different transverse and vertical positions)
it was felt that comparisons should be
made with a control group as well as the
experimental animals. This control group
of 26 randomly selected cats showed an
average weight increase of about 11 percent in 40 days with a standard deviation
of ± 8 percent. The majority of the experimental cats fell within these limits, but
animals with catalepsy, seizures and
minor infections lost weight. The group
of animals gaining weight all increased
at a rate well outside the standard deviation. The weight gaining limits in this
hyperphagic group was an increase in
weight of over 30 percent in 40 days and
just under 30 percent in 8 days postope-

ratively. To localize the region injured
most consistently in these animals, all
lesions were projected at the appropriate
level (anterior 12, Horsley-Clarke co-
ordinate) onto a map of the amygdala.
The frequency of injury was then indicated by shading as seen in text Figure 1.
The most consistently injured region is
near the junction of the basal and lateral
nuclei of the amygdala.

Unfortunately, there was no exact
control of the diet, but some observations of the feeding habits were made.
These cats did not show any particular
abnormal oral tendencies of the type
described in monkeys by Brown and
Schäfer (1888), Klüver and Bucy (1939),
and Klüver (1952) following temporal
lobe ablation. While the experimental
cats would sometimes eat rat or rabbit
food, normal cats would do so about as
frequently. They did not lick, were not
seen to indulge in coprophagy or to
explore objects with the mouth or tongue.
On the other hand, they would consume
voraciously all food put before them. In
almost all cases the same ration was given
to all cats, but in one case it was observed
that an animal ate as much as three
pounds of cat food at a single session.
Probably the weight gains would have
been much more dramatic in our series
had the cats been given food ad libitum.
In only four of the animals described was
there hypersexuality as well as hyperphagia, but the data on some of the
hypersexual animals were insufficient
and one additional animal with an extensive lesion involving the amygdala in
the same area probably did show hyperphagia as well.

(d) Catalepsy. In 11 cases, cataleptic
or catatonic manifestations were seen.
These animals appeared lethargic, moved
little in their cages, and as a rule failed
to eat voluntarily, and so lost weight.
They did not clean themselves, though
they were capable of voluntary movement. When handled, they showed typical clay-like rigidity, and their limbs

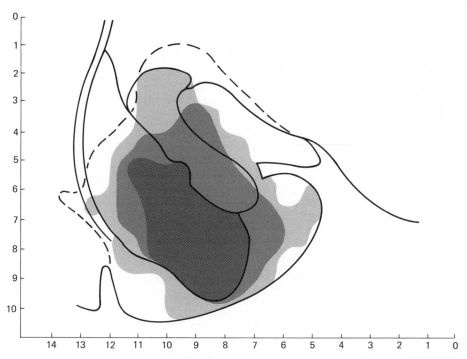

Figure 1. Superimposition of areas destroyed in animals with hyperphagia. Both sides are represented together at level A12, Horsley-Clarke plane. Successively darker areas represent 0–25, 25–50, 50–75, and 75–100 percent of incidence destruction. Thus the black zone was destroyed in 75–100 percent of the cats. Coordinates in millimeters.

could be moulded into bizarre positions which would be maintained for long periods. Vocalization, tail wagging and other manifestations of irritability were noted in some animals when they were placed in these positions. The lesions in these animals commonly involved the anterior part of the amygdala. In nine cats, there was vascular damage to the basal ganglia or internal capsule, probably due to the destruction of branches of the middle cerebral artery. In one there was damage to anterior thalamus and stria terminalis. Nine additional animals, with nonspecific lesions especially in the basal ganglia, were classified as placid or indifferent. Among the 20 animals which were placid, cataleptic and indifferent by our evaluation, 10 had involvement of the basal ganglia or

internal capsule, seven had various other adjacent lesions, and in three cases the histological findings were inadequate because the animals were found dead. This effect was considered to be nonspecific.

(e) *Aggressive behavior.* Instances of snarling, hissing and striking which appeared in animals for the first time postoperatively are included under this heading. There were 16 such animals. A very striking fact was that all 16 of these cats had seizures, and the lesion in each animal had involved the hippocampal formation to some degree. In no case did we see adversive behavior unless the hippocampal formation had been partially injured. In three cases, the hippocampus alone was involved but in the remaining 13 other areas were also injured.

This behavior was invariably directed toward the investigator or other animals, but undirected violent behavior was not observed following minor stimulation as in sham rage. Only once did we observe an animal which actually attacked, and in this instance hypersexual behavior also occurred. The aggressive attacks were much more frequent when this latter animal was thwarted, i.e., by allowing him to witness other animals running freely, by allowing him to see others copulating or by separating him from a female during copulation. These procedures progressively increased the violence of his behavior, but his reactions were strongly conditioned by territory. If the animal was allowed out of his cage during an apparent paroxysm of fury, he would often attack the observer's legs, cease abruptly, walk away and, when approached, behave in a perfectly docile fashion, only to become violent again as soon as he was returned to his cage.

Changes in sexual behavior

The term hypersexuality is used here to indicate an increase in the number of objects towards which a sex drive is exhibited. Although the term abnormal sexuality might be preferable, hypersexuality has already been used rather widely in the literature.

(a) Females. Hypersexuality was never observed in any of our females, nor did we ever see persistent estrus. In three animals, we saw a curious behavior pattern which we could not classify but which showed some resemblance to behavior observed following the administration of testosterone to prepubertal animals and also to maternal behavior. They were very active and playful, and when another animal was introduced into the cage, they would sniff its genitalia, lick it vigorously, pounce, partially mount like a male and persist in this activity even though viciously rebuffed

by the other animal. Two of these female animals, after being rejected, showed behavior indistinguishable from the after-reactions of coitus. One was found to have four fresh corpora lutea, even though she had not been mounted by a male for at least six months. This was an animal which had shown the after-reaction response. She had been observed, however, with a large inactive male which she herself had attempted to mount. Ovulation did not occur in the others.

The brain lesions involved the pyriform cortex in all three of these cases, and in two the amygdala as well. There was no activity in our females suggestive of abnormal estrus behavior as described by Gastaut (1952) and Schreiner and Kling (1953).

(b) Males. In the males, changes in sexual behavior which were distinguishable from normal behavior patterns and behavior patterns in animals treated with steroids, occurred in 20 cases. The criteria for abnormal sex behavior are summarized in columns 6 and 7 of the table. The most clear-cut difference is in the activity of the animal outside his territory, and in the behavioral changes that usually occurred abruptly three to 10 days postoperatively. In some young males, there were indications that at this time they were not expert in coitus and that they were experiencing their first mating.

There were many examples of extremely abnormal behavior. Nine days postoperatively AM58, on being released from his cage, seized an investigator by the shoe and attempted to masturbate. On the same day the animal was allowed out in the presence of six much larger normal males. Within a few moments he had attempted to mount each of them. Examples of attempted copulation with rats, guinea pigs, rabbits, teddy bears, anesthetized animals and even humans were exhibited by members of this group of lesioned male cats. These attempts were made anywhere, regardless of territory. AM2, an animal in which seizures occurred during the first week postoperatively and again six to eight weeks later, never lost his sexual abnormalities. Eventually, as he had repeated generalized seizures, it was decided to sacrifice him. Accordingly, while mounted on a teddy bear, he was given a lethal dose of nembutal. He continued to attempt coitus until he fell off the teddy bear, apparently anesthetized. When an attempt was made to remove the teddy bear, he aroused sufficiently to remount and continue for about 30 seconds, after which he died. Several animals attempted coitus with the teddy bear for periods of 20 to 45 minutes, only ceasing from exhaustion.

Castration noticeably reduced the drive in these animals, as reported by Schreiner and Kling (1954), but it took much longer for any obvious effect to appear. While normal animals lost drive in seven to ten days, the capacity for successful copulation with intromission persisted for upwards of six weeks in the animals with lesions.

One cat began to lose interest in females about four weeks after castration, but he continued to attempt copulation with a teddy bear and showed an obvious preference for the inanimate object. Two weeks later he no longer showed an interest in females but only in the teddy bear. He was then given testosterone (10 mg intramuscularly). Two days later he showed a preference for the female and one day later still had a successful intromission. He continued to be interested in the teddy bear when it alone was presented, but when both were simultaneously placed with him, he invariably chose the female. Thus, testosterone seemed to reverse his perverted tendencies.

Estradiol, stilbestrol and testosterone all restored drive to a very high level in castrated animals with lesions, and they showed remarkable persistence in attempting copulation despite repeated rebuffs by their partners. It was noted,

however, that in one animal which had been castrated for two months (but which had received a small dose of stilbestrol intramuscularly four weeks before) the experience of a fight with another male temporarily abolished his tendency to copulate. On the following day, he appeared fully restored.

Of the 20 animals which showed signs of abnormal male sex activity, 19 had involvement of the pyriform cortex, 15 had involvement of the amygdala and one a bilateral lesion in the dorsal stria terminalis. We have some reservations with regard to this last cat since it and another animal with a lesion in the stria were studied before the full importance of territory was appreciated. In the second animal with a stria terminalis lesion, apparent changes were also seen, but only when the animal was in his own cage. In six other cases where lesions were placed in or near the stria, no abnormalities were observed.

Hypersexuality was observed most consistently in animals with lesions in the pyriform cortex beneath the basal amygdaloid nuclei (Figure 2). It is noteworthy that three of these animals had no detectable injury to the amygdala and no apparent cell loss in the amygdaloid nuclei. Two of the cats had minor damage lateral to the rhinal fissure, and one suffered slight secondary vascular damage to the dentate gyrus (this was the animal which showed apparent aggressiveness associated with frustration). It is also noteworthy that all three females which showed abnormal behavior following lesions (neck grips, after reactions, etc.) had involvement of the pyriform cortex in the same area and one, the most extreme case, had involvement only of the pyriform cortex in this region. Lesions restricted to the amygdala without injury to the overlying pyriform cortex resulted in no detectable changes in sexual behavior. Thus, out of 23 animals, males and females, showing abnormal behavior there was involvement of the pyriform cortex in 22, and in four of these there

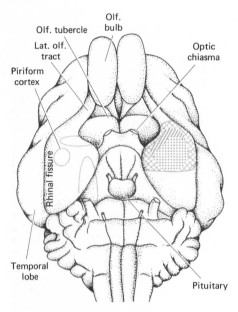

Figure 2. Ventral aspect of cat brain with projection onto surface of areas involved in animals showing various behavior patterns. At right quartile distribution of incidence of involvement of both pyriform areas in male animals with hypersexuality. Areas behind dotted line not explored. On left the three dotted zones indicate schematically that (rostral zone) lesions near anterior amygdala (branches of middle cerebral artery) produce catalepsy. Lesions at junction of basal and lateral amygdaloid nuclei produce hyperphagia and lesions in hippocampus (caudal dotted zone) are followed by seizures.

were no visible changes in the amygdala. The one case in which neither pyriform cortex nor amygdala was involved must be regarded with some reserve, but it is not felt that the stria terminalis can be excluded as playing some role in this behavioral mechanism since connections between the pyriform cortex and stria were described long ago (Volsch, 1906, 1910).

DISCUSSION
1. Normal cats
Before assessing abnormal activity in male cats, it is necessary to consider

where it occurs. The animal's own cage is territory after a fairly short interval, and the floor of the animal house becomes territory soon thereafter. The sight of other cats copulating seems to accelerate the enlargement of territory. Within territory, homosexual and tandem copulation may be expected as well as heterosexual behavior. Factors which seem to influence sex behavior in control cats are: (1) general health; (2) past general experience (i.e., cats that behave in a frightened fashion take much longer to adapt than animals that are friendly; fighting inhibits sexual activity); (3) past sexual experience (we have noticed that the greater the number of estrus females presented to normal males, the more active the males become); (4) steroid hormone levels; (5) willingness of partner; (6) size of the partner (within limits a small male seems reluctant to mate with a large female, and adapted males show little interest in kittens, though during adaptation they may attempt copulation with them); (7) sex of partner (apparently this is of little importance compared with most of the preceding); (8) age of participants; (9) state of the reproductive organs. Females seem less concerned with territory than males and to copulate somewhat more readily outside territory than in their own cages. As in males, the willingness of the partner is a major factor, and often an aggressive male is quite successful with a female showing few signs of heat when the genitalia are manipulated. Receptive females often rebuff males which are not too aggressive in their approach.

2. Sex hormones
The results we obtained in these studies were unexpected. Our findings on the effects of sex steroids in adult cats indicate that sex behavior and maturation of the reproductive tract and secondary sex characteristics may at times be distinguished. Why the steroids have different actions before and after puberty can only be conjectured. Since the effects

are reversible before puberty but irreversible after (by changing from male to female hormone) it seems unlikely that education in any ordinary sense is involved after first coitus, though, the possibility exists that the changes in behavior following the first sexual experience may be correlated with subsequent reaction to hormones. This would be the educational effect of the first coitus rather than learning in the prepubertal animal. It suggests that the type of first sexual experience may determine the subsequent behavioral reaction to hormones that have the same effect on the secondary sex characteristics and reproductive tract both before and after puberty.

The hormonal effects on behavioral changes after puberty strongly argue against the occurrence of some general metabolic change whereby the adult cat might convert the steroid hormone of the opposite sex to a substance having similar effects to its own hormone, since the effects on the reproductive tract are not changed at puberty.

It is possible that at puberty, or perhaps at the first sexual experience, some irreversible changes occur in the central excitatory mechanism—either newly-developing pathways or local metabolic changes—or that other hormones play some role in sex behavior and are not available to the prepubertal animal. It seems unlikely that the pituitary plays a direct role (Maes, 1939, 1940; Beach, 1948; Ford and Beach, 1951) but it is possible that some other endocrine organ might exert some control.

Pfeiffer (1936), on the basis of experimental transplantation of the gonads, concluded that adult male and female pituitaries developed as the result of gonadal maturation but ceased to be bipotential at puberty. Harris and Jacobsohn (1952) were able to transplant the pituitaries of adult male rats into the sellae turcicae of hypophysectomized females. Since these females were able to maintain estrus cycles and to deliver young after coitus, the conclusion was reached that the pituitary is not itself specifically sexually differentiated but rather the brain which controls the activity of the pituitary (Harris, 1954).

Our own findings seem to parallel those of Pfeiffer (1936) and Harris and Jacobsohn (1952) as far as behavior is concerned, for behavior apparently became set after puberty or sexual experience in cats,[1] so that the steroids of the opposite as well as those of the same sex increase sex behavior, while still having the same effects on the reproductive tract as before puberty. Perhaps the simplest explanation is that before sex experience, the steroids set the stage for later education and determine the animal's receptivity to another kind of experience; that is, they determine the mood of the prepubertal animal. Without full sexual experience, then, the mood is reversible; but once experience has been acquired, the pattern of behavior is set and is not changed by the administration of the steroids of the opposite sex. The steroids in the adult would thus be assumed to increase drive in a nonspecific way. Thus, only a slight modification of the hypothesis of Beach (1948) would be required to bring it into accord with our own studies.

The question of what part of the brain is modified by sexual experience remains unsettled. It may be the hypothalamus, as suggested by Harris (1954), or conceivably the pyriform cortex could be affected, perhaps by inhibition.

Sex behavior is clearly a complex of more simple behavioral patterns, some of which can be induced before puberty and others which cannot. Before normal sex behavior can be evaluated, it is necessary to consider its individual components, the variations from one animal to the next and the various external influences which can modify it. The results reported here are based only on

[1] Since most of our adults were stray animals obtained after puberty, we did not know their previous sex experience but we assumed copulation had occurred.

experiments to determine what the outside limits of behavior patterns might be, and our study of behavioral changes is incidental to the main problem. Nevertheless, they seem to suggest future possibilities for clarifying normal sex behavior in cats.

The degree of adaptation to territory seems to be the most valuable criterion by which to judge the abnormality of the sex acts in animals with rhinencephalic lesions. To a lesser extent, the tendency to copulate with unusual objects may be considered but this may sometimes be induced by the administration of sex hormones. It is apparent that the abnormal behavior patterns after lesions are not due to excessive production of male sex hormone, for if that were so, they should be stimulated by large doses of testosterone, and such was certainly not the case either in males or females. On the other hand, the sex steroids are apparently essential to the maintenance of the abnormal behavior pattern, despite the fact that it persists longer after castration than does normal male sex drive. It is emphasized that the effects of hormones shown in Table 1 represent only an occasional maximal response.

3. Seizures

The finding that the hippocampus was always involved in our animals which developed seizures must not be taken to indicate that it is the sole source of temporal lobe discharges; these observations are discussed elsewhere (Green, Clemente, and de Groot, 1957).

4. Rage, aggressiveness, and placidity

These phenomena are at once difficult to assess since rage is readily confused with fear, aggressiveness or, perhaps, frustration and even some types of playfulness, while placidity might be confused with indifference, catalepsy, catatonia, stupor, and idiocy. It must be suggested that the cataleptic or catatonic behavior seen in our animals may be confused with placidity, while the be-

havior suggestive of apprehension or fear could be considered aggressive. If this confusion is possible, our findings might serve to explain the discrepancies between the findings of Klüver and Bucy (1939) and Schreiner and Kling (1953) and those of Bard and Mountcastle (1948) for the two types of behavior clearly cannot occur together. In the case of the temporal lobectomies performed by these investigators, a rostral extension of the area removed might be expected to result in placidity whereas, if the rostral area were spared and the hippocampus involved, aggressiveness might be expected.

The behavior associated with hippocampal lesions seemed to be related to tissue irritation for it was most marked in the early postoperative stages, could be triggered by a variety of peripheral stimuli, and was progressive in the sense that the effects were more obvious with more stimulation. The latter occurred only in hypersexual males, and seemed at times dependent on territory, being more obvious in familiar surroundings. Possibly it is related to altered perceptive mechanisms or to frustrated sex drive. It seems likely that the behavior patterns which suggested fear were related to hippocampal injury. Since the latter was so frequently associated with seizures, it may well be that this behavior itself represents a type of sensory seizure discharge (Green, Clemente, and deGroot, 1957). It is hard to tell whether it can be correlated with MacLean's (1952) observation of aggression following hippocampal stimulation and Kaada, Jansen, and Andersen's (1953) observations of fear, anger and fury.[2]

[2]Hypermetamorphosis described by Klüver and Bucy was not recognized in these animals. The cats with hypersexuality were very alert and hyperactive, but the impression was gained that this might represent another manifestation of their hypersexuality. It was thought possible that the investigators' presence conditioned them to anticipate the presentation of a female.

5. Hyperphagia and
oral behavior. Hyperthermia

The evidence points to an association between hyperphagic signs and lesions of the amygdala near the junction of the lateral and basal nuclei. Although our experiments are not sufficient to ascribe the effects to specific nuclei, this area was most frequently damaged in animals showing marked weight increases. The hyperphagia was not accompanied by other signs of abnormal oral behavior, though excessive licking was seen in a few cats which did not increase in weight. In one instance at least, the excessive licking was abolished by administering salt. We did not observe excessive oral investigation by our lesioned cats or the eating of unusual substances. We consider the hyperthermia observed to have been due to seizure discharges.

6. Changes in sex behavior

The criteria for judging abnormality have been discussed above under normal cats and sex hormones. It seems clear that behavior patterns are not due simply to a high testosterone titre. The two characteristics of (a) copulating out of territory and (b) copulating with unusual objects might conceivably be due to some disorder of perception, but there were no consistent behavioral changes regularly associated with hypersexuality which might have suggested defects of intelligence. Indeed, some of these animals were very active and learned a variety of methods for escaping from their cages. Neither was the hypersexuality associated with hyperphagia. We have a better opportunity to observe male sex changes since in our series we had more males than females, but it is curious that our female cats never showed female hypersexual behavior. What we did observe in the three animals with abnormal behavior (possibly of sexual origin) is not easy to interpret on the basis of so small a sample, and it would be possible to classify it in a variety of ways. The neck grips resembled male behavior, though they could conceivably be considered maternal. The tendency to lick the other animal might again be either male or maternal, or simply oral. The curious responses resembling after reactions are impossible to evaluate, but it is noteworthy that one particular animal which showed this pattern also ovulated subsequently, though the other two did not.

Whether the hypersexual changes in males are due to irritation or destruction of the nerve tissue is difficult to assess, but the latter seems more likely since the effects last indefinitely. If this is so, the most likely explanations seem to be that either the pyriform cortex normally exerts some restraining action on sex behavior or that destruction of this localized area leads to certain perceptual changes whereby every furry object is interpreted as an estrus female in the male's territory.

The effects of lesions and stimulation of the amygdala and neighboring structures are striking, and it is remarkable that so many effects have been produced in such a small region in the brain.

Thus, we may list the following effects reported in literature:

A. Stimulation of amygdala and periamygdaloid cortex. 1. Changes in respiration: (Kaada, 1951; Vigouroux, Gastaut, and Badier, 1951; Koikegami and Fuse, 1952a, 1952b; Gastaut, 1952; Kaada, Andersen, and Jansen, 1954). 2. Inhibition of movement: (Kaada, 1951; Gastaut, Vigouroux, Corriol, and Badier, 1951; Gastaut, 1952; Koikegami, Fuse, Yokoyama, Watanabe, and Watanabe, 1955; Kaada, Andersen, and Jansen, 1954). 3. Motor effects and complex movements: (Kaada, 1951; Vigouroux, Gastaut, and Badier, 1951; Gastaut, Vigouroux, Corriol, and Badier, 1951; Gastaut, 1952). 4. Blood pressure changes: (Kaada, 1951; Morin, Naquet, and Badier, 1952a, 1952b; Koikegami, Kimoto, and Kido, 1953). 5. Seizures:

(Kaada, 1951; Vigouroux, Gastaut, and Badier, 1951; Gloor, 1955a, 1955b).
6. Pupillary changes: (Vigouroux, Gastaut, and Badier, 1951; Gastaut, 1952; Koikegami and Yoshida, 1953; Kaada, Andersen, and Jansen, 1954).
7. Pilo-erection: (Vigouroux, Gastaut, and Badier, 1951; Gastaut, 1952; Kaada, Andersen, and Jansen, 1954).
8. Gastric motility and intestinal changes: (Kaada, 1951; Vigouroux, Gastaut, and Badier, 1951; Gastaut, Vigouroux, Corriol, and Badier, 1951; Koikegami, Kushiro, and Kimoto, 1952; Gastaut, 1952; Koikegami, Kimoto, and Kido, 1953). 9. Evacuation of bladder: (Gastaut, Vigouroux, Corriol, and Badier, 1951; Kaada, 1951; Gastaut, 1952; Kaada, Andersen, and Jansen, 1954). 10. Gagging: (Gastaut, Vigouroux, Corriol, and Badier, 1951; Vigouroux, Gastaut, and Badier, 1951; Gastaut, 1952). 11. Lip and facial movement: (Gastaut, Vigouroux, Corriol, and Badier, 1951; Gastaut, 1952; Mac-Lean, 1952; Baldwin, Frost, and Wood, 1954, 1956; Kaada, Andersen and Jansen, 1954). 12. Defecation: (Gastaut, Vigouroux, Corriol and Badier, 1951; Vigouroux, Gastaut, and Badier, 1951; Kaada, Andersen, and Jansen, 1954).
13. Salivation: (Vigouroux, Gastaut and Badier, 1951; Gastaut, Vigouroux, Corriol, and Baddier, 1951; Kaada, Andersen, and Jansen, 1954; Koikegami, Fuse, Yokoyama, Watanabe, and Watanabe, 1955). 14. Fear and rage: (Gastaut, Naquet, Vigouroux, and Corriol, 1952; MacLean and Delgado, 1953; Kaada, Andersen, and Jansen, 1954). 15. Movements of eye and ears: (Takahashi, 1951; MacLean, 1952). 16. Ovulation: (Koikegami, Yamada, and Usui, 1954). 17. Uterine movements: (Koikegami, Yamada, and Usui, 1954). 18. Changes in temperature: (Koikegami, Kushiro, and Kimoto, 1952).

B. Lesions of the temporal lobe involving amygdala and periamygdaloid cortex. 1. Idiocy: (Brown and Schäfer, 1888). 2. Placidity: (Brown

and Schäfer, 1888; Klüver and Bucy, 1937, 1938, 1939; Smith, 1950; Gastaut, 1952; Anand and Brobeck, 1952; Morin, Gastaut, Vigouroux, and Roger, 1952; Schreiner and Kling, 1953, 1954). 3. Rage: (Bard and Mountcastle, 1948). 4. Temporary rage: (Woringer, Thomalske and Klingler, 1953; Sawa, Ueki, Arita, and Harada, 1954). 5. Oral behavior: (Klüver and Bucy, 1937, 1938, 1939; Spiegel, Miller, and Oppenheimer, 1940; Smith, 1950; Sawa, Ueki, Arita, and Harada, 1954). 6. Catalepsy: (Spiegel, Miller, and Oppenheimer, 1940). 7. Estrus and receptive behavior outside estrus in female: (Gastaut, 1952; Schreiner and Kling, 1953). 8. Changes in temperature: (Anand and Brobeck, 1952). 9. Hypersexuality in males: (Gastaut, 1952; Schreiner and Kling, 1953, 1954). 10. Bulimia: (Brown and Schäfer, 1888; Pribram and Bagshaw, 1953). 11. Psychic blindness: Klüver and Bucy, 1937, 1938, 1939).

It is noteworthy that at least 29 effects have been reported. Observations on stimulation and lesions of the hippocampus, cingulate, stria terminalis, septum, and entorhinal area might have been cited in a similar way. Thus, despite terminological convergence, so many effects have been described that a search for common factors is needed.

Patients with psychomotor epilepsy are notoriously prone to illusions, hallucinations, and fugues. Indeed, fugues and hallucinations could lead to a variety of other effects so that, except perhaps for ovulation, it might be possible to think of the other phenomena observed as secondary to perceptual disorientation and emotional concomitants. Alternative theories, suggesting that rhinencephalic areas control the emotions directly, are possible of course. Thus, the Papez (1937) theory of emotion may be mentioned, and the more recent concepts of Mac-Lean (1952) and Pribram and Kruger (1954) of a visceral brain. Unilateral section of the fornix, which would disrupt the Papez system, did not seem to influence the emotional behavior of humans in the cases cited by Akelaitis and collaborators (1942, 1943), however, and Garcia-Bengochea, Corrigan, Morgane, Russell, and Heath (1951) failed to observe changes in performance of a variety of psychological tests in monkeys with bilateral section of the fornix. Perhaps the hypothalamus is a final common path for higher visceral centers as suggested previously (Green, 1956) or perhaps by destruction of rhinencephalic areas there is a release of activity previously held in check by the suppressor mechanism suggested by Kaada (1951). Nevertheless, the hypersexuality of cats with pyriform cortex lesions is puzzling, for it is hard to understand why a small and localized lesion produces one single pattern of behavior which implies change of activity throughout the forebrain.

The observations of Beach (1942) and Stone (1922) show that sexual activity in rats is not abolished by the removal of the olfactory sense alone. As Le-Magnen (1953) has pointed out, they do not indicate what role olfaction plays in sex activity; only that it is dispensable. LeMagnen (1952a, 1952b) has also demonstrated special sensitivities in men and rats correlated with the degree of sexual activity. Thus, women are sensitive to synthetic musk (exaltöide) and the odor of urinary steroids (urinöide). This sensitivity increases after puberty or after administration of estrogens, decreases after castration or androgens. In the rat it is the male that is sensitive both to synthetic musk and the intensity of female odor which increases at estrus. Castration and estrogens decrease this sensitivity. We must, however, emphasize that our animals appeared easily disturbed by visual stimuli, as far as we could tell, though not by olfactory and that the effects were chronic, lasting indefinitely after lesions.

Some process leading to a loss of inhibition, whether for emotional, perceptual, visceral, or sensory reasons, seems the most reasonable explanation.

SUMMARY

1. In a series of 122 cats, lesions were placed in the amygdala-pyriform cortex and in other rhinencephalic areas in 82. Forty animals were used as controls.

2. Observed variations in normal sex behavior and sex behavior following hormone administration are described.

3. Sex hormones have behavioral effects on prepubertal animals specific to the type of hormone.

4. Sex hormones have behavioral effects in adults depending on the sex of the animal or previous conditioning, although their effects on target organs depend on the hormone.

5. Male hypersexual behavior may be induced by lesions restricted to the pyriform cortex.

6. This effort (5) is not due simply to a raised testosterone titre.

7. Hyperphagia has been produced by lesions restricted to the basal and lateral part of the amygdala.

8. Seizures observed in some animals were closely correlated with fear-like behavior and damage to the hippocampus.

9. Cataleptic changes were associated with lesions involving the rostral amygdala and basal ganglia.

10. Other phenomena observed were: hyperthermia, emotional changes, and oral behavior. These are discussed.

11. It is suggested that many of the phenomena associated with stimulation or destruction of the pyriform cortex may be secondary to the hallucinations and fugues of psychomotor epilepsy, though other changes are difficult to explain on this basis.

Literature cited

Adrian, E. D. Olfactory reactions in the brain of the hedgehog. *J. de Physiol., Paris*, 1942, **100**, 459–473.

Akelaitis, A. J. Studies on the corpus callosum VI. *Arch. Neur. Psychiat.*, 1942, **48**, 914–937.

Akelaitis, A. J. Studies on the corpus callosum VII. *J. Neuropath. Exper. Neur.*, 1943, **2**, 226–262.

Akelaitis, A. J., Risteen, W. A., Herren, R. Y., and Van Wagener, W. P. Studies on the corpus callosum Ill. *Arch. Neur. Psychiat.*, 1942, **47**, 971–1008.

Anand, B. K., and Brobeck, J. R. Food intake and spontaneous activity of rats with lesions in the amygdaloid nuclei. *J. Neurophysiol.*, 1952, **15**, 421–430.

Baldwin, M., Frost, L. L., and Wood, C. D. Investigation of the primate amygdala: Movements of the face and jaws. *Neurology*, 1954, **4**, 585–598.

Baldwin, M., Frost, L. L., and Wood, C. D. Investigation of the primate amygdala: Movements of the face and jaws 2. Effect of selective cortical ablation. *Neurology*, 1956, **6**, 288–293.

Bard, P. Central nervous mechanism for emotional behavior patterns in animals. *Res. Publ. Assn. nerv. ment. Dis.*, 1939, **19**, 190–218.

Bard, P., and Mountcastle, V. B. Some forebrain mechanisms involved in expression of rage with special reference to suppression of angry behavior. *Res. Publ. Assn. nerv. ment. Dis.*, 1948, **27**, 362–404.

Beach, F. A. Analysis of the stimuli adequate to elicit mating behavior in the sexually in-experienced male rat. *J. comp. physiol. Psychol.*, 1942, **33**, 163–207.

Beach, F. A. *Hormones and behavior*. New York and London: Hoeber, 1948.

Brown, S., and Schäfer, E. A. An investigation into the functions of the occipital and temporal lobes of the monkey's brain. *Philos. Tr. Roy. Soc. London*, 1888, **179B**, 303–327.

Eckstein, D., and Zuckerman, S. The oestrus cycle in the mammalia. In A. S. Parkes (ed.), *Marshall's physiology of reproduction*. New York: Longmans, Green, Vol. 1. Part 1, 226–396.

Ford, C. S., and Beach, F. A. *Patterns of sexual behavior*, New York: Harper & Row, 1951.

Fox, C. A., McKinley, W. A., and Magoun, H. W. An oscillographic study of olfactory, system in cats. *J. Neurophysiol.*, 1944, **7**, 1–16.

Garcia-Bengochea, F., Gorrigan, R., Morgane, P., Russell, D. Jr., and Heath, R. G. Studies on function of the temporal lobe; section on the fornix. *Tr. Amer. Neurol. Ass.*, 1951, **76**, 238–239.

Gastaut, H. Correlations entre le système nerveux végétatif et le système de la vie de relation dans le rhinencephale. *J. de Physiol., Paris*, 1952, **44**, 431–470.

Gastaut, H., Naquet, R., Vigouroux, R., and Corriol, J. Provocation de comportements emotionnels divers par stimulation rhinencephalique chez le chat avec electrodes à demeure. *Rev. Neur.*, 1952, **86**, 319–327.

Gastaut, H., Vigouroux, R., Corriol, J., and Badier, M. Effets de la stimulation electrique (par electrodes à demeure) du complexe amygdalien chez le chat non narcose. *J. de Physiol., Paris*, 1951, **43**, 740–476.

Gloor, P. Electrophysiological studies on the connections of the amygdaloid nucleus in the cat. Part I. The neuronal organization of the amygdaloid projection system. *Electroencephalog. and clin. Neurophysiol.*, 1955, **7**, 223–242. (a)

Gloor, P. Electrophysiological studies on the connections of the amygdaloid nucleus in the cat. Part II. The electrophysiological properties of the amygdaloid projection system. *Electroencephalog. and clin. Neurophysiol.*, 1955, **7**, 243–264. (b)

Green, J. D. Neural pathways to the hypophysis. In W. S. Fields (Ed.), *Hypothalamic-hypophysial interrelationships*. Springfield, Ill.: Charles C. Thomas, 1956, Pp. 9–16.

Green, J. D., and Adey, W. R. Electrophysiological studies of hippocampal connections and excitability. *Electroencephalog. and clin. Neurophysiol.*, 1956, **8**, 245–262.

Green, J. D., Clemente, C. D., and De Groot, J. Experimentally induced epilepsy with injury to Ammon's horn. *Arch. Neur. and Psychiat.*, 1957, **78**, 259–263.

Harris, G. W. The relationship between endocrine activity and the development of the nervous system. In *The biochemistry of the developing nervous system. Proc. First Int. Neurochem. Symp.* Oxford: Academic Press, 1954, Pp. 431–442.

Harris, G. W., and Jacobsohn, D. Functional grafts of the anterior pituitary gland. *Proc. Roy. Soc. London*, 1952, **139B**, 263–276.

Kaada, B. Somato-motor, autonomic and electrocorticographic responses to electrical stimulation of rhinencephalic and other structures in primates, cat and dog. *Acta Physiol. Scand.*, 1951, **24**, suppl. 83, 1–285.

Kaada, B. R., Andersen P., and Jansen, J. Stimulation of the amygdaloid nuclear complex in unanesthetized cats. *Neurology*, 1954, **4**, 48–64.

Kaada, B. R., Jansen, J., and Andersen, P. Stimulation of the hippocampus and medial cortical areas in unanesthetized cats. *Neurology*, 1953, **3**, 844–856.

Klein, M. Oestrogen level and ovarian hypophysial relationship during pseudopregnancy and pregnancy in the rabbit. *J. Endocrinol.*, 1947, **5**, xv–xxvii.

Klüver, H. Brain mechanisms and behavior with special reference to the rhinencephalon. *Lancet*, 1952, **72**, 567–574.

Klüver, H., and Bartelmez, G. W. Endometriosis in a rhesus monkey. *Surg. Gynec. and Obst.*, 1951, **92**, 650–660.

Klüver, H., and Bucy, P. C. Psychic blindness and other symptoms following bilateral temporal lobectomy in rhesus monkeys. *Amer. J. Physiol.*, 1937, **119**, 352–253.

Klüver, H., and Bucy, P. C. An analysis of certain effects of bilateral temporal lobectomy in monkeys with special reference to psychic blindness. *J. comp. Psychol.*, 1938, **5**, 33–54.

Klüver, H., and Bucy, P. C. Preliminary analysis of functions of the temporal lobes in monkeys. *Arch. Neur. and Psychiat.*, 1939, **42**, 979–1000.

Koikegami, H., and Fuse S. Studies on the functions and fiber connections of the amygdaloid nuclei and periamygdaloid cortex. Experiment on respiratory movements (1). *Folia Psychiat. neur. jap.*, 1952, **5**, 188–196. (a)

Koikegami, H., and Fuse, S. Studies on the functions and fiber connections of the amygdaloid nuclei and periamygdaloid cortex. Experiment on the respiratory movements (2). *Folia Psychiat. neur. jap.*, 1952, **6**, 94–103. (b)

Koikegami, H., Fuse, S., Yokoyama, T., Watanabe, T., and Watanabe, H. Contributions of the comparative anatomy of the amygdaloid nuclei of mammals with some experiments of their destruction or stimulation. *Folia Psychiat. neur. jap.*, 1955, **8**, 336–368.

Koikegami, H., Kimoto, A., and Kido, C. Studies on the amygdaloid nuclei and periamygdaloid cortex. Experiments on the influence of their stimulation upon motility on small intestine and blood pressure. *Folia Psychiat. neur. jap.*, 1953, **7**, 87–108.

Koikegami, H., Kushiro, H., and Kimoto, A. Studies on the functions and fiber connections of the amygdaloid nuclei and periamygdaloid cortex. Experiments on gastrointestinal motility and body temperature in cat. *Folia Psychiat. neur. jap.*, 1952, **6**, 76–93.

Koikegami, H., Yamada, T., and Usui, K. Stimulation of amygdaloid nuclei and periamygdaloid cortex with special reference to its effects on uterine movements and ovulation. *Folia Psychiat. neur. jap.*, 1954, **8**, 7–31.

Koikegami, H., and Yoshida K. Pupillary dilatation induced by stimulation of amygdaloid nuclei. *Folia Psychiat. neur. jap.*, 1953, **7**, 109–126.

LeMagnen, J. Les phénomènes olfacto-sexuels. *Arch. Sci. physiol.*, 1952, **6**, 125–160. (a)

LeMagnen, J. Les phénomènes olfacto-sexuels chez le rat blanc. *Arch. Sci. physiol.*, 1952, **6**, 295–331. (b)

LeMagnen, J. L'olfaction le fonctionnement olfactif et son intervention dans les régulations psycho-physiologiques. *J. Physiol. path. gen. Paris*, 1953, **45**, 285–326.

MacLean, P. D. Some psychiatric implications of physiological studies on fronto-temporal portion of limbic system (visceral brain). *Electroencephalog. and clin. Neurophysiol.*, 1952, **4**, 407–418.

MacLean, P. D., and Delgado, J. M. R. Electrical and chemical stimulation of fronto-temporal portion of limbic system in the waking animal. *Electroencephalog. and clin. Neurophysiol.*, 1953, **5**, 91–100.

Maes, J. P. Neural mechanism of sexual behavior in the female cat. *Nature, London*, 1939, **144**, 598–599.

Maes, J. P. Hypophysectomie et comportement sexuel de la chatte. *Comp. rend. Soc. de. biol.*, 1940, **133**, 92–94.

Morin, G., Gastaut, H., Vigouroux, R., and Roger, A. Comportement émotionnel et lésions experimentales du rhinencéphale chez le chat. *Comp. rend. Soc. de biol.*, 1952, **146**, Part 2, 1959–1961.

Morin, G., Naquet, R., and Badier, M. Stimulation electrique de la region amygdalienne et pression arterielle chez le chat. *J. de Physiol.*, Paris, 1952, **44**, 303–305. (a)

Morin, G., Naquet, R., and Badier, M. Variations de la pression arterielle par stimulation des noyaux amygdaliens et de structures voisines chez le chat. *Comp. rend. Soc. de biol.*, 1952, **146**, Part 1, 747–749. (b)

Papez, J. W. A proposed mechanism of emotion. *Arch. Neur. and Psychiat.*, 1937, **38**, 725–743.

Pfeiffer, C. Sexual differences of the hypophyses and their determination by the gonads. *Amer. J. Anat.*, 1936, **58**, 195–226.

Pribram, K. H., and Bagshaw, M. Further analysis of the temporal lobe syndrome utilizing fronto-temporal ablations. *J. comp. Neur.*, 1953, **99**, 347–375.

Pribram, K. H., and Kruger, L. Functions of the olfactory brain. *Ann. New York Acad. Sci.*, 1954, **58**, 109–138.

Sawa, M., Ueki, Y., Arita, M., and Harada, T. Preliminary report on the amygdaloidectomy on the psychotic patients, with interpretation of oral-emotional manifestation in schizophrenics. *Folia Psychiat. neur. jap.*, 1954, **7**, 309–329.

Schreiner, L., and Kling, A. Behavioral changes following rhinencephalic injury in cat. *J. Neurophysiol.*, 1953, **16**, 643–659.

Schreiner, L., and Kling, A. Effects of castration on hypersexual behavior induced by rhinencephalic injury in cat. *A. M. A. Arch. Neur. and Psychiat.*, 1954, **72**, 180–186.

Schreiner, L., and Kling, A. Rhinencephalon and behavior. *Amer. J. Physiol.*, 1956, **184**, 486–490.

Scott, P. P. The domestic cat as a laboratory animal for the study of reproduction. *J. Physiol.*, 1955, **130**, 478–488.

Scott, P. P., and Lloyd-Jacob, M. A. Some interesting features in the reproductive cycle of the cat. In R. G. Harrison (Ed.), *Studies on fertility*. Oxford: B. Blackwell (Society for the study of Fertility), 1955, **7**, 123–129.

Smith, W. K. Non-olfactory functions of the pyriform-amygdaloid-hippocampal complex. *Federation Proc.*, 1950, **9**, 118.

Spiegel, E. A., Miller, H. R., and Oppenheimer, M. J. Forebrain and rage reactions. *J. Neurophysiol.*, 1940, **3**, 538–548.

Stone, C. P. The congenital sexual behavior of the young male albino rat. *J. comp. physiol. Psychol.*, 1922, **2**, 95–153.

Takahashi, K. Experiments on the periamygdaloid cortex of cat and dog. *Folia Psychiat. neur. jap.*, 1951, **5**, 147–154.

Terzian, H., and Dalle Ore, G. Syndrome of Klüver and Bucy reproduced in man by bilateral removal of the temporal lobes. *Neurology*, 1955, **5**, 373–380.

Vigouroux, R., Gastaut, H., and Badier, M. Les formes espérimentales de l'épilepsie-provocation des principales manifestations clinique de l'épilepsie dite temporale par stimulation des structures rhinencéphaliques chez le chat non anesthésié. *Rev. Neur.*, Paris, 1951, **85**, 505–508.

Volsch, M. Zur vergleichenden Anatomie des Mandelkerns und seiner Nachbargebilde I Teil. *Arch. mikr. Anat.*, 1906, **68**, 573–683.

Volsch. M. Zur vergleichenden Anatomie des Mandelkerns und seiner Nachbargebilde II Teil. *Arch. mikr. Anat.*, 1910, **76**, 373–523.

Woringer, E., Thomalske, G., and Klingler, J. Les rapports anatomiques du noyau amygdalien et la technique de son extirpation neurochirurgicale. *Rev. Neur.*, Paris, 1953, **89**, 553–560.

Psychosexual differentiation
john money

Development and differentiation are inseparable concepts in the embryology of sex. In the psychology of sex, it is good to remember that the same applies: psychosexual development is also psychosexual differentiation as male or female.

In psychosexual theory, it has been more or less assumed that, when psychosexual development proceeds in an orderly fashion, masculinity or femininity will somehow differentiate out of an innate, instinctive bisexuality.

The origins and regulation of this psychosexual differentiation, too long neglected in research, still cannot be fully specified. In this chapter, I propose to review the present state of knowledge.

Anatomic sexual differentiation in the embryo takes place according to two plans, either of which may offer a model for psychosexual differentiation. One plan is exemplified by the gonads and subsequently repeated by the internal accessory structures. In both cases, the anlagen for both male and female are initially laid down side by side. Then one set regresses and atrophies while the other proliferates and differentiates. (See Figure 1.)

The other plan of sexual differentiation is exemplified by the external genitalia. Here the homologous male and female structures differentiate from the same embryonic anlagen. Thus, the genital tubercle becomes either a penis or a clitoris; the skin covering of the penis has the same origin as the clitoral hood and labia minora; and the labiscrotal swellings either remain divided as the labia majora or fuse in the midline to become the scrotum. (See Figure 2.)

Though complete reversal of genetic sex has been achieved in amphibian experiments, little is known about the fundamental principles of regulation of gonadal differentiation in mammals—that is, about what controls proliferation of the "rind" of the primitive gonad to become an ovary, versus proliferation of the "core" to become a testis.

Once formed, however, the gonads themselves become the source of hormonal organizer substances that regulate differentiation of the remainder of the genital system. If the embryonic gonads are removed in mammals, before the critical time of genital-duct differentiation has passed, then differentiation proceeds as female. The critical period is marvelously short. In the experiments by Jost (Chapter 2 in Jones and Scott, 1958) on the rabbit, castration before embryonic day 21 was early enough to ensure complete feminization of all the remaining reproductive system. On the twenty-fourth day, it was already too late for castration to interfere with masculine differentiation already begun. But on day 23, castration of genetic males arrested masculine differentiation in favor of resumption of feminine differentiation, with resulting hermaphroditic ambiguity of appearance.

Mammalian masculine anatomy, as these experiments show, is brought about by something added, failing which the more basic disposition of the embryo toward the feminine asserts itself. One

From *Sex Research: New Developments,* edited by John Money. Copyright © 1965 by Holt, Rinehart & Winston, Inc. Reprinted by permission of Holt, Rinehart & Winston, Inc.

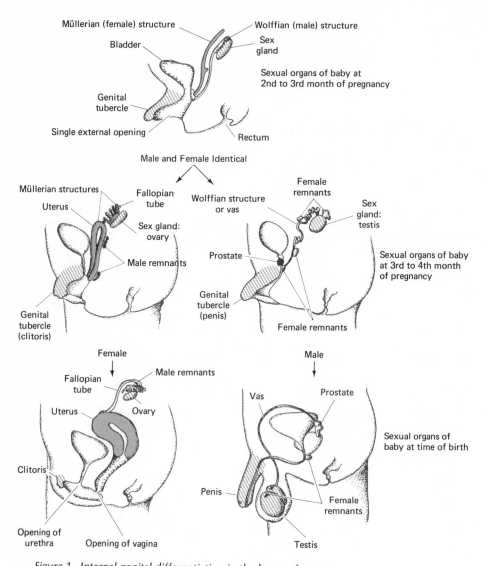

Figure 1. Internal genital differentiation in the human fetus.

wonders whether to look for a parallel in human psychosexual differentiation. In view of the alleged higher incidence of psychosexual pathologies in males, it is conceivable that masculine psychosexual differentiation is more difficult to achieve than feminine, and is more vulnerable to error and failure.

Jost did not report on the effects of the changes set in motion by embryonic castration on the subsequent differentiation of sexual behavior. More recently, however, Grady and Phoenix (1963) performed castration experiments on neonatal rats and found more feminine behavior, in response to mounting by

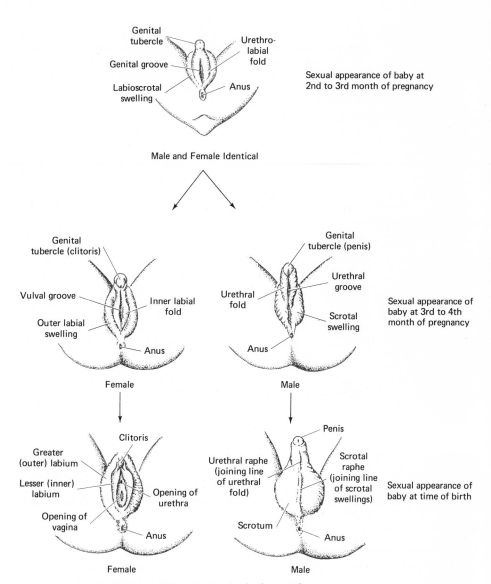

Figure 2. *External genital differentiation in the human fetus.*

intact males, in animals castrated before 10 days of age than after.

There are also behavioral reports on a type of experimental hermaphroditism easier to accomplish than that of Jost, namely masculinization of a female fetus. Phoenix, Goy, Gerall, and Young

(1959) bred hermaphroditic guinea pigs by administering testosterone to the pregnant mothers. Some of the daughters were born with male external genitalia, the internal reproductive organs being female. These animals (and to a lesser extent their morphologically normal female counterparts which had also been exposed in utero to testosterone, but in lesser amount) gained scores in various subsequent mating tests that were closer to the scores of untreated control males than to those of untreated control females. The authors ventured the hypothesis that prenatal androgen had affected neural organization and thus the organization of behavior. It is of significance to note, however, that the masculine scores of the experimental animals reflected a quantitative rather than a qualitative sex difference. The affected animals did that which normal females might do, but which normal males readily do more frequently.

The effect of early-administered androgen on subsequent mating behavior has also been studied in the female rat by Barraclough and Gorski (1962). They found that testosterone propionate administered at five days of age permanently impaired the regulation of the sexual cycle postpubertally, rendering the rats sterile and in a state of anovulatory, persistent estrus and at the same time constantly sexually unreceptive to the male. Mating behavior could not be restored by replacement therapy with estrogen and progesterone, as in the ordinary case of ovariectomized rats. When a smaller dose of testosterone propionate (10 micrograms) was used at five days of age, the results were similar, except that the rats would subsequently accept the male, though on bizarre schedules, such as nine days consecutively. The authors interpreted the findings of these and other experiments to suggest that a mating center exists in the anterior hypothalamus.

The complexities of the prenatal or neonatal influence of sex hormone on the neural basis of behavior are exemplified in the finding of Whalen and Nadler (1963), that estrogen administered subcutaneously to four-day-old female rats resulted in reduced mating in response to estrogen and proges-

terone in adulthood. Levine and Mullins (1964) replicated the result of Whalen and Nadler when they halved the dosage and injected only 100 micrograms of estradiol benzoate; 50 micrograms produced, however, an attenuated effect.

In the 100-microgram experiment, Levine and Mullins further tested their animals in adulthood by castrating them and administering testosterone. They then found an increase in the incidence of items of masculine sexual behavior, as compared with a control group, including a simulation of the male ejaculation pattern, twice, in one animal. The experimental animals also showed, after nine days of testosterone replacement therapy, masculinization of the external genitalia more extreme than that manifested by the neonatally untreated, control animals.

Levine and Mullins did also the experiment of neonatally injecting male rats with 100 micrograms of estradiol benzoate. In adulthood, these rats were mating-tested before and after castration, and again after seven days of testosterone replacement therapy. Their performance fairly well paralleled that of oil-injected control animals, except for a lesser intromission and ejaculation rate, which could be attributed to poor morphologic development of the accessory sex organs following neonatal estrogen. The mounting activity of the experimental animals was, however, bizarre: they tried to mount from the head, the side or high up on the back of the receptive female.

Testosterone to the neonatal male was found (Harris and Levine, 1962) to produce little or no effect on sexual behavior and reproductive capacity.

While admitting that there are inconsistencies which need further elucidation, Levine and Mullins suggest that the central nervous mechanism controlling gonadotropin-release in the rat will develop so as to function acyclically, that is in the male fashion, only under the influence of androgen, presumably secreted by the infantile testes. Testosterone would thus be implicated as the active hormone organizing the sexual control system, both in terms of reproductive cycles and sexual behavior. It is already known that, at a critical period earlier in embryonic life, androgen is an active organizer substance without which the internal anlagen of the female morphology do not regress and the external anlagen feminize. In other words, without androgen, nature's primary impulse is to make a female— morphologically speaking at least (see above).

The change from cyclic to acyclic release of pituitary gonadotropin in the female rat by neonatal injection of sex hormone is the product of sex-hormonal action not on the pituitary itself, but on the neural centers of the adjacent hypothalamus. Segal and Johnson (1959) took the pituitaries from female rats that had been treated neonatally with androgen and whose ovaries consequently were anovulatory and sterile. Transplanted into normal hypophysectomized hosts, these pituitaries were capable of inducing complete reproductive function, since the host animals bore young and suckled them. It was imperative, however, for the donor gland to be transplanted in contiguity with the hypothalamus of the host female, thus demonstrating that the control of cyclic pituitary function was in the hypothalamus itself.

It is theoretically important to underscore the significance of timing, and of the critical-period phenomenon, in all the above experiments. The mechanism of hypothalamic regulation of cyclic pituitary functioning, and of attendant sexual behavior, can be abolished by exogenous hormone, but only if it is injected during a critical developmental period. This period must be ascertained empirically for each species (Goy, Phoenix and Young, 1962).

There is a somewhat suggestive human parallel to the animal experiments with androgen to be found in human female hermaphrodites with the adrenogenital syndrome, virilized in utero from an excess of adrenal androgens. There is anecdotal evidence from some of these patients, who, in adulthood, have reported experiences more typically reported by normal males than females, namely, erotic arousal from visual and narrative perceptual material. The experience might be accompanied by erection of the hypertrophied clitoris and masturbation. The erotic content of the perceptual images and fantasies was suitably female, in keeping with their sex of rearing and psychosexual identity. Only the threshold and frequency of arousal followed the masculine pattern. The reaction has occurred in both the untreated and treated cases of the syndrome, but is attenuated by treatment, which consisted of feminizing clitoral surgery and hormonal correction with cortisone. There is a possibility, therefore, that there was also a residual androgenic effect, even after androgen levels were controlled to normal.

Another human parallel to the animal experiments may be looked for in another variety of hermaphroditism (Wilkins, 1965), the testicular feminizing syndrome. In this syndrome a genetic male of 46,XY chromosome constitution begins early embryonic differentiation as a male, so that the internal organs are chiefly masculine. The final stage of differentiation, that of the external genital morphology, then proceeds along entirely female lines, presumably because the necessary masculinizing principle from the fetal testes fails either to be produced or to be properly utilized. In adulthood, patients with the syndrome have completely feminine body morphology, thanks to the estrogen produced by their feminizing testes. Their psychosexual and gender-role differentiation in childhood is feminine, and remains so in adult life, which is as expected, since their sex assignment and rearing is female, in keeping with their genital appearance. One is led to speculate, however, in view of the experiments outlined in the foregoing, whether the failure of a masculinizing principle in late fetal life in some manner enhanced the capacity of the nervous system to comply with the demands of female sex assignment and rearing.

This speculation leads to another one, applicable to Klinefelter's syndrome, which is characterized by the 47,XXY chromosome anomaly, masculine morphogenesis, infertility, poor virilization at puberty (sometimes with partial feminization of the breasts), and low-powered libido. It is possible that the testicular deficit in these individuals is related to a discrepancy of some sort in neurosexual differentiation, for Klinefelter's syndrome seems to produce an excess of individuals with anomalies of psychosexual differentiation (Money, 1963; Money and Pollitt, 1964).

Whatever the ultimate experimental verdict on prenatal influences in human psychosexual differentiation, it is also true that what happens before birth can be overridden to an extraordinary degree by postnatal events. The demonstration par excellence is that of two hermaphrodites of identical diagnosis and anatomical defect, one assigned as a boy, the other as a girl. In such cases, the differentiation of gender role and pyschosexual identity ordinarily proceeds in agreement with assigned sex, particularly if three conditions are met. The first condition is that the parents resolve their ambiguities and doubts, at the time of birth, and achieve a feeling of complete conviction that they have either a son or a daughter, whom they will raise accordingly. This first condition is linked to the second: that genital surgery, at least the first stage to achieve a good cosmetic appearance, be delayed as little as possible after birth. The visual appearance of the sex organs dictates not only the expectancies of other people, but also contributes to the development of the child's own body image. This second condition is, therefore, linked to the third: that pubertal secondary sexual development be timed and regulated hormonally, possibly with adjuvant surgery, in conformity with assigned sex and psychosexual identity.

This ideal is not always attained. There are patients for whom all three conditions have not been met. Even so, some of these patients manage to achieve a unitary gender role and psychosexual identity, despite gross contradictions of bodily sex. Perhaps the most surprising of these are women with the *untreated* adrenogenital syndrome. Despite a penis-sized clitoris, an exaggerated masculine physique, excessive hirsutism, and a deep voice, it is not impossible for these girls to develop and maintain a feminine gender role and psychosexual identity.

The incongruities among the variables of sex in hermaphroditism are such as to permit one to show that psychosexual differentiation can take place in opposition to:

1. genetic sex, as revealed by either the sex-chromatin mass (Barr body) or a full chromosome count;
2. hormonal sex, in other words, a hormonal balance that is predominantly androgenic or estrogenic;
3. gonadal sex: ovarian, testicular, or mixed;
4. morphology of the internal reproductive organs;
5. morphology of the external genitals.

Psychosexual differentiation in hermaphrodites may also take place in contradiction of the sex of assignment and rearing. The same happens in cases of sexual psychopathology in people who are genetically, hormonally, and morphologically normal in all respects, according to presently known criteria.

One must make the inference that psychosexual differentiation takes place as an active process of editing and assimilating experiences that are gender-specific and that derive ultimately from the genital appearance of the body. These experiences include direct apperception—visual, tactile, and proprioceptive—of one's own sexual organs. They also include the multitudinous and cumulative experiences that derive from genital appearance as it has determined the sex of assignment and rearing—experiences that are defined by the gender of personal nouns and pronouns, clothing style, haircut, and a thousand other gender-specific expectancies and attitudes.

The evidence of hermaphroditism indicates that the condition existing at birth and for several months thereafter is one of psychosexual undifferentiation. Just as in the embryo, morphologic sexual differentiation passes from a plastic stage to one of fixed immutability, so also does psychosexual differentiation become fixed and immutable— so much so, that mankind has traditionally assumed that so strong and fixed a feeling as personal sexual identity must stem from something innate, instinctive, and not subject to postnatal experience and learning.

The error of this traditional assumption is that the power and permanence of something learned has been underestimated. The experiments of animal ethologists on imprinting have now corrected this misconception.

The basic paradigm of imprinting is that there is in a species a tendency to respond behaviorally to a certain type of perceptual stimulus, the limits of variability in both the behavior and the stimulus being phylogenetically set. Further, there is a critical period in the life history when this stimulation and responding must take place if an effective bond between the two is to occur. Finally, once the bond has been established, it has extraordinary durability for an epoch if not the entire lifetime.

The acquisition of a native language is a human counterpart to imprinting in animals. So also is the acquisition of a gender role and psychosexual identity. The critical period in establishing psychosexual identity appears to be approximately simultaneous with the establishment of native language. Planned experimental evidence is, of course, for ethical reasons impossible to come by. But there are occasional experiments of nature, namely, when infant and juvenile hermaphrodites are subjected to sex reassignment.

Psychosexual differentiation follows in agreement with a sex reassignment made in the neonatal period or up to a year or 18 months of age, provided the parents negotiate the change successfully. Thereafter, adjustment difficulties and the likelihood of residual psychopathology increase with the child's memory of life-history experiences and appreciation of gender concepts. By school age, psychosexual differentiation is so complete that a sex reassignment is out of the question, save for the rare instances of ambiguous psychosexual differentiation.

Judging by the prevalence in psychopathology of errors or partial errors of psychosexual differentiation, the process of differentiation is vulnerable to many interferences. The great vexation, scientifically, is that one knows little about the extent and precise nature of these interferences. Harlow's (1962) now famous experiments on the macaque have shown that ability to mate is adversely and lastingly affected when the young are deprived of play contact with their age mates. In the case of human beings, it is possible that any impedance of normal development and maturation, however seemingly remote from psychosexual identity, may have a noxious side-effect on psychosexual differentiation. Such impedance would include defects in the parent-child relationship and attendant hindering of normal ego mechanisms of identification and impersonation.[1]

The spread of developmental disturbance has, in the case of oral and anogenital functions, a direct counterpart demonstrated in the cortex of the "lower mammalian brain," the limbic system. MacLean has done extensive exploration of the representation of sexual function in the limbic system of the squirrel monkey by means of implanted electrodes. He writes (see Chapter 9):

> By stimulating parts of the amygdala one may obtain chewing and salivation, with partial erection occurring as a recruited response after many seconds of stimulation or as a rebound phenomenon after stimulation is terminated.

Sexual functions are directly activated by stimulation of the adjacent area of the septum. The topographical representation of the head end and the rear end of the body in such close proximity, MacLean notes, "helps in understanding the intimate interplay of behavior in the oral and sexual spheres," animal and human, normal and abnormal. In the lower mammals, one may remark, oralgenital coordination is essential to delivery of the young, and their survival, as Birch (1956) so well showed by rearing rats with a rubber ruff around the neck so as to deprive them of the experience of licking themselves. The animals subsequently failed in parturition, eating or neglecting the young instead of licking them.

With the advent of puberty, the stage is set for the completion of psychosexual differentiation in courtship, mating, and parenthood. Puberty is also the time at which prior errors and defects of psychosexual differentiation announce themselves in full and prevent continued

[1]See Brown, 1957; Kagan, 1964; Katcher, 1955; Lynn, 1959; Maccoby, in press; Mussen and Kistler, 1960; Rabban, 1950.

normal and desired completion of psychosexual maturity. Whether or not psychosexual pathologies may be induced at puberty is arguable, but it is certainly true that a great many of them have a long "psychoembryonic" period before puberty.

It is commonplace of social anthropology that, whatever their prepubertal history, a multiplicity of details of adolescent and adult gender role are specific to a particular ethnic group at a particular historical time. One may go further and say that the hormones that bring about sexual maturation do not, according to all the evidence available, have any differential determining influence on the psychosexual, male–female direction and content of perceptual, memory, or dream imagery that may trigger or be associated with erotic arousal. On the contrary, there is strong clinical and presumptive evidence (Money, 1961a, 1961b) that the libido hormone is the same for men and women and is androgen. Psychosexually, the androgenic function is limited to partial regulation of the intensity and frequency of sexual desire and arousal, but not to the cognitional patterns of arousal. In women, androgen may be secreted by the adrenal cortex or metabolically derived from the ovary's progestins, to which it is akin in chemical structure.

Sex differences in the androgen-estrogen ratio may conceivably account for some of the differences between men and women in their thresholds for erotically related behavior and activity. In the male, for instance, there is typically a greater expenditure of energy in the service of sexual searching, pursuit, and consummation. This energy expenditure extends also to adventurous, exploratory roaming, to assertiveness and aggression, and to the defense of territorial rights. Of course, the male does not have exclusive prerogative in these respects, but there does indeed seem to be a sex difference in the frequency with which these patterns of activity are manifest.

This difference is not exclusive to the human species. Harlow (1962) found that male children of the macaque monkey make many more threats toward other monkeys, boys or girls, than do the female children. The girls' threats, moreover, are reserved primarily for other girls. The young females retreat more often than the males, specifically by adopting the female sexual posture. The male youngsters initiate more play contacts, with playmates of either sex, than do females, and the males are the ones that engage in rough and tumble play. With increasing age, the male infants show increasing frequency of the male mounting position in their copulatory play. They show little grooming behavior, which in adults is more predominant in female than male sexual behavior.

Hormone-derived sex differences in behavior after puberty may be independent of social interaction, or they may be interactional, so that the behavior of the male is influenced by the hormonal cycle of the female. Michael and Herbert (1963) found that the time spent by the female rhesus monkey in grooming the male fluctuates rhythmically with the menstrual cycle and reaches a minimum at mid-cycle, near the time of ovulation. Reciprocally, it is precisely at this time that the male's grooming activity reaches a maximum, and very shortly thereafter that his mounting activity reaches its peak. These rhythmic changes in the mounting behavior of males and in the grooming activity of both sexes did not appear in one case of a nervous and excitable male, and were in all cases abolished by ovariectomy. The route by which the ovarian cycle of the female influences not only her behavior but that of the mating partner as well may conceivably be via the sense of smell, though this possibility remains to be investigated. The relationship of the ovarian cycle to sexual behavior in human beings also requires investigation. It is of interest to note that the peak of sexual desire and initiative in women has by several investigators been reported as occurring at the menstrual or progestinic phase of the cycle (Money, in press), so that one may see an analogy with the female monkey whose grooming approach to the male is intensified at this time.

In the behavior of human beings, there is evidence that the sense of smell is related to the sexual cycle in women and is hormone regulated. Women generally have greater acuity than men, and the consensus of reports (Money, 1963) is that acuity is at its peak when estrogen levels are highest, that is, between the periods of actual menstruation in the monthly cycles. Acuity is lost after overiectomy, but regained with administration of estrogen. Hypophysectomy, which suppresses ovarian function, also brings about loss of the sense of smell (Schon, 1958).

The relationship of hormonal functioning to smell acuity for sexual odor was the subject of experiments by Le-Magnen (1952) in the white rat. He confirmed that body smell varied with sex, maturation, and, in females, with the estrous cycle; conversely, test animals were able to smell these various differences and discriminate between them. Discriminatory acuity itself varied with the hormonal state of the rat making the discrimination. Capacity to distinguish the smell of the estrous female from the diestrous female and the male was lessened but not completely abolished by castration, and was not completely absent in juvenile males. Parallel findings on the female were incomplete. The effects of hormonal replacement therapy after castration were measured in terms of ability to discriminate traces of synthetic odor in drinking water. In the case of synthetic musk, there was the rather paradoxical finding that testosterone restored the male castrate to normal, but increased the acuity of the female castrate to four times that of normal. Loss of estrogen through castration had itself doubled her acuity for smelling this substance. In males, estradiol suppressed acuity for musk completely.

The odor to which a sexual response is made has recently been given the name of *pheromone*. Parkes and Bruce (1961) reviewed experiments in this new field. In one experiment, the crowding together of female mice in small groups induced pseudopregnancies, and in large groups, anestrus. The effects could be prevented by excision of the olfactory bulbs or by individual housing.

In other experiments, if the newly mated female mouse was moved from the stud male and exposed to an alien male, especially of another strain, neither pregnancy nor pseudo-pregnancy (the expected result of an infertile mating) were likely to ensue, but the mouse returned to estrus as though coitus had not occurred. The most vulnerable period comprised the first four days after the vaginal plug from the stud mating was found, and ended at the sixth day. The effect of the alien male was equally great if he was in his own cage within the compartment of the female, and not able to be in direct physical contact with her. The effect persisted if the alien male was removed from his cage and the empty cage was put in the female's compartment, but then it was imperative to replace a newly vacated, empty alien male's cage twice a day for three days. The experimental design left no doubt that odor from the alien male was the responsible agent for the arrestment of implantation and pregnancy.

Another sex difference that relates perhaps to hormonal differences pertains to perceptual distractibility. More than woman, man is in his erotic pursuits fairly promiscuously distracted from one love object to another, especially over a period of time, except perhaps when he is in the vortex of having just fallen desperately in love. The female is more steadfastly tied to a single romantic object or concept. In the act of copulation, by contrast, it is the male who has a singleness of purpose, perhaps oblivious even to noxious stimuli, and who is likely to be unable to continue if successfully distracted by a competing stimulus. This sex difference appears to hold widely in the animal kingdom (Beach, 1947, p. 264). "A marked difference between the male and female cat," wrote Horsley Gantt (1949, p. 37), "is that the female's interest in food is not inhibited by the sexual excitation of copulation, for she, as well as a bitch, will accept food not only after coitus but even during the act. . . . The female is, however, much more strongly oriented about the offspring than about the sexual act; she undergoes a great inhibition of conditional reflexes and of some unconditional reflexes postpartum, a fact which has been demonstrated several times in my laboratory with dogs."

On the relationship of sex hormones to sex-differentiated behavior, there is in animal experimentation a remarkable new development in demonstrating direct hormonal action on the brain (Michael, 1961, 1962). By implanting micro-amounts of estrogen directly into the hypothalamus of the cat, Michael was able to induce in the animal a state of sustained sexual receptivity, though without any of the other physiologic signs of estrus. Then by using C^{14}-labeled estrogen and an autoradiographic technique, he was able to demonstrate that the action of the hormone was localized and consistent with the hypothesis that certain neurons of the hypothalamus are selectively sensitive to the action of estrogen. In yet another autoradiographic experiment, Michael and Glascock (1963) were able to detect radioactivity in the brain of various mammals, including the primate, within five hours after subcutaneous administration of H^3-hexestrol, and to show that the rate of radioactive uptake peaked at the same time in the brain as in the genital tract, whereas no such peak was observed in a nontarget structure such as muscle. The effect of this estrogen uptake by the brain presented a puzzle with regard to sexual behavior, however, since the radioactivity had disappeared within 12 to 24 hours, whereas mating behavior was always postponed until at least 48 hours after administration of even large doses of estrogen.

The many difficulties inherent in unraveling the neurohormonal basis of sexual behavior, including species differences, are further exemplified in the findings of Fisher (1956) on the rat. Injecting minute amounts of testosterone directly into the preoptic area of the brains of male rats, Fisher obtained maternal and sexual behavior in a series of males. Maternal behavior included nest building and persistent retrieving and grooming of litters of young. All aspects of mating behavior were seen, sometimes accentuated. One male continuously retrieved his tail when stimulated, and then repeatedly retrieved a female in heat. When pups and paper were supplied, however, the animal built a nest and retrieved and groomed the young, neglecting the objects to which he had previously reacted. In another male, maternal and sexual behavior were activated simultaneously. When presented with a female (not in heat) and with newborn rat pups, the male attempted copulation twice while a pup he was retrieving to a nest was still in his mouth. Variations in response to injected androgen appeared to depend on small variations in placement of the cannula in the brain.

The effect of brain-implanted sex hormone is clearly related to the localization of the implant. Lisk (1962) located testosterone-sensitive centers in the region of the basal tuberal median eminence of the rat hypothalamus, where implanted testosterone brought about gonadotropin suppression and gonadal atrophy in both male and female. A similar effect was produced by means of estradiol implants (Lisk and Newlon, 1963) in the arcuate nucleus of the hypothalamus of the rat, male and female, after the implant had brought about decrease in the size of the nucleoli of the neurons of the arcuate. The implant did not suppress sexual behavior, but in females stimulated a state of constant receptivity to the male (Lisk, 1963). The sterilizing effect of the estradiol implant, alone, could be reversed by a second implant of progesterone or of testosterone, though with the latter the pregnant animals died during labor.

The human brain maintains its adult pattern of psychosexual differentiation relatively stable and constant, for the most part, though as some people gain in age and experience there may be a lifting of restraints against behavior they once tabooed. Major psychosexual changes in adulthood are not the norm, but a sign of abnormality and deterioration, well exemplified in the psychosexual regression and dedifferentiation of senility. Psychosexual deterioration may also be a symptom of other brain disease, of toxic neurological disease, and of other psychotic conditions of late onset. Otherwise, aging is a process in which the psychosexual fires simply burn low, quickly for some, but for others retaining some glow until the end.

SUMMARY

Psychosexual differentiation is an active process that takes place after birth and needs the stimulus of interaction with a behavioral environment, in much the same manner as does acquisition of a language. In certain indicative cases the behavioral environment, reinforcing the sex of assignment, can override the influence of the physical variables of sex.

Of possible significance of human psychosexual differentiation are new animal experiments on neurohormonal activity in the fetus or newborn, whereby sex hormones affect the neural organization of subsequent sexual behavior. The chief effect would appear to be that androgen is needed to induce masculine cycles and frequencies, but not types of behavior.

A second type of new experimental work is providing evidence of a direct action of sex hormone on neural centers and individual cells of the hypothalamus, which are related to phylogenetic stereotypes in sexual behavior. To date, the specificity of the relationship of estrogen and androgen to the release of feminine and masculine behavior, respectively, is none too clear; and other chemicals may prove able to simulate their neural-triggering action.

The neural component of human sexual behavior might well include a neuroperceptual sex difference. Men appear to be more responsive to visual and narrative erotic stimuli and images, women to be more dependent on touch. Males are perceptually more distractible than females in erotic pursuits. Their greater expenditure of energy in initiating erotic pursuit may bear some phylogenetic relationship to the defense of territorial rights, a type of behavior widely occurring in the mating patterns of mammals.

Women have more smell acuity than men; and it varies with the menstrual cycle. Secreted odors may be the responsible agent in controlling reciprocal mating behavior relative to the menstrual cycle, according to experiments on the macaque monkey. Odors secreted by the male have been found, in the mouse, to regulate whether copulation will succeed in successful pregnancy or not. Such excitatory odors have been named pheromones.

In human beings, psychosexual differentiation is manifested in full at adolescence and thenceforth remains relatively stable in adulthood, though changes and regression are possible, especially in senescence.

References

Barraclough, C. A., and Gorski, R. A. Studies on mating behavior in the androgen-sterilized female rat in relation to the hypothalamic regulation of sexual behavior. *J. Endocrinol.* 1962, **25**, 175–182.

Beach, F. A. A review of physiological and psychological studies of sexual behavior in mammals. *Physiol. Rev.*, 1947, **27**, 240–307.

Birch, H. G. Sources of order in the maternal behavior of animals. *Amer. J. Orthopsychiat.*, 1956, **26**, 279–284.

Brown, D. G. Masculinity-femininity development in children. *J. consult. Psychol.*, 1957, **21**, 197–202.

Fisher, A. E. Maternal and sexual behavior induced by intracranial chemical stimulation. *Science*, 1956, **124**, 228–229.

Gantt, W. H. Psychosexuality in animals. In P. H. Hoch and J. Zubin (Eds.), *Psychosexual development in health and disease.* New York: Grune and Stratton, 1949.

Goy, R. W., Phoenix, C. H., and Young, W. C. A critical period for the suppression of behavioral receptivity in adult female rats by early treatment with androgen. *Anat. Rec.*, 1962, **142**, 307.

Grady, K. L., and Phoenix C. H. Hormonal determinants of mating behavior; the display of feminine behavior by adult male rats castrated neonatally. *Amer. Zoologist*, 1963, **3**, 482–483.

Harlow, H. F. The heterosexual affectional system in monkeys. *Amer. Psychologist*, 1962, **17**, 1–9.

Harris, G. W., and Levine, S. Sexual differentiation of the brain and its experimental control. *J. Physiol.*, 1962, **163**, 42P–43P.

Jones, H. W., Jr., and Scott, W. W. *Hermaphroditism, genital anomalies and related endocrine disorders.* Baltimore: Williams and Wilkins, 1958.

Kagan, J. The acquisition and significance of sex-typing. In M. Hoffman (Ed.), *Review of child development research.* New York: Russell Sage, 1964.

Katcher, A. The discrimination of sex differences by young children. *J. genet. Psychol,* 1955, **87**, 131–143.

LeMagnen, J. Les phénomènes olfactosexuels chez le rat blanc. *Arch. Sci. physiol.,* 1952, **6**, 295–331.

Levine, S., and Mullins, R., Jr. Estrogen administered neonatally affects adult sexual behavior in male and female rats. *Science,* 1964, **144**, 185–187.

Lisk, R. D. Testosterone-sensitive centers in the hypothalamus of the rat. *Acta endocrinol.,* 1962, **41**, 195–204.

Lisk, R. D. Gonadal hormones; Effects of hypothalamic implants on reproduction in the rat. *Proc. XVI Internat. Congr. Zool.,* Washington, D.C., 1963, **2**, 136.

Lisk, R. D., and Newlon, M. Estradiol: Evidence for its direct effect on hypothalamic neurons. *Science,* 1963, **139**, 223–224.

Lynn, D. B. A note on sex differences in the development of masculine and feminine identification. *Psychol. Rev.,* 1959, **66**, 126–135.

Maccoby, E. (Ed.) *Sex role attitudes in children.* Stanford: Stanford University Press, 1965. In press.

MacLean, P. D. New findings relevant to the evolution of psychosexual functions of the brain. *J. nerv. ment. Dis.,* 1962, **135**, 289–301.

Michael, R. P. An investigation of the sensitivity of circumscribed neurological areas to hormonal stimulation by means of the application of oestrogens directly to the brain of the cat. In S. S. Kety and J. Elkes (Eds.), *Regional neurochemistry.* Oxford: Pergamon Press, 1961.

Michael, R. P. Oestrogen-sensitive systems in mammalian brains. *Excerpta Medica, International Congress Series No. 47* (containing papers read at the XXII International Congress of Physiological Sciences, Leiden, The Netherlands), 1962. Pp. 650–652.

Michael, R. P., and Glascock, R. F. The distribution of C^{14}- and H^3-labelled oestrogens in brain. *Proc. Fifth Internat. Congr. Biochem.,* 9, 11, 37. Oxford: Pergamon Press, 1963.

Michael, R. P., and Herbert, J. Menstrual cycle influences grooming behavior and sexual activity in the rhesus monkey. *Science,* 1963, **140**, 500–501.

Money, J. Components of eroticism in man: I. The hormones in relation to sexual morphology and sexual desire. *J. nerv. ment. Dis.,* 1961, **132**, 239–248. (a)

Money, J. Sex hormones and other variables in human eroticism. In W. C. Young (Ed.), *Sex and internal secretions* (3rd ed.). Baltimore: Williams and Wilkins, 1961. (b)

Money, J. Developmental differentiation of femininity and masculinity compared. In *Man and civilization: The potential of woman.* New York: McGraw-Hill, 1963.

Money, J. Influence of hormones on sexual behavior. *Ann. Rev. Med.,* Vol. 16. Palo Alto: Annual Reviews, 1965. In press.

Money, J., and Pollitt, E. Cytogenetics and psychosexual ambiguity: Klinefelter's syndrome and transvestism compared. *Arch. gen. Psychiat.,* 1964, **11**, 589–595.

Mussen, P., and Distler, L. Child-rearing antecedents of masculine identification in kindergarten boys. *Child Develpm.,* 1960, **31**, 89–100.

Parkes, A. S., and Bruce, H. M. Olfactory stimuli in mammalian reproduction. Odor excites neurohumoral responses affecting oestrus, pseudopregnancy, and pregnancy in the mouse. *Science,* 1961, **134**, 1049–1054.

Phoenix, C. H., Goy, R. W., Gerall, A. A., and Young, W. C. Organizing action of prenatally administered testosterone propionate on the tissues mediating mating behavior in the female guinea pig. *Endocrinology,* 1959, **65**, 369–382.

Rabban, M. Sex-role identification in young children in two diverse social groups. *Gen. Psychol. Monogr.,* 1950, **42**, 81–158.

Schon, M. Psychological effects of hypophysectomy in women with metastatic breast cancer. *Cancer,* 1958, **11**, 95–98.

Segal, S. J., and Johnson, D. C. Inductive influence of steroid hormones on the neural system: Ovulation controlling mechanisms. *Arch. d'Anat. micros. Morphol. expér.,* 1959, **48 bis**, 261–273.

Whalen, R. E., and Nadler, R. D. Suppression of the development of female mating behavior by estrogen administered in infancy. *Science,* 1963, **141**, 273–274.

Wilkins, L. *The diagnosis and treatment of endocrine disorders in childhood and adolescence* (3rd ed.). Springfield, Ill.: Charles C. Thomas, 1965.

Circuits
of
violence
mort la brecque

Once a relatively peaceful and cohesive nation, America turns increasingly violent. Not only has there been a rise in the rate of crimes of violence, but blood is now shed commonly during political confrontations. The death of four students at Kent State University was predictable, according to Vice President Agnew, and many observers would agree with him. Radicals of both left and right demean peaceful protest; even more ominous are the violent acts of forces empowered by society to maintain order under stress.

Until very recently, the nature of violence was studied mainly from a psychological or sociological vantage. Sociologists saw social inequities as the prime cause and recommended a change in external environment as the most effective treatment. To explain abnormal aggression, psychologists produced evidence implicating an affectionless childhood, parents who both permit and punish hostile behavior, even the active presence of a father figure; they suggested that, through conditioning, an individual can be taught to inhibit aggressive responses. Researchers in both disciplines tended to agree on one point, however: there is no physiological basis for aggression. "All that we know," said Dr. John Paul Scott, Research Professor of Psychology at Ohio's Bowling Green University, "indicates that the physiological mechanisms associated with fighting are very different from those underlying sexual behavior and eating. There is no known physiological mechanism by which spontaneous internal stimula-

From *The Sciences*, Vol. 10 No. 7, M. La Brecque, pp. 5–10, © 1970.

tion for fighting arises." (*Science*, vol. 148, p. 820).

Although no one suggests that the psychological and sociological approaches are invalid, Dr. Scott's views about physiology are now strongly disputed. "It would be naive to investigate the reasons for a riot by recording the intracerebral electrical activity of the participants," says Dr. José M. R. Delgado, Professor of Physiology at Yale University, "but it would be equally wrong to ignore the fact that each participant has a brain and that determined neuronal groups are reacting to sensory inputs and are subsequently producing the behavioral expression of violence." (*Physical Control of the Mind*, Harper and Row, 1969) The newest studies of violence have developed most dramatic experimental—and clinical—results through the administration of drugs, electrical production of brain lesions and direct brain stimulation, each technique focused upon physiological alteration of the brain.

CHEMICAL STIMULANTS OF AGGRESSION

Hormonal changes in blood chemistry are known to inhibit or stimulate aggressive behavior in human beings. Male hormone increases aggressiveness in adolescents with feelings of inferiority; stilbestrol provides striking control of irritable aggression. Concluding that the particular hormonal balance of frustration-induced irritability and aggression may sensitize certain brain areas, Drs. Douglas E. Smith, Melvyn B. King and Bartley G. Hoebel of the Department of Psychology at Princeton University set up an animal experiment to test the effects of carbachol. This drug mimics the action of acetylcholine, a brain chemical believed to play a role in transmission of nerve impulses. Twelve rats that normally never killed mice were injected with carbachol in a specific site on the lateral hypothalamus, a pea-sized area at the base of the brain that may be a center of emotion; subsequently, every rat killed mice placed in its cage. "Carbachol-induced killing had the appearance of natural killing. The kill was made with a bite through the cervical spinal cord and was not preceded by a series of incomplete or ineffective attacks. Thus, stimulation of the lateral hypothalamus with carbachol was sufficient to trigger the complete behavioral pattern involved in killing, even though these animals had never previously performed or witnessed this response." (*Science*, Feb. 6, 1970)

PHARMACOLOGICAL COOLERS

If peaceful animals become killers with synthetic acetylcholine, it might be possible to suppress killing in aggressive rats with an acetylcholine-blocking agent. Atropine methyl nitrate had exactly this effect when injected into the brains of rats who invariably killed mice less than two minutes after they were placed in the same cage. Killer rats given the drug approached, sniffed and sometimes followed the mice, but never attacked them. Drs. Smith, King, and Hoebel conclude that acetylcholine is most likely a neurohumor in an innate system of killing in rats and that similar systems may exist in other species. "This raises the practical possibility that pharmacological manipulation of such a system could be used in the treatment of pathological aggressive behavior."

In man, violence control resides in the limbic system, a marginal medial portion of the cerebral cortex, suggest Drs. Frank Ervin, Vernon H. Mark, and William H. Sweet of Massachusetts General Hospital. "Centuries of clinical observations have established the relationship between

psychomotor epilepsy originating in the temporal lobe, which contains several of the important limbic structures, and abnormal behavior, including violence," says Dr. Mark. "Many patients with tumors that impinge upon limbic structures have also been noted to show assaultive tendencies." (*Image*, Jan., 1970)

In two studies they have found indirect evidence implicating limbic system lesions as the cause of many cases of child abuse, assault, rape, manslaughter by reckless driving, and murder. The subjects of one study were convicted criminals; the subjects of the other, patients who came voluntarily to Massachusetts General because they were losing control of assaultive impulses (see Figure 1).

Eighty-four inmates from a medium-security penitentiary were given extensive medical and psychological tests for factors that might correlate with antisocial behavior. Fifty-three percent had normal electroencephalograms (EEGs) but rated high in antisocial traits on the Minnesota Multiphase Personality Inventory (MMPI); the 47 percent with abnormal EEGs averaged MMPI scores in the same low range as the general population. Some members of this group maintained that their acts seemed to result from something outside their basic

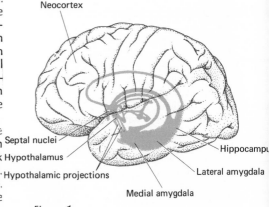

Figure 1.

personalities, a feeling shared by the 130 self-referred hospital patients. These people came to the emergency room with such complaints as "I'm afraid I'm going to break something," "I hurt people for no reason," "I want to kill my wife." Dr. Ervin, former Consultant to the National Commission on the Causes and Prevention of Violence, singled out four of their traits in combination as pathognomonic: a history of physical assault—eight had already killed—recurrent impulsive behavior, abnormal response to alcohol, and an extensive record of traffic violations and automobile accidents. Characteristically, minor incidents triggered violent responses; one man, for example, strangled a cat after a trifling argument with his wife. One-third of these patients had abnormal temporal lobe EEGs, a rate 50 times higher than the general population's, and neurological examination revealed that one-fourth had temporal lobe disease. Because diagnostic methods for detecting abnormalities deep in the brain are still relatively insensitive, Dr. Mark says that the asymptomatic two-thirds may also have neurological defects that contribute to their aggression. "Today's penologic and rehabilitative practices cannot possibly teach a person with such an organic impairment to control his destructive tendencies," Dr. Ervin concludes.

LIMBIC MODIFICATION

A wide range of earlier animal experiments have shown that attack behavior can be modified by manipulations of the limbic system. Bilateral surgical lesions in the amygdala tame the wildcat, the fierce Norway rat and other innately hostile animals, who can be handled without gloves immediately after operation. Affectionate domestic cats attack without provocation after bilateral destruction of the basal or central nucleus of the amygdala, ventromedial hypothalamus, septal region, frontal lobes, cingulum, and portions of the hippocampus, their responses well directed and

stimulus-oriented. Drs. Ervin, Mark, and Sweet have produced similar results in human patients by direct implantation of stereotactic electrodes deep in the brain that are left in place for a minimum of three weeks. Remote-control equipment permits monitoring and stimulation while the patient goes about his normal routine. "We not only detected abnormal electrical activity in limbic structures during spontaneous fits of rage and induced assaultive behavior by electric stimulation," says Dr. Mark, "but were able to turn off and prevent patients' outbursts by stimulating appropriate parts of the limbic system." The investigators found that opposite responses are elicited from different areas of the same limbic structure; temporary feelings of relaxation and relief were produced in one patient from electrode points four mm laterally above points that evoked pain and loss of control. Application of a radiofrequency current through both medial amygdalar electrodes produced therapeutic brain lesions and apparently permanent reduction of abnormal aggression.

CURRENT BEHAVIOR

Electrical stimulation of the brain (ESB), a technique pioneered largely by Yale's Dr. Delgado, offers revolutionary treatment of behavioral anomalies. In 1791, Galvani made frog muscles contract by direct electrical stimulation, proving that man can initiate and modify vital physiological processes. The first electrical stimulation of the brain, by Fritsch and Hitzig in 1870, produced body and limb movements in an anesthetized dog; well-ordered motor effects and emotional reactions were evoked in an unanesthetized cat by W. R. Hess in 1932. Dr. Delgado achieved ESB control of psychological phenomena in individual rats, cats and monkeys in 1954, evoking or inhibiting learning, conditioning, instrumental responses, pain, and pleasure. Since then, he has modified social behavior in whole colonies of animals and has influenced mental functions in human patients—including the thinking process, speech, and memory—developing the methods adopted by the Massachusetts General team.

Biological processes are related to ionic movement and electrical charges across the membranes that separate cells from the surrounding medium; cellular activity can be investigated by recording the electrical potentials appearing across the membranes or by detecting the differences in extracellular fluid potential. EEGs are normally taken by placing electrical leads, attached to recording equipment, on the scalp. If electrodes are placed in the depth of the brain, the accuracy of recordings increases, often locating the specific generator of activity. Simultaneous use of an external current establishes an external field through extracellular fluid, modifying the charge and permeability of cells and producing brain stimulation. Like the nervous system, ESB acts as a trigger for mechanisms established by evolution in the cellular structure.

TWO-WAY TRANSMISSION

The use of biologically inert materials insulated with Teflon allows electrodes to be left indefinitely inside the brain; some laboratory animals have been equipped with such apparatus for more than four years. With the development of stimoceivers, micro-miniaturized two-way radios for electrical messages to and from the brain, subjects can be completely unrestrained, and spontaneous activity is undisturbed. Anxiety, fear, suffering, hallucination, illusion, friendliness, and pleasure are among the experiences that have been examined through Dr. Delgado's physiotechnology; perhaps his most important findings concern violence. Stimulation of the lateral hypothalamus of a cat provoked aggressive displays toward subordinate animals in his group—and a careful avoidance of the most powerful feline. Monkey colonies are autocratic societies in which one animal establishes itself as boss of the group. A boss monkey stimulated in the thalamus or central gray area increased aggressiveness towards the other male who represented a challenge to his authority, but spared the little female who was his favorite partner. "Brain stimulation determined the affective state of hostility, but behavioral performance depended on the individual characteristics of the stimulated animal, including learned skills and previous experience," Dr. Delgado notes. (*Physical Control of the Mind*) In man, the expression of violence may also depend on the social setting. A human patient who appeared out of control through electrically induced aggression did not attack her doctor, indicating that she was still cognizant of his rank.

A LEVER OF FREEDOM

Dr. Delgado has also revolutionized a monkey colony by electrically controlling the violence of its boss monkey. Ali expressed his hostility symbolically by biting his own hand or threatening other group members, but radio stimulation of the caudate nucleus made him placid and easy-going. Elsa, a submissive female, discovered that a lever attached to the cage wall would stimulate Ali's caudate nucleus and pressed it whenever Ali threatened her. Although she never became the dominant animal, Elsa blocked many attacks against herself and maintained a peaceful coexistence in the colony, simultaneously achieving women's liberation and undermining a dictatorship.

Perhaps his most dramatic attempt to control natural animal violence occurred when Dr. Delgado stepped into a bull ring, directly in the path of a charging bull. Cerebral stimulation stopped the bull abruptly, and repeated stimulation produced lasting inhibition of aggressive behavior. Whether ESB can permanently alter human violence is uncertain, as is the desirability of such total control of behavior, but there is no longer doubt that physiology plays a role in violence.

higher
functions
chapter 8

The great challenge for physiological psychology lies in understanding the basis for such complex processes as communication or language in higher animals and humans. Very little is understood about sleep and dreaming. The selections in this chapter deal with recent work that has been done in attempting to understand the basis for language and concept formation. Of particular interest is the work of the Gardners with language in the chimpanzee; their research indicates that the chimpanzee might have the capacity to utilize sign language effectively in order to communicate thoughts between him and man.

The area of sleep research has been a very active one during the past 15 years. A number of advances have been made in this field. For example, it is known that there are specific electrical rhythms in the brain which signal the onset of dreaming. Through this we have learned that dreams last in reality as long as they seem to last to the dreamer, and that everyone dreams several times every night, but that only a small proportion of dreams are remembered. During dreaming both the mind and body of the individual are active; so is the electrical activity of the brain, but the person is in a state of relatively deep sleep. Even more interesting is the discovery that dreams are vital to one's mental and physical well-being and that dream deprivation leads to a greater need for dreaming. People deprived of dreams have been reported as unable to carry out organized conversations and unable to work effectively. These and other aspects of dreaming are dealt with in the last paper by Dement.

Language
name
and
concept
j. bronowski
and
ursula bellugi

The experiment of teaching a young chimpanzee to use American sign language (*1*) is an important advance on previous attempts to test the linguistic potential of primates. For the first time, a primate's capacity for a language used by some humans has been clearly separated from his capacity for making the sounds of human speech. In the nature of things, this pioneer study has been made under special conditions, and (like any single study) cannot be assumed to be perfectly representative. Nevertheless, it does offer evidence of a new kind, in the light of which it is timely to reexamine the relation between human language and the signals that animals use or can learn to use.

CHIMPANZEE AND CHILD

It has never been in doubt since the time of Aristotle that language is a characteristically human accomplishment, and that some of the capacities which it demands are either absent in other animals or are present only in the most rudimentary form. Among these is the fundamental capacity to make and interpret the intricately modulated continuum of speech sounds. Lieberman et al. (*2*) have stressed the differences between the articulatory apparatus of the chimpanzee and that of man. Thus the Gardners' decision to bypass the articulatory problems of the chimpanzee and undertake instead to teach a gesture language was a good one. They reasoned that the use of the hands is a prominent feature

From *Science,* **168**, 669–673, 8 May, 1970. Copyright 1970 by the American Association for the Advancement of Science.

in the behavior of chimpanzees, who have a rich repertoire of gestures both in the wild and in captivity. By contrast, the futile efforts to teach the chimpanzee Viki to talk (*3*) had already shown that a vocal language is not appropriate for this species. In six years of intensive training, Viki had learned to make only four sounds that grossly approximated English words. The results of the Gardners' efforts with Washoe are spectacular by comparison. By the time Washoe was about four years old she had been taught to make reliably more than 80 different signs. This comparative success therefore poses a question of substance: what is the true nature of the language performance that has been achieved by a chimpanzee (under these special conditions of training and environment) and how does it differ from that of humans?

We first describe some of the characteristics of the gesture language which Washoe was taught. The Gardners had learned sign language from dictionaries and from a teacher of sign, expressly for their experiment. They used gestures and manual configurations to represent the concepts in sign language and avoided the use of finger spelling as much as possible. All signs are arbitrary to some degree (although some have iconic origins and aspects), and American sign language has many highly arbitrary and conventionalized signs which must be learned. With the addition of finger spelling, it can be used by a literate signer as a direct translation of English in order to communicate with hearing signers; but it generally is not so used among the deaf themselves, whose rules of use may vary in different areas and may not necessarily derive from English. However, the Gardners state that, as far as they can judge, there is no message which cannot be rendered faithfully in translating from English to sign (apart from the usual problems of translating from one language into another). They also report that they tried to follow the word order of English in their signed sequences.

It might be held that ideally Washoe's progress should be compared with that of a deaf child of deaf parents who is learning sign as a native language. We cannot yet do this and so must be content to compare Washoe to children learning spoken language. There are grounds for arguing that the Gardners' method of signing makes this an appropriate comparison.

THE CHIMPANZEES' SIGNS AS NAMES

Studies of chimpanzees in their natural environment have indicated that their own communication systems are employed largely to signal motivational and emotional states of the individual. There are few if any calls given by non-human primates that convey information about their physical environment. More generally, in communicating among themselves, humans separate the components of their environment and use a great variety of names for them, and animals do not. It has therefore been argued, for example by Washburn (4) and by Lancaster (5), that the capacity for language in humans is based on a specific ability to give names to things which is absent in other primates. To quote Lancaster:

An understanding of the emergence of human language rests upon a comprehension of the factors that led to the evolution of a system of names. The ability to use names allows man to refer to the environment and to communicate information about his environment as opposed to the ability to express only his own motivational state. Object-naming is the simplest form of environmental reference. It is an ability that is unique to man.

We now see from the experiment with Washoe, however, that there is convincing evidence that a chimpanzee can be taught to use names for things. Her use of the names she has learned is not more narrow and context-bound than that of a human child. The Gardners report that in general, when introducing new signs, they have used specific referents for the initial training, and that Washoe herself then used signs in ways which extended far beyond the original training. For example, Washoe first learned the sign for *open* with a particular door. This sign she then transferred to *open* for all closed doors, then to closed containers such as the refrigerator, cupboards, drawers, briefcases, boxes, and jars. Eventually, Washoe spontaneously used it to request opening of the water faucet and of a capped bottle of soda pop. Washoe has learned distinct signs for *cat* and *dog* (primarily with pictures of each) and appropriately uses the signs while looking through magazines or books, as well as for real cats and dogs. She also used the sign for *dog* when she heard an unseen dog barking in the distance, and when someone drew a caricature of a dog for her.

There are errors in her spontaneous signing which resemble the overextensions in children's early use of words. Washoe has a sign for *hurt* which she learned first with scratches or bruises. Later she used the sign also for red stains, for a decal on the back of a person's hand, and when she saw a person's navel for the first time. Washoe used the sign for *listen* when an alarm clock rang to signal supper preparation, and then for other bells, and for watches. Washoe also signed *listen* when she found a broken watchband, and when she saw a flashlight that blinks on and off. This is characteristic of the range and extensions of words used by children in the process of first learning a language. There seems little doubt therefore that Washoe (and presumably other chimpanzees) can be taught to name in a way which strongly resembles the child's early learning of words.

We must conclude that the prolonged experiment with Washoe proves that the ability to name is not biologically confined to humans. Hence serious doubt is thrown on any theory of human language which seeks to explain its uniqueness or its origin in a human ability to name.

A CHARACTERIZATION OF LANGUAGE

A searching examination needs to step back instead from the mechanics of human language, and to ask rather what are the global features that characterize it, and differentiate it from the sharp and immediate messages that are evoked in animals either by their internal state or by their environment. One such characterization is behavioral—human utterances are more detached or disengaged from the stimuli that provoke them than those of animals—and this is a general feature of human behavior. Another characterization is logical—human languages relies on an analysis of the environment into parts which are assembled differently in different sentences. (By contrast, the signals of animals are complete utterances, which are not taken apart and assembled anew to make new messages.) Both the behavioral and the logical component must play a part in any treatment which seeks to relate the way humans shape their utterances to the way that the human brain operates in general.

One of us has formulated such a treatment (6) in terms which make it possible to see by what steps language might have developed during human evolution. Some of the steps in this sequence are:

1) a delay between the arrival of the stimulus and the utterance of the message that it has provoked or between the receipt of the incoming signal and the sending out of a signal;

2) the separation of affect or emotional charge from the content of instruction which a message carries;

3) the prolongation of reference, namely, the ability to refer backward and forward in time and to exchange messages which propose action in the future;

4) the internalization of language, so that it ceases to be only a means of social communication and becomes also an instrument of reflection and exploration with which the speaker constructs hypothetical messages before he chooses one to utter; and

5) the structural activity of reconstitution, which consists of two linked procedures—namely, a procedure of analysis, by which messages are not treated as inviolate wholes but are broken down into smaller parts, and a procedure of synthesis by which the parts are rearranged to form other messages.

The steps 1 to 4 express the behavioral ability of humans to disengage from the immediate context; without this, it would not be possible to make predicative statements; that is, to give information about the environment in a form which does not imply an instruction to act. Step 5 expresses the logical ability of humans to influence their environment by understanding it; that is, by analyzing it into parts and then making new combinations from the parts.

In this evolutionary characterization of language, the primates can be seen to share in a rudimentary form some of the necessary faculties of the human brain, for example, the delayed response. This may be the case in some small degree also for the separation of affect, the prolongation of reference and even the internalization of language. In these respects we can perhaps find examples in Washoe's use of sign language which resemble some of the earliest stages of a child's language. But the child rapidly passes beyond these precursors into the characteristically human use of language, and outstrips the chimpanzee completely. The crucial activity which the child reaches is reconstitution of the language. Human language is highly structured, and, as they grow from age about one and a half to four years, children analyze the structure of language in several distinct ways and reconstruct this structure in their own speech. In this ability the nonhuman primates are quite deficient. We have evidence for this defect, for example, in the study by Zhinkin (7) of the communication system of baboons, and it appears clearly again in the way in which Washoe forms combinations of signs.

We shall compare Washoe's development with that of a child's learning language in terms of the characterizations made above. Since the growth rate of chimpanzees is faster than that of humans, it seems reasonable to compare her development with that of children of the same age. These and other details have been discussed (8).

DISENGAGEMENT FROM CONTEXT

We make the comparison between Washoe and a human child in two parts. One is concerned with the behavioral steps 1 to 4 in which Washoe and the child appear similar at the inception of language, although within a few months the chimpanzee is left far behind. The other is the logical step 5, the reconstitution of language, in which we believe the human capacity is unique.

1) Delay between stimulus and utterance

The evidence for this will be found throughout the following sections, and no special discussion of it is required. There is a wealth of research which connects the increase in the delayed response of primates with the development of the frontal lobes of the brain (9).

2) Separation of affect from content

The child's learning of language naturally begins in situations heavily loaded with affect. Children's early sentence-words frequently have the force of command or instruction stemming from their immediate desires, discomforts, plea-

sures (*come here, give candy*). Washoe's signs are also primarily concerned with immediate situation, her desires, and her emotional states (*hurry open, gimme drink*). Yet there are some indications of a primitive ability on Washoe's part to separate affect from content of signs; for example, her spontaneous naming of objects around her when there is no indication that this involves the desire for the object or an instruction to someone else.

However, there is a great difference in this regard between the signs produced by Washoe and the sentences of a three-year-old child. By this age or before, the child is able to make cognitive statements, including those which he may not have heard before. He is able to understand and interpret correctly cognitive sentences without emotional charge. He has mastered the difference between "I want that" and "She fed him," and can separate out the immediate pleasures and emotional components of words from their objective meanings in sentences. There is by now good evidence with children of only two years which attests to the ability to understand cognitive statements, including novel ones (10).

3) Prolongation of reference

Children's early one- and two-word sentences (like Washoe's signing) are based almost entirely on the immediately perceptible context. They are often uninterpretable as messages without reference to the situation as context. They are primarily in the present, about objects, persons, or events which are in the here and now. However, they do include rudimentary references to situations in the immediate past (*all gone juice*) or demands for something not present (*more cookie*). In this respect, the chimpanzee and young child are not far different. Washoe, for example, signed *listen* when an alarm clock stopped ringing and signed *more food* when there was no food in sight.

At three years old the child comes to

present a markedly more advanced picture. He does far more than "name" objects and events not immediately present, as Washoe does. He makes statements which are predicational and cognitive and may refer to events in the more distant past, which have a future sense or intent but are not just demands for action and which involve pretense or possibility. These have been documented for a group of children (11).

4) Internalization

There are few indications that gesture language is used as an instrument of reflection by Washoe. She has been seen to name objects while looking through a picture book, and occasionally corrects the signs she makes. Washoe has been observed on several occasions signing spontaneously to herself, in front of a mirror, or in bed at nap time. The Gardners have described these signs as idle chatter.

Weir (12) collected tape-recorded samples of her two and one-half-year old son alone in his room and found that the child clearly uses language as an instrument of exploration. His monologues show a great deal of syntactic play, arrangements and rearrangements, transformations of sentence types, substitution of words in fixed sentence frames, and so forth. It is not just idle chatter, although it has no social function, no content to instruct someone else, and consists in large part of explorations of structure. It is in fact the extreme form of that "distancing" from any immediate context which characterizes behavioral modes 1 to 4.

THE CHILD'S SENTENCES

In turning now to the last of the five characterizations of human language, reconstitution, we face a process which is different in kind from the preceding four. In its full meaning it implies an analysis of the sentences the child hears (and indeed of the environments in which the child experiences their meanings) as a condition for the child's formation of his own sentences. In the first place, however, we shall confine ourselves to the child's construction of sentences in a meaningful way from primitive signs or names which are already known. Then later we shall ask how the child (and the human mind in general) is able to extract signs or names from their context—is able, in fact, to form concepts by an inner analysis of cognitive sentences.

The most subtle yet crucial way in which Washoe's performance falls short of that of a hearing child is in the failure so far to develop any form of sentence structure. The Gardners report that they did not make deliberate attempts to elicit combinations, but almost as soon as Washoe had eight or 10 signs in her repertoire, she began to use them in combinations. It is common for her to sign in combinations now, and by June 1968, the Gardners had recorded 330 different strings of two or more signs. A number of these combinations may be spontaneous and original with Washoe; that is, it is unlikely that they are direct imitations of sentences which she has observed. We may compare her combinations of signs with the sequences of words produced by a child of three. The comparison makes clear both the limitations of the chimpanzee's utterances and the nature of the capacity and the steps by which a child learns his first language.

1) The child of three already gives evidence that he has a concept of a sentence, which includes an understanding of grammatical relations (such as subject of a sentence, predicate of a sentence, object of a verb). These are not only clearly understood but are well marked in the child's own speech. McNeill (13) suggests that these relations are present before the first combinations of words into utterances in children's speech, and he considers them as a part of children's linguistic predispositions. Our evidence

indicates that a child of three years expresses the basic sentence relations with great precision in English (where these are often signaled by word order in simple sentences) (14).

The Gardners in their diary studies report that, for many combinations, all orders of signs have been observed. Various orderings seem to be used indiscriminately by Washoe and do not differentiate the basic grammatical relations. The signs for *me, you,* and *tickle,* for example, have occurred in all possible orders in Washoe's signed sequences. These different orders do not seem to refer to different situations in any systematic way. For the same situation (requesting someone to tickle her), Washoe signed *you tickle* and *tickle you.* Washoe signed *me tickle* for someone tickling her and again *me tickle* to indicate that she would tickle someone. Washoe's spontaneous signed combinations seem so far rather like unordered sequences of names for various aspects of a situation.

2) Children of about three years seem to have well-developed means for expressing the full range of basic sentence types. They not only make demands and commands, they also negate propositions and ask innumerable questions. Children seem to have rudimentary ways of asking questions and of negating from the early stages of language development. What develops, along with more complex meanings, are the grammatical rules for expressing those meanings (15).

The Gardners in the past year have concentrated on the question-answer process with Washoe. They write (1), "We wanted Washoe not only to ask for objects but to answer questions about them and also to ask us questions." They have taught Washoe to respond to questions of several types (for example, *What you want? Who that? Where Susan?*) and in the process Washoe has seen many models. Despite the ample opportunity to learn about questions (and certainly some opportunity to learn negative sentences as well), there is no evidence in the diary summaries that Washoe either asks such questions or negates.

3) The child of three organizes his vocabulary into categories and subcategories which resemble in some respects the categories of the adult language. These are combined into sentences not as unordered naming but according to grammatical principles, which include hierarchical organization of the parts of a sentence (16).

We find in general that the child forms or extracts rules from the sentences he hears, and resystematizes them in his own speech. The child is not taught and does not need to be taught specifically the underlying rules of grammatical structure, yet careful study of his development shows that he gradually reconstructs the system for himself (often not precisely the same system as in the adult language, but by stages approaching the complexity of the adult system). Children seem to develop rules of maximum generality, often applying them at first in more instances than required, and only gradually learning the proper domain for their application. For example, three- and four-year-old children say things like *He comed yesterday, It breaked, I falled; two mans, my foots, many sheeps.* It is clear that these are not phrases that children have heard; they have generalized the past tense and plural forms from regularities like *walked* and *cats.* Children do not need to be taught the rules of grammatical structure because they discover them for themselves, just as they discover and do not need to be taught the rules of correspondence for recognizing the same object under different conditions of light and position. We see that small children whose cognitive powers are limited in many respects show a remarkable ability to reconstruct the language they hear, just as they reconstruct (give structure to) their experience of their physical environment; the process and the capacity are not specifically linguistic, but are expressions of a general human ability to construct general rules by induction. What is involved is not just the capacity to learn names as they are specifically taught by the humans around the child in the early stages. Far more basic and important is the child's ability to analyze out regularities in the language, to segment novel utterances into component parts as they relate to the world, and to understand these parts again in new combinations. It is this total activity, analysis and synthesis together, which is described in the term reconstitution. We conclude by considering this in more philosophical terms.

LANGUAGE AND CONCEPT

It has been proposed (6) that the human practice of naming parts of the environment presupposes and rests on a more fundamental activity, namely, that of analyzing the environment into distinct parts and treating these as separate objects. That is, there is implied in the structure of cognitive sentences a view of the outside world as separable into things which maintain their identity and which can be manipulated in the mind, so that even actions and properties are reified in words. In this philosophical sense, predication is not merely putting together words in syntactical patterns, nor even the manipulation in the mind of ready-made objects and categories. Rather, predication is in the first place a way of analyzing the environment into parts, and only after that can they be regrouped in new arrangements and new sentences.

Thus a child may first learn the word for chair with one particular chair, and may extend it at first to all pieces of furniture without being specifically taught to do so. Through his analysis of sentences about chairs in his parents' speech and his experiences with these sentences ("Please sit in this chair, Mrs. Jones," "John, move your chair around") the child may gradually narrow his use to the range of objects that we might also describe as chairs. It is important to note that there is no way to give a definition of chair in terms of size, dimensions, color, material, or other aspects of physical measurements. To recognize another object we have not seen before as a chair, we must ignore many aspects of the differences between chairs, and attend to criteria which include something like the following: a movable seat that is designed to accommodate one person, and usually has four legs and a back. Notice that a chair is a man-made object designed for a specific function or action, and that this is part of its implicit definition. Learning the word for objects like chair is considered to be one of the simplest problems of language learning. Yet for the child to understand his parents' sentence "The chair broke," he must first analyze out the state of being of the chair at the time of the utterance, and then interpret the meaning of the word broke (perhaps violently separated into parts, no longer functioning) from this. He can construct the sentence "The toy broke" for himself only after having analyzed out the relevant aspects of the environment in the parts of the sentence above. The new predication can result only after the definitive attributes of break and chair have been taken apart as independent units, and the activity of predication presupposes this kind of analysis.

What we have been describing in the child is a general characterization of the relation of human thought to the environment. For humans, the environment consists of objects, properties and actions, and we are tempted to assume that these exist ready-made in the outside world, and present themselves simply and directly to the senses. But this is a naive simplification of the complex of interlocking processes by which we are persuaded of the existence and the persistence even of so unitary a natural object as a tree or a bird. Most of what we regard as objects in our environment, however, are far more so-phisticated concepts than these. Thus the logic by which a child unravels the sentences he hears and his experience of the environment together is much more than a capacity for language and expresses in miniature a deeper human capacity for analyzing and manipulat-ing the environment in the mind by subdividing it into units that persist when they are moved from one mental context into another.

What language expresses specifically in this scheme is the reification by the human mind of its experience, that is, an analysis into parts (including actions and properties) which, as concepts can be manipulated as if they were objects. The meaning that these concepts have de-rives from their construction (as parts of reality) and cannot be displayed by a direct appeal to the senses, singly or in combination. Very few concepts derive directly from the senses, as the word *cold* does; the great majority are at least as indirect and intellectual as the word *two*. They are constructions of the mind from a variety of contexts, and in making them, the mind acts exactly as the child does who learns to give meaning to a word by analyzing the variety of sen-tences in which he hears it. Concepts are artifacts extracted by reification from the contexts or sentences in which they occur. Some of them, like *two*, can be taught to animals, but they remain arti-facts of the human mind. We may even speculate that the human mind began to reify objects by their function when man began to make tools as functional arti-facts for future use.

If the reification of the environment serves to manipulate its parts in the mind, then the laws which distinguish admissible from inadmissible rearrange-ments round out and complete the same mental process as a necessary part—as the addition *one* and *one* belongs to the concept *two*. That is, we cannot sep-arate the naming of concepts (objects, actions, and properties) from the rules which govern their permissible arrange-ments—the two form an interlocking whole. Looking for these rules is in es-sence the search for structural relations in the environment which characterizes the human mind and is the same as the procedure of generalization which in science is called inductive inference (in the widest, nonpartisan sense). For humans, the division of the environment into parts only has meaning if they obey rules of structure, so that permissible arrangements can be distinguished from arrangements which are not permissible. So in human language, words and gram-matical structure form an interlocking whole, from which nonsense words and ill-formed sentences are equally ex-cluded. The match between a sentence and the reality that it maps strikes us now, when we know the language, as made by putting the sentence together; but it begins in the first place, in the begin-ning of language, by taking reality apart. And it is taken apart into words and grammatical rules together (concepts and structural laws)—just as we create a scientific theory of, say, the atomic structure of the physical world by infer-ring the existence of the elementary particles and the laws of their combi-nation at the same time.

In short, we must not think of sen-tences as assembled from words which have an independent existence already, separate from any kind of sentence. This puts the matter in linguistic terms; in more philosophical terms, we must not think of the external world as already existing in our consciousness as a pre-viously analyzed assembly of conceptual units, such as things, actions, and quali-ties. The experience of learning about the world consists of an inner analysis and subsequent synthesis. In this way, human language expresses a specifically human way of analyzing our experience of the external world. This analysis is as much a part of learning language as is the more obvious synthesis of sentences from a vocabulary of words. In short, language expresses not a specific linguistic faculty but a constellation of general faculties of the human mind.

When we watch the way a child learns to speak from his point of view, we become aware of his mental activity in finding for himself inductive rules of usage which constitute both a grammar of language and a philosophy of the structure of reality. The child does not "recapitulate" the evolution of language, of course; instead, he demonstrates the logic which binds the development of language to the evolution of the human faculties as a whole. What the example of Washoe shows in a profound way is that it is the process of total reconstitution which is the evolutionary hallmark of the human mind, and for which so far we have no evidence in the mind of the non-human primate, even when he is given the vocabulary ready-made.

References and notes

1. Gardner, A. R., and Gardner, B. T. *Science*, 1969, **165**, 664. The Gardners obtained an infant chimpanzee from the wild when she was about one year old and began their project in June 1966. The above-mentioned paper describes the first 22 months of the project. The first six diary summaries (unpublished) contain full reports of all new signs and new combinations of signs observed until Washoe was about three years old. This article is based primarily on these materials, and we thank the Gardners for supplying them. The interpretations we have made are our own.

2. Lieberman, P. H., Klatt, D. H., and Wilson, W. H. *Science*, 1969, **164**, 1185.

3. Hayes, C. *The ape in our house.* New York: Harper & Row, 1951.

4. Washburn, S. L. *The study of human evolution.* Eugene: Univ. of Oregon Press, 1968.

5. Lancaster, J. B. In P. C. Jay, (Ed.), *Primates.* New York: Holt, Rinehart and Winston, 1968. Pp. 439–457.

6. Bronowski, J. In *To honor Roman Jakobson, I.* The Hague: Mouton, 1967. Pp. 374–394.

7. Zhinkin, N. I. In R.-G. Busnel (Ed.), *Acoustic behavior of animals.* Amsterdam: Elseiver, 1963. Pp. 132–180.

8. Bronowski, J., and Bellugi, U. In T. G. Bever and W. Weksel (Eds.), *The structure and psychology of language, II.* New York: Holt, Rinehart and Winston. In press.

9. Warren, J. M., and Akert, K. (Eds.), *The frontal granular cortex and behavior.* New York: McGraw-Hill, 1964.

10. Bever, T. G., Mehler, J., and Vaiian, V. In T. G. Bever and W. Weksel, (Eds.), *The structure and psychology of language, II.* New York: Holt, Rinehart and Winston. In Press.

11. Cromer, R. F. Thesis. Harvard University, 1968.

12. Weir, R. H. *Language in the crib.* The Hague: Mouton, 1962.

13. McNeill, D. *Explaining linguistic universals,* paper presented at the 19th International Congress of Psychologists in London, 1969.

14. Brown, R., Cazden, C., and Bellugi, U. In J. P. Hill (Ed.), *Minnesota Symposia on Child Psychology.* Minneapolis: Univ. of Minnesota Press, 1969. Pp. 28–73.

15. Bellugi, U. *How children say no.* Cambridge, Mass.: MIT Press. In press.

16. Brown, R., and Bellugi, U. In E. H. Lenneberg, (Ed.), *New directions in the study of language.* Cambridge, Mass.: MIT Press, 1964, Pp. 131–161.

Teaching sign language to a chimpanzee
r. allen gardner
and
beatrice t. gardner

The extent to which another species might be able to use human language is a classical problem in comparative psychology. One approach to this problem is to consider the nature of language, the processes of learning, the neural mechanisms of learning and of language, and the genetic basis of these mechanisms, and then, while recognizing certain gaps in what is known about these factors, to attempt to arrive at an answer by dint of careful scholarship (1). An alternative approach is to try to teach a form of human language to an animal. We chose the latter alternative and, in June 1966, began training an infant female chimpanzee, named Washoe, to use the gestural language of the deaf. Within the first 22 months of training it became evident that we had been correct in at least one major aspect of method, the use of a gestural language. Additional aspects of method have evolved in the course of the project. These and some implications of our early results can now be described in a way that may be useful in other studies of communicative behavior. Accordingly, in this article we discuss the considerations which led us to use the chimpanzee as a subject and American Sign Language (the language used by the deaf in North America) as a medium of communication; describe the general methods of training as they were initially conceived and as they developed in the course of the project; and summarize those results that could be reported with some degree

of confidence by the end of the first phase of the project.

PRELIMINARY CONSIDERATIONS

The chimpanzee as a subject

Some discussion of the chimpanzee as an experimental subject is in order because this species is relatively uncommon in the psychological laboratory. Whether or not the chimpanzee is the most intelligent animal after man can be disputed; the gorilla, the orangutan, and even the dolphin have their loyal partisans in this debate. Nevertheless, it is generally conceded that chimpanzees are highly intelligent, and that members of this species might be intelligent enough for our purposes. Of equal or greater importance is their sociability and their capacity for forming strong attachments to human beings. We want to emphasize this trait of sociability; it seems highly likely that it is essential for the development of language in human beings, and it was a primary consideration in our choice of a chimpanzee as a subject.

Affectionate as chimpanzees are, they are still wild animals, and this is a serious disadvantage. Most psychologists are accustomed to working with animals that have been chosen, and sometimes bred, for docility and adaptability to laboratory procedures. The difficulties presented by the wild nature of an experimental animal must not be underestimated. Chimpanzees are also very strong animals; a full-grown specimen is likely to weigh more than 120 pounds (55 kilograms) and is estimated to be from three to five times as strong as a man, pound-for-pound. Coupled with the

From *Science*, **165** (3894), 664–672, 15 August 1969. Copyright 1969 by the American Association for the Advancement of Science.

wildness, this great strength presents serious difficulties for a procedure that requires interaction at close quarters with a free-living animal. We have always had to reckon with the likelihood that at some point Washoe's physical maturity will make this procedure prohibitively dangerous.

A more serious disadvantage is that human speech sounds are unsuitable as a medium of communication for the chimpanzee. The vocal apparatus of the chimpanzee is very different from that of man (2). More important, the vocal behavior of the chimpanzee is very different from that of man. Chimpanzees do make many different sounds, but generally vocalization occurs in situations of high excitement and tends to be specific to the exciting situations. Undisturbed, chimpanzees are usually silent. Thus, it is unlikely that a chimpanzee could be trained to make refined use of its vocalizations. Moreover, the intensive work of Hayes and Hayes (3) with the chimpanzee Viki indicates that a vocal language is not appropriate for this species. The Hayeses used modern, sophisticated, psychological methods and seem to have spared no effort to teach Viki to make speech sounds. Yet in six years Viki learned only four sounds that approximated English words (4).

Use of the hands, however, is a prominent feature of chimpanzee behavior, manipulatory mechanical problems are their forte. More to the point, even caged, laboratory chimpanzees develop begging and similar gestures spontaneously (5), while individuals that have had extensive contact with human beings have displayed an even wider variety of communicative gestures (6). In our choice of sign language we were influenced more by the behavioral evidence that this medium of communication was appropriate to the species than by anatomical evidence of structural similarity between the hands of chimpanzees and of men. The Hayeses point out that human tools and mechanical devices are constructed to fit the human hand, yet chimpanzees have little difficulty in using these devices with great skill. Nevertheless, they seem unable to adapt their vocalizations to approximate human speech.

Psychologists who work extensively with the instrumental conditioning of animals become sensitive to the need to use responses that are suited to the species they wish to study. Leverpressing in rats is not an arbitrary response invented by Skinner to confound the mentalists; it is a type of response commonly made by rats when they are first placed in a Skinner box. The exquisite control of instrumental behavior by schedules of reward is achieved only if the original responses are well chosen. We chose a language based on gestures because we reasoned that gestures for the chimpanzee should be analogous to bar-pressing for rats, key-pecking for pigeons, and babbling for humans.

American sign language

Two systems of manual communication are used by the deaf. One system is the manual alphabet, or finger spelling, in which configurations of the hand correspond to letters of the alphabet. In this system the words of a spoken language, such as English, can be spelled out manually. The other system, sign language, consists of a set of manual configurations and gestures that correspond to particular words or concepts. Unlike finger spelling, which is the direct encoding of a spoken language, sign languages have their own rules of usage. Word-for-sign translation between a spoken language and a sign language yields results that are similar to those of word-for-word translation between two spoken languages: the translation is often passable, though awkward, but it can also be ambiguous or quite nonsensical. Also, there are national and regional variations in sign languages that are comparable to those of spoken languages.

We chose for this project the American Sign Language (ASL), which, with certain regional variations, is used by the deaf in North America. This particular sign language has recently been the subject of formal analysis (7). The ASL can be compared to pictograph writing in which some symbols are quite arbitrary and some are quite representational or iconic, but all are arbitrary to some degree. For example, in ASL the sign for "always" is made by holding the hand in a fist, index finger extended (the pointing hand), while rotating the arm at the elbow. This is clearly an arbitrary representation of the concept "always." The sign for "flower," however, is highly iconic; it is made by holding the fingers of one hand extended, all five fingertips touching (the tapered hand), and touching the fingertips first to one nostril then to the other, as if sniffing a flower. While this is an iconic sign for "flower," it is only one of a number of conventions by which the concept "flower" could be iconically represented; it is thus arbitrary to some degree. Undoubtedly, many of the signs of ASL that seem quite arbitrary today once had an iconic origin that was lost through years of stylized usage. Thus, the signs of ASL are neither uniformly arbitrary nor uniformly iconic; rather the degree of abstraction varies from sign to sign over a wide range. This would seem to be a useful property of ASL for our research.

The literate deaf typically use a combination of ASL and finger spelling; for purposes of this project we have avoided the use of finger spelling as much as possible. A great range or expression is possible within the limits of ASL. We soon found that a good way to practice signing among ourselves was to render familiar songs and poetry into signs; as far as we can judge, there is no message that cannot be rendered faithfully (apart from the usual problems of translation from one language to another). Technical terms and proper names are a problem when first in-troduced, but within any community of signers it is easy to agree on a convention for any commonly used term. For example, among ourselves we do not finger-spell the words *psychologist* and *psychology*, but render them as "think doctor" and "think science." Or, among users of ASL, "California" can be finger-spelled but is commonly rendered as "golden playland." (Incidentally, the sign for "gold" is made by plucking at the earlobe with thumb and forefinger, indicating an earring—another example of an iconic sign that is at the same time arbitrary and stylized.)

The fact that ASL is in current use by human beings is an additional advantage. The early linguistic environment of the deaf children of deaf parents is in some respects similar to the linguistic environment that we could provide for an experimental subject. This should permit some comparative evaluation of Washoe's eventual level of competence. For example, in discussing Washoe's early performance with deaf parents we have been told that many of her variants of standard signs are similar to the baby-talk variants commonly observed when human children sign.

Washoe

Having decided on a species and a medium of communication, our next concern was to obtain an experimental subject. It is altogether possible that there is some critical early age for the acquisition of this type of behavior. On the other hand, newborn chimpanzees tend to be quite helpless and vegetative. They are also considerably less hardy than older infants. Nevertheless, we reasoned that the dangers of starting too late were much greater than the dangers of starting too early, and we sought the youngest infant we could get. Newborn laboratory chimpanzees are very scarce, and we found that the youngest laboratory infant we could get would be about two years old at the time we planned to start the project. It seemed preferable to obtain a wild-caught infant. Wild-caught infants are usually at least eight to 10 months old before they are available for research. This is because infants rarely reach the United States before they are five months old, and to this age must be added one or two months before final purchase and two or three months for quarantine and other medical services.

We named our chimpanzee Washoe for Washoe County, the home of the University of Nevada. Her exact age will never be known, but from her weight and dentition we estimated her age to be between eight and 14 months at the end of June 1966, when she first arrived at our laboratory. (Her dentition has continued to agree with this initial estimate, but her weight has increased rather more than would be expected.) This is very young for a chimpanzee. The best available information indicates that infants are completely dependent until the age of two years and semi-dependent until the age of four; the first signs of sexual maturity (for example, menstruation, sexual swelling) begin to appear at about eight years, and full adult growth is reached between the ages of 12 and 16 (8). As for the complete life-span, captive specimens have survived for well over 40 years. Washoe was indeed very young when she arrived; she did not have her first canines or molars, her hand-eye coordination was rudimentary, she had only begun to crawl about, and she slept a great deal. Apart from making friends with her and adapting her to the daily routine, we could accomplish little during the first few months.

Laboratory conditions

At the outset we were quite sure that Washoe could learn to make various signs in order to obtain food, drink, and other things. For the project to be a success, we felt that something more must be developed. We wanted Washoe not only to ask for objects but to answer questions about them and also to ask us questions. We wanted to develop behavior that could be described as conversation. With this in mind, we attempted to provide Washoe with an environment that might be conducive to this sort of behavior. Confinement was to be minimal, about the same as that of human infants. Her human companions were to be friends and playmates as well as providers and protectors, and they were to introduce a great many games and activities that would be likely to result in maximum interaction with Washoe.

In practice, such an environment is readily achieved with a chimpanzee; bonds of warm affection have always been established between Washoe and her several human companions. We have enjoyed the interaction almost as much as Washoe has, within the limits of human endurance. A number of human companions have been enlisted to participate in the project and relieve each other at intervals, so that at least one person would be with Washoe during all her waking hours. At first we feared that such frequent changes would be disturbing, but Washoe seemed to adapt very well to this procedure. Apparently it is possible to provide an infant chimpanzee with affection on a shift basis.

All of Washoe's human companions have been required to master ASL and to use it extensively in her presence, in association with interesting activities and events and also in a general way, as one chatters at a human infant in the course of the day. The ASL has been used almost exclusively, although occasional finger spelling has been permitted. From time to time, of course, there are lapses into spoken English, as when medical personnel must examine Washoe. At one time, we considered an alternative procedure in which we would sign and speak English to Washoe simultaneously, thus giving her an additional source of informative cues. We rejected this procedure, reasoning that, if she should come to understand speech sooner or more easily than ASL, then she might not pay sufficient attention to our gestures. Another alternative, that of speaking English among ourselves and signing to Washoe, was also rejected. We reasoned that this would make it seem that big chimps talk and only little chimps sign, which might give signing an undesirable social status.

The environment we are describing is not a silent one. The human beings can vocalize in many ways, laughing and making sounds of pleasure and displeasure. Whistles and drums are sounded in a variety of imitation games, and hands are clapped for attention. The rule is that all meaningful sounds, whether vocalized or not, must be sounds that a chimpanzee can imitate.

TRAINING METHODS

Imitation

The imitativeness of apes is proverbial, and rightly so. Those who have worked closely with chimpanzees have frequently remarked on their readiness to engage in visually guided imitation. Consider the following typical comment of Yerkes (9):

Chim and Panzee would imitate many of my acts, but never have I heard them imitate a sound and rarely make a sound peculiarly their own in response to mine. As previously stated, their imitative tendency is as remarkable for its specialization and limitations as for its strength. It seems to be controlled chiefly by visual stimuli. Things which are seen tend to be imitated or reproduced. What is heard is not reproduced. Obviously an animal which lacks the tendency to reinstate auditory stimuli—in other words to imitate sounds—cannot reasonably be expected to talk. The human infant exhibits this tendency to a remarkable degree. So also does

the parrot. If the imitative tendency of the parrot could be coupled with the quality of intelligence of the chimpanzee, the latter undoubtedly could speak.

In the course of their work with Viki, the Hayeses devised a game in which Viki would imitate various actions on hearing the command "Do this" (10). Once established, this was an effective means of training Viki to perform actions that could be visually guided. The same method should be admirably suited to training a chimpanzee to use sign language; accordingly we have directed much effort toward establishing a version of the "Do this" game with Washoe. Getting Washoe to imitate us was not difficult, for she did so quite spontaneously, but getting her to imitate on command has been another matter altogether. It was not until the 16th month of the project that we achieved any degree of control over Washoe's imitation of gestures. Eventually we got to a point where she would imitate a simple gesture, such as pulling at her ears, or a series of such gestures—first we make a gesture, then she imitates, then we make a second gesture, she imitates the second gesture, and so on—for the reward of being tickled. Up to this writing, however, imitation of this sort has not been an important method for introducing new signs into Washoe's vocabulary.

As a method of prompting, we have been able to use imitation extensively to increase the frequency and refine the form of signs. Washoe sometimes fails to use a new sign in an appropriate situation, or uses another, incorrect sign. At such times we can make the correct sign to Washoe, repeating the performance until she makes the sign herself. (With more stable signs, more indirect forms of prompting can be used —for example, pointing at, or touching, Washoe's hand or a part of her body that should be involved in the sign; making the sign for "sign," which is equivalent to saying "Speak up"; or asking a question in signs such as "What do you want?" or "What is it?") again, with new signs, and often with old signs as well, Washoe can lapse into what we refer to as poor "diction." Of course, a great deal of slurring and a wide range of variants are permitted in ASL as in any spoken language. In any event, Washoe's diction has frequently been improved by the simple device of repeating, in exaggeratedly correct form, the sign she has just made, until she repeats it herself in more correct form. On the whole, she has responded quite well to prompting, but there are strict limits to its use with a wild animal—one that is probably quite spoiled, besides. Pressed too hard, Washoe can become completely diverted from her original object; she may ask for something entirely different, run away, go into a tantrum, or even bite her tutor.

Chimpanzees also imitate, after some delay, and this delayed imitation can be quite elaborate (10). The following is a typical example of Washoe's delayed imitation. From the beginning of the project she was bathed regularly and according to a standard routine. Also, from her second month with us, she always had dolls to play with. One day, during the 10th month of the project, she bathed one of her dolls in the way we usually bathed her. She filled her little bathtub with water, dunked the doll in the tub, then took it out and dried it with a towel. She has repeated the entire performance, or parts of it, many times since, sometimes also soaping the doll.

This is a type of imitation that may be very important in the acquisition of language by human children, and many of our procedures with Washoe were devised to capitalize on it. Routine activities—feeding, dressing, bathing and so on—have been highly ritualized with appropriate signs figuring prominently in the rituals. Many games have been invented which can be accom-

panied by appropriate signs. Objects and activities have been named as often as possible, especially when Washoe seemed to be paying particular attention to them. New objects and new examples of familiar objects, including pictures, have been continually brought to her attention, together with the appropriate signs. She likes to ride in automobiles, and a ride in an automobile, including the preparations for a ride, provides a wealth of sights that can be accompanied by signs. A good destination for a ride is a home or the university nursery school, both well stocked with props for language lessons.

The general principle should be clear: Washoe has been exposed to a wide variety of activities and objects, together with their appropriate signs, in the hope that she would come to associate the signs with their referents and later make the signs herself. We have reason to believe that she has come to understand a large vocabulary of signs. This was expected, since a number of chimpanzees have acquired extensive understanding vocabularies of spoken words, and there is evidence that even dogs can acquire a sizable understanding vocabulary of spoken words (11). The understanding vocabulary that Washoe has acquired, however, consists of signs that a chimpanzee can imitate.

Some of Washoe's signs seem to have been originally acquired by delayed imitation. A good example is the sign for "toothbrush." A part of the daily routine has been to brush her teeth after every meal. When this routine was first introduced Washoe generally resisted it. She gradually came to submit with less and less fuss, and after many months she would even help or sometimes brush her teeth herself. Usually, having finished her meal, Washoe would try to leave her highchair; we would restrain her, signing "First, toothbrushing, then you can go."

One day, in the 10th month of the project, Washoe was visiting the Gardner home and found her way into the bathroom. She climbed up on the counter, looked at our mug full of toothbrushes, and signed "toothbrush." At the time, we believed that Washoe understood this sign but we had not seen her use it. She had no reason to ask for the toothbrushes, because they were well within her reach, and it is most unlikely that she was asking to have her teeth brushed. This was our first observation, and one of the clearest examples, of behavior in which Washoe seemed to name an object or an event for no obvious motive other than communication.

Following this observation, the toothbrushing routine at mealtime was altered. First, imitative prompting was introduced. Then as the sign became more reliable, her rinsing-mug and toothbrush were displayed prominently until she made the sign. By the 14th month she was making the "toothbrush" sign at the end of meals with little or no prompting; in fact she has called for her toothbrush in a peremptory fashion when its appearance at the end of a meal was delayed. The "toothbrush" sign is not merely a response cued by the end of a meal; Washoe retained her ability to name toothbrushes when they were shown to her at other times.

The sign for "flower" may also have been acquired by delayed imitation. From her first summer with us, Washoe showed a great interest in flowers, and we took advantage of this by providing many flowers and pictures of flowers accompanied by the appropriate sign. Then one day in the 15th month she made the sign, spontaneously, while she and a companion were walking toward a flower garden. As in the case of "toothbrush," we believed that she understood the sign at this time, but we had made no attempt to elicit it from her except by making it ourselves in appropriate situations. Again, after the

first observation, we proceeded to elicit this sign as often as possible by a variety of methods, most frequently by showing her a flower and giving it to her if she made the sign for it. Eventually the sign became very reliable and could be elicited by a variety of flowers and pictures of flowers.

It is difficult to decide which signs were acquired by the method of delayed imitation. The first appearance of these signs is likely to be sudden and unexpected; it is possible that some inadvertent movement of Washoe's has been interpreted as meaningful by one of her devoted companions. If the first observer were kept from reporting the observation and from making any direct attempts to elicit the sign again, then it might be possible to obtain independent verification. Quite understandably, we have been more interested in raising the frequency of new signs than in evaluating any particular method of training.

Babbling

Because the Hayeses were attempting to teach Viki to speak English, they were interested in babbling, and during the first year of their project they were encouraged by the number and variety of spontaneous vocalizations that Viki made. But, in time, Viki's spontaneous vocalizations decreased further and further to the point where the Hayeses felt that there was almost no vocal babbling from which to shape spoken language. In planning this project we expected a great deal of manual "babbling," but during the early months we observed very little behavior of this kind. In the course of the project, however, there has been a great increase in manual babbling. We have been particularly encouraged by the increase in movements that involve touching parts of the head and body, since these are important components of many signs. Also, more and more frequently, when Washoe has been unable to get something that she wants, she has burst into a

TABLE 1. SIGNS USED RELIABLY BY CHIMPANZEE WASHOE[1]

Signs	Description
Come-gimme	Beckoning motion, with wrist or knuckles as pivot.
More	Fingertips are brought together, usually overhead. (Correct ASL form: tips of the tapered hand touch repeatedly.)
Up	Arm extends upward, and index finger may also point up.
Sweet	Index or index and second fingers touch tip of wagging tongue. (Correct ASL form: index and second fingers extended side by side.)
Open	Flat hands are placed side by side, palms down, then drawn apart while rotated to palms up.
Tickle	The index finger of one hand is drawn across the back of the other hand. (Related to ASL "touch.")
Go	Opposite of "come-gimme."
Out	Curved hand grasps tapered hand; then tapered hand is withdrawn upward.
Hurry	Open hand is shaken at the wrist. (Correct ASL form: index and second fingers extended side by side.)
Hear-listen	Index finger touches ear.
Toothbrush	Index finger is used as brush, to rub front teeth.
Drink	Thumb is extended from fisted hand and touches mouth.
Hurt	Extended index fingers are jabbed toward each other. Can be used to indicate location of pain.
Sorry	Fisted hand clasps and unclasps at shoulder. (Correct ASL form: fisted hand is rubbed over heart with circular motion.)
Funny	Tip of index finger presses nose, and Washoe snorts. (Correct ASL form: index and second fingers used; no snort.)
Please	Open hand is drawn across chest. (Correct ASL form: fingertips used, and circular motion.)
Food-eat	Several fingers of one hand are placed in mouth. (Correct ASL form: fingertips of tapered hand touch mouth repeatedly.)
Flower	Tip of index finger touches one or both nostrils. (Correct ASL form: tips of tapered hand touch first one nostril, then the other.)
Cover-blanket	Draws one hand toward self over the back of the other.
Dog	Repeated slapping on thigh.

[1]Within 22 months of the beginning of training. The signs are listed in the order of their original appearance in her repertoire (see text for the criterion of reliability and for the method of assigning the date of original appearance).

Context
Sign made to persons or animals, also for objects out of reach. Often combined: "come tickle," "gimme sweet," etc.
When asking for continuation or repetition of activities such as swinging or tickling, for second helpings of food, etc. Also used to ask for repetition of some performance, such as a somersault.
Wants a lift to reach objects such as grapes on vine, or leaves; or wants to be placed on someone's shoulders; or wants to leave potty-chair.
For dessert; used spontaneously at end of meal. Also, when asking for candy.
At door of house, room, car, refrigerator, or cupboard; on containers such as jars; and on faucets.
For tickling or for chasing games.
While walking hand-in-hand or riding on someone's shoulders. Washoe usually indicates the direction desired.
When passing through doorways; until recently, used for both "in" and "out" Also, when asking to be taken outdoors.
Often follows signs such as "come-gimme," "out," "open," and "go," particularly if there is a delay before Washoe is obeyed. Also, used while watching her meal being prepared.
For loud or strange sounds: bells, car horns, sonic booms, etc. Also, for asking someone to hold a watch to her ear.
When Washoe has finished her meal, or at other times when shown a toothbrush.
For water, formula, soda pop, often combined with "sweet."
To indicate cuts and bruises on herself or on others. Can be elicited by red stains on a person's skin or by tears in clothing.
After biting someone, or when someone has been hurt in another way (not necessarily by Washoe). When told to apologize for mischief.
When soliciting interaction play, and during games. Occasionally, when being pursued after mischief.
When asking for objects and activities. Frequently combined: "Please go," "Out, please," "Please drink."
During meals and preparation of meals.
For flowers.
At bedtime or naptime, and, on cold days, when Washoe wants to be taken out.
For dogs and for barking.

TABLE 1. (continued)

Signs	Description
You	Index finger points at a person's chest.
Napkin-bib	Fingertips wipe the mouth region.
In	Opposite of "out."
Brush	The fisted hand rubs the back of the open hand several times. (Adapted from ASL "polish.")
Hat	Palm pats top of head.
I-me	Index finger points at, or touches, chest.
Shoes	The fisted hands are held side by side and strike down on shoes or floor. (Correct ASL form: the sides of the fisted hands strike against each other.)
Smell	Palm is held before nose and moved slightly upward several times.
Pants	Palms of the flat hands are drawn up against the body toward waist.
Clothes	Fingertips brush down the chest.
Cat	Thumb and index finger grasp cheek hair near side of mouth and are drawn outward (representing cat's whiskers).
Key	Palm of one hand is repeatedly touched with the index finger of the other. (Correct ASL form: crooked index finger is rotated against palm.)
Baby	One forearm is placed in the crook of the other, as if cradling a baby.
Clean	The open palm of one hand is passed over the open palm of the other.

flurry of random flourishes and arm-waving.

We have encouraged Washoe's babbling by our responsiveness; clapping, smiling, and repeating the gesture much as you might repeat "goo goo" to a human infant. If the babbled gesture has resembled a sign in ASL, we have made the correct form of the sign and have attempted to engage in some appropriate activity. The sign for "funny" was probably acquired in this way. It first appeared as a spontaneous babble that lent itself readily to a simple imitation game—first Washoe signed "funny," then we did, then she did, and so on. We would laugh and smile during the interchanges that she initiated, and initiate the game ourselves when some-thing funny happened. Eventually Washoe came to use the "funny" sign spontaneously in roughly appropriate situations.

Closely related to babbling are some gestures that seem to have appeared independently of any deliberate training on our part, and that resemble signs so closely that we could incorporate them into Washoe's repertoire with little or no modification. Almost from the first she had a begging gesture—an extension of her open hand, palm up, toward one of us. She made this gesture in situations in which she wanted aid and in situations in which we were holding some object that she wanted. The ASL signs for "give me" and "come" are very similar to this, except that they in-

Context
Indicates successive turns in games. Also used in response to questions such as "Who ticklet?" "Who brush?"
For bib, for washcloth, and for Kleenex.
Wants to go indoors, or wants someone to join her indoors.
For hairbrush, and when asking for brushing.
For hats and caps.
Indicates Washoe's turn, when she and a companion share food, drink, etc. Also used in phrases, such as "I drink," and in reply to questions such as "Who tickle?" (Washoe: "you"); "Who I tickle?" (Washoe: "Me.")
For shoes and boots.
For scented objects: tobacco, perfume, sage, etc.
For diapers, rubber pants, trousers.
For Washoe's jacket, nightgown, and shirts; also for our clothing.
For cats.
Used for keys and locks and to ask us to unlock a door.
For dolls, including animal dolls such as a toy horse and duck.
Used when Washoe is washing, or being washed, or when a companion is washing hands or some other object. Also used for "soap."

volve a prominent beckoning movement. Gradually Washoe came to incorporate a beckoning wrist movement into her use of this sign. In Table 1 we refer to this sign as "come-gimme." As Washoe has come to use it, the sign is not simply a modification of the original begging gesture. For example, very commonly she reaches forward with one hand (palm up) while she gestures with the other hand (palm down) held near her head. (The result resembles a classic fencing posture.)

Another sign of this type is the sign for "hurry," which, so far, Washoe has always made by shaking her open hand vigorously at the wrist. This first appeared as an impatient flourish following some request that she had made in signs;

for example, after making the "open" sign before a door. The correct ASL for "hurry" is very close, and we began to use it often, ourselves, in appropriate contexts. We believe that Washoe has come to use this sign in a meaningful way, because she has frequently used it when she, herself, is in a hurry—for example, when rushing to her nursery chair.

Instrumental conditioning

It seems intuitively unreasonable that the acquisition of language by human beings could be strictly a matter of reiterated instrumental conditioning— that a child acquires language after the fashion of a rat that is conditioned, first, to press a lever for food in the presence of one stimulus, then to turn a wheel in the presence of another stimulus, and so on until a large repertoire of discriminated responses is acquired. Nevertheless, the so-called "trick vocabulary" of early childhood is probably acquired in this way, and this may be a critical stage in the acquisition of language by children. In any case, a minimal objective of this project was to teach Washoe as many signs as possible by whatever procedures we could enlist. Thus, we have not hesitated to use conventional procedures of instrumental conditioning.

Anyone who becomes familiar with young chimpanzees soon learns about their passion for being tickled. There is no doubt that tickling is the most effective reward that we have used with Washoe. In the early months, when we would pause in our tickling, Washoe would indicate that she wanted more tickling by taking our hands and placing them against her ribs or around her neck. The meaning of these gestures was unmistakable, but since we were not studying our human ability to interpret her chimpanzee gestures, we decided to shape an arbitrary response that she could use to ask for more tickling. We noted that, when being tickled, she tended to bring her arms together to cover the place being tickled. The result was a very crude approximation of the ASL sign for "more" (see Table 1). Thus, we would stop tickling and then pull Washoe's arms away from her body. When we released her arms and threatened to resume tickling, she tended to bring her hands together again. If she brought them back together, we would tickle her again. From time to time we would stop tickling and wait for her to put her hands together by herself. At first, any approximation to the "more" sign, however crude, was rewarded. Later, we required closer approximations and introduced imitative prompting. Soon, a very good version of the "more" sign could be obtained, but it was quite specific to the tickling situation.

In the sixth month of the project we were able to get "more" signs for a new game that consisted of pushing Washoe across the floor in a laundry basket. In this case we did not use the shaping procedure but, from the start, used imitative prompting to elicit the "more" sign. Soon after the "more" sign became spontaneous and reliable in the laundry-basket game, it began to appear as a request for more swinging (by the arms) —again, after first being elicited with imitative prompting. From this point on, Washoe transferred the "more" sign to all activities, including feeding. The transfer was usually spontaneous, occurring when there was some pause in a desired activity or when some object was removed. Often we ourselves were not sure that Washoe wanted "more" until she signed to us.

The sign for "open" had a similar history. When Washoe wanted to get through a door, she tended to hold up both hands and pound on the door with her palms or her knuckles. This is the beginning position for the "open" sign (see Table 1). By waiting for her to place her hands on the door and then lift them, and also by imitative prompting, we were able to shape a good approximation of the "open" sign, and would reward this by opening the door. Originally she was trained to make this sign for three particular doors that she used every day. Washoe transferred this sign to all doors; then to containers such as the refrigerator, cupboards, drawers, briefcases, boxes, and jars; and eventually—an invention of Washoe's—she used it to ask us to turn on water faucets.

In the case of "more" and "open" we followed the conventional laboratory procedure of waiting for Washoe to make some response that could be shaped into the sign we wished her to acquire. We soon found that this was not necessary; Washoe could acquire signs that were first elicited by our holding her hands, forming them into the desired configuration, and then putting them through the desired movement. Since this procedure of guidance is usually much more practical than waiting for a spontaneous approximation to occur at a favorable moment, we have used it much more frequently.

RESULTS

Vocabulary

In the early stages of the project we were able to keep fairly complete records of Washoe's daily signing behavior. But, as the amount of signing behavior and the number of signs to be monitored increased, our initial attempts to obtain exhaustive records became prohibitively cumbersome. During the 16th month we settled on the following procedure. When a new sign was introduced we waited until it had been reported by three different observers as having occurred in an appropriate context and spontaneously (that is, with no prompting other than a question such as "What is it?" or "What do you want?"). The sign was then added to a checklist in which its occurrence, form, context, and the kind of prompting required were recorded. Two such checklists were filled out each day, one for the first half of the day and one for the second half. For a criterion of acquisition we chose a reported frequency of at least one appropriate and spontaneous occurrence each day over a period of 15 consecutive days.

In Table 1 we have listed 30 signs that met this criterion by the end of the 22nd month of the project. In addition, we have listed four signs ("dog," "smell," "me," and "clean") that we judged to be stable, despite the fact that they had not met the stringent criterion before the end of the 22nd month. These additional signs had, nevertheless, been reported to occur appropriately and spontaneously on more than half of the days in a period of 30 consecutive days. An indication of the variety of signs that Washoe used in the course of a day is given by the following data: during the 22nd month of the study, 28 of the 34 signs listed were reported on at least 20 days, and the smallest number of different signs reported for a single day was 23, with a median of 29 (12).

The order in which these signs first appeared in Washoe's repertoire is also given in Table 1. We considered the first appearance to be the date on which three different observers reported appropriate and spontaneous occurrences. By this criterion, four new signs first appeared during the first seven months, nine new signs during the next seven months, and 21 new signs during the next seven months. We chose the 21st month rather than the 22nd month as the cutoff for this tabulation so that no signs would be included that do not appear in Table 1. Clearly, if Washoe's rate of acquisition continues to accelerate, we will have to assess her vocabulary on the basis of sampling procedures. We are now in the process of developing procedures that could be used to make periodic tests of Washoe's performance on samples of her repertoire. However, now that there is evidence that a chimpanzee can acquire a vocabulary of more than 30 signs, the exact number of signs in her current vocabulary is less significant than the order of magnitude—50, 100, 200 signs, or more—that might eventually be achieved.

Differentiation

In Table 1, column 1, we list English equivalents for each of Washoe's signs. It must be understood that this equivalence is only approximate, because equivalence between English and ASL, as between any two human languages, is only approximate, and because Washoe's usage does differ from that of standard ASL. To some extent her usage is indicated in the column labeled "Context" in Table 1, but the definition of any given sign must always depend upon her total vocabulary, and this has been continually changing. When she had very few signs for specific things, Washoe used the "more" sign for a wide class of requests. Our only restriction was that we discouraged the use of "more" for first requests. As she acquired signs for specific requests, her use of "more" declined until, at the time of this writing, she was using this sign mainly to ask for repetition of some action that she could not name, such as a somersault. Perhaps the best English equivalent would be "do it again." Still, it seemed preferable to list the English equivalent for the ASL sign rather than its current referent for Washoe, since further refinements in her usage may be achieved at a later date.

The differentiation of the signs for "flower" and "smell" provides a further illustration of usage depending upon size of vocabulary. As the "flower" sign became more frequent, we noted that it occurred in several inappropriate contexts that all seemed to include odors; for example, Washoe would make the "flower" sign when opening a tobacco pouch or when entering a kitchen filled with cooking odors. Taking our cue from this, we introduced the "smell" sign by passive shaping and imitative prompting. Gradually Washoe came to make the appropriate distinction between "flower" contexts and "smell" contexts in her signing, although "flower" (in the single-nostril form) (see Table 1) has continued to occur as a common error in "smell" contexts.

Transfer

In general, when introducing new signs we have used a very specific referent for the initial training—a particular door for "open," a particular hat for "hat." Early in the project we were concerned about the possibility that signs might become inseparable from their first referents. So far, however, there has been no problem of this kind: Washoe has always been able to transfer her signs spontaneously to new members of each class of referents. We have already described the transfer of "more" and "open." The sign for "flower" is a particularly good example of transfer, because flowers occur in so many varieties, indoors, outdoors, and in pictures, yet Washoe uses the same sign for all. It is fortunate that she has responded well to pictures of objects. In the case of "dog" and "cat" this has proved to be important because live dogs and cats can be too exciting, and we have had to use pictures to elicit most of the "dog" and "cat" signs. It is noteworthy that Washoe has transferred the "dog" sign to the sound of barking by an unseen dog.

The acquisition and transfer of the sign for "key" illustrates a further point. A great many cupboards and doors in Washoe's quarters have been kept secure by small padlocks that can all be opened by the same simple key. Because she was immature and awkward, Washoe had great difficulty in learning to use these keys and locks. Because we wanted her to improve her manual dexterity, we let her practice with these keys until she could open the locks quite easily (then we had to hide the keys). Washoe soon transferred this skill to all manner of locks and keys, including ignition keys. At about the same time, we taught her the sign for "key," using the original padlock keys as a referent. Washoe came to use this sign both to name keys that were presented to her and to ask for the keys to various locks when no key was in sight. She readily transferred the sign to all varieties of keys and locks.

Now, if an animal can transfer a skill learned with a certain key and lock to new types of key and lock, it should not be surprising that the same animal can learn to use an arbitrary response to name and ask for a certain key and then transfer that sign to new types of keys. Certainly, the relationship between the use of a key and the opening of locks is as arbitrary as the relationship between the sign for "key" and its many referents. Viewed in this way, the general phenomenon of transfer of training and the specifically linguistic phenomenon of labeling become very similar, and the problems that these phenomena pose for modern learning theory should require similar solutions. We do not mean to imply that the problem of labeling is less complex than has generally been supposed; rather, we are suggesting that the problem of transfer of training requires an equally sophisticated treatment.

Combinations

During the phase of the project covered by this article we made no deliberate attempts to elicit combinations or phrases, although we may have responded more readily to strings of two or more signs than to single signs. As far as we can judge, Washoe's early use of signs in strings was spontaneous. Almost as soon as she had eight or ten signs in her repertoire, she began to use them two and three at a time. As her repertoire increased, her tendency to produce strings of two or more signs also increased, to the point where this has become a common mode of signing for her. We, of course, usually signed to her in combinations, but if Washoe's use of combinations has been imitative, then it must be a generalized sort of imitation, since she has invented a number of combinations, such as "gimme tickle" (before we had ever asked her to tickle us), and "open food drink" (for the refrigerator—we have always called it the "cold box").

Four signs—"please," "come-gimme," "hurry," and "more"—used with one or more other signs, account for the largest share of Washoe's early combinations. In general, these four signs have functioned as emphasizers, as in "please open hurry" and "gimme drink please."

Until recently, five additional signs—"go," "out," "in," "open," and "hear-listen"—accounted for most of the remaining combinations. Typical examples of combinations using these four are,

"go in" or "go out" (when at some distance from a door), "go sweet" (for being carried to a raspberry bush), "open flower" (to be let through the gate to a flower garden), "open key" (for a locked door), "listen eat" (at the sound of an alarm clock signaling mealtime), and "listen dog" (at the sound of barking by an unseen dog). All but the first and last of these six examples were inventions of Washoe's. Combinations of this type tend to amplify the meaning of the single signs used. Sometimes, however, the function of these five signs has been about the same as that of the emphasizers, as in "open out" (when standing in front of a door).

Toward the end of the period covered in this article we were able to introduce the pronouns "I-me" and "you," so that combinations that resemble short sentences have begun to appear.

Concluding observations

From time to time we have been asked questions such as, "Do you think that Washoe has language?" or "At what point will you be able to say that Washoe has language?" We find it very difficult to respond to these questions because they are altogether foreign to the spirit of our research. They imply a distinction between one class of communicative behavior that can be called language and another class that cannot. This in turn implies a well-established theory that could provide the distinction. If our objectives had required such a theory, we would certainly not have been able to begin this project as early as we did.

In the first phase of the project we were able to verify the hypothesis that sign language is an appropriate medium of two-way communication for the chimpanzee. Washoe's intellectual immaturity, the continuing acceleration of her progress, the fact that her signs do not remain specific to their original referents but are transferred spontaneously to new referents, and the emergence of rudimentary combinations all suggest that significantly more can be accomplished by Washoe during the subsequent phases of this project. As we proceed, the problems of these subsequent phases will be chiefly concerned with the technical business of measurement. We are now developing a procedure for testing Washoe's ability to name objects. In this procedure, an object or a picture of an object is placed in a box with a window. An observer, who does not know what is in the box, asks Washoe what she sees through the window. At present, this method is limited to items that fit in the box; a more ingenious method will have to be devised for other items. In particular, the ability to combine and recombine signs must be tested. Here, a great deal depends upon reaching a stage at which Washoe produces an extended series of signs in answer to questions. Our hope is that Washoe can be brought to the point where she describes events and situations to an observer who has no other source of information.

At an earlier time we would have been more cautious about suggesting that a chimpanzee might be able to produce extended utterances to communicate information. We believe now that it is the writers—who would predict just what it is that no chimpanzee will ever do—who must proceed with caution. Washoe's accomplishments will probably be exceeded by another chimpanzee, because it is unlikely that the conditions of training have been optimal in this first attempt. Theories of language that depend upon the identification of aspect of language that are exclusively human must remain tentative until a considerably larger body of intensive research with other species becomes available.

SUMMARY

We set ourselves the task of teaching an animal to use a form of human lan-

guage. Highly intelligent and highly social, the chimpanzee is an obvious choice for such a study, yet it has not been possible to teach a number of this species more than a few spoken words. We reasoned that a spoken language, such as English, might be an inappropriate medium of communication for a chimpanzee. This led us to choose American Sign Language, the gestural system of communication used by the deaf in North America, for the project.

The youngest infant that we could obtain was a wild-born female, whom we named Washoe, and who was estimated to be between eight and 14 months old when we began our program of training. The laboratory conditions, while not patterned after those of a human family (as in the studies of Kellogg and Kellogg and of Hayes and Hayes), involved a minimum of confinement and a maximum of social interaction with human companions. For all practical purposes, the only verbal communication was in ASL, and the chimpanzee was maximally exposed to the use of this language by human beings.

It was necessary to develop a rough-and-ready mixture of training methods. There was evidence that some of Washoe's early signs were acquired by delayed imitation of the signing behavior of her human companions, but very few if any, of her early signs were introduced by immediate imitation. Manual babbling was directly fostered and did increase in the course of the project. A number of signs were introduced by shaping and instrumental conditioning. A particularly effective and convenient method of shaping consisted of holding Washoe's hands, forming them into a configuration, and putting them through the movements of a sign.

We have listed more than 30 signs that Washoe acquired and could use spontaneously and appropriately by the end of the 22nd month of the project. The signs acquired earliest were simple demands. Most of the later signs have been names for objects, which Washoe has used both as demands and as answers to questions. Washoe readily used noun signs to name pictures of objects as well as actual objects and has frequently called the attention of her companions to pictures and objects by naming them. Once acquired, the signs have not remained specific to the original referents but have been transferred spontaneously to a wide class of appropriate referents. At this writing, Washoe's rate of acquisition of new signs is still accelerating.

From the time she had eight or ten signs in her repertoire, Washoe began to use them in strings of two or more. During the period covered by this article we made no deliberate effort to elicit combinations other than by our own habitual use of strings of signs. Some of the combined forms that Washoe has used may have been imitative, but many have been inventions of her own. Only a small proportion of the possible combinations have, in fact, been observed. This is because most of Washoe's combinations include one of a limited group of signs that act as combiners. Among the signs that Washoe has recently acquired are the pronouns "I-me" and "you." When these occur in combinations the result resembles a short sentence. In terms of the eventual level of communication that a chimpanzee might be able to attain, the most promising results have been spontaneous naming, spontaneous transfer to new referents, and spontaneous combinations and recombinations of signs.

References and notes

1. See, for example, E. H. Lenneberg, *Biological foundations of language.* New York: Wiley, 1967.

2. Bryan, A. L. *Curr. Anthropol.*, 1963, **4**, 297.

3. Hayes, K. J., and Hayes, C. *Proc. Amer. Phil. Soc.*, 1951, **95**, 105.

4. Hayes, K. J. Personal communication. Dr. Hayes also informed us that Viki used a few additional sounds which, while not resembling English words, were used for specific requests.

5. Yerkes, R. M. *Chimpanzees* New Haven: Yale Univ. Press, 1943.

6. Hayes, K. J., and Hayes, C. In J. A. Gavan (Ed.), *The nonhuman primates and human evolution.* Detroit, Wayne Univ. Press, 1955. P. 110 Kellogg, W. N., and Kellog, L. A. *The ape and the child.* New York: Hafner, 1967; originally published by New York: McGraw-Hill, 1933. Kellogg, W. N. *Science*, 1968, **162**, 423.

7. Stokoe, W. C., Casterline, D., and Croneberg, C. G. *A dictionary of american sign language* Washington, D.C.: Gallaudet College Press, 1965. McCall, E. A. Thesis, University of Iowa, 1965.

8. Goodall, J. In I. DeVore (Ed.), *Primate behavior*, New York: Holt, Rinehart and Winston, 1965. P. 425. Riopelle, A. J., and Rogers, C. M. In A. M. Schrier, H. F. Harlow, F. Stollnitz (Eds.), New York: Academic Press, 1965. P. 449.

9. Yerkes, R. M., and Learned, B. W. *Chimpanzee intelligence and its vocal expression.* Baltimore: Williams and Wilkins, 1925. P. 53.

10. Hayes, K. J., and Hayes, C. *J. comp. physiol. Psychol.*, 1952, **45**, 450.

11. Warden, C. J., and Warner, L. H. *Quart. Rev. Biol.*, 1928, **3**, 1.

12. The development of Washoe's vocabulary of signs is being recorded on motion-picture film. At the time of this writing, 30 of the 34 signs listed in Table 1 are on film.

The effect of dream deprivation

william dement

About a year ago, a research program was initiated at the Mount Sinai Hospital which aimed at assessing the basic function and significance of dreaming. The experiments have been arduous and time-consuming and are still in progress. However, the results of the first series have been quite uniform, and because of the length of the program, it has been decided to issue this preliminary report.

In recent years, a body of evidence has accumulated which demonstrates that dreaming occurs in association with periods of rapid, binocularly synchronous eye movements (Aserinsky and Kleitman, 1955; Dement and Wolpert, 1958a; Goodenough, Shapiro, Holden, and Steinschriber, 1959; Wolpert and Trasman, 1958; Dement, 1955; Dement and Kleitman, 1957b; Dement and Wolpert, 1958a). Furthermore, the amount and directional patterning of these eye movements and the associated dream *content* are related in such a way as to strongly suggest that the eye movements represent scanning movements made by the dreamer as he watches the events of the dream (Dement and Kleitman, 1957b; Dement and Wolpert, 1958b). In a study of undisturbed sleep (Dement and Kleitman, 1957a), the eye-movement periods were observed to occur regularly throughout the night in association with the lightest phases of a cyclic variation in depth of sleep, as measured by the electroencephalograph. The length of individual cycles averaged about 90 minutes, and the mean duration of single periods of eye

From *Science*, **131**, 1705–1708, 10 June 1960. Copyright 1960 by the American Association for the Advancement of Science.

movement was about 20 minutes. Thus, a typical night's sleep includes four or five periods of dreaming, which account for about 20 percent of the total sleep time.

One of the most striking facts apparent in all the works cited above was that a very much greater amount of dreaming occurs normally than had heretofore been realized—greater both from the standpoint of frequency and duration in a single night of sleep and in the invariability of its occurrence from night to night. In other words, dreaming appears to be an intrinsic part of normal sleep and, as such, although the dreams are not usually recalled, occurs every night in every sleeping person.

A consideration of this aspect of dreaming leads more or less inevitably to the formulation of certain rather fundamental questions. Since there appear to be no exceptions to the nightly occurrence of a substantial amount of dreaming in every sleeping person, it might be asked whether or not this amount of dreaming is in some way a necessary and vital part of our existence. Would it be possible for human beings to continue functioning normally if their dream life were completely or partially suppressed? Should dreaming be considered necessary in a psychological sense or a physiological sense of both?

The obvious attack on these problems was to study subjects who had somehow been deprived of the opportunity to dream. After a few unsuccessful preliminary trials with depressant drugs, it was decided to use the somewhat drastic method of awakening sleeping subjects immediately after the onset of dreaming and to continue this procedure throughout the night, so that each dream period would be artificially terminated right at its beginning.

SUBJECTS AND METHOD

The data in this article are from the first eight subjects in the research program, all males, ranging in age from 23 to 32. Eye movements and accompanying low voltage, nonspindling electroencephalographic patterns (Dement and Kleitman, 1957a) were used as the objective criteria of dreaming. The technique by which these variables are recorded, and their precise relationship to dreaming, have been extensively discussed elsewhere (Dement, 1955; Dement and Kleitman, 1957a). Briefly, the subjects came to the laboratory at about their usual bedtime. Small silver-disk electrodes were carefully attached near their eyes and on their scalps; then the subjects went to sleep in a quiet, dark room in the laboratory. Lead wires ran from the electrodes to apparatus in an adjacent room upon which the electrical potentials of eye movements and brain waves were recorded continuously throughout the night.

Eye movements and brain waves of each subject were recorded throughout a series of undisturbed nights of sleep, to evaluate his base-line total nightly dream time and over-all sleep pattern. After this, recordings were made throughout a number of nights in which the subject was awakened by the experimenter every time the eye-movement and electroencephalographic recordings indicated that he had begun to dream. These "dream-deprivation" nights were always consecutive. Furthermore, the subjects were requested not to sleep at any other time. Obviously, if subjects were allowed to nap, or to sleep at home on any night in the dream-deprivation period, an unknown amount of dreaming would take place, off-

setting the effects of the deprivation. On the first night immediately after the period of dream deprivation, and for several consecutive nights thereafter, the subject was allowed to sleep without disturbance. These nights were designated "recovery nights." The subject then had a varying number of nights off, after which he returned for another series of interrupted nights which exactly duplicated the dream-deprivation series in number of nights and number of awakenings per night. The only difference was that the subject was awakened in the intervals between eye-movement (dream) periods. Whenever a dream period began, the subject was allowed to sleep without interruption, and was awakened only after the dream had ended spontaneously. Next, the subject had a number of recovery nights of undisturbed sleep equal to the number of recovery nights in his original dream-deprivation series. Altogether, as many as 20 to 30 all-night recordings were made for each subject, most of them on consecutive nights. Since, for the most part, tests could be made on only one subject at a time, and since a minute-by-minute all-night vigil was required of the experimenter to catch each dream episode immediately at its onset, it can be understood why the experiments have been called arduous and time-consuming.

Table 1 summarizes most of the pertinent data. As can be seen, the total number of base-line nights for the eight subjects was 40. The mean sleep time for the 40 nights was seven hours and two minutes, the mean total nightly dream time was 82 minutes, and the mean percentage of dream time (total dream time to total sleep time × 100) was 19.4. Since total sleep time was not held absolutely constant, percentage figures were routinely calculated as a check on the possibility that differences in total nightly dream time were due to differences in total sleep time. Actually, this is not a plausible explanation for any

TABLE 1. SUMMARY OF EXPERIMENTAL RESULTS. *TST*, TOTAL SLEEP TIME; *TDT*, TOTAL DREAM TIME

Mean and Range, Base-Line Nights			Dream Deprivation Nights (No.)	Awakenings (No.)	
TST	*TDT*	Percent		First Night	Last Night
				Subject W. T.	
6^h36^m	1^h17^m	19.5	5	8	14
6^h24^m–6^h48^m	1^h10^m–1^h21^m	17.0–21.3			
				Subject H. S.	
7^h27^m	1^h24^m	18.8	7	7	24
7^h07^m–7^h58^m	1^h07^m–1^h38^m	15.4–21.8			
				Subject N. W.	
6^h39^m	1^h18^m	19.5	5	11	30
5^h50^m–7^h10^m	1^h11^m–1^h27^m	17.4–22.4			
				Subject B. M.	
6^h59^m	1^h18^m	18.6	5	7	23
6^h28^m–7^h38^m	0^h58^m–1^h35^m	14.8–22.2			
				Subject R. G.	
7^h26^m	1^h26^m	19.3	5	10	20
7^h00^m–7^h57^m	1^h13^m–1^h46^m	16.9–22.7			
				Subject W. D.	
6^h29^m	1^h21^m	20.8	4	13	20
5^h38^m–7^h22^m	1^h08^m–1^h32^m	17.8–23.4			
				Subject S. M.	
6^h41^m	1^h12^m	17.9	4	22	30
6^h18^m–7^h04^m	1^h01^m–1^h23^m	16.2–19.3			
				Subject W. G.	
6^h16^m	1^h22^m	20.8	3	9	13
6^h08^m–6^h24^m	1^h17^m–1^h27^m	20.7–20.9			

*Second recovery night (see text).

but quite small differences in dream time, because the range of values for total sleep time for each subject turned out to be very narrow throughout the entire study. When averaged in terms of individuals rather than nights, the means were: total sleep time, six hours 50 minutes; total dream time, 80 minutes; percentage of dream time, 19.5; this indicates that the figures were not skewed by the disparate number of base-line nights per subject. The remarkable uniformity of the findings for individual nights is demonstrated by the fact that the standard deviation of the total nightly dream time was only plus or minus seven minutes.

PROGRESSIVE INCREASE IN DREAM "ATTEMPTS"

The number of consecutive nights of dream deprivation arbitrarily selected as a condition of the study was five. However, one subject left the study in a flurry of obviously contrived excuses after only three nights, and two subjects insisted on stopping after four nights but consented to continue with the recovery nights and the remainder of the

	Dream-Deprivation Recovery Nights					
	First Night			First Control Recovery Night		
No.	TST	TDT	Percent	TST	TDT	Percent
(4-base-line nights) 1	6^h43^m	2^h17^m	34.0	6^h50^m	1^h04^m	15.6
(5 base-line nights) 2	8^h02^m	2^h45^m	34.2	8^h00^m	1^h49^m	22.7
(7 base-line nights) 5	6^h46^m	1^h12^m	17.8	7^h10^m	1^h28^m	20.2
(6 base-line nights) 5	7^h25^m	1^h58^m	26.3	7^h48^m	1^h28^m	18.8
(10 base-line nights) 5	7^h14^m	2^h08^m	29.5	7^h18^m	1^h55^m	26.3
(4 base-line nights) 3	8^h53^m	2^h35^m	29.0			
(2 base-line nights) 6	5^h08^m 6^h32^{m*}	1^h01^m 1^h50^{m*}	19.8 28.1*	6^h40^m	1^h07^m	16.8
(2 base-line nights)						

schedule. One subject was pushed to seven nights. During each awakening the subjects were required to sit up in bed and remain fully awake for several minutes. On the first nights of dream deprivation, the return to sleep generally initiated a new sleep cycle, and the next dream period was postponed for the expected amount of time. However, on subsequent nights the number of forced awakenings required to suppress dreaming steadily mounted. Or, to put it another way, there was a progressive increase in the number of attempts to dream. The number of awakenings required on the first and last nights of deprivation are listed in Table 1. All the subjects showed this progressive increase, although there was considerable variation in the starting number and the amount of the increase. An important point is that each awakening was preceded by a minute or two of dreaming. This represented the time required for the experimenter to judge the emerging record and make the decision to awaken the subject after he first noticed the beginning of eye movements. In some cases the time was a little longer, as when an eye-movement period started while the experimenter was looking away from the recording apparatus. It is apparent from this that the method employed did not constitute absolute dream deprivation but, rather, about a 65- to 75-percent deprivation, as it turned out.

NIGHTLY DREAM TIME
ELEVATED AFTER DEPRIVATION

The data on the first night of the dream deprivation recovery period are summarized for each subject in Table 1. As was mentioned, one subject had quit the study. The mean total dream time on the first recovery night was 112 minutes, or 26.6 percent of the total mean sleep time. If the results for two subjects who did not show marked increases on the first recovery night are excluded, the mean dream time is 127 minutes or 29 percent, which represents a 50-percent increase over the group base-line mean. For all seven subjects together, on the first recovery night the increase in percentage of dream time over the base-line mean (Table 1, column 3, mean percentage figures; column 10, first recovery night percentages) was significant at the $p > .05$ level in a one-tail Wilcoxin matched-pairs signed-ranks test (Siegel, 1956).

It is important to mention, however, that one (S. M. in Table 1) of the two subjects alluded to above as exceptions was not really an exception because, although he had only one hour one minute of dreaming on his first recovery night, he showed a marked increase on *four* subsequent nights. His failure to show a rise on the first recovery night was in all likelihood due to the fact that he had imbibed several cocktails at a party before coming to the laboratory so that the expected increase in dream time was offset by the depressing effect of the alcohol. The other one of the two subjects (N. W. in Table 1) failed to show a significant increase in dream time on any of five consecutive recovery

nights and therefore must be considered the single exception to the over-all results. Even so, it is hard to reconcile his lack of increase in dream time on recovery nights with the fact that during the actual period of dream deprivation he showed the largest build-up in number of awakenings required to suppress dreaming (11 to 30) of any subject in this group. One may only suggest that, although he was strongly affected by the dream loss, he could not increase his dream time on recovery nights because of an unusually stable basic sleep cycle that resisted modification.

The number of consecutive recovery nights for each subject in this series of tests was too small in some cases, mainly because it was naively supposed at the beginning of the study that an increase in dream time, if it occurred, would last only one or two nights. One subject had only one recovery night, another two, and another three. The dream time was markedly elevated above the base-line on all these nights. For how many additional nights each of these three subjects would have maintained an elevation in dream time can only be surmised in the absence of objective data. All of the remaining four subjects had five consecutive recovery nights. One was the single subject who showed no increase, two were nearing the base-line dream time by the fifth night, and one still showed marked elevation in dream time. From this admittedly incomplete sample it appears that about five nights of increased dreaming usually follow four or five nights of dream suppression achieved by the method of this study.

EFFECT NOT DUE TO AWAKENING

Six of the subjects underwent the series of control awakenings—that is, awakenings during nondream periods. This series exactly duplicated the dream-deprivation series for each subject in number of nights, total number of awakenings, and total number of awakenings per successive night. The dream time on these nights was slightly below base-line levels as a rule. The purpose of this series was, of course, to see if the findings following dream deprivation were solely an effect of the multiple awakenings. Data for the first recovery nights after nights of control awakenings are included in Table 1. There was no significant increase for the group. The mean dream time was 88 minutes, and the mean percentage was 20.1. Subsequent recovery nights in this series also failed to show the marked rise in dream time that was observed after nights of dream deprivation. A moderate increase found on four out of a total of 24 recovery nights for the individuals in the control-awakening group was felt to be a response to the slight reduction in dream time on control-awakening nights.

BEHAVIORAL CHANGES

Psychological disturbances such as anxiety, irritability, and difficulty in concentrating developed during the period of dream deprivation, but these were not catastrophic. One subject, as was mentioned above, quit the study in an apparent panic, and two subjects insisted on stopping one night short of the goal of five nights of dream deprivation, presumably because the stress was too great. At least one subject exhibited serious anxiety and agitation. Five subjects developed a marked increase in appetite during the period of dream deprivation; this observation was supported by daily weight measurements which showed a gain in weight of three to five pounds in three of the subjects. The psychological changes disappeared as soon as the subjects were allowed to dream. The most important fact was that *none* of the observed changes were seen during the period of control awakenings.

The results have been tentatively interpreted as indicating that a certain amount of dreaming each night is a necessity. It is as though a pressure to dream builds up with the accruing dream deficit during successive dream-deprivation nights—a pressure which is first evident in the increasing frequency of attempts to dream and then, during the recovery period, in the marked increase in total dream time and percentage of dream time. The fact that this increase may be maintained over four or more successive recovery nights suggests that there is a more or less quantitative compensation for the deficit. It is possible that if the dream suppression were carried on long enough, a serious disruption of the personality would result.

References and notes

1. E. Aserinsky and N. Kleitman, *J. Appl. Physiol.* **8**, 1 (1955); W. Dement and E. Wolpert, *J. Nervous Mental Disease* **126**, 568 (1958); D. Goodenough, A. Shapiro, M. Holden, L. Steinschriber, *J. Abnormal Social Psychol.* **59**, 295 (1959); E. Wolpert and H. Trosman, *A.M.A. Arch. Neurol. Psychiat.* **79**, 603 (1958).

2. W. Dement, *J. Nervous Mental Disease* **122**, 263 (1955).

3. W. Dement and N. Kleitman, *J. Exptl. Psychol.* **53**, 339 (1957); W. Dement and E. Wolpert, *ibid.* **55**, 543 (1958).

4. W. Dement and N. Kleitman, *Electroencephalog. and Clin. Neurophysiol.* **9**, 673 (1957).

5. S. Siegel, *Nonparametric Statistics for the Behavioral Sciences* (McGraw-Hill, New York, 1956).

6. The research reported in this paper was aided by a grant from the Foundations' Fund for Research in Psychiatry.

index

72 73 74 7 6 5 4 3 2 1